The Family Context of Parenting in Children's Adaptation to Elementary School

MONOGRAPHS IN PARENTING SERIES
Marc H. Bornstein, Series Editor

To order, please call our toll-free number 1-800-926-6579 www.erlbaum.com

The Family Context of Parenting in Children's Adaptation to Elementary School

Edited by

Philip A. Cowan and Carolyn Pape Cowan
University of California, Berkeley

Jennifer C. Ablow
University of Oregon

Vanessa Kahen Johnson
WestChester University

Jeffrey R. Measelle
University of Oregon

 LAWRENCE ERLBAUM ASSOCIATES, PUBLISHERS
2005   Mahwah, New Jersey   London

Lawrence Erlbaum Associates, Inc., Publishers
10 Industrial Avenue
Mahwah, New Jersey 07430
www.erlbaum.com

Cover design by Kathryn Houghtaling Lacey

Library of Congress Cataloging-in-Publication Data

The family context of parenting in children's adaptation to elementary
   school / edited by Philip A. Cowan ... [et al.].

   p. cm. — (Monographs in parenting series)

Includes bibliographical references and index.

ISBN 0-8058-4157-1 (alk. paper)

1. Readiness for school. 2. Parent and child. 3. Education, Elementary—
   Parent participation.   I. Cowan, Philip A.   II. Series.

LB1132.F36   2005
372.21'—dc22   2004056444

Books published by Lawrence Erlbaum Associates are printed on acid-
free paper, and their bindings are chosen for strength and durability.

Printed in the United States of America
10   9   8   7   6   5   4   3   2   1

For our children by birth and by marriage:
Joanna, Kennen, Dena, Tom, Jon,
Jennifer, Eli, Sam, Abby, and Noa.

And for our grandchildren:
Kailey, Kiegan, Alexandra, Jordyn,
Caitlin, Jamie, and Spencer.

Contents

III. THE FAMILY CONTEXT OF PARENTING

IV. INTERVENTIONS AS TESTS OF CAUSAL
MODELS OF FAMILY INFLUENCE ON CHILDREN'S
ADAPTATION TO SCHOOL

V. INTEGRATIONS

Series Foreword
Monographs in Parenting

Parenting is fundamental to the survival and success of the human race. Everyone who has ever lived has had parents, and most adults in the world become parents. Opinions about parenting abound, but surprisingly little solid scientific information or considered reflection exists about parenting. *Monographs in Parenting* intends to redress this imbalance: The chief aim of this series of volumes is to provide a forum for extended and integrated treatments of fundamental and challenging contemporary topics in parenting. Each volume treats a different perspective on parenting and is self-contained, yet the series as a whole endeavors to enhance and interrelate studies in parenting by bringing shared perspectives to bear on a variety of concerns prominent in parenting theory, research, and application. As a consequence of its structure and scope, *Monographs in Parenting* will appeal, individually or as a group, to scientists, professionals, and parents alike. Reflecting the nature and intent of this series, contributing authors are drawn from a broad spectrum of the humanities and sciences — anthropology to zoology—with representational emphasis placed on active contributing authorities to the contemporary literature in parenting.

Parenting is a job whose primary object of attention and action is the child—children do not and cannot grow up as solitary individuals—but parenting is also a status in the life course with consequences for parents themselves. In this forum, parenting is defined by all of children's principal caregivers and their many modes of caregiving. *Monographs in Parenting* encompass central themes in parenting . . .

WHO PARENTS?

Biological and adoptive mothers, fathers, single parents, divorced and remarried parents can be children's principal caregivers, but when siblings, grandparents, and nonfamilial caregivers mind children, their "parenting" is pertinent as well.

WHOM DO PARENTS PARENT?

Parents parent infants, toddlers, children in middle-childhood, and adolescents, but special populations of children include multiple births, preterm, ill, developmentally delayed or talented, and aggressive or withdrawn children.

THE SCOPE OF PARENTING

Parenting includes genetic endowment and direct effects of experience that manifest themselves through parents' beliefs and behaviors; parenting's indirect influences take place through parents' relationships with each other and their connections to community networks; the positive and negative effects of parenting are both topics of concern.

FACTORS THAT AFFECT PARENTING

Evolution and history; biology and ethology; family configuration; formal and informal support systems, community ties, and work; social, educational, legal, medical, and governmental institutions; economic class, designed and natural ecology, and culture—as well as children themselves—each helps to define parenting.

THE NATURE, STRUCTURE, AND MEANING OF PARENTING

Parenting is pleasures, privileges, and profits as well as frustrations, fears, and failures.

Contemporary parenting studies are diversified, pluralistic, and specialized. This fragmented state needs counterforce in an arena that allows the extended in-depth exploration of cardinal topics in parenting. *Monographs in Parenting* vigorously pursues that goal.

—*Marc H. Bornstein*
Series Editor

Acknowledgments

This study, and the previous one on which it was based, have been supported by a grant from the National Institute of Mental Health (MH31109). We are very grateful for the ongoing support.

We wish to express our appreciation and respect for the Intervention Staff Couples: Deborah Rafael, LCSW, and Gary Whitmer, LCSW; Susan Brand, PhD, and Ben Kanne, MFCC; Michelle Holt, MFCC, and Michael Haas, MFT; and Paul Guillory, PhD, and Donna Guillory, MFCC.

Our sincere gratitude goes to the following: Gertrude Heming, our original Data Manager, whose loyal, dedicated, thoughtful assistance managing the data made these analyses possible; Penny Marsh, our recent Data Manager and Project Coordinator, whose grace and diligent work with the families and the data made our task so much smoother; and Natalya Maisel, our current Data Manager, for her quiet and skillful assistance on the tables and figures for this volume.

We could not have conducted the visits with the parents or children in the early years of the longitudinal study without the skilled expertise of the following: Jennifer Ablow, Victoria Bondar, Isabel Bradburn, Stacy Chang, Monica Garcia, Emily Gerber, Cheryl Herbsman, Jeanette Hsu, Yun Hsu, Dannie Johnson, Vanessa Kahen Johnson, Joan Kaplan, Margaret Kuklinski, Susan Lyon, Lisa Marchitelli, Jonathan Mattanah, Laura Mayorga, James McHale, Clark McKown, Jeff Measelle, Kaly Nguyen, Adele Pratt, Daniel Silver, and Lynna Tsou.

Our planning of the entire study was helped immeasurably by consultations with Michael Pratt of Wilfrid Laurier University and Yona Teichman of Tel Aviv University.

We are indebted to Marc Bornstein for his detailed, challenging, and stimulating editorial review of the Monograph.

About the Authors

Jennifer C. Ablow (PhD, 1997, University of California, Berkeley) is Assistant Professor in the Department of Psychology at the University of Oregon. Ablow's work focuses on understanding how the psychological and physiological properties of emotional arousal and styles of emotional regulation in one subsystem of the family shape similar processes in other familial subsystems.

Isabel Bradburn (PhD, 1997, University of California, Berkeley) is a Clinical Psychologist in Blacksburg, VA. Her current work includes research and educational consulting on issues pertaining to young children and their families.

Carolyn Pape Cowan (PhD, 1985, Center for Psychological Studies, Albany, CA) is Adjunct Professor of Psychology and Codirector of the Becoming a Family Project and the Schoolchildren and Their Families Project at the University of California, Berkeley. For the past 30 years, Dr. Cowan has collaborated with Philip Cowan on two longitudinal intervention studies of families undergoing transitions. The first is summarized in *When Partners Become Parents: The Big Life Change for Couples*, the second in this Monograph. Both studies emphasize the significant role of parents' marital quality in parent–child relationships and children's development and evaluate the effectiveness of early interventions on parents' and children's subsequent adaptation.

Philip A. Cowan (PhD, 1963, University of Toronto) is a Professor of Psychology at the University of California, Berkeley. He was Director of the

Clinical Training Program and Psychology Clinic for 12 years, and recently completed a 5-year term as Director of the Institute of Human Development. For the past three decades, Cowan has collaborated with Carolyn Pape Cowan on two longitudinal studies of families making major life transitions. The first is summarized in *When Partners Become Parents: The Big Life Change for Couples*. The current Monograph summarizes a new second study of children's transition to elementary school. Both studies emphasize the role of the parents' marital quality in influencing parent–child relationships and children's development, and the importance of intervention studies for testing correlational models of family process and children's outcomes.

Vanessa K. Johnson (PhD, 1998, University of California, Berkeley) is Assistant Professor in the Department of Psychology at WestChester University in WestChester, PA. Johnson's teaching and research interests focus on the role of family relationships in children's social and emotional development, and on the design of interventions to prevent maladjustment in both childhood and adolescence.

Gertrude Heming (PhD, 1985, University of California, Berkeley) is a Staff Psychologist in the Student Health Service at Stanford University. Her areas of specialization include college mental health and the prevention and treatment of sexual assault trauma.

Jeanette Hsu (PhD, 1995, University of California, Berkeley) is a Staff Psychologist and Coordinator of the Specialized Mental Health Consultation Team at the Veterans Affairs Palo Alto Health Care System. Hsu has also served as a part-time faculty member at Stanford University, San Jose State University, and Santa Clara University. Her current work centers on mental health services integration and the supervision of interns and postdoctoral trainees. She has interests in training and supervision issues, multicultural competence, behavioral medicine, and addiction treatment, and is a Board Member of the Association for Psychology Postdoctoral and Internship Centers (APPIC).

Jonathan Mattanah (PhD, 1999, University of California, Berkeley) is Associate Professor of Psychology at Towson University, MD. Mattanah's teaching and research focus on exploring the process of separation and individuation during late adolescence, and parents' roles in facilitating or inhibiting that process, specifically during the college transition.

Jeffrey R. Measelle (PhD, 1997, University of California, Berkeley) is Assistant Professor and Codirector of Clinical Training, Department of Psychology, University of Oregon. Measelle's work currently focuses on investigating how psychobiological and family processes interact to shape young children's socioemotional well-being, in particular, the cognitive and physiological bases of emotion regulation in early family relationships.

Marc Schulz (PhD, 1994, University of California, Berkeley) is Associate Professor of Psychology at Bryn Mawr College. Schulz's current research focuses on emotion regulation and conflict resolution processes in marital and adolescent–parent relationships, and on the effects of marital conflict on children.

I

INTRODUCTION
AND METHOD

1

Family Factors in Children's Adaptation to Elementary School: Introducing a Five-Domain Contextual Model

Philip A. Cowan, Carolyn Pape Cowan, Jennifer C. Ablow,
Vanessa K. Johnson, and Jeffrey R. Measelle

Each year, in late August or early September, a ritual takes place at the entrance to America's elementary schools. Mixed in with confident and casual first, second, and third graders streaming toward the school building are sets of both eager and anxious 5-year-olds approaching their first day of kindergarten. Some stride off to their designated classrooms without a backward glance. Some smile tentatively at their parents and hesitate before stepping into the unknown. Several cling tightly to mother's hand or father's leg. A closer look suggests that it is not only the children who are experiencing anxiety. Some parents' memories of their own passage into the world of elementary school make it difficult for them to let their children go easily. The school bell rings. The older children begin to form lines and move into their classrooms. As most of the kindergartners get the idea, they form a ragged not-quite-line, and with guidance from a teacher, they too disappear into the building. Their parents stand around in small clusters. Some mothers and fathers look lost, not quite ready to leave the school grounds, and a few surreptitiously brush away a tear as they begin to move on to the rest of their morning.

INTRODUCTION

Entrance to kindergarten is widely believed to represent a significant developmental milestone for a child (Perry & Weinstein, 1998; Vecchiotti, 2003), and, as the preceding vignette illustrates, it is often an emotionally charged event in the life of a family (Elizur, 1984). Although kindergarten is not the first school experience for increasing numbers of children (U.S. Department of Education, 1993), the entrance to elementary school involves a journey into a significantly larger and more anonymous world than that of the day-care or preschool environment. Children face increased demands for learning and performance rather than the freedom to play that is the hallmark of most preschool and day-care settings. Parents of elementary school children experience many fewer opportunities for direct involvement in their children's school day. Pianta and his colleagues (Pianta, Rimm-Kaufman, & Cox, 1999, p. 3) observed that, because of the importance and disequilibrating quality of the child's entrance to kindergarten, "almost every school in the United States has some program or set of practices related to helping ease this transition, although research indicates that these practices are by and large cursory and not well-suited for families' needs."

This volume describes a longitudinal study of children's transition to elementary school, with a special focus on parenting in the context of family factors that enhance or interfere with children's ability to make the transition successfully. Our study—the Schoolchildren and Their Families Project—began in the year before the families' first child entered kindergarten, and followed the family over the next 2 years as the children completed kindergarten and first grade. As we show, these were ordinary families living in many different communities in the larger San Francisco Bay area. They were not selected because they were experiencing difficulties, and we believe that they are comparable to families in other studies of this transition in different areas of the country (e.g., Belsky & MacKinnon, 1994).

Our study is unusual, not only because it gathers extensive information about family relationships before and during children's early years of elementary school, but also because it contains a preventive intervention component. Two thirds of the parents, randomly selected, met weekly in couples groups for 4 months before the children entered kindergarten. Led by mental health professionals, the groups were designed to help men and women discuss and deal with issues faced by contemporary American parents rearing young children. The story of why preventive interventions may be helpful to ordinary families unfolds throughout this volume as we document the fact that a sizable number of individuals and relationships in these families with young children are already showing signs of risk or actual distress as their children begin their formal schooling.

In this chapter, we introduce our central research questions, describe the primary theoretical models that guide the design (family systems, developmental psychopathology, and prevention science), outline the main design and measurement features of the study, and present a brief review of prior research on family factors in children's adaptation to school.

Missing: Longitudinal Studies of the Child's Transition to Elementary School

An important developmental milestone. An emotional time for the family. A disequilibrating period that could benefit from family-based preventive intervention. In the late 1980s, when we began to design the study reported in this volume, we were surprised to find that the transition to elementary school had received surprisingly little systematic attention from researchers, with the exception of Entwisle and Alexander's landmark study, which started in first grade (Alexander & Entwisle, 1988). As our work proceeded, we began to see signs of growing interest in this period. A new book on the importance of the kindergarten transition—*The Transition to Kindergarten* (Pianta, Cox, & National Center for Early Development & Learning, 1999)—and reports of systematic studies (Denton & West, 2002; Entwisle & Alexander, 1993) brought new focus to the importance of the early years of elementary school, but provided little information about the role of family relationships in children's adaptation to school. Entwisle and Alexander (1993, 1996) described parents' expectations and family structure as they were associated with achievement in first grade, but neither their work nor the work of Denton and West assessed the children or their families before the children entered school.

In the mid-1990s, three new books provided extensive reviews of studies of the family's contribution to children's intellectual and social adaptation to school—*The Family–School Connection: Theory, Research, and Practice* (Ryan, Adams, Gullotta, Weissberg, & Hampton, 1995), *Family-School Links: How Do They Affect Educational Outcomes?* (Booth & Dunn, 1996), and *The Five To Seven Year Shift: The Age of Reason and Responsibility* (Sameroff & Haith, 1996). A search of the books' contents and a review of earlier and later studies (discussed later) revealed plentiful studies of the transition to middle school, junior high school, and high school, but few longitudinal studies with assessments before and after children's entrance to kindergarten. The few that focused on the transition to kindergarten emphasized continuity and stability over time in children's intellectual abilities (F. A. Campbell, Pungello, Miller-Johnson, Burchinal, & Ramey, 2001) or peer relationships (Ladd & Price, 1987; Pettit, Harrist, Bates, & Dodge, 1991). Belsky and MacKinnon (1994) noted that very few studies examine the quality of family relationships in the preschool period as predictors of both academic and social behavior in kindergarten or first grade. This situation has not changed appreciably over the past decade.

The paucity of longitudinal studies of family–school linkage around the child's transition to elementary school is doubly surprising because it represents a missed opportunity to clarify the contribution of family processes to children's earliest school performance and behavior. James Coleman's report

on factors associated with school success more than three decades ago presented evidence that inequalities stemming from home, neighborhood, and
peer groups account for much more of the variance in children's academic
achievement than variations in school environments do (Coleman et al.,
1966). Although school environments also make an important difference in
children's lives (Weinstein, 2002), recent investigations continue to present
correlations that authors interpret as evidence for the strong role of family relationships in shaping children's achievement test scores (Phillips, Brooks-
Gunn, Duncan, Klebanov, & Crane, 1988; Rodriguez, 2002), and in influencing the presence or absence of behavior problems in the classroom (Smith,
Prinz, Dumas, & Laughlin, 2001). The difficulty with these interpretations is
that almost all studies of family–school linkage begin after children enter elementary school. It is always possible that the correlations are driven by the
fact that the child's behavior problems and school failure create disruptions
in family relationships. The missed opportunity, then, is one of assessing family relationships before children enter elementary school to measure both stability and change over the transition period.

Family Factors in Children's Adaptation to School:
A Five-Domain Model

Current studies of connections between what occurs inside the family and
what happens to the child at school tend to focus on one, or at most two, domains of family functioning (e.g., parents' depression, marital conflict, divorce, or parent–child relationships) and the correlation between adaptation
in those domains and children's academic or social competence or problem
behaviors. The central theme of the study presented here is that parenting behavior and parent–child relationships operate in a five-domain context of relationships within the family, and between family members and the larger social systems in which they live, love, work, and play (P. A. Cowan, Powell, &
Cowan, 1998). The conceptual and measurement model in the Schoolchildren and Their Families Project is based on a multidomain, theoretical family
systems model developed in previous research (Belsky, 1984; C. P. Cowan et
al., 1985; Heinicke, 2002). It assumes (see Figs. 1.1 to 1.6) that predicting and
understanding the quality of a child's school adaptation requires information
about change, adjustment, and distress in five domains or aspects of family
functioning (P. A. Cowan et al., 1998):

1. The psychological adjustment of individual family members.
2. The quality of each parent's relationship with the child.
3. The quality of the parents' relationship as a couple.
4. The transmission of relationship patterns across three generations.
5. The balance of stressors and supports outside the family.

We recognize that an important sixth domain of family functioning is the child's relationship with his or her siblings (Dunn, Slomkowski, & Beardsall, 1998). Although Measelle (this volume) includes sibling relationships in analyses presented in chapter 7, these relationships do not play a central role in this volume, partly because about one third of the children had no siblings at the time they made their transition to kindergarten, and partly because the siblings of the remaining two thirds varied in age (M age = 2.3 years; SD = .31), making the systematic study of sibling interaction extremely complex in an already complex study.

We begin in Fig. 1.1 with nuclear families comprised of two parents and their oldest child. We recognize the fact that not all children have two biological parents in the home, but in this study with an emphasis on the relationship of the parents as a couple, all children were living in a two-parent nuclear family when the study began. We assume that parents' or children's characteristics as individuals, and their level of psychological development and behavioral tendencies in the preschool period, each play a role in the child's subsequent behavior and academic achievement at school. In Fig. 1.1, and in all of the other models we present here, the arrows connecting domains of family functioning point both ways to indicate that we expect the influences of one on the other to operate in both directions. For example, parents' characteristics influence children, and children's characteristics influence parents (Bell, 1968).

From the individual level of analysis, we then move to an examination of the role of family relationships in children's adaptation to school. Judging by the volume of research on parenting and the availability of countless self-help books and articles on bookstore shelves and magazine racks, parent–child relationships are regarded as the key to understanding children's development (Fig. 1.2). Again, the double-headed arrows imply that parents and children influence each other in ways that shape the quality of their relationship, and

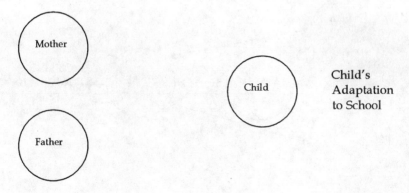

FIG. 1.1. Family members' individual characteristics and the child's adaptation to school.

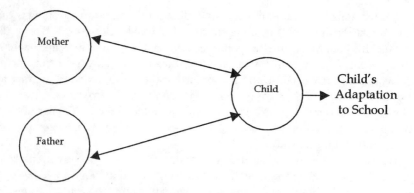

FIG. 1.2. Parent–child relationships, individual characteristics, and the child's adaptation to school.

the quality of the relationship provides a context for the development and well-being of the two individuals.

Over the last two decades, it has become increasingly clear that the relationship between the parents also affects the child's adaptation to school (e.g., Grych, Fincham, Jouriles, & McDonald, 2000). Our model (Fig. 1.3) includes couple relationship qualities such as high, unresolved conflict or cold disengagement between the parents that can influence the child—directly by creating fear and distraction, and indirectly by affecting the quality of one or both parents' relationship with the child. For example, living in a conflict-filled marriage may make it more difficult for a parent to be patient and nurturant with the child. The bidirectional arrows recognize the fact that chronic problematic behavior on the part of the child can also disrupt the relationship between the parents.

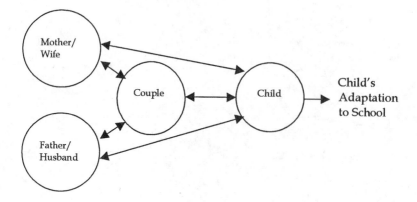

FIG. 1.3. Marital quality, parent–child relationships, individual characteristics, and the child's adaptation to school.

From a close-up on parents and children during the preschool period, our model expands to an intergenerational perspective on parenting that unfolds across time (Fig. 1.4). We expected to find that when mothers and fathers had difficult relationships with their parents when they were growing up, they would still be experiencing the effects of those early struggles and might find it more difficult to establish a positive connection with their partners or children. We predicted that children of those parents would be at increased risk for academic and peer relationship difficulties. The influence is bidirectional in this domain, too. Although current difficulties with the child could not affect what had occurred earlier in the parents' families of origin, these difficulties could affect both memories of the past and current relationship quality among children, parents, and grandparents.

So far we have described the model in terms of family risks for children's difficulties or problems in the classroom. Each figure in the model could tell the family–school story in terms of positive effects: Warm and nurturant relationships in the parents' families of origin should increase the probability of harmony in marital and parent–child relationships, which should facilitate children's adaptation to the academic and social challenges at school.

Our model also suggests (Fig. 1.5) that family relationships are influenced over time by parents' daily experiences in the world outside the family, represented in this study primarily by the balance between stress at work and other settings, and support from coworkers and friends. We expected these experiences of the parents to contribute to their children's adaptation to school and also recognized the possibility that children's adaptation and family relationships might have reverberating effects on their parents' experiences at work and in other key settings outside the family.

Finally, Fig. 1.6 provides a five-domain model of family–school linkage that summarizes Figs. 1.1 to 1.5. First, the model as a whole suggests that measures of adaptation in different domains will be correlated. This cross-domain correlation may result simply from the fact that, like multiple drillings

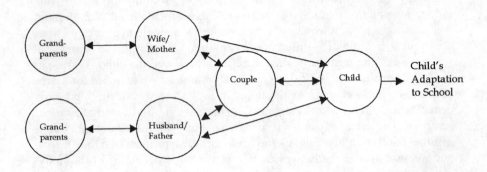

FIG. 1.4.   A three-generational perspective on the child's adaptation to school.

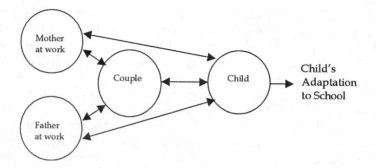

FIG. 1.5. Work–family connections and the child's adaptation to school.

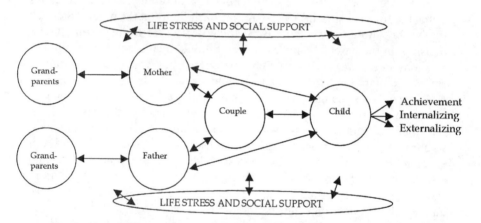

FIG. 1.6. The full Family–School Model for this study.

of the same ground, measurement at any point locates the same vein of gold or dross beneath the surface. Another possibility—our working hypothesis in this study—is that information from each aspect of family life will provide unique information, and a combination of assessments from each domain will provide a more adequate understanding than single measures of what contributes to individual differences in children's adaptation to school.

The use of the term *adaptation* to refer to how well the child is faring in kindergarten and first grade deserves some comment. We searched for a construct that would encompass the range of indicators we had in mind (academic achievement, social competence, internalizing and externalizing behaviors). The term *outcomes* is used frequently in the literature, but it assumes that the child's abilities and behaviors are a product of family forces, and we were not yet ready to make that claim at the beginning of the study. *Competence* is often used as a generic term to describe variations in performance, but we wanted to reserve it for assessments of the child's social competence in getting along with peers and academic competence as measured by teachers' ratings or achievement tests. *Adjustment* is another term in common usage, but it often has the connotation that the child who is well-adjusted is conforming to the demands of the system rather than showing originality, creativity, and an ability to solve problems by changing circumstances and overcoming barriers. We settled on the term adaptation although it too has sometimes been used to describe accommodation and adjustment. In both biology (Darwin, 1875) and psychology (Emery, 1999; Greenspan, 1981; Lazarus, 1999; Scar, 1996), adaptation has a long and honorable history as a term to describe an active process in which an organism modifies itself and the environment in ways that enhance its ability to manage, given environmental conditions.

The model of family–school linkage in Fig. 1.6 is consistent with Bronfenbrenner's attempts to understand children's adaptation in an ecological framework (Bronfenbrenner, 1979, 1986; Bronfenbrenner & Ceci, 1994) and with other authors' contextual analyses of multiple aspects of family life (see Belsky, 1984; Conger, Elder, Lorenz, Simons, & Whitbeck, 1994; Cox, Paley, Payne, & Burchinal, 1999; Heinicke, 1984; Parke & Tinsley, 1987; Walsh, 2003). The model presented here also resembles more specific models of family–school connections (Barth & Parke, 1996; Epstein, 1996; Green, 1995; Ladd, Price, & Hart, 1988; Pianta et al., 1999; Ryan & Adams, 1995). Some of these models state or imply that parents' characteristics or the quality of parent–child and marital relationships are factors in children's adaptation. A few mention the possibility that intergenerational cycles from grandparent to parent to child affect children's learning. Some models also acknowledge the potential for stress, support, and general resources outside the family (e.g., work, illness, socioeconomic status, social networks) to affect children's achievement and socioemotional development. Despite this overall level of consensus in conceptual terms, we have been unable to find other longitudinal studies that examine data from all five domains as potential predictors of children's academic, social, and emotional adaptation to elementary school.

A Developmental Psychopathology Approach: Risks, Transitions, and Trajectories

Risk Models and Developmental Psychopathology. Our approach to the study of family–school connections is informed by the concept of risk and protective factors that are central to the emerging field of developmental psychopathology. About two decades ago, developmental psychopathologists adopted a relatively new research paradigm (Sroufe & Rutter, 1984) that attempts to predict who will and will not succumb to disease or natural disasters, based on concepts drawn from the fields of public health and epidemiology (Kleinbaum, Morgenstern, & Kupper, 1982). Rather than beginning with studies of people in distress and looking back to identify potential ante-cedents or causes, these researchers follow people over time to describe four potential developmental pathways: (a) those initially at high risk of malad-justment who wind up in distress, (b) those at high risk who fare relatively well, (c) those at low risk who wind up in distress, and (d) those at low risk who unexpectedly move toward serious maladjustment (Cicchetti & Cohen, 1995a, 1995b). Risks, then, are markers of biological, psychological, or social processes that forecast an increased probability of a disorder or a negative outcome in a population, but risks are not always followed by negative out-comes. Sometimes protective factors intervene, so that, for example, risks as-sociated with marital conflict might be mitigated by effective relationships between each parent and child. Developmental psychopathologists are inter-ested in understanding the mechanisms that connect risks, protective factors, and outcomes, and the trajectories that people follow as they negotiate major challenges and transitions in their lives. As developmental psychopatholo-gists, we set out to identify a set of risk and protective factors that occur rela-tively early in family life, to help us understand the child's journey toward or away from academic and social adaptation to the first 2 years of elementary school.

Trajectories.   Longitudinal prospective studies are essential to develop-mental psychopathologists because they enable them to identify earlier risks for later maladaptation. In their longitudinal studies of children's academic competence, Alexander and Entwisle's results (1988) suggested that children follow a fairly consistent trajectory from the time they enter elementary school. Despite the fact that children make significant changes as they move through elementary school, middle school, and junior and senior high school, they tend to stay in the same rank order on measures of adaptation, relative to their age cohort. In longitudinal studies that followed children rather than families, and did not focus explicitly on children's adaptation to school, the trajectory hypothesis received substantial support in both middle-class sam-ples (Baumrind, 1991; Bennett et al., 1999; Gjerde, Block, & Block, 1988) and low-income samples (Alexander & Entwisle, 1988; Asher & Coie, 1990; Jimerson, Egeland, Sroufe, & Carlson, 2000; Kellam, Ling, Merisca, Brown, & Iaolongo, 1998; Lambert, Hartsough, Sassone, & Sandoval, 1987; Rich-man, Stevenson, & Graham, 1982; Werner & Smith, 1992). In a summary of studies of preschool children who already had behavior problems and were followed over time, Campbell (1995, p. 119) claimed that "children identified as hard to manage at ages 3 or 4 have a high probability (probably some-where around 50:50) of continuing to show difficulties throughout the ele-mentary school years and into early adolescence." Overall, then, children's ability to grapple with academic material and get along with peers in kinder-garten and first grade should be good predictors of educational, social, and mental health outcomes a dozen years later as they finish high school. Because the proportion of children experiencing identifiable difficulty is substantial, this finding of stability is a cause for concern. Studies indicate that as many as 20%[1] of the children in kindergarten have problems serious enough to warrant intervention (Babinski, Hartsough, & Lambert, 1999), although most do not receive special help of any kind (Saxe, Cross, & Silverman, 1988). The trajectory hypothesis suggests that, without help, many of these children will show signs of difficulty throughout their school careers and into adulthood.

Children are not the only ones who tend to follow relatively fixed trajectories. Adults' personality traits and symptom patterns persist over time (J. Block, 1971; Livson & Peskin, 1981), and couples at the maritally satisfied and dissatisfied ends of the continuum tend to be in similar places years later (Bradbury, 1998; Gottman & Levenson, 1999; Skolnick, 1981). We assumed that parent–child relationships, too, would follow a consistent trajectory, but to our surprise, we found no observational data of parenting styles during the 5- to 7-year-old period in previous studies to establish whether there is consistency of parenting over the period when most children make the transition to elementary school.

Transitions, Trajectories, and Risks. We focused our study on the child's transition to elementary school, in part because we believe there are methodological advantages of studying families as one or more members move through major life transitions. Major shifts in the life course precipitate disequilibration that challenges family members' coping patterns—cognitively, socially, and emotionally. Not all changes represent major life transitions. We view transitions as occurring when there are qualitative shifts in the individual's self-concept and world view, major life roles, and central relationships (P. A. Cowan, 1991). As these shifts occur during transitions, adaptive and maladaptive strategies and outcomes are highlighted and become more visible to researchers and to family members themselves. Transitions tend to provoke crises—not in the catastrophic negative sense, but in the sense of the Chinese pictograph for crisis, which embodies both danger and opportunity. At the same time that transitions heighten the risk for negative outcomes, they provide a stimulus and challenge for increased competence and developmental growth.

---

[1]Perry and Weinstein (1988) provided an excellent, brief discussion of the literature on the estimates of incidence and prevalence of difficulties in adjusting to kindergarten and first grade. The estimates range from 1% to 35%, depending on the domain of difficulty, the criterion used, the setting of the problem, the informant, and the sampling method. Almost all investigators who address these issues agree that these difficulties for children are long-lasting and that there are few services available to help parents deal with them.

Even when the rank order of people's adaptation remains relatively constant, the adaptation gap tends to widen over time, as transitions spread people farther apart. Alexander and Entwisle (1988, p. 99) offered an apt metaphor to describe what happens: "As in a bicycle race, people cluster together along the straightaway but pull apart when they go up a hill." Using a different metaphor, biologist C. H. Waddington (1957) made a similar point. He presented a model of developmental transitions as occurring in an epigenetic landscape—a terrain of hills and valleys with a succession of forks in each road, with the right or left path to be chosen by the traveler. Over time, small developmental deviations heading toward or away from adaptation become cumulative; the traveler who makes a small turn in the road at an early transitional choice point may ultimately wind up far from his or her desired destination. People who begin their journey at the high end of the adaptation continuum may make small positive changes that cumulate into large effects and lead to even more positive adaptations over time. At the high-risk end, small setbacks early in development can be amplified by subsequent negative shifts that ultimately produce large-scale negative effects on later adaptation.

Preventive Intervention: A Program for Science and Practice

The Schoolchildren and their Families Project was conceived within the framework of prevention science (Coie, Watt, West, & Hawkins, 1993). One of our goals was to intervene early in risk–outcome processes in families—before the difficulties become intractable—to reduce distress and dysfunction and enhance children's competence and performance in the classroom. Using a developmental psychopathology framework, we identified family risk indicators (e.g., unresolved marital conflict, ineffective parenting) associated with maladaptation to school, and evaluated a preventive intervention designed to reduce those risks and to enhance the factors that appear to protect children and promote their adjustment and competence as they embark on their school careers (Kazdin, 1997).

Several converging ideas led to the conclusion that a major life transition, such as the first child's entrance to school, would be an ideal time to mount a family-based preventive intervention program. Not only are family members and relationships more likely to be changing during a period of disequilibrium, but parents who face new challenges may also be motivated to accept help if it is offered. Our decision to study "nonclinical" families with young children about to enter school meant that for many families, we were intervening to bolster family processes long before negative, maladaptive patterns had become "set in stone." Intervention for families with a preschooler holds the promise of short-term gains for parents and children as the children enter school and long-term gains as the students follow trajectories set in motion as they embark on their academic careers.

In chapter 11, we report on the results of two variations of a 16-week semistructured couples group led by mental health professionals, randomly offered to parents in the year before their first child entered kindergarten. In one variation, during the open-ended part of the sessions, the leaders helped parents focus specifically on their relationships with their child, whereas in the other, leaders helped parents focus specifically on their relationship as a couple. The intervention design, embedded in a longitudinal study, has implications for both scientific theory and practice. On the theoretical side, we know that a longitudinal design by itself does not solve the problem of determining direction of effects or causal connections—whether family processes affect children's development or children's characteristics affect the family. The quality of family relationships during the preschool period is undoubtedly influenced by even earlier characteristics of the child (P. A. Cowan & Cowan, 2002b). Nevertheless, we can help answer questions about the causal connections in a set of correlations with an intervention design that includes random assignment to conditions. As we describe in chapter 11, our results show some differential impact of the two variations of the intervention on the parents and their children. This allows us to move beyond correlational models to speculate about the causal influence of specific family relationships on children's adaptation to school. The comparison of interventions with two different foci (parenting or marital relationships) allowed us to tease apart the close connection between parent–child and couple relationships and examine whether intervention-induced changes in one of the five domains triggered changes in others.

The benefits of using intervention designs to address issues of causality are not without costs. Because some of the participants may follow different paths by virtue of their assignment to intervention or control conditions, the overall curves of their trajectories over time are confounded with possible intervention effects. We do our best throughout the volume to control for these effects statistically, but as we discuss in the concluding chapter, research designs always involve trade-offs and compromises. Without the intervention, we lose the benefit of examining causal mechanisms that induce or facilitate change. With the intervention, we have a more difficult time drawing conclusions about consistency and stability over time. In our view, there is no single perfect design that allows a simultaneous view of both issues. In our case, we provide the appropriate caveats and await new studies that will provide information about the generality and replicability of the patterns that we found in our study.

We want to emphasize the fact that the intervention component of our study also had practical goals. One was to encourage parents to help their children get a more positive start on their trajectories of adaptation as they made the transition to kindergarten and first grade. A longer-term goal was to enable children to "catch the wave"—to take advantage of the possibility that the family and peer relationship qualities that help to maintain trajectories of adaptation over time would help to maintain any initial gains promoted by the intervention. For example, if the children develop a sense of their own competence and effectiveness in their first year of school, the reactions of both parents and peers may be positive in ways that help to support and stimulate curiosity, academic achievement, and effectiveness with peers over the next few years. Conversely, if children begin kindergarten with academic difficulties or angry aggressive behavior, subsequent family and peer reactions may function to maintain these maladaptive outcomes over time.

A number of early intervention programs for families considered at high risk by virtue of poverty, single parenthood, or minority status have focused on mothers and their relationships with their babies. A few of these have followed the children into school to assess the longer-term impact of the interventions (see P. A. Cowan et al., 1998, for a review). As far as we know, the preventive intervention in this study for "low-risk" families with children about to enter kindergarten is unique. Before we focus on the intervention results in chapter 11, we examine different perspectives on the family context of parenting during the preschool period, and explore how multiple aspects of family functioning predict children's academic achievement, social competence, and internalizing and externalizing behaviors in kindergarten and first grade.

OVERVIEW OF THE SCHOOLCHILDREN
AND THEIR FAMILIES PROJECT

This volume contains 13 chapters that describe links among different aspects of families' lives as their first children make the transition to elementary school. Details about recruitment, design, and measures are provided in chapter 2. Here we describe the editors, authors, participants, and general research approach to orient the reader to the study.

Two of us (Philip and Carolyn Cowan) are the directors of the Schoolchildren and Their Families Project. We served as editors of this volume along with Jennifer Ablow, Vanessa Johnson, and Jeffrey Measelle. At the time the data were gathered, Ablow, Johnson, and Measelle, and most of the other contributing authors (Isabel Bradburn, Jeanette Hsu, Jonathan Mattanah, and Marc Schulz), were graduate students working on various phases of the project. All are now involved in professional academic and clinical careers in various parts of the country. Gertrude Heming served as the Data

Manager for the entire study, which was planned and carried out with a great deal of collaboration among us. Each of the authors contributed to the design, measurement protocol, data gathering, data processing, and analyses presented here. Each of the reports in the separate chapters focuses on a specific subset of family variables as they relate to children's outcomes, with chapter 12 presenting an integrative model, similar to Fig. 1.6, that includes data from all five domains in our family systems model of adaptation to school. It is our hope that, taken together, the chapters convey the breadth and utility of the model that guided this research enterprise.

Design and Measurement Features

The volume reports on 100 families that began the study in the year before their first child entered kindergarten (mean age of 5.0), 84 of whom remained with the study until the first child completed first grade (mean age of 7.0). The chapters in this volume focus on associations between various aspects of family relationships in the prekindergarten period and major indicators of children's adaptation to kindergarten and first grade—academic achievement, social competence, and both internalizing and externalizing problem behaviors at school (shyness, withdrawal, and depression and anger and aggression).

   In addition to its depth of focus on the content of the family-to-school linkages, the volume makes a number of methodological contributions. First, in each domain of family life, with the exception of the parents' perceptions of relationships with their parents where we have no observations of interactions between the parents and grandparents, measurements are taken from multiple perspectives that include self-reports from mothers, fathers, and children, observations from experimenters and teachers, and family members' descriptions of each other and their relationships. Second, developmental researchers have found it difficult to obtain reliable and valid assessments of self-appraisals and perceptions of family relationships in very young children. With few exceptions, existing measures have been limited to use with children who are 8 years old or older. The Berkeley Puppet Interview (Ablow & Measelle, 1993) created for this study (see chapter 2) made it possible to assess children's appraisals of key family relationships and their own competence and difficulties before and after they entered elementary school. Third, children in the study attended more than 80 different kindergarten and first-grade classrooms in northern California. Teachers' ratings of the target children in the study were standardized against their ratings of the same-sex children in their classrooms. This approach allowed us to control for differences in teacher rating bias, and to evaluate the adaptation of the 100 children in the study relative to the 1,000 to 1,500 children in the same grades and schools in 27 cities and towns within a 40-mile radius of the study site at the University of California at Berkeley.

The two-parent families participating in the study were recruited from day-care centers, preschools, and announcements in local media in the years 1990 to 1993. Because our recruitment materials did not mention the couples group intervention (see chapter 11), parents' attraction to the study at the outset was not to seek help in the mental health system, although some have done so since then. Of the parents who entered the study, 84.0% are European American, 6.6% are African American, 7.0% are Asian American, and 2.5% are Latin American. Although we did not exclude cohabiting couples, all but two of the participant couples were married when they entered the study.

The median yearly total family income of the families ($78,000) indicates a relatively affluent sample, with three qualifications: First, in the recruitment of two-parent families with a first child about to enter kindergarten, we attracted mostly two-job families (71% of the women were employed at least half-time). Second, there was enormous variability in the income levels (with the *SD* of the sample more than $30,000 per year), so there was certainly a range of income levels represented in the sample. And, despite the high central tendency in family income, 21% of the participants' incomes were below the median family income in the San Francisco Bay area ($53,000), and thus are more representative of two-parent families at the lower end of the income scale.

Based on several considerations that we describe in more detail in chapter 2, we believe that the results of this study are relevant to a large proportion of the population of entering schoolchildren: The sample is not skewed either toward the adaptive or maladaptive ends of the continuum, and the children were perceived by their teachers in 80 different classrooms as no different from their peers in social competence, internalizing behaviors, or externalizing behaviors. In other words, the children in this study were essentially "typically developing children." Nevertheless, because this is the first longitudinal study with a preventive intervention for two-parent families with a first child entering kindergarten, we treat the findings cautiously as sources of hypotheses to be tested for generalizability.

FAMILY FACTORS IN CHILDREN'S ADAPTATION TO SCHOOL: A REVIEW OF RESEARCH

In our brief review of previous research on family factors in children's adaptation, we group the studies on the basis of their focus on one of the five family domains in our conceptual model (Figs. 1.1 to 1.5). Whenever possible, we rely on results from studies with longitudinal research designs.

Characteristics of Individual Family Members and Children's Adaptation to School

Children's Characteristics.   Given that longitudinal studies have established considerable continuity between toddlerhood and middle childhood or adolescence (e.g., J. H. Block & Block, 1980; Carlson et al., 1999), it should not be surprising to find that children's characteristics assessed during the preschool period predict their later academic achievement and social competence. Children's preschool IQ and language skills forecast their cognitive abilities in kindergarten and their actual grades in later elementary school (Hess, Holloway, Dickson, & Price, 1984; Olson, Bates, & Kaskie, 1992; Walker, Greenwood, Hart, & Carta, 1994). Personality or temperament characteristics (Bates, 1986), biases in cognitive information processing (Dodge, 1990), and social skills such as cooperation observed in preschool classrooms (Ladd & Price, 1987) predict patterns of friendship and peer status in kindergarten. Children's attachment status (secure vs. insecure) measured in infancy is a precursor of kindergarten teachers' rating of their emotional health and aggression with peers (Renken, Egeland, Marvinney, & Mangelsdorf, 1989; Sroufe, Egeland, & Kreutzer, 1990).[2] Behavior problems identified at age 3 or 4 tend to persist into first and second grade (Campbell, 1995; Richman et al., 1982). In sum, children who are more competent or better adjusted before they enter elementary school generally show higher levels of adaptation in kindergarten and the early elementary school grades. Findings on this point from this study are presented in chapter 3.

Parents' Characteristics.   Individual differences in parents have been assessed in two ways—"background" or "social address" indicators that function as proxies for measures of resources such as socioeconomic status (SES), minority status, or single parenthood; and psychological characteristics such as parents' intelligence, personality, or psychopathology:

1. Background variables—There is considerable evidence that children of parents who are low in SES, members of minority groups, or single parents are likely to have lower academic achievement scores (Astone & McLanahan, 1991; Entwisle & Alexander, 1993). There has been extensive debate about explanations of these findings, with some making a plausible case for the hypothesis that minority status and single parenthood are often confounded with low income and education, and that the risk factors associated with poverty are responsible for disrupting children's learning process at school (but

---

[2]It is not clear whether we should think of attachment as a characteristic of the child, because attachment categories are based on observations of children's behavior in response to parents' reentry after a brief separation in the laboratory, or whether we should think of attachment as a quality of the parent–child relationship, as the theory describes it (Bowlby, 1988).

see Ogbu, 2003, for a controversially different view). Although most studies of family background variables have focused on their links to academic achievement, there is suggestive evidence that SES may also be associated with children's acceptance by peers (C. J. Patterson, Griesler, Vaden, & Kupersmidt, 1992). Because of the relative homogeneity of our sample, these background variables were not examined as part of this study.

2. Psychological characteristics—In investigations of both academic achievement and internalizing or externalizing in school-age children, it is clear that diagnosed psychopathology in parents (e.g., schizophrenia, depression, antisocial personality) is associated with their children's academic and social problems, including problems with learning, aggression, shyness, low self-esteem, and depression (e.g., G. R. Patterson & Capaldi, 1991; Sameroff, Seifer, Baldwin, & Baldwin, 1993; Zahn-Waxler, Duggal, & Gruber, 2002). We were unable to find any studies showing direct links between specific personality traits of parents and children's school outcomes in nonclinical samples. However, a number of studies show that broader constructs—diagnosed psychopathology; broadband measures of personality characteristics, such as neuroticism, extraversion, and agreeableness; and measures of developmental maturity, complexity, and adjustment—are related in the expected direction to observed and reported parenting style (see Belsky & Barends, 2002; Vondra & Belsky, 1993, for reviews). By assessing both mothers' and fathers' personality before the birth of a first child, and then observing their parenting style at 1 month and 4 years postpartum, Heinicke and his colleagues (summarized in Heinicke, 2002) were able to show that the link between personality and parenting did not stem solely from children's rather than parents' characteristics. Because parenting is linked to children's adaptation (Conger, Conger, Elder, & Lorenz, 1992; and see the next section, Heinicke, 2002), the assumption is that links between parents' personality characteristics and children's adaptation may be mediated by the quality of the parent–child relationship. Chapter 12 examines the contribution of parents' psychological symptoms, along with other family domains, to predictions of their children's adaptation to school.

Parent–Child Relationships and Children's Adaptation to School

In light of the voluminous literature on parenting and children's development, and the emergence of recent reviews of this topic (P. A. Cowan et al., 1998; Kuczynski, 2003), including Bornstein's (2002) second edition of his comprehensive *Handbook of Parenting*, we have been extraordinarily selective in our summary in this section. What makes the task even easier is the unfortunate fact that, as we noted at the beginning of this chapter, there is very little systematic information about parenting in the preschool period as a predictor of children's early school adaptation.

In reviewing this large body of research, Darling and Steinberg (1993) made a useful contribution by distinguishing between parenting practices as parents' specific behaviors with their children, and parenting style as a descriptor of the general context or climate of the parent–child relationship. A third type of research bearing on issues of links between parent–child relationships and children's adaptation, not quite fitting either in the parenting practices or parenting styles approach, is the literature on attachment.

Parenting Practices.   Maternal warmth, support, and responsiveness in infancy (Coates & Lewis, 1984; Olson et al., 1992) and the preschool years (Pianta, Smith, & Reeve, 1991) and fathers' physical play during the preschool period (Barth & Parke, 1996) predicted children's social competence in kindergarten. Maternal intrusion and seductive behavior with their 6-month-old and 2-year-old children accounted for significant variations in the children's hyperactivity in kindergarten (Jacobvitz & Sroufe, 1987). Lack of cognitive stimulation in the preschool home, and negative, conflicted parent–child relationships, were antecedents of lower achievement in first grade (Bradley & Caldwell, 1984; Estrada, Arsenio, Hess, & Holloway, 1987).

Over the past four decades, researchers have consistently found significant correlations between parenting practices and children's behavior problems. Children's internalizing behavior has been attributed to their parents' depression, lack of care, overinvolvement, overprotection, overcontrol, or loss of a parent (Cummings, DeArth-Pendley, Du Rocher Schudlich, & Smith, 2001; Rutter & Sroufe, 2000). Children's externalizing behavior has been linked to parents' harsh, coercive, or inconsistent discipline practices (Kremen, 1996; Loeber & Dishion, 1983), rejection of the child (Rothbaum & Weisz, 1994), and mothers' hostility and intrusiveness (Lyons-Ruth, Alpern, & Repacholi, 1993; Pettit et al., 1991).

Parenting Style.   Well-established connections between the quality of parent–child relationships and children's school adaptation are found in studies stimulated by Baumrind's work on parenting styles (1973), although few focus specifically on the transition to elementary school. Baumrind's conceptualization, subsequently reinforced by Maccoby and Martin's comprehensive review (1983), was that two orthogonal dimensions summarize much of the variance in parents' behavior toward their children: warmth and responsiveness, and structure and control. Furthermore, the combination of high parental warmth and high, but not punitive, control during the preschool period, characterized as authoritative parenting, tends to be associated with children's instrumental competence, including academic skills and social competence, 6 years later in middle school (Baumrind, 1989; P. A.

Cowan, Cowan, Schulz, & Heming, 1994). Parents' appropriate granting of autonomy to children—explicit in the conceptualization of authoritative parenting but not usually separated out in the measurement of the construct—has also been regarded as a central ingredient of academic and social competence in the classroom (e.g., Grolnick, Ryan, & Deci, 1991).

Higher levels of behavior problems of the internalizing and externalizing type have been associated with authoritarian or uninvolved parenting styles (Maccoby & Martin, 1983; Steinberg, 2001). One possible explanation of these findings lies in Dix's argument (1991) that an essential ingredient in parenting styles is the way in which emotions aroused in parents lead them to regulate their children's emotions. That is, within the general context of parenting styles, there are specific parenting practices that help to shape both adaptive and maladaptive behavior in children. Because few studies examine links between parenting style and both internalizing and externalizing in children, it is not clear whether specific parenting styles make unique contributions to one outcome or the other. A number of chapters in this volume (4, 5, 6, 8, 10, 11, and 12) describe links between qualities of parent–child relationships and measures of children's academic competence and problem behaviors of the internalizing and externalizing type, as described by their teachers in kindergarten or first grade.

Attachment. "Although attachment, by definition, is not a parenting style or practice, classical and modern directions in attachment research are fundamentally about parenting" (Cummings & Cummings, 2002, p. 38). In a "generational" transmission of theory from Bowlby (1951) to Ainsworth (Ainsworth & Wittig, 1969) to Main (Main & Goldwyn, 1984), a number of investigators who attempt to describe essential features of the relationship between parents and children focus on how infants and young children react to a parent when reunited after a separation—whether they seek out the parent as a "secure base." Some children characterized as "insecurely attached" avoid the parent anxiously, others react angrily and resist the parent's overtures, and a few show disorganized behavior after the parent's return. Bowlby's assumption was that children develop "working models" of whether they can expect to be responded to when they are upset and that these models tend to shape expectations and interactions with parents, peers, and others in their social environment.

Belsky's review (1999) concluded that there are clear differences in parenting when mother–child pairs representing these attachment categories are observed: (a) Securely attached infants have mothers who are observed to be warmer and more responsive and sensitive than mothers of insecurely attached infants; (b) infants with avoidant attachments have mothers who are observed to be intrusive, controlling, and excessively stimulating; and (c) infants with resistant attachments have mothers who appear to be unresponsive and underinvolved with them. Results of longitudinal studies, most notably those by Sroufe, Egeland, and their colleagues (Sroufe, Duggal, Weinfield, & Carlson, 2000; Weinfield, Sroufe, & Egeland, 2000), reveal that infants with an early history of secure attachment, usually to the mother, have a variety of more adaptive characteristics later on, but the outcomes are almost all socioemotional rather than academic because the investigators did not focus specifically on the child's adaptation to school. Because the children in our study were almost 5 years of age when the study began, we do not have information about the early attachment patterns in the parents' relationships with the children. Story-stem measures for this age group (Steele, Steele, Croft, & Fonagy, 1999) had not yet been published. We did examine the recalled attachment relationships between the parents in our study and their parents, using the Adult Attachment Interview (George, Kaplan, & Main, 1985, discussed later), which we describe in chapter 8.

Marital Conflict and Children's Adaptation to School

Here we move to the context of parenting from a family systems perspective (Fig. 1.3). In the early years of the development of family systems theories by clinicians working with disturbed families, couple relationships were thought to be the primary influence in shaping communication patterns in the family. For example, Satir (1972) described the couple metaphorically as the "architects" of family life, and S. Minuchin (1974) focused on the strength of the parents' alliance as a couple in his treatment of problems in children and adolescents. Ironically, the idea that couple relationships were important to children's adaptation did not spread to the design of family studies until investigators became concerned about the potentially negative effects of parents' divorce on their children (Hetherington, Cox, & Cox, 1982; Wallerstein & Kelly, 1980).

The role of couple relationship quality in intact families has become an important topic in child development research only in the last two decades. Research on links between parents' marital quality and the quality of their relationships with their children or the children's adaptation have been described in several recent comprehensive reviews of family research (e.g., Cox, Paley, & Harter, 2001; Cummings & Davies, 1994; Emery, 1999; Fincham, 1998). Parents' marital disharmony appears to place young children at risk for developing both internalizing and externalizing behaviors and disorders (Amato & Keith, 1991; P. A. Cowan et al., 1994; Fincham, Grych, & Osborne, 1994; Katz & Gottman, 1993). As far as we know, only the Cowan et al. (1994) and the Katz and Gottman (1993) studies assessed marital conflict using observational methods before children entered school and then assessed child outcomes after the children had made their transition to school.

Despite the fact that correlational links between marital quality and children's peer competence have been well established, the mechanisms by which marital conflict influences school adaptation have not been clearly delineated. The most frequently held hypothesis is that the parents' marital conflict and distress "spill over" into one or both of the parent–child relationships, with resulting negative effects on the child (Cummings & Davies, 1994; Erel & Burman, 1995; Wilson & Gottman, 1995). More specific hypotheses have been advanced about how the role of emotional security (Davies & Cummings, 1994) and emotion (dys)regulation patterns (Crockenberg & Langrock, 2001) help to explain links between patterns in the parents' interactions as a couple and children's difficulties adapting to peers and classroom challenges. Barth and Parke (1993) speculated further that (a) marital conflict affects parents' ability to provide social support or alleviate their children's stress by limiting parents' emotional and physical availability to their children, and (b) maritally discordant parents affect children's school achievement through their lack of involvement with their children's school.

We should note that the impact of marital conflict and distress need not always be negative. Forehand, Armistead, and Klein (1995) pointed out that some individual and family processes can buffer children from the negative impact of their parents' divorce. Five chapters in this volume (6, 7, 8, 11, and 12) explore direct links between parents' marital quality and children's adaptation, examine various individual and family processes that operate to protect or buffer children from the negative impact of their parents' unresolved conflict, and suggest some indirect mechanisms that link parents' marital quality with their children's adjustment.

Three-Generational Relationship Quality and Children's Competence at School

Intergenerational relationships provide another perspective on the family context of parenting (Fig. 1.4). Clinical theories of family dynamics emphasize the idea that both adaptation and maladaptation tend to cycle from generation to generation (Bowen, 1978; Framo, 1982; P. Minuchin, 1988; S. Minuchin, 1974; Rolland & Walsh, 1996). In this study, we are not concerned with the transmission of individual psychopathology through genetic and other biological means (Plomin & McClearn, 1993), although that is certainly one of the powerful mechanisms behind intergenerational transmission. We focus on the repetition of family relationship patterns from one generation to another. Evidence of intergenerational repetition of patterns comes from several sources. Large-scale sociological studies and meta-analyses of results of smaller studies find that adult children whose parents divorced are more likely to end their own marriages in divorce (Amato, 1996). Similarly, maritally dissatisfied couples are more likely to have unhappily married parents (Amato & Booth, 2001; Schneewind & Ruppert, 1998), and marital violence in the family of origin tends to be repeated in the next generation (Stith et al., 2000). Parenting patterns, too, are likely to be repeated. When parents abuse their children, the children are at risk of repeating the pattern as grownups with their own children (Cicchetti, Toth, & Maughan, 2000; Newcomb & Locke, 2001; Pears & Capaldi, 2001). Caspi and Elder (1988) showed that intergenerational cycles can involve multiple aspects of family life. They found evidence across four generations of maladaptive patterns that included parents' irritability as individuals, conflict as a couple, difficulties with their children, and subsequent behavioral difficulties in the children.

All of these studies chronicle repetitive patterns and provide speculation, although no systematic information, about potential mechanisms to explain the repetition of these cycles or evidence that transmission across generations is not inevitable. Many men and women manage to create new families that are significantly different in style and adaptation from the families in which they grew up. Because it is difficult to obtain data directly from members of both generations, investigators interested in intergenerational continuities and discontinuities have begun to examine parents' working models of their early relationships with their parents using the Adult Attachment Interview (AAI; George et al., 1985). This 90-min semistructured interview was developed to assess adults' states of mind regarding parent–child attachment, by means of a detailed analysis of both the content of the narrative and the coherence of the responses to a series of questions about the adults' early and current relationships with their parents. Based on the pattern of coding on continuous scales, the interviewed individual is described as having a secure state of mind regarding parent–child relationships, or an insecure state of mind, which can include a style of either dismissing the importance of such relationships or expressing anger in ways that disrupt the coherence of the narrative (see chapters 2 and 8 for more details). It is not necessary to assume that the interview elicits an accurate picture of the individual's early experience. One need only assume that the interview questions call forth a set of cognitive and affective schemas that represent the adult's current working model of intimate relationships (cf. Main, Kaplan, & Cassidy, 1985).

A large number of studies now show that there is a strong correspondence between parents' working models of their relationships with their parents and their children's security of attachment or adaptation (cf. Van IJzendoorn, Kranenburg, Zwart-Woudstra, & Van Busschbach, 1991). The question is how such linkage occurs. Our preliminary answer (Cowan, Bradburn, & Cowan, chapter 8, this volume) is that representations of parent–child relationships in both parents' families of origin are connected directly and indirectly with the quality of their marital and parent–child relationships in the family they create in the present generation.

Life Stress and Social Support As Predictors of Children's Competence at School

Although Green (1995, p. 208) described the family as "the original and primary classroom experience in a child's life," families do not constitute the only influence on children's adjustment to school (Fig. 1.5). Some research suggests that children's experiences in day care, preschool programs, and peer relationships in the neighborhood affect their academic achievement and social skills in the early elementary school grades, but this conclusion continues to be debated, especially when it centers on the amount and quality of day care (Ladd, 1996; Lazar & Darlington, 1982; NICHD Early Child Care Research Network, 2003). A comprehensive review sponsored by the National Research Council and the Institute of Medicine (Shonkoff & Phillips, 2000, p. 311) concluded the following: "The findings from this literature are consistent. Intensive, high quality, center-based interventions that provide learning experiences directly to the young child have a positive effect on early learning, cognitive and language development, and school achievement." School follow-ups on the impact of these preschool programs on children's subsequent social development have rarely been done (see, however, Ramey & Ramey, 1992).

Most studies that explore outside-the-family influences on children's school adjustment focus on stressors or supports, primarily those that directly affect parents, some aspects of family dynamics, or children's adaptation during the transition to school. In addition to the general association between SES and school outcomes, Barth and Parke (1996) noted that acute stressors experienced by the family before children enter school are associated with kindergarten teachers' negative perceptions of the children and peers' rejection of them. Parents' chronic work stress and dissatisfaction are also associated with negative child outcomes (McLoyd, 1990; Repetti & Wood, 1997). Conversely, there is some suggestion that social supports and positive maternal attitudes toward work promote children's cognitive, social, and behavioral functioning (Crockenberg, 1988; Gottfried, Gottfried, & Bathurst, 1988). In other words, what happens in parents' lives outside the family tends to have spillover effects that amplify or reduce the quality of the transactions among family members at home. Chapter 9 examines parents' daily stress at work as it is related to the children's adaptation, and chapter 12 examines links between parents' general life stress and social support and children's early school outcomes.

Putting Humpty Dumpty Back Together Again

We have been describing risk and protective factors associated with children's adaptation one domain at a time. Some investigators have assumed that a multiple risk model will account for more variance in children's development and adaptation than will any single risk model (e.g., Sameroff, Seifer, & Zax, 1982; Werner & Smith, 1992). Often, multiple risk models assess the presence or absence of risk, and simply add the number of risks together to create a single index. The assumption underlying this approach is that risks have impact only in terms of their presence or absence rather than degree of seriousness, and that any single risk operates much like any other (Greenberg et al., 1999). The idea that marital, parenting, and outside the family supportive relationships could be linked in different ways with different outcomes has not been tested in this additive risk model approach. Furthermore, as Kraemer and her colleagues (Kraemer, Stice, Kazdin, Offord, & Kupfer, 2001) aptly pointed out, there are numerous ways in which multiple risk factors might coexist (e.g., as proxies for one another, independently, or as mutual mediators or moderators), the precise specification of which is vitally necessary for effective prevention or intervention.

Within the field of developmental psychopathology, risk models are beginning to emerge that resemble the family systems model that we presented in Figs. 1.1 to 1.6. For example, in chapter 9 of their text, *Developmental Psychopathology and Family Process: Theory, Research, and Clinical Implications*, Cummings, Davies, and Campbell (2000) proposed a model describing how parental depression can affect children. They summarized evidence from their own and other studies linking genetic intergenerational factors, parents' personality, diagnosed depression, marital conflict, parent–child attachment, parenting practices, children's emotional security, outside-the-family social support, and child adjustment. The research they cited generally deals with two or three of these links at a time, rather than with tests of the model as a whole.

In this volume, we attempt to put the Humpty Dumpty of family risk factors together by testing a five-domain model applied to a nonclinical population, with a focus on children and families undergoing a normative transition. As we noted, there have been no studies of the family factors associated with the transition to school that examined information from all five domains. Based on a few existing studies containing information about two or three domains at a time, we had reason to expect that the five-domain model would be useful in describing the family context of parenting in relation to children's adaptation. In data from an earlier longitudinal family study (P. A. Cowan et al., 1994), structural equation models revealed that a combination of prebirth and postbirth family measures assessing self-reported and observed marital quality, observed parenting style, and parents' reports of life stress predicted 52% of the variance in the children's academic achievement scores in kindergarten. Measures of mothers' and fathers' working models of attachment, in combination with observational measures of their parenting and marital quality, predicted from 39% to 60% of the variance in teachers' ratings of the children's internalizing and externalizing behaviors in kindergarten (P. A.

Cowan, Cohn, Cowan, & Pearson, 1996). Because these earlier articles were based on overlapping data sets and small samples (*ns* ranged from 27 to 44), they almost certainly contained inflated estimates of explained variance. Nevertheless, studies by other investigators who used similar multidomain models to look at children of other ages revealed a similar pattern of findings. For example, Katz and Gottman (1993) showed that, taken together, marital conflict and compromised parenting, assessed when children were 5 years old in kindergarten, predicted the children's behavior problems in second grade 2 years later. Stressors outside the family appear to disrupt the quality of the marriage and each parent's effectiveness with their child in ways that predict the child's lower academic achievement and social competence, and higher levels of aggression or shy, withdrawn, or depressed behavior with peers in both childhood and adolescence (e.g., Conger, Ge, Elder, & Lorenz, 1994). We consider data from combinations of family domains in many chapters of this volume, but focus on the full five-domain context of parenting in chapters 12 and 13.

The Importance of Sex and Gender in Understanding Family Processes

Until late in the 20th century, "parent" in studies of parent–child relationships usually meant "mother" (Lamb, 2000; Parke, 1996). Recent research indicates that fathers also make important, often unique contributions to their children's development (Bronstein & Cowan, 1988; Lamb, 2000; Parke, 1996; Tamis-LeMonda & Cabrera, 2002), despite the fact that fathers generally spend much less time than mothers as "hands-on" caregivers (Coltrane, 1996). This study examined the role of both father–child and mother–child relationships in predicting children's adaptation to elementary school. Introducing fathers into the study of family processes, as we do in this study, adds complexity because of the intricate interplay of both sex and gender in the unfolding of family processes.

For the purposes of clarity and consistency, we refer to sex solely as biological femaleness or maleness, gender as a social construct referring to the social aspects of being of one or the other sex, gender-role as the social expectations and overt expressions of gender, and the personality dimensions of masculinity and femininity as general predispositions that may influence behavior and are typically associated with one gender or the other (Al-Issa, 1982).

The first and most obvious question about the role of sex and gender in families is whether mothers and fathers or boys and girls show significantly different mean scores in their responses to interviews, tests, and questionnaires, or in their behavioral responses in laboratory or naturalistic settings. Although there are usually many similarities between men and women or boys and girls, as well as extensive overlaps in the distribution of abilities and characteristics, it is also the case that there are mean differences between the sexes in areas that are central to this study. For example, in many countries and cultures, women and girls have a greater likelihood than men and boys of experiencing depression, anxiety, and internalizing symptoms (Angold, Er-kanli, Silberg, Eaves, & Costello, 2002; Weissman, 2001), whereas men and boys tend more than women and girls to show more overt signs of aggression (Asher & Coie, 1990). In chapter 3, we provide data from our study to com-pare mothers and fathers on self-report measures of adaptation, and boys and girls on both self-report and observer measures of adaptation.

A second question about sex differences is whether the sex of the partici-pants makes a difference to the quantity or quality of a relationship or trans-action. In this case, we are interested in mean differences in the quality of dyadic interactions among the four dyadic combinations: mothers and daughters, mothers and sons, fathers and daughters, and fathers and sons. Previous research on parents' relationships with young children has not pro-vided unequivocal answers (J. H. Block, 1976; Leaper, 2000, 2002; Lytton, 2000; Maccoby, 2000). Some of the ambiguity in the literature comes from the fact that studies look for differences between fathers and mothers or be-tween sons and daughters but rarely examine all four combinations. In chap-ter 5, we explore whether parents' reactions to children's sex-stereotyped be-havior depends on the sex of the parent and the sex of the child.

A third question that we investigate in this volume is whether children's sex-typed behavior and parents' reaction to it play a role in the development of internalizing behavior problems more typical of girls, and externalizing be-havior problems more typical of boys (see chapters 7 and 8). A final question concerning the role of sex and gender in family patterns is whether sex func-tions as a moderator, affecting the strength of the links between two or more family domains. Does sex of parent or child play a role in the size of the corre-lations between parent–child relationship quality and children's behavior? For example, in one prospective longitudinal study, girls whose parents used a primarily authoritarian parenting style were rated as more overcontrolled in childhood and early adolescence (J. H. Block & Block, 1980), but families with boys did not show this pattern (Kremen, 1996). Sex of parent and child may also influence the connections between marital and parent–child rela-tionships. Kerig and colleagues (1993) found that maritally dissatisfied fa-thers of girls were much more negative toward their daughters than unhap-pily married fathers were toward their sons. In this volume, we present several examples of family relationship patterns that played out differently depending on the sex of parent and child, and some instances in which the sex of the family member did not make a difference (chapters 3, 4, 5, and 10).

In this section, our focus has been on sex differences in the relationships between parents and young children. Information about sex differences in adult attachment patterns (focused on schemas of relationships between adults and their parents), especially differences in correlations between adult attachment and children's adaptation, is remarkably sparse in the literature. Although it is clear from interview studies that adult women do much more of the caregiving and relationship work with their parents than men do with theirs, and that both men and women are more connected with their mothers than with their fathers (Zarit & Eggebeen, 1998), it seems that men and women have very similar distributions of secure or insecure models of attachment (Hesse, 1999) as coded from the AAI (George et al., 1985). We should note that in the coding of this interview, the attachment category is assigned to the overall interview, despite the fact that the interview asks for information about the adults' relationships with both mother and father, and that some of the continuous scales used in the process of coding focus separately on relationships with each parent. A few studies of intergenerational patterns examine links between men's and women's working models of attachment to their parents (AAI) and children's security of attachment to each parent (Strange Situation; Ainsworth & Wittig, 1969). There appear to be stronger links from mother's attachment to the child's security of attachment than there are from father's attachment (Fonagy, Steele, & Steele, 1991), but, as far as we know, the sex of the child was not considered in this or other studies. In chapter 8, we trace different pathways from preschool measures of the parents' working models of attachment to their parents, through marital and parent–child relationship quality, to the children's internalizing and externalizing problem behaviors in kindergarten.

The issue of sex and gender is centrally relevant to the title of this volume in its focus on the family context of parenting. To what extent can we make generalizations about "parents" and to what extent must we consider parent–child relationships as "gendered"? Although we did not have this question in mind when we began designing our study, the findings kept leading us to consider ways in which sex affects what we can say about links between family factors and children's adaptation to school. Our research design made it possible to compare patterns for mothers and fathers of boys and girls.

ORGANIZATION OF THIS VOLUME

Here, we introduce one caveat about the chapters that follow. The volume is written as an integrated one because the reports presented here were part of a single project with an overall organizing set of assumptions. Nevertheless, because the analyses in each chapter were completed at slightly different time periods, in some cases as part of the author's dissertation, the construction of the measures and the focus of the analyses vary somewhat to fit each author's specific aims. Despite this variation, the general constructs and measures are quite similar from chapter to chapter. The volume is divided into five sections.

Section I: Introduction and Method

In addition to this introductory chapter, section I includes a description of the methods of the larger Schoolchildren and Their Families Project (chapter 2). Written by the editors, these chapters serve as the general introduction and method section for all of the subsequent research reports.

Section II: How Things Change Yet Stay the Same

This section contains a chapter by Philip Cowan and Gertrude Heming describing similarities and differences between mothers and fathers and sons and daughters—in measures of individual functioning and family relationships, and in changes in these measures from preschool to kindergarten and from kindergarten to first grade. The chapter addresses the question of whether the child's entrance to elementary school constitutes a major life transition—for the child or for the family as a whole.

Section III: The Family Context of Parenting

Section III begins with two studies of parenting style and children's adaptation to school. Authoritative parenting, based on the dimensions of warmth and control, has been cited consistently as a primary factor in children's academic and social competence, at least in middle-class European American samples. In chapter 4, Jonathan Mattanah goes beyond authoritative parenting to examine parents' encouragement of children's autonomy as an additional ingredient in children's development of competence in the early school years. In chapter 5, Jeanette Hsu looks separately at mothers' and fathers' parenting of sons and daughters to help explain the differential incidence of internalizing and externalizing behaviors in girls and boys in their first year of elementary school.

Following the progression of Figs. 1.1 to 1.5, shown earlier, the model of family–school connections becomes even more complex and differentiated. Two chapters focus on children's perceptions—of themselves and their parents' relationship as a couple—as linking transactions in marital and parenting relationships and children's adaptation to school. In chapter 6, Jeffrey Measelle tests the hypothesis that links among marital conflict, parenting style, and children's school outcomes are mediated and moderated by children's perceptions of themselves. In chapter 7, Jennifer Ablow investigates how parents' reports of their style of resolving marital conflict, and children's perceptions of their parents' conflict resolution, are associated with children's adjustment with their peers in the first year of elementary school.

In chapter 8, Philip Cowan, Isabel Bradburn, and Carolyn Pape Cowan add the perspective of the intergenerational transmission of patterns to children's school adjustment. Then, in chapter 9, as one example of establishing links among family dynamics, outside-the-family circumstances, and children's adaptation to school, Marc Schulz explores links among parents' day-to-day work stress, their reactions to one another and the children at home, and children's competence at school. Finally, in chapter 10, Vanessa Johnson tests the hypothesis that the parents' perceptions of their functioning as a whole family (mother, father, and child) before the children entered elementary school are predictive of the children's problematic behaviors in kindergarten 1 year later.

Section IV: Interventions As Tests of Causal Models of Family Influence on Children's Adaptation to School

In chapter 11, Carolyn Pape Cowan, Philip Cowan, and Gertrude Heming describe the results of a 16-week couples group intervention offered to parents through random assignment after they had expressed interest in the study. This chapter shows that a family-based preventive intervention led by mental health professionals offers the potential of improving the position of children as they set out on their school career trajectories, and illustrates how an intervention design can be useful in testing hypotheses about causal links between the quality of two key family relationships and children's adaptation to school.

Section V: Integrations

In chapter 12, Philip Cowan and Carolyn Pape Cowan present an integrative structural equation model that examines the combined contribution of data from all five family domains to predicting children's adaptation to the first 2 years of elementary school. In a concluding chapter 13, the editors spell out the implications of the findings for understanding the family context of parenting and children's adaptation to school.

2

Recruitment, Design, and Measures

Philip A. Cowan, Carolyn Pape Cowan, Jennifer C. Ablow,
Vanessa K. Johnson, and Jeffrey R. Measelle

The Schoolchildren and their Families study began in 1990 with a recruitment process that included announcements and fliers, and public service announcements in local media to parents of preschool age children. Interested parents were asked to complete and return by mail a brief questionnaire and were invited to an initial interview with a staff couple. This resulted in an initial participant sample of 100 two-parent families. Using a random selection procedure, parents were invited to (a) participate along with four or five other couples in a 16-week couples group with a marital emphasis ($n = 28$), in groups led by a male–female team of mental health professionals; or (b) a 16-week couples group intervention with a parenting emphasis ($n = 27$), led by the same staff; or (c) the opportunity for a once-yearly consultation ($n = 25$) with the same staff couples in the 3 years surrounding their first child's transition to elementary school. The parents were not aware of the variation in emphasis in the different couples groups (see details in chapter 11). An additional 20 couples who became a self-selected "no-intervention" comparison group when they refused the couples group intervention but agreed to be followed were not included in the intervention analyses, except for one intention-to-treat examination of the data. In almost all cases, the 4-month couples groups ended just before the children entered kindergarten.

Families were assessed in the spring of the year before their first child entered school. The assessment included a set of interviews with the parents and with the child, questionnaire booklets for the parents, a family interaction session in our project playroom laboratory, and a home visit interview and test session for the child. A similar set of assessments occurred 1 year later in the spring of the kindergarten year, with the addition of a teacher checklist description of the study child and each child in his or her classroom. Assessments in first grade included interviews with parents and children, questionnaires for the parents, and ratings by the teachers, but no observations of parent–child, couple, or family interaction in the laboratory. An overall retention rate of 84% from preschool to first-grade assessments resulted in a complete data set for 84 families followed over the first child's transition to school—from the last preschool year to the end of first grade.

RECRUITMENT AND DESIGN

Phase 1

Couples were initially recruited through day-care centers, preschools, pediatricians' offices, and public service announcements in the media throughout the larger San Francisco Bay area. They entered the study in three yearly waves, based on their child's school entry in fall 1990, 1991, or 1992. Although the project included an evaluation of a preventive intervention, it is important to note that the recruitment publicity did not mention the intervention but focused on the fact that we were attempting to learn more about parents' and children's experiences of the first child's transition to elementary school. In other words, the participants were not drawn to the study by an explicit expectation of receiving help.

Of initial inquiries from parents in more than 300 families, 198 couples met the initial selection criteria: (a) two parents who were living together with a first child who would enter kindergarten the next fall, and (b) two parents who completed an initial four-page questionnaire booklet containing measures of marital adjustment (Short Marital Adjustment Test; Locke & Wallace, 1959), symptoms of depression (CES-D or Center for Epidemiological Studies in Depression Scale; Radloff, 1977), parenting stress (Parenting Stress Index; Abidin, 1980), a checklist of negative experiences in their family of origin, and a checklist of concerns about their child starting school (the latter checklists created for this project). Despite their making an initial call to the project, some parents were not available for even one initial interview. These scheduling difficulties reduced the pool by 6 couples to a total of 192 who participated in Phase 2.

Phase 2

Couples who completed Phase 1 were invited for an interview with a staff couple. Before the interview, and without letting the interviewers know the scores, the data manager arranged couples in order based on their Locke-

Wallace marital satisfaction scores (discussed later) and placed them randomly in three groups with roughly equal scores. This stratified approach to random selection made certain that, overall, couples in the three study conditions (maritally-focused intervention, parenting-focused intervention, brief consultation) had a similar range of marital satisfaction scores, with each couple winding up in their assigned condition by random assignment.

Each couple was initially interviewed by one of four staff couples—all licensed mental health professionals who were psychologists, social workers, or marriage, family, and child counselors. Participant couples who were assigned to a couples group were further subdivided randomly into two variations of the group intervention: one focusing more on marital issues, the other focusing more on parenting issues during the open-ended portion of each meeting.

The Marital Focus. A weekly couples group met with a staff couple for 16 weeks prior to the children's entrance to kindergarten, with leaders emphasizing marital issues in the open-ended part of each evening.

The Parenting Focus. A weekly couples group met with a staff couple for 16 weeks prior to the children's entrance to kindergarten, with leaders emphasizing parenting issues in the open-ended part of each evening. (Chapter 11 contains more detailed descriptions of the intervention and its variations.)

Assignment to couples groups with the differing emphasis on marital or parenting issues was known only by the two senior authors, the data manager, and staff leaders; participating couples were not made aware that different couples groups would have slightly different emphases. Over the course of the entire study, each staff couple led some maritally-focused groups and some parenting-focused groups, and conducted some brief consultations. The co-investigators met with the four staff couples as a group twice a month throughout the intervention phase to discuss any questions or problems, and to insure that the prescribed emphasis of the two variations of the couples groups were upheld.

Of 153 couples offered a couples group at the end of their initial interview, 61 (40%) accepted; 32 of those 61 couples had been randomly assigned to one of eight maritally-focused intervention groups, and 29 had been assigned to the parenting-focused groups. Of those who initially accepted the invitation to participate in a group, 4 couples assigned to the maritally-focused groups and 2 couples assigned to the parenting-focused intervention did not ultimately attend the group meetings, leaving the final number of couples participating in the group intervention as 28 marital and 27 parenting, or 35.9% of those initially offered a couples group. Twenty couples who declined the offer

TABLE 2.1
Retention From Initial Phase 2 to First Grade

	Interviewed and Offered	Initially Agreed	Began Phase 2 (Prekindergarten)	Completed First Grade Follow-Up
Marital focus	80	32	28	22
Parenting focus	73	29	27	22
Consultation	39	25	25	22
Self-selected controls	(from the above cells)	36	20	18
Total in study	192	122	100	84

of a couples group[1] agreed to allow us to follow their families over time, thus constituting a self-selected no-intervention comparison sample (see Table 2.1). To make the study fit the Randomized Clinical Trials design, data from this self-selected comparison were not used in evaluating the impact of the intervention.

In sum, of 100 couples (200 parents) who proceeded with the study after their initial inquiry, there were 28 couples in the maritally-focused intervention, 27 in the parenting-focused intervention, 25 in the brief consultation, and 20 in the self-selected no-intervention comparison group. The families in each condition were comparable on various measures of adaptation during their children's last preschool year. Once couples agreed to continue in Phase 2, there was a relatively small attrition rate averaging 16%; 84% of the intervention couples ($n = 46$), 80% of the consultation couples ($n = 20$), and 90% of the self-selected controls ($n = 18$), remained in the study over the next 2 years. Because of scheduling difficulties, equipment failures, and occasional missing questionnaires, data from approximately 88 families were available at the kindergarten follow-ups and 80 to 84 families at first grade for most of the analyses. From the 100 families who agreed to participate in Phase 2 of the study before their first child entered kindergarten, we have almost complete data from 84 at both kindergarten and first grade.

For specific reasons having to do with the measures that are the focus of a particular set of analyses, three chapters in this volume report on a somewhat

---

[1]Most couples who declined the offer of a weekly couples group gave time constraints as their reason. For example, there were a few couples in which one partner worked daytime hours and the other worked night shifts. A few couples said that they had no evening when both partners were free to meet with our staff. Several parents claimed that they had never left their preschooler with a baby sitter other than a family member, and the obligation for 16 weeks of regular weekday evening child care felt too problematic for them. Because the groups were held in the evening to make it possible for working fathers and mothers to attend, we were unable to offer child care at the university during hours when most of the children needed to be put to sleep. We did offer to defray the costs of child care for couples who said that this would be a hardship for the 16 weeks. There was no charge for the groups.

reduced data set (ns = 60 to 73; chapters 6, 8, and 9). The remaining chapters (3, 4, 5, 7, 10, 11, and 12) are based on analyses of the full sample.

Participants

Of the 100 couples initially participating in Phase 2 of the study, 59 had a male first child (age M = 4.91, SD = .56) and 41 had a female first child (age M = 5.10, SD = .55).[2] The average age of the fathers at entry was 38.07 years (SD = 7.44) and of the mothers 36.88 years (SD = 5.75). According to their self-descriptions, 84.0% are European American, 6.6% are African American, 7.0% are Asian American, and 2.5% are Latin American. At the time they entered the study, the parents and children were not involved in seeking help in the mental health system, although some have done so since then. Although we did not exclude unmarried cohabiting couples, all but two participant couples were married when they entered the study.

The couples lived in 27 cities and towns within a 40-mile radius of the University of California at Berkeley. As we noted in chapter 1, the median yearly total household income of the families indicates a relatively affluent sample of two-parent, mostly two-job or two-career families with a first child about to enter kindergarten, although 21% of the participant couples earned below the median family income in the San Francisco Bay area. Thus, although the sample is clearly not representative of families in poverty, it does contain a substantial range of family incomes.

The Logic of the Assessment Procedure

We were guided in selecting measures for this study by findings from an earlier longitudinal study of families from pregnancy through the first child's completion of kindergarten (C. P. Cowan & Cowan, 1992), by discussions with couples in a preventive intervention project that was part of the graduate program in Clinical Psychology at the University of California at Berkeley (Chavez et al., 1988), and by material gathered in interviews with parents of children about to enter elementary school (Brand, Cowan, & Cowan, 1994). The measurement strategy was based on four general principles. First, consistent with a family systems model (see chapter 1), we measured adaptive and maladaptive functioning in each of five family domains (individual, marital, parent–child, three-generations, and outside the family). Second, two or more measures from each of the central constructs in the study were included (questionnaire instruments from different sources, or one self-report and one

---

[2]A χ^2 of 5.32 (4, N = 100) revealed no significant differences in the proportion of boys and girls in the Phase 1 families who did not continue, the families in the marital intervention, the parenting intervention, the brief consultation, and the self-selected controls.

observational measure). Third, in individual, marital, parent–child, and sibling domains, information was obtained from multiple perspectives, including self-report data, reports by other family members, and observations by nonfamily members—mainly our research staff and the children's teachers. Fourth, to evaluate family trajectories during the child's transition to elementary school, we engaged in extensive assessments of each family member and the relationships among family members during the preschool period and at the end of kindergarten and first grade.

In the prekindergarten and preintervention period (PRE), families participated in extensive assessments that included (a) structured interviews; (b) structured observations of marital, parent–child, sibling, and whole family interaction, all conducted on site in our project playroom; (c) a questionnaire booklet filled out separately by mothers and fathers; and (d) separate observations of the children by project staff, once in our project playroom and once at each family's home during the summer. These assessments were repeated during the kindergarten year (POST1). In the spring and summer following first grade (POST2), we repeated questionnaires and interviews with the parents and home visits with the children, but not the observations of the couple, the child, or the whole family at our project. Families were paid $100 each year for participation in these activities after parents returned their questionnaire booklets.

In this chapter, we describe the measures used in the studies in the volume. Table 2.2 provides a schematic list of measures and when they were obtained. For the questionnaires and rating scales created for this study, we provide evidence of validity—in most cases from their use in other studies. We expect that readers will use the remaining sections of this chapter as a reference library, referring back to these fuller descriptions of each measure when it is described more briefly in the chapters that follow.

MEASURES OF CHILDREN'S ADAPTATION TO SCHOOL

Academic Achievement

Our measure of academic achievement was derived from the widely-used Peabody Individual Achievement Test (PIAT; Markwardt, 1989). The PIAT was administered individually to each child at home by a member of our research staff in the summer after the completion of kindergarten and first grade. The Peabody Individual Achievement Test–Revised (PIAT–R) has five subscales with standardized scores that measure reading recognition, reading comprehension, mathematics, spelling, and general information, which are used to create an overall standardized achievement score.

TABLE 2.2
Schoolchildren and Their Families Project Measures

Questionnaire Name	Acronym	Child	Mother	Father	Observer	Teacher
Children's Adaptation						
Peabody Individual Achievement Test	PIAT	P, 1, 2				
Berkeley Puppet Interview: Self concept	BPI	P, 1, 2				
Child Adaptive Behavior Inventory: Six dimensions	CABI		P, 1, 2	P, 1, 2	P, 1, 2	P, 1, 2
Parent's Adaptation						
Adjective Check List: Self-esteem	ACL		P, 1, 2	P, 1, 2		
Brief Symptom Inventory: Anxiety	BSI		P, 1, 2	P, 1, 2		
Center for Epidemiological Studies in Depression	CES-D		P, 1, 2	P, 1, 2		
Marital Relationship						
Self Report						
Who Does What	WDW		P, 1, 2	P, 1, 2		
Locke–Wallace Marital Satisfaction	MAT		P, 1, 2	P, 1, 2		
Couple Communication			P, 1, 2	P, 1, 2		
Observed						
Couple problem-solving discussion					P, 1, 2	
Coparenting rating scale		P, 1, 2				
Berkeley Puppet Interview					P, 1	

(Continued)

TABLE 2.2
(Continued)

Questionnaire Name	Acronym	Child	Mother	Father	Observer	Teacher
Parent–Child Relationship						
Self Report						
Ideas About Parenting	IAP		P, 1, 2	P, 1, 2		
Parenting Stress Index	PSI		P, 1, 2	P, 1, 2		
Observed						
Parenting Style Rating Scale					P, 1	
Family Adaptation						
Family of origin						
Adult Attachment Interview			P	P		
Family Relationship Questionnaire			P, 2	P, 2		
Traumatic Events Checklist			P	P		
Whole Family						
Moos Family Environment Scale			P, 2	P, 2		
Outside the family						
Work and Family Life			P, 2	P, 2		
Recent Life Events: Life stress			P, 1, 2	P, 1, 2		
Important People In Your Life: Social support			P, 1, 2	P, 1, 2		

Note. P = Pre-intervention; 1 = Post-intervention 1; 2 = Post-intervention 2. P = PRE Preschool. 1 = PO1 kindergarten. 2 = PO2 Gr.

Children's Views of Their School Adaptation:
The Berkeley Puppet Interview

Rather than attempt to assess all known facets of the young child's self-concept, the goal was to develop an age-appropriate instrument that could be used easily to measure young children's perceptions of their adjustment at school. The Berkeley Puppet Interview (BPI), created by Ablow and Measelle (1993), was used to measure children's academic and social self-perceptions late in the year before they entered kindergarten and again at the end of kindergarten and first grade. The BPI adopts a multidimensional approach to the measurement of young children's self-perceptions (Shavelson, Hubner, & Stanton, 1976), and builds on the theoretical idea that children can provide domain-specific descriptions and self-judgments when asked about salient aspects of their lives (Damon & Hart, 1982; Markus & Wurf, 1987).

In the BPI, children are questioned by two identical hand puppets (tan-colored puppy dogs named "Iggy" and "Ziggy," as indicated on their visible nametags). The interview begins with Iggy and Ziggy saying, "I'm going to tell you some things about me," and then, "We want to learn about you." Three to four neutral practice items (e.g., "I like pizza," or "I don't like pizza") are administered to acclimate the child to the BPI method. During the interview, one puppet says, "I have lots of friends at school." The second puppet says, "I don't have lots of friends at school," and then the child would be asked by one of the puppets, "How about you _____ (child's name)?"

Similar to Harter's self-concept measures (Harter, 1982, 1999), each BPI item consists of a pair of opposing, bipolar statements designed to reflect the positive and negative ends of different behaviors and attributes. An equal number of items focus on positive attributes and behaviors (e.g., "I'm good at making friends" or "I'm not good at making friends") and negative attributes and behaviors (e.g., "I tease other kids" or "I don't tease other kids"). Items were counterbalanced so that children heard the positive half of an item first as often as they heard the negative half first from the puppets. Positive and negative attributes were also divided equally between the two puppets so that the children would not identify exclusively with either puppet.

The BPI method does not use a forced-choice response format or recognition task as do most other self-perception measures for children this age (Elder, 1990; Harter & Pike, 1984; Marsh, Craven, & Debus, 1991). Rather, children are allowed to respond in a way that is comfortable for them. They typically responded verbally or made partial verbal statements that paralleled or modified one of the statements made by the puppets. A few of the preschool children responded nonverbally by pointing to a puppet or by shaking their head in agreement or disagreement. If a child's nonverbal manner of responding was ambiguous, the puppeteer was trained to establish a clearer means of communication with the child through the puppet. For example, if a child nodded or shook his or her head "yes" or "no," the puppets encouraged the child to point to the particular puppet as well.

Two coders scored all BPI interviews from videotaped interviews. Based on the degree to which children's responses paralleled one of the puppet's statements, responses were coded on a 7-point (1–7) Likert-type scale. On the BPI's 7-point scale, the numbers 2 and 6 represent responses that are equivalent to one of the statements made by either puppet. For example, if a child responded at the negative end by endorsing the item, "I think I'm not smart," the response was coded 2, because it directly reflected the statement made by one puppet. However, if a child amplified the original negative statement by stating, "I'm really stupid," this response was scored 1 to represent a more negative response than the puppet's original statement. If the child expressed a less emphatic negative perception (e.g., "*Sometimes* I think I'll get along well with other kids, but not always") or felt the need to qualify the response (e.g., "When I'm at preschool I don't get along, but on my street I do"), the response was scored 3. Positive response were coded on the 5 to 7 range of the scale, with 5 representing a less emphatic positive response than a 6, and 7 representing a more positive response than the puppet's original statement. If children indicated that "both" options pertain to them or that they are "in the middle," their responses were coded 4. Two additional codes (8 and 9) were reserved for unable-to-code responses. Absolute agreement among coders' ratings of children's preschool responses on the BPI was high (90.3%). The average Pearson correlation between raters of the preschool, kindergarten, and first-grade BPIs was .86.

Both a rational grouping of the 41 items and a factor analysis supported the division of items into six scales: academic competence, achievement motivation, social competence, peer acceptance, depression-anxiety, and aggression-hostility. With the exception of the social competence scale, alpha reliabilities ranged from .70 to .78, quite good considering the age of the children.

Research with the BPI on this sample (Measelle, Ablow, Cowan, & Cowan, 1998) showed that the method was sensitive to normative changes and individual differences during the 4½- to 7½-year-old period. The validity of the BPI was supported by the fact that there were consistent patterns of association between children's self-perceptions and ratings by adult informants. For example, children's self-descriptions of their academic competence, achievement motivation, peer acceptance, depression-anxiety, and aggression-hostility, were correlated with kindergarten teachers' ratings on the Child Adaptive Behavior Inventory (CABI) of the same constructs, $rs(86) = -.31$ to .42, and also with first-grade teachers' ratings, $rs(86)^3 = .31$ to .44. The only scale

---

[3]Note that the n here is 88, although we generally have complete data only from 84 families with first graders. A few families permitted us to obtain teachers' ratings but did not participate in the laboratory family interactions.

that did not show significant correlations between children's and teacher's descriptions was social competence.

In a three-city study of children from clinic-referred families and community families, an expanded version of the BPI self-description scale was constructed with an additional 18 items focusing on symptoms (Ablow et al., 1999). Six of the nine scales (depression, overanxious, separation anxiety, oppositional defiant, conduct problem, overt hostility) discriminated between children referred for mental health problems and children who were not referred. Further evidence concerning the validity of the BPI is presented in the course of this volume.

Teachers' View of the Child: The Child Adaptive Behavior Inventory (CABI)

CABI Items. Instruments for the assessment of social–emotional behavior in school-age children tend to focus either on competence or problematic behavior, but not both. For example, in the widely-used Child Behavior Check List (CBCL; Achenbach & Edelbrock, 1983), 118 of 138 items describe problem behavior, with little attention to positive adaptation. To create an instrument that would do justice to both adaptation and maladaptation, we obtained descriptions of the children from their teachers in kindergarten and first grade using the CABI, an instrument used in an earlier study (C. P. Cowan & Cowan, 1992) and adapted further for this investigation (P. A. Cowan, Cowan, & Heming, 1995).

The 106 items included in the CABI were selected from several sources (see the Appendix for the complete list). A 60-item Adaptive Behavior Inventory (Schaefer & Hunter, 1983), containing both positive and negative descriptors of academic and social competence in the classroom (e.g., "is smart for his or her age," "has trouble concentrating on what he or she is doing," "is shy or bashful with other children," "acts as a leader"), was used in its entirety. Each item is rated on a 4-point scale ranging from (1) *Not at all like this child*, to (4) *Very much like this child*. To this 60-item scale, 46 items were added, 16 to assess attributes usually assessed in sociometric measures of peer status (social isolation, peer rejection, social skills), and 30 items to measure problem behavior, selected from the downward extension of the Quay-Peterson Behavior Problem Checklist (O'Donnel & Van Tuinen, 1979) and Achenbach and Edelbrock's (1983) CBCL.

A Normative Sample. The children attended 85 different schools in the larger San Francisco-Oakland Bay area. In late fall and late spring of kindergarten and first grade, children's teachers were asked to fill out the CABI on each child in the classroom without being told which child was a participant in the study. Depending on the assessment period, approximately 60% of the teachers agreed to complete the CABI on all of the children in their classroom. An additional 20% to 25% of the teachers, depending on grade and time of year (fall, spring), agreed to complete the checklists on at least five children of the same gender as the target child, with the children chosen by us from the teacher's list to keep the identity of the target child anonymous. Finally, from 1% to 9% of the teachers at each assessment period agreed to describe only the target child, in which case, we asked the parents' permission to identify their child to the teacher. Teachers were paid $40 for each set of ratings of the whole class in fall and spring.

In total, then, we gathered teachers' descriptions of all 100 of the study children and their classmates in the fall and 93 in the spring of kindergarten year, and of 94 of the study children in the fall and 85 in the spring of first grade. Thus, we have a large normative sample of CABI teacher ratings at 4 points: kindergarten fall ($n = 1,723$; average n per classroom $= 17.23$); kindergarten spring ($n = 1,433$; average n per classroom $= 15.31$); first grade fall ($n = 1,490$; average n per classroom $= 15.85$); first grade spring ($n = 1,297$; average n per classroom $= 15.26$). The averages hide the fact that the distribution of the number of children rated per classroom was bimodal, centering around 28 in classrooms in which the teacher rated all of her students and around 10 for classrooms in which a teacher rated a much smaller subset.

Scale Reliability. We have reported on the use of the CABI in other publications (e.g., P. A. Cowan et al., 1994; Johnson, Cowan, & Cowan, 1999), but because the CABI is the source of most of our information about children's adaptation to school throughout the volume, we provide details here about reliability and validity. The 106 items of the CABI were grouped into 22 scales, each containing from 3 to 7 items. The first 16 scales were taken from Schaefer and Hunter's (1983) original arrangement of 60 items (e.g., fair, anxious, hyperactive, intelligent, creative).

From a content-based classification of new items, six additional scales were created (imitative, impaired in physical development, social isolated, socially rejected, socially perceptive, socially skilled). We calculated the item alphas for each of the 22 scales at four assessment periods—fall and spring, kindergarten and first grade—for the Schoolchildren and Their Families sample and for the entire large sample of children at each assessment (see Tables 2.3a and 2.3b). Two of the new scales, imitative and impaired in physical development, had relatively low reliabilities and were not used in further analyses. The remaining 20 scales showed adequate to high interitem consistency, with alphas ranging from .60 to .93. Over all four assessment periods (fall kindergarten, spring kindergarten, fall first grade, spring first grade), median alphas for teachers' ratings of the children included in our study ranged from .78 to .80, and median teachers' ratings of the whole sample of 1,297 to 1,723 children ranged from .79 to .82, depending on the assessment period.

TABLE 2.3A
Kindergarten Teacher Child Adaptive Behavior Inventory Alphas

Scales	First Grade Spring	First Grade Fall	First Grade Spring	First Grade Fall
Main scales				
Fair	.68	.75	.81	.78
Calm	.65	.54	.64	.63
Kind	.80	.82	.85	.85
Anxious	.85	.80	.78	.77
Hyperactive	.83	.83	.86	.87
Antisocial	.84	.86	.86	.87
Oppositional	.83	.88	.86	.87
Hostile	.88	.90	.88	.88
Intelligent	.81	.83	.85	.85
Creative	.73	.77	.78	.81
Task	.76	.71	.80	.78
Distractible	.85	.83	.88	.88
Extroverted	.86	.87	.86	.85
Introverted	.89	.90	.86	.86
Depressed	.91	.93	.87	.88
Somaticizes	.82	.83	.77	.78
Imitative	.56	.42	.52	.45
Impaired in physical development	.56	.60	.65	.65
Socially isolated	.85	.87	.87	.86
Socially rejected	.78	.82	.82	.79
Socially perceptive	.77	.75	.80	.78
Socially skilled	.65	.73	.68	.69
Composite dimensions				
Academic competence	.89	.86	.89	.88
Social competence	.89	.90	.89	.88
Externalizing-aggressive	.92	.92	.92	.92
Externalizing-hyperactive	.71	.83	.77	.77
Internalizing-social isolation	.89	.88	.85	.86
Internalizing-anxious and depressed	.80	.74	.74	.72

Because classrooms vary in the distribution of both academic and social competence (Kellam, Rebok, Mayer, Ialongo, & Kalodner, 1994), scores were created that reflected the standing of the target child relative to his or her same-sex classmates. For each target child, a standardized score was created by subtracting the mean scale score from the mean scale scores of all same-sex classmates and dividing by the standard deviation of the classroom. For the small proportion of target children whose teachers filled out the checklist on them alone, we standardized their scores relative to all the study children of the same grade and sex. This standardization procedure follows the advice of Feshbach, Adelman, and Fuller (1977), who found stronger correlations between achievement tests and standardized teachers' ratings than

TABLE 2.3B
Kindergarten Teacher Child Adaptive Behavior Inventory Alphas

Scales	First Grade Spring	First Grade Fall	First Grade Spring	First Grade Fall
Fair	.78	.75	.80	.80
Calm	.64	.62	.68	.65
Kind	.87	.89	.87	.86
Anxious	.81	.75	.81	.81
Hyperactive	.87	.88	.89	.88
Antisocial	.87	.88	.87	.87
Oppositional	.88	.85	.89	.88
Hostile	.91	.88	.88	.89
Intelligent	.82	.82	.89	.87
Creative	.72	.75	.90	.80
Task	.81	.80	.83	.83
Distractible	.86	.90	.91	.90
Extroverted	.81	.81	.84	.83
Introverted	.86	.84	.86	.86
Depressed	.86	.86	.85	.85
Somaticizes	.76	.79	.83	.81
Imitative	.48	.58	.58	.60
Impaired in physical development	.52	.72	.60	.61
Socially isolated	.89	.86	.87	.86
Socially rejected	.77	.86	.84	.83
Socially perceptive	.87	.79	.85	.83
Socially skilled	.69	.77	.76	.75
Composite dimensions				
Academic competence	.85	.83	.89	.87
Social competence	.92	.93	.92	.92
Externalizing-aggressive	.94	.90	.93	.93
Externalizing-hyperactive	.78	.74	.80	.78
Internalizing-social isolation	.87	.88	.83	.85
Internalizing-anxious and depressed	.77	.74	.78	.76

between tests and raw scores: "The loss in discrimination entailed in assuming equivalence between classes is more than balanced by the gain resulting from eliminating error variance due to the tendency of some teachers to systematically avoid low ratings" (p. 301). A further justification follows from the point that classrooms vary in the distribution of both academic and social competence (Kellam et al., 1994), so that a child judged as relatively low in competence in one class might actually be seen as highly competent in another.

To reduce the item-based scales to a manageable number of aspects of adaptation, we composited 20 of the 22 standardized scale scores into six dimensions. Our grouping was based on a previous factor analysis of the scale on a similar population (C. P. Cowan & Cowan, 1992; see the Appendix for specific scales included in each dimension): (a) academic competence; (b) social competence; (c) externalizing-aggression; (d) externalizing-hyperactivity; (e) internalizing-social withdrawal, isolated; and (f) internalizing-psychological symptoms (anxiety, depression, tension). The interitem consistencies of these composite dimensions were very high. Median αs of the teachers' ratings across all six dimensions ranged from .84 to .86 over fall and spring kindergarten and first grade, in both the smaller sample that included only the children in our study, and in the larger sample that included their classmates (see Tables 2.3a and 2.3b).

Test–Retest Reliability (Fall–Spring Correlations). To examine the test–retest reliability of teachers' ratings over time, we correlated target children's fall and spring ratings in kindergarten and again in first grade. Because the remaining children in the class were not identifiable to us, we could not match the fall and spring teachers' ratings for the larger sample. The median fall–spring correlations (across 5 months within the same school year) over 20 scales were generally high (kindergarten αs (93) ranged from .35 to .87, median .63; first-grade αs (83) ranged from .46 to .80, median .64).

Reflecting the fact that composite scores are likely to be more reliable measures than individual scales, the fall–spring correlations for the six composite dimensions on the CABI were even higher than the single scales. Kindergarten correlations (Pearson) across 6 months for academic competence, social competence, externalizing-aggression, externalizing-hyperactivity, internalizing-withdrawal, and internalizing-psychological symptoms correlations $(df = 93)$ ranged from .67 to .80, with a median of .75. First grade rs (84) ranged from .69 to .84, with a median of .77.

Validity. The available evidence suggests that the CABI provides meaningful measures of children's variations along each of six major dimensions of adaptation. First, the already-noted stability of the teachers' ratings, not only from fall to spring with the same teacher, but also from kindergarten to first grade (.49 to .58) with different teachers (see Table 3.3 in chapter 3), indicates that the instrument appears to be sensitive to children's characteristics regardless of observer or classroom. Second, teachers' ratings using the CABI were correlated with other sources of information concerning the same or similar constructs in this and other studies:

1. Academic competence—There was low to moderate agreement between teachers' ratings of the children and their scores on academic achievement tests administered by project staff. When kindergarten and first grade teachers described the child as more academically competent on CABI items, the child's Peabody Individual Achievement total score was higher (spring kindergarten, $r(91) = .38$, $p < .001$; fall first grade, $r(91) = .26$, $p < .05$; and

spring first grade, $r(83) = .32$, $p < .001$).[4] The teacher's rating of academic competence was also correlated with the child's view of himself or herself as competent in school as assessed by the BPI in both kindergarten, $r(86) = .34$, $p < .01$; and first grade, $r(86) = .31$, $p < .01$.

2. Externalizing and internalizing—Further evidence for the validity of the externalizing and internalizing CABI factors comes from a study by Katz and Gottman (1993), who compared a single teacher's ratings of 7- to 8-year-olds on two different instruments and reported significant correlations between internalizing and externalizing on the CBCL and the CABI (internalizing $r = .49$, $p < .001$; externalizing $r = .68$, $p < .001$). A study of 4-year-olds by Wood, Cowan, and Baker (2002) found moderate to high correlations between teachers' ratings of externalizing on the CABI and sociometric measures of peer rejection, $r(36) = .46$, $p < .01$ for girls and $r(38) = .64$, $p < .01$ for boys.

We note that the correlations among teachers' CABI ratings, parents' CABI ratings, the child's self-description on the BPI, and tested academic achievement (PIAT), are not always high. Nevertheless, despite the fact that the child was being assessed in different settings by different observers using different methods, these correlations are consistent and almost all are statistically significant.

A central criterion of validity for a new measuring instrument like the CABI is whether it is associated with a network of measures predicted by theory. In our earlier longitudinal study, with a different sample of children and parents, we showed that indicators of parents having a secure working model of attachment, low marital conflict, and authoritative rather than authoritarian parenting styles, assessed when children were 3½ years old, predicted higher academic achievement and lower levels of both internalizing and externalizing 2 years later when they were in kindergarten (P. A. Cowan et al., 1996; P. A. Cowan et al., 1994). The combined predictive power of the family relationship measures explained more than 50% of the variance in these CABI measures of adaptation to elementary school. As we show, the findings from this study reveal similarly strong linkages between family processes and children's outcomes, providing additional support for the usefulness of the CABI as a measure of children's academic competence, social competence, and problem behaviors.

---

[4]Note that there was no significant correlation between teachers' views obtained in fall kindergarten and the child's tested achievement in spring of the same year. The lack of correspondence is not simply a matter of time between observation and testing, because teachers' ratings in fall first grade were correlated with Peabody Individual Achievement Test scores in the spring. The issue seems to be that in the disequilibrating early months of entrance to elementary school, it is difficult for teachers to judge academic competence.

Parents' View of the Child

A CABI identical to that filled out by the teachers was completed in the spring of each year by fathers and mothers. At the pretest only, the parents' Phase 1 booklet also included "My Child's Entrance to Kindergarten," a questionnaire that we created about a number of possible concerns about school (e.g., choosing between public and private schools, whether the classroom will have enough structure for the child), the teacher (e.g., whether he or she will like and accept my child, be critical of my child), and the child's adaptation (e.g., whether he or she will succeed academically, make friends, be too shy, be too aggressive).

MEASURES OF ADAPTATION IN THE FAMILY

Parents' Views of Themselves

Self-Concept and Identity. The "Pie" (C. P. Cowan & Cowan, 1991) was developed to represent the more contextual, social aspects of the self or identity-in-relationships. Beside a circle 4 in. in diameter, each participant was asked to list the main roles in his or her life right now, and to divide the circle (Pie) so that each section reflects the salience or importance of each aspect of self, not the amount of time spent in that role. Content analysis yielded a coding scheme that included the following: family roles such as parent and partner or lover, worker and student roles, leisure roles such as artist and gardener, and "core" aspects of the self such as "me" or "myself alone" (C. P. Cowan et al., 1985b). Partners completed one Pie for "Me as I am" and another for "Me as I'd like to be" at each phase of the study. One index of the validity of this instrument is that the self as depicted on the Pie changes in meaningful ways over the course of a major life transition. For example, in a study of the transition to parenthood in contrast with self-esteem on the Adjective Check List (ACL), which remained stable over the course of the transition to parenthood (C. P. Cowan et al., 1985a), men's and women's self-descriptions on the Pie showed systematic and meaningful shifts: the parent piece increased between pregnancy and 18 months postpartum for both men and women; the worker piece increased for men, but decreased for women; and the partner or lover aspect of self grew smaller for new mothers and fathers.

Adaptation. The ACL (Gough & Heilbrun, 1965, 1980) contains 300 adjectives that can be endorsed to describe oneself. Gough and Heilbrun created and normed 36 scales by validating them extensively with other self-report and observational instruments. At each assessment period, mothers and fathers in the Schoolchildren and Their Families Project completed two ACLs to describe "Me as I am" and "Me as I'd like to be." Self-esteem was inferred from discrepancies between actual and ideal descriptions on eight of the subscales, using a self-esteem index (Gough, Fioravanti, & Lazzari, 1983). Extensive studies of the validity of the instrument are reported in the ACL Manual (Gough & Heilbrun, 1965, 1980). The ACL provides an individually-focused, essentially context-free description of self. The context-independent nature of the ACL may be one reason that self-descriptions remain so stable over time (e.g., correlations between late pregnancy and 18 months postpartum in an earlier sample of 94 parents of young children were .67 for men and .75 for women; C. P. Cowan & Cowan, 1992).

We used two measures of psychological symptoms—the Brief Symptom Inventory (BSI; Derogatis & Melisaratos, 1983) and the CES-D (Radloff, 1977). On the BSI, parents indicated which of 53 symptoms they had experienced in the past 4 weeks (nervousness, feeling that most people can't be trusted, feelings of guilt, feeling that something is wrong with your mind), as well as how much discomfort that problem caused, using ratings from 0 (*not at all*) to 4 (*extreme*). The total symptom score on the BSI was used as a global index of each parent's psychological distress. Evidence suggests that, although the individual subscales are highly intercorrelated and provide poor discriminant validity, the global scale provides a valid general indicator of psychopathology (Boulet & Boss, 1991).

On the CES-D, parents indicated which of 20 symptoms of depression applied to them in the past week, with intensity ranging from 0 (*rarely or none of the time/less than 1 day*) to 3 (*most or all of the time/5–7 days*); items included affective ("I felt depressed"), interpersonal ("I felt lonely"), behavioral ("I talked less than usual"), and somatic ("My sleep was restless") correlates of depression. The scale has been shown to discriminate between psychiatric and nonpsychiatric samples (Husaini et al., 1980; Radloff, 1977). The total CES-D score was used as an index of the severity of each parent's self-reported symptoms of depression.

Parent–Child Relationships

Observed Parenting Style.   Parenting style was assessed with observers' ratings of the interaction between mother and child, and father and child, as each of the parent–child dyads worked and played together in 40-min sessions in the project playroom. The order of parent was randomly selected at PRE, and then reversed at POST1 for each family. Comparable activities for each parent were presented by one of the experimenters in a prescribed order, but each parent was invited to use his or her own judgment about how to order the tasks and how long to continue each activity. The parent's first task was to ask the child to retell a brief story that he or she had just been told by one experimenter outside the playroom while the parent was being briefed by a second experimenter inside the room (see Pratt, Kerig, Cowan, & Cowan, 1988, for details). Next, the children were to traverse a complex maze by using two knobs to direct a pointer on an "Etch-A-Sketch" board, or to tilt a ball bearing around slotted tracks without letting it drop through several holes in the tracks on a "Labyrinth" game. During a third task, parents were asked to instruct the child in counting techniques or in a Piagetian conservation of number task. A fourth task involved the parent asking the child to tell the story from a children's book with vivid illustrations but no words (one of Mercer Mayer's "frog stories" used frequently in studies of psycholinguistic development around the world; Berman et al., 1994). Finally, each parent and child "built a world" together in a 3 ft. × 3 ft. sand tray by choosing from hundreds of miniature figures and structures.

Two observers rated each parent's behavior on 17 items adapted from scales initially created by Block and Block (1980) and later modified by Erickson, Sroufe, and Egeland (1985). In addition to rating the typical level of that behavior over the entire visit, each behavior was also rated on a 5-item Likert-type scale for the highest level of that behavior observed at any time during the visit. Most items were also rated for lowest level observed.

The current study focused on six composite scales that directly assess emotional climate (warmth, responsiveness, anger) and parental control, the two central dimensions of authoritative parenting according to many authorities (e.g., Baumrind, 1989; Maccoby & Martin, 1983). In addition, there were ratings of autonomy encouragement as a separate dimension of parenting style:

1. Emotional climate—Warmth was assessed on two scales in the system: warmth–coldness and pleasure–displeasure. Warmth–coldness was rated on a 7-point scale ranging from high coldness to high warmth. Parents high in warmth demonstrated affection for their child openly and clearly, and a feeling of connectedness was apparent between parent and child. Parents seen as high on coldness interacted with the child in a withdrawn and aloof fashion and some rejected their child's overtures for closeness. Pleasure–displeasure assessed how readily the parent accepted his or her role as parent and conveyed that acceptance to the child. Parents high on pleasure appeared to enjoy their role as parents and interacted with their child in a playful, humorous, and enthusiastic manner; parents low on pleasure seemed to accept their role as parents grudgingly and displayed boredom or ill feeling when interacting with the child. The composite variable for warmth summed parents' typical level of warmth and pleasure; internal consistency was high (mothers' α = .86; fathers' α = .83).

Negative emotions expressed toward the child were assessed with a composite of four scales (anger, displeasure, coldness, and anxiety), which had a high level of internal consistency (mothers' α = .88; fathers' α = .89).

2. Control—Parents' setting of limits was coded on two scales in this system: limit-setting and maturity demands. The limit-setting scale assessed how well the parent established, maintained, and followed through on limits set during the interaction. The variable was rated on a 4-point scale ranging from 1 (*very low limit-setting*) to 4 (*high limit-setting*). Parents high on limit-setting established limits for their children's behavior, maintained those limits in the face of defiant or difficult behavior on the child's part, and were consistent in the application of their limits. The maturity demands scale assessed the parent's expectations of developmentally or familial or culturally appropriate behavior from the child, expectations that can be conveyed verbally (e.g., "don't lean back in your chair") or nonverbally (with facial gestures, frowns, etc.). The tone in which these expectations were conveyed was not considered in making the rating. Rated on the same 4-point scale, parents high on maturity demands expected a high standard of performance within the child's capacity. From these ratings, a composite variable for control was created by summing parents' scores on their typical and lowest levels on limit-setting and maturity demands. The composite made up of these four measures was highly internally consistent (mothers' α = .91; fathers' α = .85).

Because authoritative parenting represents a style that combines high warmth and high control (Baumrind, 1989; Hinshaw, Zupan, Simmel, Nigg, & Melnick, 1997; Miller, Cowan, Cowan, & Hetherington, 1993), we created a composite variable that summed parents' scores on the warmth and control composite variables. Thus, parents high on authoritative parenting were seen as making developmentally appropriate demands for mature behavior and setting firm limits (from the limit-setting composite)—while remaining warm and seeming to take pleasure in their child (from the warmth composite). Separately or in composite form, the warmth and control ratings have been shown to be connected with both positive academic outcomes and problem behavior outcomes in children in preschool (Pratt et al., 1988) and kindergarten (P. A. Cowan et al., 1994; Miller et al., 1993).

Interrater reliabilities (αs) for the warmth, negative emotion, and structure or control composite scales were high, as was the authoritative parenting construct. Median α for mothers was .82 at the PRE assessment and .86 at the POST1 (kindergarten) follow-up. Median α for fathers was .87 at PRE and .88 at POST1.

3. Active autonomy encouragement (see chapter 4).

Self-Reported Parenting.

1. Ideas about parenting—This questionnaire (G. Heming, P. A. Cowan, & C. P. Cowan, 1990) combines items from scales by Baumrind (1971), Block (1971), and Cohler, Grunebaum, Weiss, and Moran (1971). Fathers and mothers were asked to indicate the extent of their own agreement or disagree-

ment with each item, and what they believed were their partners' opinions. Items factored into two scales that reflect authoritative parenting and authoritarian parenting, $\alpha = .73$ and $.56$, respectively. A permissiveness scale had an unacceptably low α of $.35$, and was not used in this study. In a study of children with and without an Attention Deficit Hyperactivity Disorder (ADHD) diagnosis (Anderson, Hinshaw, & Simmel, 1994), the authoritative parenting scale filled out by mothers predicted overt and covert externalizing behavior in ADHD boys observed during their participation in a summer camp. The authoritarian scale differentiated girls with both attention and hyperactivity disorders from girls who were diagnosed as inattentive but not hyperactive (Hinshaw, 2002).

2. Parenting Stress Index—A 35-item revised version (Loyd & Abidin, 1985) of the original 150-item Parenting Stress Index (Abidin, 1980) asks parents to indicate the extent of their agreement or disagreement with statements describing themselves as stressed, their child as difficult to manage, and a lack of fit between what they expected and the child they have. The scale has been validated extensively by comparing parents who have known stressors in childrearing (children with developmental delay, oppositional defiance, or difficult temperaments) and parents who do not have these stressors (Abidin, 1997).

The Marital Relationship

The parents' marital relationship, a central construct in the studies reported here, was assessed in a variety of ways, including self-evaluations by the partners, observations by the research staff, and descriptions by the couples' children.

Observed Marital Interaction.

1. A couple problem-solving discussion—Because most of the robust findings linking children's adaptation and marital discord show that it is overt marital conflict that affects children negatively (Cummings & Davies, 1994), we videotaped husbands and wives during two 10-min conflict resolution tasks, using the procedures for marital discussions developed by Gottman and Levenson (1986). Following separate 90-min interviews with each parent (at PRE, the Adult Attachment Interview; at POST1, a Couple Attachment Interview), both partners came together and responded to a checklist of common marital and parenting problems. In a room in which two video cameras were mounted inside a cabinet, interviewers explained the problem-focused procedure and outlined three discussion segments. Partners were asked to do the following: (a) discuss how the issues raised in the separate interviews (their family of original relationships or their marital relation-

ship history) were affecting their lives now, (b) review a list of marital and parenting problems and choose one of each type to discuss together, and (c) attempt to make some progress toward resolution of the two problems. At PRE, in the year before the child entered kindergarten, the order in which parenting and marital problem lists were given to the parents was randomly selected. At POST1, couples discussed marital and parenting issues in the reverse order. One of the experimenters helped the couple choose an issue to discuss, worked with them to focus some of the areas of disagreement, and then left the room. A knock on the door after 10 min signaled the end of the time to discuss the first problem and the beginning of the time to discuss the second problem.

Nine scales to assess each participant's strategies for coping with marital conflict were developed by Bradburn (1997), based on concepts reflecting central features of intimate attachment relationships. Scales describing constructive problem solving, supportiveness, and collaboration were thought of as more typical of individuals with a secure or coherent state of mind regarding attachment. Scales describing avoidance, minimizing, and rejection were thought to be more typical of individuals with a dismissive approach to close relationships. Scales describing blaming, rumination, and controlling strategies were thought to typify individuals with a preoccupied state of mind. Behaviorally-anchored ratings were given to the coders for each of nine 7-point scales. Average interrater reliabilities were .62 (*range* = .29–.76) for the men and .68 for the women (*range* = .57–.72). The scales with low interrater reliabilities for men (minimizing and ruminating) reflected low frequencies of occurrence of the behavior.

It is traditional to discard scales that are not rated reliably, but at this stage in the development of our rating system, we were reluctant to eliminate scales solely because they contained low frequency behaviors. We created two aggregate scales based on the assumption that composite measures would be more reliable, and that an overall effect on family interaction would be more likely if each partner showed more negative behaviors toward the other. The first scale summed all behaviors described as positive (supportive, constructive problem solving, collaborative), and the second summed all behaviors described as negative (avoidant, minimizing, rejecting, blaming, ruminating, controlling). Preliminary data on the validity of these two scales come from Bradburn's dissertation (1997), which showed that these scales are correlated in the expected direction with security of attachment as measured by the Adult Attachment Interview (George, Kaplan, & Main, 1985).

2. Observed marital interaction in the context of coparenting—As part of the 2½-hour family visit to our project playroom in preschool period and again in the spring of the kindergarten year, mothers and fathers spent 40 min together working and playing with their oldest child (the target child) and any

younger siblings. The child was presented with a number of challenging tasks and the parents were invited to help as they typically would at home. In the first task, the family played "Jenga," a game in which members take turns removing one piece at a time from the center of a tower of small wooden blocks, placing each removed piece on top of the tower. The object of the game is to stack the pieces on top to make the tower as high as possible before it collapses. A second task focused on the child, asking him or her to replicate a difficult picture made of triangular puzzle pieces. In a third task, the family was asked to build a structure of their own using a set of colorful abstract cardboard design pieces from a set called "Pablo." A fourth task required family members to pass a tennis ball held under their chins from one person to another without using their hands. The tasks were designed to elicit cooperation, competition, problem-solving style, humor, and physical contact. Two of the four tasks were designed to be challenging for the child. Despite the fact that the other two tasks were designed to be fun for family members, some families were tense throughout the session.

After the playroom-laboratory visit, two observers who had been present behind a bookcase barrier where they observed the family interaction on a TV monitor, filled out global rating scales on eight constructs to describe parents' behavior toward each other. Each scale was rated for both highest level of the behavior shown during the interaction (e.g., high warmth) and the typical level shown overall (e.g., moderate warmth).[5] Raters used 5-point scales to rate highest level of pleasure and displeasure, and 7-point scales to rate the overall level of pleasure and displeasure, from very high on one end, through "neither predominates," to very high on the other end. This procedure was also used for the bipolar constructs warmth–coldness and cooperation–competition. Unipolar constructs (anger, interactiveness, responsiveness, clarity, and disagreement) were rated for both highest and typical level of the behavior on 5-point scales, from very low to very high.

The 10 items with highest and typical rating items used in forming composite measures had a median interrater reliability (α) of .80 at PRE and .88 at POST1. Two composite measures used in this study also had high inter-item consistency: negative emotion (including items assessing displeasure and coldness; $\alpha = .90$ at PRE and .91 at POST1); and conflict (including items assessing anger, competition, and disagreement, scale $\alpha = .91$ at PRE and .92 at POST1). Evidence concerning validity comes from studies by Gottman and

---

[5]In the original plan for the scales, we included a high point that indicated "excessive" levels of the behavior (e.g., warmth that appeared to be smothering), but in this sample, these points were used extremely rarely (fewer than .3% of the ratings). Scatter plots failed to reveal curvilinear associations with measures of children's adaptation. We concluded that in this nonclinical sample, the coding system was not able to differentiate between high levels of a positive parenting behavior, and extremely high but maladaptive manifestations of that behavior.

colleagues in which the two composite measures of the coparenting relation-ship in the presence of the child were good predictors of both the quality of couple interaction when the parent partners discussed a marital problem (Gottman, 1993), and the children's internalizing and externalizing behavior as described by second-grade teachers (Gottman & Katz, 1989). Additional evidence comes from our previous longitudinal study in which earlier marital warmth and conflict in the context of coparenting were linked in theoretically expectable ways with the observed quality of parent–child interaction and with children's academic achievement and problem behaviors in kindergar-ten (P. A. Cowan et al., 1994).

3. The marriage from the child's perspective—In addition to the use of the BPI for the assessment of children's self-perceptions, different items were cre-ated to obtain a picture of how the children viewed their parents' relationship as a couple (Ablow & Measelle, 1993; Measelle et al., 1998). The BPI items assessing the parents' marital quality were drawn from Grych and Fincham's work in assessing older children's perceptions of their parents' marital con-flict (Grych, Seid, & Fincham, 1992). For example, Iggy might say, "My par-ents fight a lot," whereas Ziggy might say, "My parents don't fight a lot," and then, "How about you _____?" (to the target child). As with the self-description items, children's responses to the interview were videotaped and later coded on a 7-point scale, based on which statement children said was most like them. Endpoints on the Likert-type scale represent *very negative* (1) and *very positive* (7) perceptions. If a child responded at the negative end by endorsing the item, "When my parents have a fight, I think it's my fault," the response was coded 2, because it directly reflected the statement made by one puppet. If a child amplified the original negative statement by stating, "When my parents have a fight, I *always* think it's my fault," this response was scored 1 to represent a more negative response than the puppet's original statement. If the child expressed a less emphatic negative perception (e.g., "When my parents have a fight, *sometimes* I think it's my fault, but not al-ways") or felt the need to qualify the response (e.g., "When my parents have a fight *about me*, I think it's my fault"), the response was scored 3. Positive re-sponses were coded on the 5 to 7 range of the scale, with 5 representing a less emphatic positive response than a 6 (e.g., "*Usually* I don't think it's my fault" versus "I don't think it's my fault") and 7 representing a more positive re-sponse than the puppet's original statement (e.g., "It's *never* my fault"). If children indicated that "both" options pertained to them or that they were "in the middle," their responses were coded 4. The average interrater reliabil-ity, $r(83)$, was .89. Children's perceptions of marital conflict on the BPI were more highly correlated with our observations of the parents as they worked and played together with the child than were the parents' self-reports of their marital conflict (Ablow, 1997b).

Self-Report Instruments.

1. Division of labor: Who Does What—This 44-item self-report question-naire (C. P. Cowan & Cowan, 1991) assessed each partner's perception of the partners' division of roles for family and household responsibilities along three dimensions: (a) 12 household and family tasks, including laundry, cooking, paying bills, and care of plants or yard; (b) 12 issues in family decision making, including handling finances, how often to see family and friends, and plans for vacations; and (c) the division of 20 tasks involved in the caring and rearing of children, including feeding, dressing, taking them to activities, responding to their distress, and scheduling baby sitters and medical appointments. On each item, parents described who does what on a 9-point scale ranging from 1 (*she does it all*) through 5 (*we do this about equally*) to 9 (*he does it all*). Parents indi-cated the relative actual division of tasks and decisions and then how they would like the ideal division to be. The discrepancy between "How it is now" and "How I'd like it to be" was used as an index of each partner's satisfaction with each task and with the relative division overall.

At the beginning of the study, when the children were in preschool, moth-ers' and fathers' mean responses to "How it is now" for household and family tasks were respectively 4.67 and 4.97, and for child-related tasks, 3.43 and 3.77. Mothers and fathers showed general agreement in their description of the division of household tasks, $r(94) = .72$, $p < .001$, and child-related tasks, $r(94) = .73$, $p < .001$. Both partners acknowledged that mothers did substan-tially more family work, with each partner given himself or herself credit for somewhat more work than the spouse did. Because mothers are typically much more involved than fathers in caring for young children (ratings of less than 5), we interpreted higher scores (toward *he does it all*) as indicative of a more egalitarian sharing of tasks. The lower the score (toward *she does it all*), the greater the role differentiation by gender.

Parents' gender-role differentiation as assessed by "Who Does What?" has been shown to increase during the transition to parenthood: Both men and women described a more traditional division of family labor over the first months and years of parenthood, and more traditional arrangements for car-ing for the children than they had predicted in pregnancy, regardless of where the couple began on the traditional-to-egalitarian continuum (C. P. Cowan & Cowan, 1992; C. P. Cowan et al., 1985a). Furthermore, both husbands' and wives' satisfaction with their role arrangements as assessed by this measure was related to their marital satisfaction, self-esteem, and parenting stress at various points during the transition to parenthood (C. P. Cowan & Cowan, 1988).

2. Marital Adjustment and Satisfaction: Short Marital Adjustment Test (MAT; Locke & Wallace, 1959)—This 16-item, widely-used questionnaire

was used to assess partners' overall adjustment or satisfaction with the marital relationship. Half of the questions address how much the couple disagrees on a variety of topics related to their life as a couple, including the handling of finances, friends, and their sexual relationship. The remaining questions ask about the amount of happiness in and commitment to the relationship, style of settling disagreements, partners' preferences for staying home or being "on the go," and whether they would choose the same or a different partner again. Rationally-derived weights are assigned to the items, and total marital adjustment and satisfaction is calculated by summing the weighted items. Higher scores represent greater adjustment or satisfaction, and scores below 100 suggest considerable marital conflict or distress. The MAT differentiates clinically distressed and nondistressed couples, and is related to observed differences in quality of marital interaction of couples above and below the cutoff for marital distress (see Gottman, 1993).

3. Marital Conflict and Problem-Solving: Couple Communication Questionnaire (C. P. Cowan & Cowan, 1982a)—Each partner's perception of conflict and style of resolving conflict in the couple relationship was assessed using a 64-item questionnaire. First, on a 1 to 7 scale, with 1 representing *a lot* and 7 representing *none*, each partner was asked to rate the amount of conflict and disagreement with the partner over the last month on typical issues of conflict: division of workload in the family, amount of time spent together as a couple, the sexual relationship, management of family money, the quality of time spent together as a couple, relationships with in-laws, ideas about how to rear children, willingness to work for improvement in the relationship, communication between the partners, work outside the home, child(ren)'s schooling, and "other."

Second, partners were given a list of 25 possible strategies to tackle problems in their relationship and asked to endorse the ones they tend to use (e.g., "we talk about it to clarify the problem," "we delay action," "one or both of us pushes, grabs, or shoves the other"). Seven of the items were adapted from the Conflict Tactics Scale (Straus, 1979), which is designed to assess marital violence, and the other 18 describe less volatile strategies. Responses related to the couple's style of resolving conflict were factor analyzed using a principal components varimax rotation. Results yielded four factors for both wives' and husbands' perceptions of their problem-solving style, three of which had acceptably high levels of internal consistency: validating patterns, α for mothers = .82, α for fathers = .74; conflict avoidant patterns, α for mothers = .73, α for fathers = .76; and volatile patterns, α for mothers = .80, α for fathers = .81. Husbands and wives with high validating scores endorsed items describing discussion of both points of view, compromise, and acceptance of differences. Partners with high avoidance of conflict scores endorsed items describing delaying, ignoring the problem, and lacking a way of resolving differences. Couples with high volatile scores described yelling, insulting, throwing things, or hitting each other. All three reliable scales were significantly correlated with overall marital satisfaction on the Locke-Wallace Marital Adjustment Test (Locke & Wallace, 1959) at the beginning of the study (PRE): couple validation, mothers, $r(98) = .33$, $p < .01$, fathers, $r(98) = .34$, $p < .01$; avoidance, mothers $r(98) = -.26$, $p < .01$, fathers $r(98) = -.29$, $p < .01$; and volatility, mothers $r(98) = -.41$, $p < .01$, fathers $r(98) = -.44$, $p < .01$.

Parents' Views of Their Family of Origin

The Adult Attachment Interview. In visits during the spring of the child's prekindergarten year, each parent was interviewed individually with the Adult Attachment Interview (AAI; George et al., 1985; Hesse, 1999). Assessing the adult's current state of mind with regard to early attachment, the AAI elicited (a) specific descriptors of the adult's early relationship with each parent, (b) anecdotes that illustrate the descriptors, (c) information about separations from and loss of parents and other important attachment figures, (d) speculations about why the parents behaved as they did, and (e) descriptions of change in the relationship of each adult with his or her parents since childhood.

All interviews were transcribed verbatim, with transcribers trained to pay close attention to exact phrasing. The category classification of attachment status on the AAI is based on an analysis of the entire transcript. In the first pass through the coding procedure, the coder makes a series of continuous ratings. Five rating scales are intended to capture the probable quality of early experiences, separately with mother and with father (e.g., loving, rejecting, neglecting). An additional 12 scales describe the individual's current state of mind regarding those experiences (e.g., idealizing, involving anger, derogation of attachment, and coherence of the narrative). Some state of mind scales are rated separately for the participants' descriptions of experiences with their mothers and fathers (e.g., idealizing, involving anger).

In a second pass through the materials, the coder uses a configurational analysis of these scales that is thought to represent dominant discourse strategies, to determine a primary attachment category. Two-thirds of the interviews were coded by Isabel Bradburn of the University of California, Berkeley, and one third by Nina Koren-Karie of Haifa University. Both coders had previously met the reliability criterion for 30 AAI interviews established by Mary Main and Erik Hesse (1999). A reliability subsample of 23 transcripts coded by both raters showed a mean percentage of agreement across four categories (secure, dismissing, preoccupied, unresolved) of 77%, kappa = .68. Disagreements between the two coders were resolved in consultation with Mary Main and Erik Hesse. On another sample of 15 transcripts, percentage agreement between Isabel Bradburn and Erik Hesse was 93% across two and three categories, kappa = .70, $p < .01$, and .90, $p < .001$. Disagreements were resolved by consensus.

This interview has now been used in a great many studies. Evidence of validity of the AAI comes primarily from studies reporting strong correspondence between mothers' security of working models of attachment and measures of (a) observed parenting style, and (b) their children's security of attachment (Hesse, 1999; van IJzendoorn, 1995) as assessed in the "Strange Situation" (Ainsworth, Blehar, Waters, & Wall, 1978; Ainsworth & Wittig, 1969).

"Family Relationships" is a structured questionnaire (C. P. Cowan & Cowan, 1982b), designed to assess adults' global perceptions of the positive or negative tone of relationships in their families of origin—with father, with mother, and between father and mother. Each adult in our study rated those relationships, as they recalled them from childhood and as they perceived them currently, using six 7-point bipolar scales (uninvolved–involved, high conflict–low conflict, unhappy–happy, distant–close, cold–warm, unsatisfying–satisfying). Alpha reliabilities for the six scales describing both past and present relationships were very high, ranging from .85 to .95. In this sample, there was reasonably high stability of the parents' retrospective and current reports over a 2-year period (preschool to first grade) with Pearson correlations ranging from .75 to .84.

Because the questions on "Family Relationships" involve more conscious memories, whereas the codes for the AAI are assumed to tap some unconscious material, we did not expect correlations between the quality of experience scales from the questionnaire or the in-depth interview and men's or women's categorical attachment category of secure or insecure. The data bore out those predictions. Nevertheless, there were significant correlations between men's and women's self-reports of the global quality of their relationships with their parents in the past on the questionnaire and the experience scale scores on the in-depth AAI. For example, mothers who described their early relationships with a parent as warm and low in conflict on the Family Relationships questionnaire described that parent on the AAI as loving, mother $r(72) = 62$, $p < .001$, father $r(72) = .51$, $p < .001$; and not rejecting, mother $r(72) = -.45$, $p < .001$, father $r(72) = -.43$, $p < .001$. As we expected, there was no correlation between descriptions of either parent on the Family Relationships questionnaire and overall security of attachment. Similarly, fathers' descriptions of their early relationships with their parents on the Family Relationships questionnaire were correlated with their AAI ratings of their parents as loving, mother $r(72) = .30$, $p < .001$, father $r(72) = .48$, $p < .001$; and not rejecting, mother $r(72) = -.56$, $p < .001$, father $r(72) = -.59$, $p < .001$, but not with their security of attachment. Thus, the questionnaire and interview methods converged on specific descriptions of the quality of positive and negative early relationships with each parent.

Potentially Traumatic Events in the Family of Origin. In the Phase 1 questionnaire booklet only, we included a list of 12 potentially traumatic events that were experienced prior to each parent's 18th birthday, including the following: your mother or father not being there when you needed them; chronic illness or disability of either parent; alcoholism of either parent; physical hurt from more than an occasional spanking; and extreme or chronic conflict between my parents. We did not expect interitem consistency on this measure and we had no prior validation information.

Whole Family Relationships

Parents completed a shortened version of the Family Environment Scale (FES; Moos & Moos, 1976) to describe their current nuclear family in the year before their first child entered kindergarten. The FES was developed to assess the social climate of the family. The original measure is a 90-item self-report scale measuring three dimensions of the family: (a) Relationships (cohesion, expressiveness, and conflict); (b) System Maintenance (organization and control); and (c) Personal Growth (independence, achievement, intellectual-cultural orientation, active-recreational orientation, and moral-religious emphasis). The FES, standardized on 1,000 individuals using a sample of 285 families, discriminates between families with adaptive and dysfunctional characteristics.

The shortened version of the FES in our study was completed separately by each mother and father to describe their current family in the year before their first child entered kindergarten. The 63 items assessed various aspects of family cohesion and relatedness and family structure, and loaded onto the following 7 of the original 10 FES subscales: cohesion, expressiveness, conflict, independence, achievement orientation, organization, and control. The seven FES scales were combined to create two composite variables. Family relatedness combined the cohesion, conflict, and expression scales, to assess the commitment, help, and support family members provide for one another, how much family members are encouraged to act openly to express their feelings directly, and the amount of openly expressed anger, aggression, and conflict among family members. Family structure combined the importance of clear organization and structure in planning family activities and responsibilities, the extent to which set rules and procedures were used to run family life, the extent to which family members were assertive, self sufficient, and made their own decisions, and the extent to which activities such as school and work were cast into an achievement-oriented or competitive framework.

Outside the Family: Work, Life Stress, and Support

Work Investment. A three-item scale adapted from previous studies (Ladewig & White, 1984; Lodahl & Kejner, 1965) measured the degree of self-investment parents had in their work. The items in the scale were as follows: (a) How well I perform on my job is extremely important to me; (b) I live, eat and breathe my job (I am very personally involved in my work); and (c) Work is only a small part of who I am. Participants rated the accuracy of each of these statements using a 4-point Likert-type scale (1 = *agree strongly*; 4 = *disagree strongly*). The first two items were reverse-coded so that high scores on this measure reflect a high degree of work investment.

A Cronbach's α coefficient of .60 indicated an adequate level of internal consistency for this three-item scale. Evidence of the validity of the scale was provided by its moderate level of positive correlation with a standard measure of internal work motivation—a related but distinct construct. Men's and women's level of work investment were both correlated with the internal work motivation scale of the Job Diagnostic Survey (JDS), $r(55) = .54$, $p < .01$; $r(55) = .50$, $p < .01$.

Work Autonomy. All measures of parents' work come from the pre-kindergarten family assessments. Work autonomy was assessed with a three-item self-report scale measuring the degree to which participants believed that their job provided independence, discretion, and freedom in determining how to carry out the work. Respondents were asked to rate the accuracy of two items ("I don't have any chance to use my personal initiative or judgment in carrying out my work [reverse scored]" and "I have considerable opportunity for independence and freedom in how I do my work") on a 7-point Likert-type scale (1 = *very inaccurate* and 7 = *very accurate*). The third item asked respondents to indicate on a 7-point Likert-type scale the extent to which their work permits them to decide on their own how to go about doing their jobs (1 = *very little*, my work gives me almost no personal "say" about how and when the work is done; 7 = *very much*, my work gives me almost complete responsibility for deciding how and when the work is done). The work autonomy scale is part of the short form of the JDS, which has been demonstrated to have good divergent and predictive validity (Hackman & Oldham, 1975). In this study, the scale demonstrated adequate internal consistency, α = .60. To distinguish between general autonomy over the way one does one's work and control over the hours a person works, participants were also asked whether they had control over the hours they worked (Schedule Control; *yes* = 1; *no* = 0).

Satisfaction With Partner Support for Work Outside the Home (SPSW). Participants indicated their degree of agreement or disagreement on a 4-point Likert-type scale (1 = *Agree strongly*; 4 = *Disagree strongly*) with the following statement: "I am satisfied with the support my partner has given me in my decisions about working outside the home." Scores on this item were reversed so that high scores indicated satisfaction with partner's level of support. Evidence for the validity of SPSW was provided by its positive correlation with participants' reports of marital satisfaction (Locke & Wallace, 1959). Participants who were more maritally satisfied were also more likely to be satisfied with the support they received from a spouse for working outside the home: women, $r(57) = .36, p < .01$; men, $r(57) = .39, p < .001$. These correlations suggest a modest degree of overlap between marital satisfaction and partner support for work, but also a large degree of independence.

Life Stress. We chose to ask about stressful events occurring outside the family unit using a life events scale developed by Horowitz, Schaefer, Hiroto, Wilner, and Levin (1977), with items weighted not only for their potential stress value but also according to how recently they had occurred.

Social Support. Curtis-Boles (1979) developed the "Important People" questionnaire, which asks partners to describe four people who are currently important in their lives as potential sources of support. A combination of multiple-choice items and rating scales assessed how frequently and how satisfactorily these people provided support in the form of information, advice, material benefits, and emotional support. A positive support index was created by combining frequency of support with rated satisfaction.

Balance of Life Stress and Social Support. Based on the hypothesis that stressful events have a negative impact in the absence of adequate social support (e.g., Nuckols, Cassel, & Kaplan, 1972), an overall index was created to reflect the balance of life stress and social support from a cross-tabulation of the life stress and social support scores (Heming, 1985). A high positive balance was ascribed to those in the bottom one third of the sample on life stress and the top one third on social support. In our earlier longitudinal study (C. P. Cowan & Cowan, 1992), multiple regression equations indicated that this balance index accounted for a significant proportion of the variance in men's and women's marital satisfaction (Locke & Wallace, 1959) at 6 and 18 months after birth, over and above their level of life stress or social support.

SELECTION BIAS, ATTRITION BIAS, AND REPRESENTATIVENESS

Selection Bias

As we noted at the beginning of this chapter, we obtained completed initial questionnaire booklets from 192 potential participant couples whose families were classified in five study conditions: people who did not participate further in the study after submitting the booklets ($n = 92$); maritally-focused group participants (randomly selected, $n = 28$); parenting-focused group participants (randomly selected, $n = 27$); consultation controls (randomly selected, $n = 25$); and self-selected controls ($n = 20$). We used two-way, mixed model analyses of variance (ANOVAs; sex as a within-subjects effect[6] and condition as a between-subjects effect) to test for preexisting differences on any of the five measures obtained in the initial questionnaire booklet (Locke-Wallace marital adjustment test, CES-D, Abidin's Parenting Stress Index, checklists that we created concerning traumatic experiences in parents' families of origin, and concerns about their child starting school). We found no significant differences on parents' responses to these measures among the study conditions. That is, the 100 couples who participated fully in the study were not statistically different on these initial self-report measures from the 92 who subsequently refused further participation. Similar mixed model ANOVAs comparing couples who went on to complete the Phase 1 questionnaire revealed that the self-selected controls were not statistically different from either the random controls or the intervention participants in their description of their marital relationships (Marital Adjustment Test), their Ideas About Parenting (Heming, Cowan, & Cowan, 1990), or the quality of their past or current relationships with their mothers or fathers (Family Relationships).

Attrition Bias

Sixteen percent of the 100 families agreeing to participate in the intervention and control conditions did not participate in the first-grade follow-up assessments (POST2). To determine whether those parents who dropped out were significantly different in any way from those who continued, we performed a set of t tests on pretest measures from the five conceptual domains of the study (individual, marital, parent–child, three-generations, and outside the family). Pretest measures were chosen for two reasons: (a) we needed to establish whether those who dropped out were in some way identifiable at the beginning of the study, and (b) because the pretest occurred before the intervention began, participation in the intervention could not reasonably affect dropout or retention. We chose 33 variables from instruments and observations that assessed mothers' and fathers' adaptation (identical for both parents), and four measures of observed couple interaction quality for a total of 70 t tests.

---

[6]In this and all subsequent analyses, we treat data obtained from husbands and wives as related measures.

Individual: The Pie, self-esteem (ACL), anxiety (Brief Symptom Inventory), depression (CES-D)

Parent–child: Parenting Stress Index, Ideas About Parenting, observed parenting style

Three-generation: Past and current relationships in the family of origin (Family Relationships)

Couple: Marital adjustment and satisfaction (Locke & Wallace, 1959), division of labor (Who Does What?), observed marital interaction

Outside the family: Work hours, Life Stress, Social Support (Important People).

Setting the significance level at alpha = .05, we found only one significant difference for mothers (women who later dropped out described having less positive relationships with their parents when they were young, $t(98) = -2.00$, $p < .05$), one for fathers (men who later dropped out described lower levels of positive social support, $t(98) = -2.17$, $p < .05$), and one for couples (couples who later dropped out were described as less clear in their communication while they were working and playing with their child $t(98) = -2.00$, $p < .05$). The number of "significant" differences was 3/70 or 4%, around the level one would expect by chance with this alpha ($p = .05$). The remaining nonsignificant results have not been tabled in the interest of saving space, but they are available from the authors.

Given the fact that the general practice is to correct for family-wise error by setting the significance boundary higher, we think that it is safe to conclude that the couples who dropped out of the study were similar to those who continued in their self-descriptions, parenting style, and couple communication. Thus, the data in chapter 3 about stability and change over time were not biased by the patterns of attrition in the participants.

Representativeness of the Sample: Issues of Generalization

We acknowledge that the families in this study do not constitute an epidemiological, representative sample of the United States population with respect to marital status, economic status, or ethnic and cultural diversity. Nevertheless, with the exception of marital status, there is considerable range in the demographic characteristics. Based on a number of considerations, we believe that the results of this study are generalizable to a substantial proportion of two-parent American families:

1. Although the median household income of the participants was relatively high compared with U.S. norms, the characteristics of this sample were shaped in large part by our initial decision to focus on the role of couple relationships in family life. In a cultural climate in which dual-worker couples are the norm, two parents are more likely to earn above-average household incomes than single parents.

2. The sample of parents was not markedly skewed in the direction of optimal functioning. Despite the stereotype of moderate- to high-income families as faring relatively well, we show in chapter 3 that a significant proportion of the parents in this study were experiencing clinically significant levels of stress and distress. That is, in this "nonclinical" sample drawn from a population that was not in treatment in the mental health system, we found individual family members and whole families reporting a range of difficulties that appeared to be playing a part in their children's earliest adjustment to elementary school.

3. The sample of parents was not markedly skewed in the direction of being especially troubled. The couples in this study did not apply to participate in the hopes of receiving some form of psychological help because the intervention was not mentioned in any recruitment materials. Couples responded to an invitation to participate in a study of families with a child making the transition to kindergarten, with no mention of intervention until the end of the initial interview with a staff couple.

4. In teacher-reported measures of children's adaptation, the children in our study were remarkably similar to their classmates. We noted earlier that a large majority of teachers filled out CABIs on all children or a substantial subset of children in their classrooms. Teachers used the full range of the scales (1–4) in describing both the children participating in the study and their classmates. To examine whether the children of the families participating in our study were viewed differently from their classmates, we performed six 2×2 General Linear Modeling (GLM) analyses (study child versus classmates, boys versus girls) on each CABI scale within each grade (see Table 2.4 for the cell means). We found that children in the study sample were described by their teachers as more academically competent than their classmates in kindergarten, $F(1, 90) = 17.90$, $p < .001$, and first grade, $F(1, 82) = 8.65$, $p < .001$, although the effect size was very small ($eta = .03$). On the other five CABI scales (social competence, externalizing-aggression, externalizing-hyperactivity, internalizing-social withdrawal, internalizing-psychological symptoms), there were no significant differences between children in the study and their classmates in the larger sample in either kindergarten or first grade.

Furthermore, the children in our study appeared at the extremes in proportions similar to those of children in the larger sample. In Table 2.5, we present the proportion of children in the study sample falling at the 10th, 20th, 80th, and 90th percentile scores of the first-grade spring assessment (83

TABLE 2.4
Comparison of Study Children and Their Classmates on
Six Child Adaptive Behavior Inventory Factor Scales

Child Adaptive Behavior Inventory		Kindergarten			First Grade		
		Girls	Boys	Combined	Girls	Boys	Combined
Academic	Our sample	3.53	3.41	3.47[b]	3.44	3.34	3.39[b]
competence	Classmates	3.31	3.16	3.23[b]	3.28	3.14	3.19[b]
	combined	3.41[a]	3.28[a]		3.29	3.12	
Social	Our sample	3.40	3.21	3.30	3.52	3.15	3.33
competence	Classmates	3.36	3.10	3.22	3.40	3.15	3.27
	combined	3.38[a]	3.15[a]		3.40[a]	3.15[a]	
Externalizing-	Our sample	1.42	1.70	1.56	1.46	1.70	1.59
aggressive	Classmates	1.47	1.74	1.60	1.53	1.73	1.64
	combined	1.44[a]	1.73[a]		1.52[a]	1.73[a]	
Externalizing-	Our sample	1.69	1.98	1.84	1.70	2.02	1.87
hyperactive	Classmates	1.72	1.98	1.85	1.77	2.04	1.95
	combined	1.71[a]	1.98[a]		1.76[a]	2.04[a]	
Internalizing-	Our sample	1.87	2.01	1.94	1.90	2.05	1.98
social isolation	Classmates	1.96	1.99	1.98	1.91	1.98	1.95
	combined	1.92	2.00		1.91	1.98	
Internalizing-	Our sample	1.78	1.78	1.78	1.69	1.69	1.69
symptoms	Classmates	1.68	1.69	1.68	1.71	1.71	1.71
	combined	1.73	1.74		1.71	1.71	

[a]Adjacent cell means significantly different. [b]Adjacent cell means significantly different.

TABLE 2.5
Proportion of Study Children With Scores at Different Cutoffs in Larger Sample

Study Sample	Cutoff Scores for Classmates			
	10th Percentile	20th Percentile	80th Percentile	90th Percentile
Academic competence	5.0%	7.8%	25.0%	15.5%
Social competence	9.7%	19.6%	22.3%	10.0%
Externalizing-aggressive	10.0%	17.5%	18.4%	11.7%
Externalizing-hyperactive	6.8%	19.4%	21.4%	8.7%
Internalizing-social isolation	6.8%	20.4%	24.3%	11.7%
Internalizing-anxiety/depression	8.7%	11.7%	23.4%	14.4%

participants and 1,297 classmates). In many standardized checklist instruments (e.g., the CBCL; Achenbach & Edelbrock, 1983), a score above the 90th percentile in negative or undesirable behavior or below the 10th percentile in positive behavior is treated as an indicator of psychopathology. As the GLM analysis of means suggested, there were fewer study children at the bottom of the distribution in ratings of academic competence compared with their first-grade classmates and slightly more at the top. Only 5% of the children in the study sample received ratings as low as the bottom 10% in the larger sample, but 15.5% received ratings above the 90th percentile score in the larger sample. By contrast, the study participants' extreme ratings matched the larger sample in social competence, with 10% of the children in the study in the top 10% of the larger sample and 9.7% of the study participants in the bottom 10%. Similarly, on the more problematic dimensions of the CABI, from 8.7% to more than 14% of the children in our study had externalizing or internalizing scores above the 90th percentile.

In sum, although we do not claim that the results of this study can be generalized to the population at large (few studies can), we feel that they apply to the significant number of American families with two parents and working-to middle-class lifestyles. Because this is the first longitudinal study with a preventive intervention for couples with a first child making the transition to elementary school, we feel that it is reasonable to treat the findings as sources of hypotheses to be tested for generalizability in future replications—some with similar families and others with low-income families or families from different ethnic and cultural groups.

STATISTICAL CONSIDERATIONS

In contrast with survey studies of families, in which many participants are assessed on a few variables, the 80 to 100 participants in this study were assessed intensively with many instruments at three points in time. We deal here with three issues: the power of analyses to detect significant differences with this number of participants, the issue of overestimating "significant" findings when many analyses are performed on the same data set with the same participants, and the use of Latent Variable Partial Least Squares (LVPLS) structural equation modeling in many of the chapters in this volume.

Power

The primary analyses presented in this section consist of tests based on the chi-square distribution (goodness-of-fit tests, contingency tests), standard normal distribution, and the t distribution. For analyses based on the sample of families with full data from PRE to POST2 ($n = 84$) with α set to .05, two-tailed, we have limited power ($> .25$) to detect small effects ($r = .10$), using Cohen's (1988) criteria for describing the magnitude of effects. However, we have sufficient power ($> .90$) to detect medium effect sizes ($r = .30$) with α set to .05, two-tailed. We have reasonable power ($> .70$) to detect small to medium effects sizes ($r = .20$) for specific analyses involving single degree-of-freedom contrasts ($p < .05$) using the complete sample, and sufficient power

(> .95) to detect medium effect sizes ($r = .30$). For single degree-of-freedom contrasts ($p < .05$) with subsamples, for example those that divide children according to gender (e.g., $n = 33$ girls or 51 boys), our power is low (> .53) for detecting medium effect sizes for samples including only girls, but adequate (> .75) to detect medium effect sizes in the boys. Further, power is more than adequate to detect large effect sizes for both girls (> .85) and boys (> .94). It is clear that we need to interpret the absence of statistical significance in analyses of subsamples divided by sex of child with caution.

Specific power analyses for some of the multivariate models presented in this monographic are particularly difficult to compute (Cohen, 1988). As an estimate for the multivariate models for the smaller subsamples ($n = 45$), we have modest power (> .65, alpha = .05) to detect medium effects (incremental $r^2 = .10$) for up to seven predictors. Within the context of models containing seven predictors where $R = .40$, we have adequate power to detect αs as small as .30 under a range of full model effects. We have reasonable power (> .70; $\alpha = .05$) to detect small effects (incremental $R^2 = .07$) for up to seven predictors for the complete longitudinal sample of $n = 84$. Although these power estimates do not address the complexities involved in the Partial Least Squares structural models that we develop and test, we believe that they provide meaningful indexes. That is, in general, we have a reasonable amount of power to address the primary research questions in identifying clinically significant effects. In addition, because we are sensitive to the ratio of parameter estimates to N, we attempted to have at least 10 cases per parameter.

The Use of LVPLS Models for Data Analysis

Because many of the studies throughout the volume use structural equation modeling to examine links among multiple family factors and children's adaptation to school, we provide a brief overall description of the method here. Structural modeling helps to reduce data in a process guided by a priori theoretical constructs. These constructs help to define latent variable composites created from combinations of two or more manifest (measured) variables of the kind described earlier. Multiple indicants increase the stability of measures while reducing measurement error, and in most cases, they increase our ability to detect underlying relations (Rushton, Brainerd, & Pressley, 1983). Unlike multiple regression techniques, which reveal the combined power of independent variables to account for variance in a dependent variable (direct effects), structural models enable us to examine both direct and indirect pathways. For example, the models may reveal that, although there is no significant correlation between parents' characteristics (e.g., attachment histories) and children's outcomes, there is a chain of associations in which parents' attachment histories are associated with marital and parenting relationship qualities, which, in turn, are highly related to children's adaptation to school.

Throughout this volume, we employed Latent Variable Path Analysis with Partial Least Squares estimation procedure (LVPLS), or "soft modeling" (Falk & Miller, 1992; Lohmoeller, 1989; Wold, 1982), specifically because it allows us to explore hypothesized relations among constructs without imposing certain restrictive statistical and structural assumptions that underlie the widely-used LISREL structural modeling programs (Joreskog, 1985). Whereas this procedure is appropriate for the analysis of relatively small samples, it requires that the number of participants be adequate for the number of latent variables in the model. Although the model is very flexible, the program will not run when the number of manifest variables approaches the number of participants. In data sets like this one, with a high ratio of measures to participants, one must make theoretically-driven choices about which measures to include in a latent variable.

The reliability of the measurement model can be evaluated by inspecting the factor loadings of the manifest variables on the specified latent construct and the communality index (h2). Communality indexes range from 0 to 1 and reflect the percentage of variance of a manifest variable that is related to its latent construct. LVPLS provides a summary communality index, which represents the average of all communalities. Falk and Miller (1992) suggested that a mean communality (h2) of less than .50 indicates a poorly measured model in which less than 50% of the variance of each manifest variable is captured by its latent construct.

Once the latent constructs have been measured reliably, the relations among latent variables are estimated by conducting simultaneous multiple regressions in which the path weights are adjusted to provide the optimal linear coefficient among predictor and predicted components in the model. Composite weights provide a smoothing function that creates the plane of best fit between the constructs using the least square criteria. The iterative process results in maximizing the prediction of dependent composite variables from both the manifest data and the relationships specified in the model (Falk & Miller, 1992; Wold, 1982).

Although LVPLS does not provide a test to determine when a modeled path weight (standardized beta weight between variables) is too small to merit inclusion, Falk and Miller (1992) recommended deleting paths that contribute less than 2% to the variance of a predicted variable. Due to the exploratory nature of this study, we took a more conservative approach in which paths were deleted if they did not explain more than 5% of the variance of an endogenous variable, after which the model was rerun. Only the modified or trimmed models are presented in this volume.

LVPLS models have become more commonly used in developmental and family research (Brody & Flor, 1997; Isley et al., 1999) despite one acknowledged drawback: There is no significance test for the precise fit of the chosen paths to the data. Falk and Miller (1992) argued that, although the best test of a PLS model is replication in another sample, three important steps can be taken to evaluate the adequacy of the model beyond citing the communality coefficients of the measurement model: (a) evaluation of the root-mean-square-covariance (RMS COV E,U), (b) calculation of whether the amount of explained variance is statistically significant, and (c) testing alternative models and calculating the significance of the added explained variance.

The coefficient root-mean-square-covariance (RMS COV [E,U]) describes the average correlation between the residuals on the manifest and latent variables that is not accounted for by the model relations (Falk & Miller, 1992). The lower the correlation, the more adequate the model; in a model that perfectly describes the relations among all the variables, this coefficient is zero, whereas a coefficient above .20 is evidence of an inadequate model. All of the models reported in this volume have a value for RMS COV E,U of less than .10, indicating that the data fit the models adequately or better.

A second, more widely-used index of model adequacy can be derived from the fact that PLS provides a summation of the amount of variance in the dependent (latent) variable explained by all the independent variables taken together. This R^2 can be tested for significance in the same way as can a multiple regression coefficient.

Third, it is possible to test the significance of adding a critical latent variable to the model through comparisons of the difference between two regressions, one that includes the specific latent variable, the other that excludes the variable. For example, in chapter 11, we test the impact of the preventive intervention by comparing models with and without the intervention effect. This procedure, using nested parameters, provides a calculation of R^2 change as in a hierarchical regression that tests the increase in variance explained by a new variable, over and above the variables already entered in the model. Examples of these comparisons can be found in chapters 8 and 11.

We do not regard PLS or any other structural equation program as a panacea. PLS models are always additive, and they are not adequate to test multiplicative, moderator effects. Despite the language of causality commonly used in describing results (direct and indirect effects), these models are fundamentally correlations, and path links cannot be used to test hypotheses about direction of effects. The PLS models are used in this volume as a way of organizing complex data to describe connections among central dimensions of the family system as they relate to children's adaptation to school. Only intervention designs can be used to test the causal implications of the patterns they reveal, and we attempt to do this in chapter 11.

APPENDIX

Composition of the Child Adaptive Behavior
Inventory Scales and Factors

Child Adaptive Behavior Inventory Scales

The names of the 22 scales and the items that comprise them are as follows:

(1) Fair
  14 Always plays fair with other children.
  41 Is willing to wait his/her turn.
  67 Can be depended on to do what he/she is supposed to do.
(2) Calm
  9 Is not easily bothered or upset.
  31 Is calm and easy-going.
  62 Keeps cool no matter what happens.
(3) Kind
  12 Is concerned about the feelings of others.
  34 Tries not to do or say anything that would hurt another.
  65 Is sympathetic toward others' hurts or misfortunes.
(4) Anxious
  8 Is nervous or highstrung.
  27 Cries a lot.
  30 Worries a lot.
  61 Is afraid of a lot of things.
  80 Gets easily upset.
(5) Hyperactive
  15 Is restless; can't sit still.
  23 Hums and makes other odd noises.
  42 Has a hard time waiting when he/she wants something.
  66 Sometimes breaks or ruins things.
  68 Is always getting into things.
  83 Exhibits oddness or bizarre behavior.
  89 Is noisy and loud; never seems to stop talking.
(6) Antisocial
  11 Tends to disobey or break rules.
  13 Hangs around with kids who might be a bad influence.

35 Sometimes takes things that don't belong to him/her.
58 Punishment doesn't affect his/her behavior.
90 Doesn't always tell the truth.

(7) Oppositional
25 Acts "smart."
36 Seeks attention; "shows off."
39 Is uncooperative in group situations with adults.
40 Is uncooperative in group situations with children.
60 Expects others to conform to his/her wishes.
88 Is stubborn or irritable.

(8) Hostile
33 Has a hot temper.
52 Argues; quarrels.
59 Is deliberately cruel to others.
64 Gets into fights with other children.

(9) Intelligent
1 Is smart for his/her age.
18 Catches on quickly; e.g. is quick at learning new games.
45 Is able to follow directions; remembers what he/she is told.
76 Understands difficult words.
82 Learns new skills to cope with new situations or problems.

(10) Creative
3 Is always asking questions.
20 Explores and navigates things.
38 Shows creativity in art or crafts work.
46 Thinks up interesting things to do.
77 Has good ideas about how to do things or make things.

(11) Task oriented
2 Doesn't seem very interested in things (scoring reversed).
16 Often works quietly at an activity for a long time.
43 Works carefully and does his/her best.
51 Adapts to changes in routine.
69 Listens well when someone explains something.

(12) Distractible
17 Has trouble concentrating on what he/she is doing.
44 Is easily distracted from what he/she's doing.
54 Is unable to work independently; needs constant attention.
55 Acts like he/she is much younger; immature, "childish."
70 Quickly loses interest in an activity.

(13) Extroverted
6 Makes friends quickly and easily.
22 Acts like a leader.

　　28　Likes to meet new people.
　　49　Has an outgoing personality.
(14)　Introverted
　　　4　Is shy or bashful with adults.
　　21　Is shy or bashful with children.
　　24　Withdraws; prefers solitary activities.
　　26　Takes a while to get comfortable with others.
　　37　Is self-conscious; easily embarrassed.
　　47　Finds it hard to talk with strangers.
　　53　Has difficulty leaving parent to come to school.
(15)　Depressed
　　　5　Seems unhappy or depressed.
　　19　Often sits around doing nothing.
　　48　Often seems lonely.
　　78　Doesn't smile or laugh much.
　　84　Is often sad.
　　86　Has a fixed expression; lack of emotional reactivity.
(16)　Somaticizes
　　　7　Often complains of stomach aches or headaches.
　　29　Comes running to me with every little bump or scratch.
　　50　Says he/she's sick when he/she doesn't want to do something.
　　71　Daydreams a lot; often has a "far away look."
　　79　Often complains about not feeling well.
(17)　Imitative
　　56　Is highly involved in play fantasies.
　　57　Tends to imitate other children.
　　85　Takes on emotions or moods of people around him/her.
(18)　Impaired in physical development
　　72　Is clumsy, awkward; runs poorly; falls or stumbles.
　　73　Speech is difficult to understand.
　　74　Does not seem to hear well.
　　75　Does not seem to see well.
　　81　Has toileting problems; wets or soils him/herself.
(19)　Socially isolated
　　87　Doesn't stand up for him/herself.
　　96　Has a difficult time initiating play with a group.
　　97　Liked by other children, who seek him/her out for play. (scoring reversed).
　101　Isolates himself/herself from the peer group.
　102　Tends to be ignored by other children, who act like he/she is not there.
　103　Usually plays or works with only one other child.

104 Usually plays or works alone.
(20) Socially rejected
    10 Is picked on by other children.
    32 Is often left out by other children.
    63 Lets other children push him/her around.
    92 Gets along well with peers of the same sex. (scoring reversed).
    94 Is reluctant to share things with peers.
    99 Actively disliked by other children, who reject him/her from their play.
    106 Makes a lot of comments that are not related to what the group is doing; many of these comments are self-related.
(21) Socially perceptive
    95 Is very good at understanding other people's feelings.
    98 Is good at interpreting what peers are trying to do and in understanding their intentions.
    100 Is very aware of the effects of his/her behavior on others.
(22) Socially skilled
    91 Is kind to younger children.
    93 Gets along well with peers of the opposite sex.
    105 Takes a few seconds to size up a group situation, but then joins them smoothly and confidently, and without disrupting them.

Child Adaptive Behavior Inventory Composite Dimensions

The direction of scoring each scale before including in the composite follows the name of each scale.

(1) Academic competence
Intelligent (+)
Creative (+)
Task oriented (+)
(2) Social competence
Kind (+)
Fair (+)
Socially rejected (−)
Socially skilled (+)
Socially perceptive (+)
(3) Externalizing - aggressive
Anti-social (+)
Hostile (+)
Oppositional (+)

(4) Externalizing - hyperactive
   Distractible (+)
   Hyperactive (+)
   Calm (−)
(5) Internalizing - social isolation
   Socially isolated (+)
   Introverted (+)
   Extroverted (−)
(6) Internalizing - anxious and depressed
   Depressed (+)
   Somaticizes (+)
   Anxious (+)

II

HOW THINGS CHANGE
YET STAY THE SAME

3

How Children and Parents Fare During the Transition to School

Philip A. Cowan and Gertrude Heming

A central premise of this study is that the transition to elementary school represents a major transition for children, one that has potential ripple effects throughout the family system. In chapter 1, we argued that even when children have had extensive experience in preschool, their experiences in kindergarten and first grade present qualitatively new demands for them and their families. In contrast with the relatively free choice of activities and movement available for children in home day care, day-care centers, and preschools, elementary schools require children to sit still for long periods, focus their attention, do what the teacher asks, make sense of instructions, and adjust to the styles of other children. Teachers of kindergarten and first grade are more likely to be regarded as authority figures in ways that their parents, child-care providers, and preschool teachers were not. Elementary school teachers are more likely to provide children with evaluative feedback on the quality of their work and the appropriateness of their behavior. Furthermore, because teachers' evaluations lead to children's placement in groups that are based on ability, and because ability group classification is remarkably stable over time, these evaluations have potential long-term consequences for children's lives within the school system (Entwisle & Alexander, 1993; Perry & Weinstein, 1998).

In addition to getting to know the kindergarten classroom, children must learn to maneuver within a large, heterogeneous institution with new and complex sets of values, rules, practices, and rituals (Belsky & MacKinnon, 1994). They must cope with the loss of contact with siblings and familiar friends from their preschool days and face the challenge of establishing new friendships in a large group of strangers (Ladd, 1990). For some children, school entrance also requires mastering a new language or dialect. In short, the school is a new culture to which children and their families must assimilate (Ladd, 1996). Sameroff and Haith (1996) summarized these ideas dramatically: "Second to birth and death, this may be one of the most striking transitions that a person experiences during his or her lifetime" (p. 440).

For the parents, too, with only their own entrance to kindergarten to look back on as a guide, the first child's transition to elementary school represents a major developmental milestone. Along with their excitement, almost all of the 192 couples we interviewed in Phase 2 of the study (see chapter 2) expressed some concerns about whether their child could meet the challenges posed by elementary school and whether the school could meet any special challenges posed by their child. In the 1990s, parents' concerns were heightened by what appeared to be a deepening sense of societal unease about the state of public schools. Trust in public education had been declining over the preceding decades, and criticism of the educational system had increased (Fuller, 1999). Some of the parents' concerns were based on data from cross-national research indicating that children in the United States were at a disadvantage compared with their age-mates in other countries (e.g., Stevenson, Chen, & Lee, 1993). Local newspapers published stories about social unrest being reflected even in early elementary school classrooms.

Although we and the parents in our study were under the impression that many families were fleeing from public schools to parochial and private schools, we later learned that the proportion of children actually enrolled in public and private schools has remained relatively constant over two decades (NCES, 1998). Nevertheless, from interviews with almost 200 couples who were parents of preschoolers at that time (those who continued past the initial contact and those who did not), we believe that more parents were considering options outside the public school system, a trend that we believe is continuing. Because private schools tend to be expensive, and because there are no "objective" criteria or test scores to inform parents about whether these educational alternatives might be better in the long run than those available in their local public school, many parents faced with the possibility of choice experience significant tension in the months preceding their child's entrance to school.

CENTRAL QUESTIONS

This chapter addresses five central questions about the transition to elementary school—the period that begins in the year before children enter kindergarten (age 4½ to 5½) and ends when they complete first grade (ages 6½ to 7½):

1. As a group, do children and parents change for better or worse in their adjustment as individuals, relationships with their families of origin, marital relationship quality, parent–child relationship quality, and out-side-the-family stress and support during the first child's transition to elementary school?
2. Regardless of whether the average child or parent changes in positive or negative directions during the transition to elementary school, do in-dividuals and relationships maintain their position in a developmental trajectory of adaptation by remaining in the same rank order relative to one another during this time?
3. Are there sex differences in mothers', fathers', sons', and daughters' ad-aptation as the family's first child makes the transition to school?
4. What is the level of risk and actual distress in a sample of relatively ad-vantaged families as the first child makes the transition to school?
5. Based on answers to questions 1 to 4, does managing the changes and uncertainties of the transition to elementary school constitute a major life transition for children and their parents?

Questions about whether individuals and families change during the first child's transition to school are more complex than they seem initially, be-cause change over time is evaluated in two qualitatively different ways (for a helpful discussion of this point, see Bornstein & Suess, 2000). First, we can ask whether the group mean of a sample, representing the average level of functioning, remains the same from Time 1 to Time 2. If the average level of functioning does not change, we can conclude that the group shows continu-ity with respect to what is being measured. If the mean scores show signifi-cant change, we would say that the group shows discontinuity. Predictability of later adaptation depends on knowing the trajectory of group means over time. Second, we can ask whether the individuals in the group remain in the same rank order from Time 1 to Time 2. If they do, they are described as showing stability. If the rank order is not maintained, there is instability with reference to what is being measured. Predictability of later adaptation here refers to knowing the trajectories of individuals' scores over time and whether those individuals maintain their place on that trajectory relative to each other.

The fact that continuity–discontinuity and stability–instability are inde-pendent ways of looking at change makes matters more complex. Even when the mean level of group functioning shifts in an upward or downward direc-tion (discontinuity), individuals within the group may be stable over time. For example, although there is evidence that parents' marital satisfaction de-clines during the transition to parenthood (Belsky & Pensky, 1988; C. P. Cowan & Cowan, 1995), it is also true that happily married and unhappily married couples tend to remain in the same relative position across the years.

Conversely, the mean of the group could remain continuous from Time 1 to Time 2 (with no change in level), but individuals within the group could change idiosyncratically so that there is no stability of individuals' scores over that same period.

Hypotheses

Continuity and Discontinuity. In the absence of previous systematic research, it was not clear what to expect about individual and family continuity as children enter elementary school. Would the stresses surrounding the child's transition to school reverberate in negative ways through the family? Would parents' well-being and quality of life in the family remain static or perhaps improve during the first child's transition from preschool to more formal schooling—as children become more independent and parents have some increased freedom to make choices based on their own needs? Another alternative also seems possible—that the disequilibration experienced by the child results in discontinuity, but does not produce change in mean level of adaptation in the parents. It seems, then, that there are reasonable arguments to support expectations of increased distress and maladjustment, decreased distress and dysfunction, increased positive development, and no significant change during the first child's transition to school. Given these possibilities, we approached the analyses of continuity–discontinuity over time from a hypothesis-generating rather than a hypothesis-testing perspective.

Stability and Instability. Regardless of whether families change in positive or negative ways or remain the same during the first child's transition to school, it is important to find out whether there is stability in their rank order of adaptation over time. The answer is central to the issue of whether there are connections between risks occurring during the preschool period and later school-related outcomes. Although data are lacking on this question during the elementary school transition, there are several reasons to expect that family members will maintain their relative level of adaptation over this 2-year period. First, predictability within a context of change tends to be the rule in major life transitions (Caspi & Roberts, 1999; P. A. Cowan, 1991). After transitions we tend to be much like we were before, perhaps more so. Second, Alexander and Entwisle's (1988) trajectory hypothesis, cited in chapter 1, asserts that children tend to maintain their level of functioning throughout their academic careers from kindergarten through high school. Third, data from longitudinal studies of early to midadulthood (J. Block, 1971; Vaillant, 1995) reveal stability of rank order over time. Based on the evidence from these and similar studies, we predicted relative stability (high correlations) in the functioning of children and parents and in the quality of their relationships from the preschool period through the kindergarten and first-grade years.

Differences Among Mothers, Fathers, Sons, and Daughters. In chapter 1, we noted the enduring controversy about whether there are consistent sex differences in various domains of children's functioning (J. H. Block, 1976; Leaper, 2000, 2002; Lytton, 2000; Maccoby, 2000) or in adults' functioning (Kornstein & Clayton, 2002). Outside of the ubiquitous findings that boys tend to be more overtly aggressive than girls, that men tend to have more aggressive-externalizing behavior problems than women (A. Campbell, 1993), and that women tend to have more internalizing, self-doubting, and depressive symptoms than men (Kessler, 2003), we had little basis for making specific predictions about main-effect sex differences in the measures used in our study or in patterns of change across the child's transition to school.

Risk and Distress in a Well-Functioning Sample. As we noted in chapter 2, most of the two-parent families in our study were relatively advantaged by virtue of their level of education, income, and personal resources. Furthermore, we did not recruit families from mental health facilities where we would be more likely to find a high proportion of individuals, couples, or families in serious distress. The initial recruitment focused on asking families with children using day-care and preschool settings to participate in a study of the first child's transition to school. Furthermore, the parents were not offered the opportunity to take part in an intervention until the end of their initial interview. Thus, we had no a priori expectation that the parents or their children would be especially troubled.

Two-parent, "low risk" families like the ones in this study are often cited as a kind of ideal comparison group with which to contrast the state of families at "high risk" because of single parenthood, poverty, or divorce (Mason, Skolnick, & Sugarman, 2003; Popenoe, 1993). This quick assumption, that two-parent families are at low risk, ignores the fact that the national divorce rate is estimated at between 40% and 50% (Amato, 2001; Hetherington & Kelly, 2002), suggesting that up to half of all marriages are at risk of dissolution. Young children entering elementary school may also be at more risk than we initially assumed. As Perry and Weinstein (1998) suggested, the incidence and prevalence of children's school adjustment problems vary from 1% to 35%, depending on the domain of difficulty, the criterion used (e.g., impairment vs. disorder), the setting of the problem (e.g., home or school), and the informant. A national assessment that was not limited to a high risk children sample (cited in Perry & Weinstein, 1998) found that 20% to 30% of the children showed clinically significant levels of internalizing and externalizing behavior. Our earlier study of similar families with a first child entering kindergarten (C. P. Cowan & Cowan, 1992) found that about half the marriages were showing clinically significant levels of distress and 10% of the children were already diagnosed by the school or mental health system with learning difficulties, depression, or Attention Deficit Hyperactivity Disorder (ADHD), by the end of the kindergarten year. We were not certain exactly what incidence of risk and distress to predict in our current sample of families as their first child entered kindergarten, but we expected to be concerned about the child's future academic and social trajectory in a meaningful number of families.

Our concern about the children is related to the answers to our questions about the extent of continuity and stability of adaptation over the child's transition to school. If all of the "nonclinical" families who participated in this study were essentially well-functioning, then a slight average decline in adaptation might not be worrisome. Neither would the finding that individuals and families follow a relatively fixed trajectory, because even those at the low end would be doing well in absolute terms. However, if some of the families showed marked levels of stress, distress, or maladaption in the period when the first child is entering elementary school, and if individual and relationship trajectories appear to be relatively fixed, then it is possible to identify some individuals and families at risk of distress and diagnosable difficulties in the early elementary school years. This possibility made the idea of evaluating an intervention that might affect children's trajectories even more important.

The Child's Entrance to School Constitutes a Major Life Transition. We define a life transition (P. A. Cowan, 1991) as involving changes in the self and in one's central relationships:

1. Alterations in the individual's view of both self and world (including self-concept, values, and affect regulation).
2. Increases or decreases in personal competence in response to new challenges.
3. Reorganization (adding, subtracting, reorganizing, or shifting the importance) of central life roles.
4. Change in the quality of central relationships.

Transitions in themselves are neither positive nor negative. Developmental theorists (e.g., Erikson, 1950) and community psychologists and psychiatrists (Caplan, 1964) have described transitions as necessary for growth and development because disequilibrium stimulates the replacement of old ineffective patterns with new, more differentiated responses to new challenges. It is also the case that inadequate attempts to meet the challenges associated with transitions can bring stress, distress, and dysfunction. In that sense, transitions have within them the potential for crisis in that they embody both opportunity and danger.

With the exception of a short-term longitudinal study by Barth and Parke (1996), and our own earlier study following families from a first pregnancy through the child's completion of kindergarten (P. A. Cowan et al., 1994), we know of no longitudinal studies that provide a foundation for hypotheses about what happens to family relationships and family members during this important developmental period. We used the data from the answers to the first four questions to arrive at a tentative conclusion about whether the findings about change fit the definition of a major life transition.

METHODS

The measures that we used to assess continuity–discontinuity and stability–instability in individual, parent–child, marital, three-generational, and outside-the-family domains of our model (chapter 1, Fig. 1.1 to 1.6) were described in chapter 2. Because we found no significant differences in marital satisfaction, depression, or parenting stress at pretest between self-selected controls who rejected the intervention and those who were randomly assigned to the consultation conditions, all participants followed over time were included in these analyses, not merely those in the randomized design to the intervention or control subsamples. The ns for most of the analyses ranged from 80 to 90.

We used General Linear Modeling two-way, mixed model, multivariate analyses of covariance (MANCOVAs) to evaluate continuity from preschool to first grade, with Time as a within-subjects effect and Sex of child as a between-subjects effect. In the analysis of parents' change, Sex of parent was treated as a within-subjects effect because of the consistent correlations that we found between many aspects of mothers' and fathers' self-reports and observed behaviors. We needed to rule out the possibility that discontinuity or instability between assessments at PRE (prekindergarten) and POST1 (kindergarten) or POST2 (first grade) were attributable to the fact that parents participated in one of the two kinds of couples groups. A vector variable (dummy coded +1 or –1) differentiating those families with parents who participated in either the maritally-focused or parenting-focused couples group (+1) from families who did not (–1) served as a covariate control for the possible impact of the interventions on mean change over time.

We used partial correlations to evaluate stability of adaptation in mothers, fathers, and children, from preschool to first grade. From the Pearson correlations between Time 1 and Time 2, Time 2 and Time 3, or Time 1 and Time 3, the intervention vector was partialled out to control for the effect of the intervention on predictability across time. In recognition of the fact that many analyses of predictability and change were performed, we included in the relevant tables only effect sizes described by Cohen as moderate ($r < .30$) or large ($r < .50$).

RESULTS

Overview

The findings we report in this chapter tell a reasonably coherent but complex story about how children and their parents fared during the transition to elementary school. The complexity is in part attributable to the fact that the answer to many of our questions about continuity and stability depend on the source of the information: test scores, children's or adults' self-reports, teachers' reports, or observations by our staff. We found both continuity and discontinuity in children and parents over the course of the transition. The majority of statistically significant changes in mean level of functioning indicated that, in general, adaptation was improving over time. Important exceptions were that 5- to 7-year-old girls' perceptions revealed that they thought their academic competence had declined as they made the transition to elementary school, and mothers' and fathers' depression scores increased whereas satisfaction with their relationships as couples declined over the same period of time.

We found strong support for the trajectory hypothesis in that children and parents tended to remain in the same rank order relative to others in the sample. The overwhelming majority of measures showed moderate to high stability over a 1-year period (prekindergarten to kindergarten, kindergarten to first grade) or 2-year period (prekindergarten to first grade). An important exception was the low stability in observed parenting style. Finally, we found a number of important sex differences both in children and in parents, and a very few significant Time × Sex interactions. That is, there were both differences and similarities in how boys and girls, or fathers and mothers, changed over time.

Continuity–Discontinuity and Stability–Instability in Children Across the Transition to School

Achievement Test Scores. As measured by the standardized Peabody Individual Achievement Test (PIAT), children's achievement in reading, spelling, and math (see Table 3.1) increased significantly from the end of kindergarten to the end of first grade: reading, $F(1, 80) = 11.12, p < .001$; math, $F(1, 80) = 15.66, p < .001$; and spelling, $F(1, 80) = 11.28, p < .001$. Boys had significantly higher math scores than girls (see discussion of sex differences

TABLE 3.1

Continuity–Discontinuity in Achievement Test Scores Over Time

Peabody Individual Achievement Test Scores	Kindergarten	First Grade	Estimated Marginal Means
Reading			
Girls $n = 37$	97.8	105.2	101.5
Boys $n = 47$	104.1	108.7	106.4
Estimated marginal means	101.0[a]	107.0[a]	
Mathematics			
Girls	99.9	108.0	104.6[b]
Boys	110.8	117.5	114.0[b]
Estimated marginal means	105.4[a]	112.3[a]	
Spelling			
Girls	97.7	104.7	101.2
Boys	103.6	106.8	105.1
Estimated marginal means	100.6[a]	105.8[a]	

[a]Means significantly different, $p < .001$. [b]Means significantly different, $p < .01$.

later), but there were no significant Time × Sex interactions. Because intervention vectors were included in the GLM analysis as covariates, we can conclude that, over and above any impact of their parents' participation in a couples group, the achievement of the children in our sample went up from 5 to 8 standardized score points in the year between kindergarten and first grade.

Despite the discontinuity revealed by significant group increases in achievement scores, children generally maintained the stability of their place in the achievement trajectory relative to their peers. Tested academic achievement on the PIAT was highly predictable from the end of kindergarten to the end of first grade (see Table 3.2): reading, $r(82) = .77$; math, $r(82) = .71$; and spelling, $r(82) = .82$, all $ps < .001$.

Children's Self-Reports: Berkeley Puppet Interview (BPI). The data concerning continuity and stability of children's self-perceptions during their transition to elementary school come in part from a previously published report. Measelle et al. (1998) found that, whereas boys' and girls' average level of self-reported academic competence (BPI) did not change over the elementary school transition period, their perceptions of their achievement motivation and acceptance by peers became significantly more positive between prekindergarten and kindergarten, but did not change further between kindergarten and first grade. Children's positive perceptions of their social competence increased significantly over the 2-year period between prekindergarten and first grade.

Self-reported depression and aggression were not assessed with the BPI during the preschool period. From kindergarten to first grade, there were no

TABLE 3.2
Stability–Instability of Children's Adaptation Over Time

	Prekindergarten Spring to Kindergarten Spring	Kindergarten Spring to First-Grade Spring	Prekindergarten Spring to First-Grade Spring
Peabody Individual Achievement Test Scales			
Reading		.77***	
Math		.71***	
Spelling		.82***	
Berkeley Puppet Interview[a]			
Academic competence	.29*	.32**	
Achievement motivation	.41***	.54***	.25*
Social competence	.46***	.51***	.30**
Peer acceptance	.49***	.55***	.31**
Depression-anxiety	—	.58***	—
Aggression-hostility	—	.56***	—

	Mothers	Fathers	Mothers	Fathers	Mothers	Fathers
Parents' Child Adaptive Behavior Inventory (CABI) Scales						
Academic competence	.47***	.64***	.59***	.60***	.64***	.57***
Social competence	.62***	.67***	.76***	.80***	.71***	.69***
Externalizing-aggressive	.73***	.67***	.72***	.71***	.68***	.64***
Externalizing-hyperactive	.72***	.68***	.75***	.75***	.62***	.63***
Internalizing-social isolation	.70***	.72***	.84***	.72***	.70***	.64***
Internalizing-anxiety and depression	.58***	.67***	.65***	.74***	.67***	.57***
Teachers' CABI Scales						
Academic competence			.35**			
Social competence			.30*			
Externalizing-aggressive			.53***			
Externalizing-hyperactive			.41***			
Internalizing-social isolation			.41***			
Internalizing-anxiety and depression			ns			

[a]Data concerning Berkeley Puppet Interview scores are adapted from Table 4.1 (Measelle, Ablow, Cowan, & Cowan, 1998, p. 1567).

*$p < .05$. **$p < .01$. ***$p < .001$.

significant shifts in either of these self-report measures. Counteracting this rather optimistic picture of increases in measures of positive functioning, and declines or no change in measures of negative functioning, was the finding that girls' sense of academic competence declined significantly (see discussion of sex differences later) over the transition to elementary school period.

Despite the fact that several aspects of their self-perceptions were changing significantly, on the average, children's descriptions of themselves on the BPI were generally predictable over time (Measelle et al., 1998; see Table 3.3). From preschool to kindergarten, the four scales assessing academic and social competence showed an average $r = .41$. From kindergarten to first grade,

TABLE 3.3

Time of Assessment by Sex of Parent

	Mothers			Fathers			Time × Sex	Parents			Time	Sex		Sex
	PRE	PO1	PO2	PRE	PO1	PO2	F	PRE	PO1	PO2	F	Women	Men	F
Individual Parent														
Self concept														
The Pie														
Parent	155.5	145.4	132.0	94.6	104.2	97.8		125.7	124.8	114.9	5.49*	144.3	98.9	47.13***
Partner or lover	52.7	59.1	63.8	69.9	66.7	67.3		61.3	62.9	65.5		58.5	67.9	8.01**
Housewife or househusband	22.3	27.7	18.9	24.3	16.2	11.2	3.82*	23.4	21.5	15.1	3.78*	23.1	16.9	
Worker	59.0	59.3	66.9	121.9	127.1	134.3		90.4	93.2	100.6	4.81*	61.7	127.8	64.82***
Adaptation														
Self-esteem: ACL	100.7	99.2	96.7	83.0	78.8	77.3		91.8	89.0	87.0	7.89**	99.0	80.0	5.78*
Anxiety: BSI	.6	.5	.4	.6	.4	.4		.6	.5	.4		.5	.5	
Depression: CES-D	10.0	10.4	12.4	9.5	10.4	11.6		9.8	11.2	12.0	4.19*	11.5	10.5	
Parent–Child relationship														
Observed														
Authoritative	2.5	2.6		2.4	2.6		4.74*	2.5	2.6	33.49***		2.7	2.5	5.81*
Authoritarian	.5	.5		.6	.6			.5	.5			.6	.4	14.91***
Warmth	3.8	3.7		3.6	3.6		5.00**	3.7	3.7			3.8	3.6	14.17***
Negative emotion	1.9	1.6		2.0	1.6		5.23**	1.9	1.6		44.59***	1.8	1.8	
Structure and limits	3.5	3.6		3.5	3.8		8.95**	3.5	3.7		37.54***	3.7	3.5	4.64*
Respect for autonomy	3.8	3.8		3.7	3.7			3.8	3.8			3.9	3.7	7.42**
Self report														
Ideas About Parenting														
Authoritative	6.8	6.8		6.7	6.5		5.9**	6.8	6.6		6.78**	6.8	6.6	6.38*
Authoritarian	4.4	4.6		4.6	4.9			4.5	4.8		12.97***	4.5	4.8	4.25*
Parenting Stress Index	139.7	138.1	140.9	140.5	137.8	139.1		140.1	137.9	140.0		139.6	139.1	

(Continued)

TABLE 3.3
(Continued)

	Mothers			Fathers			Time × Sex	Parents			Time	Sex		Sex
	PRE	PO1	PO2	PRE	PO1	PO2	F	PRE	PO1	PO2	F	Women	Men	F
Marital relationship														
Observed														
Conflict	—	—	—	—	—	—		1.80	1.79					
Negative emotion	—	—	—	—	—	—		2.21	2.27					
Positive emotion	—	—	—	—	—	—		3.43	3.41					
Clarity	—	—	—	—	—	—		3.51	3.75		31.68***			
Self report														
Who Does What Task division	5.2	5.1	5.1	5.4	5.4	5.4		5.3	5.3	5.3		5.1	5.4	
Decision division	4.8	4.8	4.8	4.9	4.9	4.9		4.9	4.8	4.8		4.8	4.9	
Child-care division	3.5	3.5	3.5	3.8	3.8	3.8		3.6	3.7	3.6		3.5	3.8	16.28***
Task dissatisfaction	1.5	1.7	1.2	1.1	1.1	.9	3.84*	1.3	1.2	1.1	10.64***	1.3	1.1	8.80**
Decision dissatisfaction	.8	.8	.8	.7	.7	.8		.8	.7	.8		.8	.7	
Child-care dissatisfaction	1.2	1.1	1.1	.8	.7	.7		1.0	.9	.9	4.37*	1.1	.7	39.99***
Conflict (L-W)[a]	37.2	37.4	37.0	36.6	36.5	35.0	4.91*	36.9	36.9	36.0		37.2	36.0	5.24*
Power struggle	1.1	1.0	1.4	1.1	1.2	1.5		1.1	1.1	1.4	4.10*	1.2	1.3	
Conflict avoidance	1.0	1.4	1.2	1.2	1.5	1.3		1.1	1.4	1.2	4.93**	1.2	1.3	
Marital satisfaction (L-W)[a]	111.0	110.3	107.3	108.4	107.6	103.0		109.7	108.9	105.2	3.68*	109.5	106.3	

							F				F			F
Family of Origin														
Family Relationship questionnaire														
With mother past	29.1	29.4	30.8	31.3	29.9	30.3						29.2	31.0	4.13**
With father past	26.0	26.3	27.9	28.0	27.0	27.2						26.1	28.0	
Between parents past	25.5	25.8	28.3	27.9	26.9	26.9						25.7	28.1	
With mother now	30.4	30.1	30.0	30.0	30.2	30.0						30.3	30.0	
With father now	27.0	27.2	30.8	29.8	28.9	28.1						27.1	29.9	
Between parents now	26.8	28.3	31.0	30.1	28.8	29.3	9.21**					27.7	30.6	
Outside Family														
Work														
Work hours (per week)	26.7	—	26.7	44.2	—	45.2	4.3*	35.1	—	35.8	7.1**	26.3	44.7	81.09***
Income (median)	22,000	—	36,349	51,500	—	68,500		78,500	—	90,000		29,179	60,000	15.8***
Life stress and support														
Total life stress	21.5	18.8	18.3	20.4	19.1	18.9	5.23*	36.9	37.0	36.0	5.6**	19.24	18.89	5.23*
Positive social support	192.1	—	189.2	145.9	—	144.09		168.0	—	166.6		190.7	145.0	83.06***

Note. PRE = prekindergarten; PO1 = POST1 or kindergarten; PO2 = POST2 or first grade; ACL = Adjective Check List; BSI = Brief Symptom Inventory; CES-D = Center for Epidemiologic Study of Depression scale.

[a]Lower numbers = higher conflict.

*$p < .05$. **$p < .01$. ***$p < .001$.

the six BPI scales (now including depression and aggression) showed an average $r = .51$. This effect size compares very favorably with stability coefficients using other measures of self-concept in children this age (Harter, 1999). It represents a "large" effect size, but it means that there is still a great deal of change in rank order of children's self-descriptions over the transition from preschool through first grade.

Parents' Reports of Children's Adaptation.   Mothers' and fathers' ratings on the Child Adaptive Behavior Inventory (CABI) of children's academic competence, social competence, and externalizing and internalizing problem behaviors, showed no statistically significant changes as the children moved from preschool through kindergarten and first grade (results not tabled).

Parents' descriptions of their child were more stable in rank order over time than were the children's descriptions of themselves (see Table 3.2). The median correlation between parents' CABI descriptions at ages 5 to 6—from late preschool to end of kindergarten—was $r(88) = .68$, $p < .001$, for mothers, and $r(88) = .67$, $p < .001$, for fathers. Kindergarten to first-grade consistency was slightly higher for both mothers $r(82) = .76$, $p < .001$, and fathers $r(82) = .73$, $p < .001$.

Tests for the significance of the difference between stability correlations of children's BPI self-descriptions (reported earlier) and parents' CABI descriptions of their child on four similar scales showed significantly higher stability over time for parents' ratings of academic competence and social competence (both parents) and internalizing-anxiety (fathers' ratings). Only the externalizing aggressive descriptions of children by themselves and their parents showed similar levels of stability over time. It is possible that the higher stability in parents' reports than in children's reports is attributable to the different measuring instruments (CABI versus BPI). It is more likely, however, that 5- to 6-year-old children's identities and self-concepts are less stable and more open to contextual fluctuations (P. A. Cowan, 1978) than are parents' impressions of their children's abilities and personalities, at least in this early period of schooling. What is noteworthy here—and we see this phenomenon in most of the measures—is that the correlations over the 2-year period were not much different in size than the correlations over a single year. That is, as the test–retest period grew longer, the ratings did not become less stable. Once the child's place on the continuum of self-reported adaptation relative to peers is established in kindergarten, it tends to remain at that level at least through the first grade.

Teachers' Reports of Children's Adaptation.   For most reports in this study, scales on the CABI completed by teachers were normed by creating z scores that compared the children in our study with their same-sex classmates (see Method, Chapter 2). Because the mean of the z scores is set to 0 for each assessment period, this procedure ruled out the possibility of finding changes over time. Therefore, for the analyses in this chapter, we used the teachers' raw scores on each item, averaged for each of six scales, in spring of kindergarten and first grade: academic competence, social competence, externalizing-aggressive, externalizing-hyperactive, internalizing-socially isolated, and internalizing-psychological symptoms (anxiety, depression, somatization, withdrawal into fantasy). In two-way GLM analyses of covariance, with Time as a within factor and child Sex as a between factor, similar to the parents' CABI descriptions across the same time span, we found no significant mean differences between spring kindergarten and spring first-grade ratings for any of the six scales (results not tabled).

In chapter 2, we reported that for all six factor scores on the CABI, the fall–spring correlations within each year were quite high, with the median test–retest reliability for kindergarten children, $r = .75$, and for first-grade children, $r = .77$. Because a year had passed and different teachers were now doing the ratings, correlations between kindergarten and first-grade descriptions of the children were substantially lower than the within-year correlations. The median correlation between spring kindergarten and spring first-grade ratings was .38, with a range from internalizing-anxiety and depression, $r(82) = .21$ (not significant), to externalizing-aggressive, $r(82) = .53$, $p < .001$. In contrast with high stability coefficients for tested academic achievement (same child, same test), and moderate to high stability coefficients for parents' perceptions of academic achievement (same child, same observer), the effect size for teachers' ratings of academic competence across time were moderate but substantially lower, $r(82) = .35$, $p < .01$, same child, different raters. Tests revealed that all differences between parents' and teachers' stability coefficients were statistically significant except for fathers' and teachers' ratings of externalizing aggression (where both coefficients showed substantial stability (see Table 3.2).

Sex Differences in Children's Adaptation to School. We saw that whether children's adaptation was continuous or discontinuous depended on the source of the information and the index of adaptation. A similar conclusion can be drawn about whether boys and girls differ in adaptation as they enter elementary school:

1. Academic and social competence—At both kindergarten and first-grade assessment points, there were no differences between boys and girls in reading and spelling achievement test scores, but boys were more than 10 standard score points higher in math scores in both kindergarten and first grade, $F(1, 90) = 12.25$, $p < .001$. There were no significant Time × Sex interactions for any of the three achievement test measures. We noted, however, in

the previous report on the same participants by Measelle et al. (1998), that boys' self-perceptions of academic competence remained continuous, whereas girl's views of their academic competence declined from kindergarten to first grade.

Analysis of the CABI scores, including a composite measure of academic competence, showed that there were no significant main effects of sex of parent or child and no statistically significant interactions. Parents' reports did not reflect the decline in academic competence from preschool to first grade that their daughters reported.

In chapter 2, Table 2.5, we presented the cell means for teachers' ratings of the target children in our study and their classmates on each of the six CABI scales. Over the whole sample, teachers gave girls significantly higher ratings than they gave boys on academic competence in kindergarten, $F(1, 1429) = 5.70$, $p < .05$, and on the social competence scale in both kindergarten, $F(1, 1429) = 17.51$, $p < .001$, and first grade, $F(1, 1293) = 21.63$, $p < .001$. In other words, whether boys or girls were at an advantage in academic achievement early in the elementary school grades depended on the source of the information. Math test scores and children's perceptions of their own academic competence favored boys. Teachers' reports of academic competence favored girls. Parents of daughters described academic competence no differently than parents of sons.

2. Problem behavior—Measelle et al. (1998) reported that at both kindergarten and first grade, consistent with gender stereotypes, girls described themselves on the BPI as being significantly less aggressive and significantly more depressed and withdrawn than did the boys. The sex difference in externalizing behavior was consistent with the teachers' views. Girls were given significantly lower ratings than boys on the externalizing-aggressive scale and the externalizing-hyperactive scales, kindergarten $Fs(1, 1429) = 16.92$ and 21.37, $ps < .001$; first-grade $Fs(1, 1293) = 8.71$ and 17.49, $ps < .001$. The trends we report here held for both the Schoolchildren and their Families sample and for their classmates; there were no statistically significant interactions between sample and sex of child.

Could teachers' views of problem behaviors have influenced their perceptions of the children's academic competence? We found that, at each rating period (kindergarten fall and spring, first grade fall and spring), teachers' ratings of items reflecting children's academic competence were moderately negatively correlated with their ratings of externalizing-aggression (rs from $-.31$ to $-.47$) and highly negatively correlated with their ratings of children's externalizing-hyperactivity (rs from $-.58$ to $-.73$). Although correlations do not provide evidence of directionality, the findings are consistent with the notion that kindergarten and first-grade teachers judge academic competence in part on the ability of children to sit still, stay on task, and not be oppositional, defiant, or aggressive. This description of the academically competent student seems more characteristic of 5-year-old girls than boys, and may account for the fact that teachers see girls as more academically competent than boys.

Consistent with the parents' reports, but not with the children's, teachers viewed girls and boys as having similar levels of symptoms of anxiety and depression. Perhaps because these behaviors are less overt and less disruptive of classroom or family environments, neither teachers' nor parents' ratings reflected the fact that girls were reporting more feelings of sadness and depression than were boys. We discuss some implications of these findings about children's continuity and stability later.

Parents' Continuity–Discontinuity and Stability–Instability as Their Children Enter School

In this section, we focus on what is happening to parents in the period during which children make the transition to elementary school.

Individual Functioning.

1. Self concept—We chose to examine continuity–discontinuity in four aspects of parents' self concept as measured by "The Pie" (parent, partner or lover, housewife or househusband, worker). In separate two-way MANCOVAs, three of the four aspects of self showed significant change over time (i.e., they demonstrated discontinuities). Although it remained a salient aspect of fathers' and mothers' identities, the parent aspect of self declined significantly from preschool through first-grade follow-ups, $F(2, 78) = 3.13$, $p < .05$. Despite the decline in psychological salience of the parent aspect of the self, on average slightly more than 30% of the parents' Pies continued to be allocated to that piece of the circle when their children were in first grade.

As the children moved from preschool through kindergarten to first grade, there was also a significant decrease in the salience of women's and men's housewife or househusband selves, $F(2, 78) = 3.78$, $p < .05$, and a significant increase in both parents' identity as workers $F(2, 78) = 4.81$, $p < .05$. Inspection of the means in Table 3.3 suggested that these changes were more likely to occur in the kindergarten to first-grade year than in the preschool to kindergarten year, but post hoc multiple comparisons (LSD) showed that only the linear trends were statistically significant ($p < .05$). There were no significant mean changes over time in the size of the partner or lover aspect of either mothers' or fathers' identities as their children made the transition to school.

In Table 3.4, we can see that, although women's and men's parent, partner or lover, and worker pieces of The Pie were changing over time on the group level, individual differences remained stable from the preschool period to kin-

TABLE 3.4
Parents' Stability: Correlations Across Time

	Mothers			Fathers		
	PRE-PO1	PO1-PO2	PRE-PO2	PRE-PO1	PO1-PO2	PRE-PO2
Individual parent						
Self concept						
The Pie						
Parent	.39**			.45***	.34**	.35**
Partner or lover	.49***			.39**	.33**	.31**
Housewife or househusband	.38***		.32**	.55**	.34*	.38
Worker	.58***	.40***	.53***			
Adaptation						
Self-esteem	.71**	.78**	.71*	.70**	.73**	.79*
Adjective Check List						
Anxiety: Brief Symptom Inventory	.32*	.59*	.42*	.42***	.58*	.44**
Depression: CES-D		.39*	.40**		.54***	

	Mothers			Fathers		
	PRE	PO1	PO2	PRE	PO1	PO2
Parent–Child relationship						
Observed						
Authoritative		—	—	.40***	—	—
Authoritarian		—	—		—	—
Warmth		—	—	.40**	—	—
Negative emotion	.30*	—	—		—	—
Structure and limits		—	—		—	—
Respect for autonomy	.33*	—	—		—	—

	Couples					
Self report						
Ideas about Parenting						
Authoritative			.53***			.63***
Authoritarian			.72***			.70***
Parenting Stress Index			.67**			.72***
Marital relationship						
Observed						
Conflict	.37***	—	—	—	—	—
Negative emotion	.39***	—	—	—	—	—
Positive emotion	.34**	—	—	—	—	—
Clarity	.34**	—	—	—	—	—
Marital relationship						
Self report						
Who Does What Tasks	.83***	.82***	.79***	.69***	.69***	.71***
Decisions	.74***	.75***	.66***	.71***	.72	.65**
Child care	.78***	.84***	.77***	.82***	.85***	.79***
Task dissatisfaction	.67***	.80***	.65***	.70***	.53***	.47***
Decision dissatisfaction	.58***	.63***	.65***	.57***	.55***	.58***
Child-care dissatisfaction	.56***	.72***	.66***	.60***	.55***	.58***
Conflict (L-W)[a]	.60***	.77***	.63***	.58***	.60***	.60***
Power struggle	.58***	.49***	.48***	.57***	.41***	.63***
Conflict avoidance	.53***	.60***	.49***	.41***	.68***	.32***
Marital satisfaction (L-W)[a]	.70***	.81***	.60***	.55***	.66***	.51***

(Continued)

97

TABLE 3.4
(Continued)

	Mothers			Fathers		
	PRE	PO1	PO2	PRE	PO1	PO2
Family of origin						
Family Relationship questionnaire						
With mother past	—	—	.83***	—	—	.79***
With father past	—	—	.76***	—	—	.78***
Between parents past	—	—	.80***	—	—	.83***
With mother now	—	—	.75***	—	—	.77***
With father now	—	—	.81***	—	—	.72***
Between parents now	—	—	.84***	—	—	.84***
Outside Family						
Work						
Work Hours (per week)	—	—	.62***	—	—	.69***
Income	—	—	.32**	—	—	.83***
Life stress and support						
Total life stress	.49***	.61***	.60***	.67***	.78***	.71***
Positive social support	—	—	.67***	—	—	.63***

Note. PRE-PO1 = ; PO1-PO2 = ; PRE-PO2 = ; PRE = prekindergarten; PO1 = POST1 or kindergarten; PO2 = POST2 or first grade; CES-D = Center for Epidemiologic Study of Depression scale.

[a]Lower numbers = higher conflict.

*p < .05. **p < .01. ***p < .001.

dergarten. The PRE and POST1 correlations were statistically significant, although the effect sizes were moderate for parent and partner or lover. Over the next year, as the parent aspect of self grew smaller and the worker piece grew larger, the worker aspect of identity for women, $r(82) = .40, p < .01$, and men $r(86) = .34, p < .001$, remained moderately stable. For fathers, parent and househusband pieces of The Pie also tended to remain the same size relative to other fathers: parent, $r(82) = .34, p < .01$; househusband, $r(82) = .33 p < .01$. That is, how men and women saw themselves at the POST2 assessment depended in part on how they saw themselves at the start of the study. This interpretation should be treated cautiously, because, as we shall see, these statistically significant correlations are among the lowest stability coefficients we obtained of any of the measures. The pattern of findings suggests that, although there was some degree of predictability in parents' psychological aspects of self, there was also substantial idiosyncratic fluctuation over this period of time for mothers and fathers.

2. Adaptation—Adjective Check List measures of self-ideal discrepancies indicated that mothers' and fathers' self-esteem were both continuous and stable (Tables 3.3 and 3.4). For the group, average self-esteem scores remained at the same level over the 2-year period from prekindergarten, when the children were 5, to the end of first grade, when they were approximately 7. Similar to other studies of self-esteem (Wylie, 1989), parents' self-esteem was highly stable across time; the $r(86)$ from prekindergarten to kindergarten was .71 for mothers and .70 for fathers, with even higher correlations for fathers across the 2-year period from preschool through first grade, $r(82) = .79, p < .001$.

Changes in both mothers' and fathers' perceptions of their own adaptation occurred in mixed positive and negative directions. Parents' symptoms of anxiety on the Brief Symptom Inventory (BSI) and depression on the Center for Epidemiological Study of Depression Scale (CES-D) declined significantly between the preschool and kindergarten transition, and anxiety showed a further decline between the kindergarten and first-grade assessments: anxiety symptoms, $F(2, 78) = 7.89, p < .01$. Despite the changes in group means, mothers' and fathers' scores on anxiety (BSI) tended to remain in the same relative rank from PRE to POST1 to POST2 (rs from .32 to .59).

By contrast, symptoms of depression rose over the same period, $F(2, 78) = 3.87, p < .05$, primarily in the preschool to kindergarten period. Mothers' symptoms of depression (CES-D) showed moderate stability from the preschool to first-grade period, $r(82) = .40, p < .01$, but not in the preschool to kindergarten period. Similarly, fathers' reports of symptoms of depression were not at all stable during their child's transition from preschool to kindergarten, but they were highly stable over the following year, $r(82) = .57, p < .001$. In sum, this seems to be a disequilibrating period in terms of parents' views of themselves, with self-esteem remaining stable, symptoms of anxiety declining, and symptoms of depression rising.

Parent–Child Relationships.

1. Observed parenting style—Our observational measures of parent–child interaction were obtained only at the prekindergarten and kindergarten assessments, when children were ages 5 and 6. According to observers' ratings of family interaction in our project playroom, both mothers and fathers were significantly more authoritative (warm, structured, and autonomy encouraging) with their child during their second visit to our project playroom in kindergarten than they were during the visit 1 year earlier, $F(1, 85) = 33.49$, $p < .001$, whereas for the sample as a whole, qualities of authoritarian parenting (high in structure, low in warmth) remained continuous over the same period. From an analysis of the separate scores included in the authoritative index, it appears that the shift was due to a reduction in negative emotion expressed to the child in the playroom interaction, $F(1, 85) = 44.59$, $p < .001$, and an increase in structuring or setting limits during the visit, $F(1, 85) = 37.54$, $p < .001$. There were consistent differences between mothers and fathers in their patterns of change, and these are discussed later in the section on sex differences.

Despite the continuity of group averages, the behavior of mothers and fathers with their children in two sessions 1 year apart did not show a great deal of stability in rank order. Individual differences in mothers' scores showed some consistency over time in expression of displeasure and anger, $r(86) = .31$, $p < .05$, and in respect for the child's autonomy, $r(86) = .33$, $p < .05$. The cross-year correlation with authoritarian parenting style was statistically significant but below our effect size cutoff for inclusion in Table 3.4. Fathers' interactions with their children as preschoolers and kindergartners showed significant predictability across the year, but the correlations were moderate at best. Fathers who were more authoritative at PRE with their 5-year-olds also tended to be more authoritative at POST1 with their 6-year-olds $r(86) = .40$, $p < .001$; most of this effect was carried by a consistency in warmth, $r(86) = .43$, $p < .001$. Correlations over the year with the expression of negative emotion and with structuring the laboratory tasks were statistically significant but below our effect size cutoff.

We hoped to place these findings on stability of parenting style over time in context by comparing them with results of other studies. To our surprise, despite the existence of parents' reports of their parenting style over time, we could find no published studies of observations of parent–child interaction over time, to assess whether parent–child relationships follow the trajectories we have seen in other relationships. In a personal communication (2000), Diana Baumrind confirmed our impression that there are no published studies of whether parents who are observed to be authoritative or authoritarian at Time 1 remain in the same category at Time 2 or 3. Studies of children's attachment classifications suggest that there is a high level of stability across time (although this has been questioned by Belsky, Campbell, Cohn, & Moore, 1996), but these classifications are made primarily on the basis of the child's behavior during a reunion with the parent, not on the parent's behavior. In sum, further research is necessary to establish whether the rather low consistency of parenting style over 1 year in this study is typical of parent–child relationships during the period when children are making the transition to school.

2. Self-reports of parent–child relationships—In response to the Ideas About Parenting questionnaire, parents changed in a direction apparently opposite to their observed behavior with the child in a playroom setting. Both mothers and fathers showed a decline in endorsement of authoritative attitudes, which include statements about the parents' freedom of emotional expression, confidence, maturity demands, and satisfaction with parenting, $F(2, 78) = 6.78$, $p < .05$, and an increase in endorsement of authoritarian statements, which emphasize items about parental control of child behavior and emotional expression, $F(2, 78) = 12.39$, $p < .001$. One possible explanation of the contrast between observed and self-reported parent–child relationships is that the Ideas About Parenting scale was administered only during the preschool period and first grade, whereas the parenting observations were done in preschool and kindergarten. That is, a move away from authoritative and toward authoritarian attitudes could have taken place in the year between kindergarten and first grade. A second possibility is that the measures differ not only in source (self-report versus observation) but also in context. The self-report measures ask general questions that are relatively context-free, whereas the observational measures focus on a specific set of interactions around tasks in a playroom. It is also true that the playroom observations were observed by project staff, but they were observed at both periods. Unless we assume that the parents were becoming more self-conscious, this does not explain why there was a reduction in negative emotion and an increase in limit-setting.

By contrast with the observations of parents with their children, which were not highly stable in rank order, parents' reports about their ideas about how to handle children were uniformly and highly consistent across time during their child's transition to school. On the Ideas About Parenting questionnaire, mothers' authoritative and authoritarian parenting attitudes were highly stable across a 2-year period, authoritative, $r(82) = .53$, $p < .001$; authoritarian, $r(82) = .72$, $p < .001$, as were fathers' attitudes, authoritative, $r(82) = .63$, $p < .001$; authoritarian, $r(82) = .72$, $p < .001$.

Finally, we found no significant change in scores on the Parenting Stress Index during the period of the child's transition to school. As with the Ideas About Parenting scale over the same 2-year period, both mothers' and fathers' self-reported parenting stress was highly predictable, $rs(82) = .67$ for mothers and .72 for fathers.

Why were parents' descriptions of their relationship with their children so much more stable over time than our staff observations of parent–child interaction? One reason may be that there were different staff observers at each data point. Another may be related to the fact that the playroom observations, however artificial, were better predictors of children's adaptation to school than were the parents' reports (analyses performed but not reported elsewhere in this volume). Parents may be holding somewhat stereotypic or generalized views that minimize both systematic and idiosyncratic changes in their relationships with their children over time.

The Marital Relationship.

1. Observed marital interaction—Over the year between preschool and kindergarten, the clarity with which partners talked to each other in front of their child increased significantly, $F(1, 82) = 31.68, p < .001$, but there was no change in the other three composite measures of marital interaction during the family visits—positive emotion, negative emotion, and conflict. The group means, then, primarily demonstrated continuity. In correlational tests of stability of adaptation relative to others, we found that partners tended to behave similarly toward each other at the preschool and kindergarten assessments. All four measures of marital interaction quality demonstrated statistically significant levels of stability in rank order from PRE to POST1, but the correlations were in the low moderate range (.34 to .39).

2. Who Does What?—As we followed parents of 5- to 7-year-olds, we found no significant systematic shifts in their reports of their division of household tasks, family decisions, or care of the child. In Table 3.3, a mean score between 1 and 5 signifies that mothers are doing more of the tasks than fathers are, a score between 5 and 9 signifies that fathers are doing more than mothers are; a score of 5 represents equal sharing of tasks in a given domain. On the average, household and family tasks and family decisions were shared fairly equally in this sample (5.3 for household tasks and 4.8 for decision making), but, as expected, both partners reported that mothers did more than fathers in caring for the child (mothers = 3.5; fathers = 3.8; both substantially below 5.0).

A previous study of mothers' and fathers' family roles in the earlier childrearing years (C. P. Cowan & Cowan, 1988) indicated that more egalitarian arrangements were accompanied by higher levels of marital satisfaction for both fathers and mothers. In this study, despite the lack of change over time in the sharing of child-care tasks, and with most mothers working outside the home at least 20 hours per week, both mothers and fathers showed increasing satisfaction with their division of household tasks as their first child entered kindergarten and first grade, $F(2, 78) = 10.64, p < .001$, and increasing satisfaction with the sharing of child-related tasks, $F(2, 78) = 4.37$,

$p < .05$. Our measure of "Who Does What?" assesses mothers' involvement in family work relative to fathers' involvement. As children grew older and more self-sufficient and parents' increasing incomes allowed them to purchase more help outside the family, accompanying the decline in salience of housework, there may have been a decline in the absolute amount of family work. Such a reduction could be responsible for mothers' and fathers' increasing satisfaction with their division of household and family labor during the transition to elementary school.

Over the transition to school period, fathers' and mothers' descriptions of their division of household and family tasks, family decisions, and child-related tasks on the Who Does What? questionnaire were highly stable over time (median correlation over 1 year = .79 for women and .71 for men). Across-time correlations for satisfaction with their division of labor in each of these domains were also high (discrepancy between actual and ideal ratings: mothers = .63, fathers = .64).

3. Self-reported marital quality—In contrast with the positive changes described earlier, and consistent with the increase in symptoms of depression, several self-report indicators suggest a systematic decline in both husbands' and wives' descriptions of marital quality during their first child's transition to elementary school. Compared with their reports during the preschool period, both fathers and mothers of kindergartners were more likely to report that they avoided further discussion when they disagreed, $F(2, 78) = 4.93, p < .01$. During the next year, when the children were in first grade, both fathers and mothers reported more power struggles over their disagreements, $F(2, 78) = 4.10, p < .05$. An increase in marital conflict as measured on the Locke–Wallace Marital Adjustment Test was only marginally significant ($p = .08$), but there was a significant overall main effect for marital satisfaction declining over time, $F(2, 78) = 3.68, p < .05$. Post hoc tests (LSD) revealed no significant change in marital satisfaction (Locke & Wallace, 1959) as children moved from prekindergarten to kindergarten, but a significant decline over the kindergarten to first-grade year for both fathers and mothers. These findings are consistent with the cross-sectional literature (e.g., Spanier & Lewis, 1980) and with more than 20 longitudinal studies (see C. P. Cowan & Cowan, 1997) in suggesting that self-reported marital satisfaction continues to decline from pregnancy throughout the years of rearing young children.

Mirroring the pattern of parents' descriptions of their relationship with their child over time, their reports of their relationship as a couple were much more consistent than were staff observations of their interactions. Men's and women's satisfaction with marriage (Locke & Wallace, 1959) over a 1-year period showed typically high (Spanier & Lewis, 1980) stability coefficients: mothers PRE to POST1, $r(86) = .70, p < .001$, and POST 1 to POST 2, $r(86) = .81, p < .001$; fathers PRE to POST1, $r(86) = .55, p < .001$, and POST 1 to POST 2, $r(86) = .66, p < .001$. Predictability of husbands' and wives' reports of marital conflict over the same periods were slightly lower, but still strong (see Table 3.4).

Relationships With the Family of Origin.   Neither the past nor the present quality of each parent's reported relationship with his or her parents showed significant change in the two assessments using the Family Relationships Questionnaire in the preschool period and 2 years later during first grade. Continuity was also evident in each partner's perception of his or her parents' marriage in the past. One exception to continuity is that their parents' current marital relationship quality was described more positively over time by women, but not by men, Time × Sex, $F(1, 78) = 9.21, p < .01$.

On the Family Relationship Scale, the rank order in which qualities of past and present family relationships were described was highly stable, $rs(82)$ ranged from .72 to .84 (see Table 3.4). Although there were indications from interviews and discussions in the couples groups (see chapters 8 and 11) that many parents were struggling to make sense of their early relationships with their parents and to renegotiate their current relationships with them, the quantitative data reflected both stability and consistency of men's and women's descriptions of their relationships with their parents in the period of their first child's transition to elementary school.

Outside the Nuclear Family.

1. Parents' work—At the beginning of the study, before their first child entered kindergarten, 7% of the mothers were unemployed; 67% of the mothers were working more than 20 hours per week, with an average work week of 28.3 hours. Almost all fathers were employed, with only 2% out of work; 98% of the fathers worked more than 20 hours per week, with an average work week of 44.5 hours. Two years later, as their children completed first grade, the figures describing work hours for both mothers and fathers were virtually unchanged. There was, however, an increase in family incomes. Mothers' average incomes increased by more than $4,000 per year, whereas fathers' average incomes rose by more than $17,000 per year. The main effect for Time was significant, $F(1, 78) = 5.6, p < .01$, but so was the Time × Sex interaction, $F(1, 78) = 7.1, p < .01$. The mothers' increase in income was not statistically significant, probably due to the high variability in mothers' incomes. In the 2 years between the prekindergarten period and the end of first grade, parents' work hours were relatively stable in rank order: mothers, $r(82) = .62, p < .001$; fathers, $r(82) = .69, p < .001$. In contrast to mothers' incomes, which were only moderately stable over time, $r(82) = .32, p < .001$, fathers' incomes were highly stable over the transition to school period, $r(82) = .83, p < .001$.

2. Life stress and social support—Parents of children entering elementary school reported declining life stress (Horowitz, Schaefer, Hiroto, Wilner, &

Levin, 1977) from prekindergarten to the first grade year, $F(2, 78) = 5.6, p <$ .05, and their reports of positive social support (Curtis-Boles, 1979) remained continuous over the 2-year transition. Both of these measures showed high stability over time, with correlations ranging from $r = .49$ to $r = .78$. In sum, as their children were beginning their school careers, parents' work hours, social support, and life stress were relatively stable and predictable. Despite the similarity in mothers' and fathers' reports of these parts of their lives, fathers' incomes rose moderately yet significantly, but mothers' incomes did not.

A Note on Differences Between Parents

Although there were very few Time × Sex interaction effects, and therefore few sex differences in parents' change over time, there were a number of significant main effect differences between the mothers and fathers in this study (see Table 3.3). In terms of their self-concepts, mothers had a significantly larger piece of The Pie labeled parent, $F(1, 78) = 47.13, p < .001$, and smaller pieces labeled partner or lover, $F(1, 78) = 8.01, p < .01$, and worker, $F(1, 78) = 64.82, p < .001$, than did fathers. In fact, mothers' worker piece of The Pie averaged slightly less than half the size of fathers'. There were no differences between parents in reports of symptoms of anxiety or depression, but mothers had significantly lower self-esteem (Adjective Check List), $F(1, 78) = 4.77, p < .05$.

In parenting style, mothers were observed to be more authoritative than fathers, $F(1, 78) = 4.77, p < .05$—warmer, more structuring of tasks, with greater respect for the child's autonomy (see Table 3.3). In their self-reports, the women expressed more authoritative, $F(1, 78) = 6.38, p < .01$, and less authoritarian, $F(1, 78) = 4.25, p < .05$, parenting attitudes than their husbands, did, in part because the fathers endorsed more of the angry and punitive items on the Ideas About Parenting scale.

Each partner described himself or herself as doing significantly more of the child-care tasks than the other, $F(1, 78) = 16.23, p < .001$. Women were significantly more dissatisfied than their partners on their division of both household, $F(1, 78) = 8.80, p < .01$, and child-related tasks, $F(1, 78) = 39.99, p < .001$. None of the other measures of marital functioning revealed sex differences in response (division of household tasks and decision making, conflict avoidance, power struggle, and marital satisfaction).

Finally, consistent with The Pie data measuring psychological involvement in work, mothers were actually working many fewer hours per week than fathers (28.3 hours versus 44.5 hours), $F(1, 78) = 81.09, p < .001$, getting paid much less when they did work, $F(1, 78) = 15.83, p < .001$, and reporting more stressful life events, $F(1, 78) = 5.23, p < .05$. On the other hand, mothers were reporting much more positive social support from others outside the nuclear family than were their husbands, $F(1, 78) = 83.06, p < .01$. This combination of divergent experiences for mothers and fathers of very young school-age children may well be contributing to their declines in satisfaction with their overall relationships as couples.

Incidence of Risk in a Low-Risk Sample

So far, we have presented data concerning continuity and stability using the prekindergarten period as a baseline and assessing positive or negative change from that point in time forward. Measures of adaptation in children and their parents showed either no change or improvement over time, with a few, but important, indicators reflecting a decline in satisfaction or sense of well-being. It seems fair to say that for the families in our study, meeting the challenges of the first child's entrance to elementary school was somewhat disequilibrating at some points, but overall not debilitating.

Are these findings simply a natural consequence of the fact that these are relatively "low-risk," advantaged, two-parent families, most of whom have two incomes that place them in middle and upper-middle socioeconomic status categories? In our view, there are several reasons to be more cautious in drawing optimistic conclusions about the sample as a whole, and some reasons to be concerned about families who may have advantages in terms of demographic characteristics but are at the bottom of the sample distribution in terms of individual and relationship adaptation. We have been considering mean change relative to a prekindergarten baseline. Before drawing final conclusions about how families are faring during the first child's transition to school, we need to pay more attention to a number of issues arising from the pattern of individual differences within this sample, and to the meaning of the scores at the low end of the distribution. We shall see that from this perspective, a significant proportion of this low-risk sample is actually at high risk for future difficulties, and that some participants are already showing signs of distress or dysfunction by the time the child completes first grade.

First, girls' mathematics scores on the individually administered PIAT achievement test were significantly lower than boys' scores in both kindergarten and first grade. Although their math scores actually increased over the next year, their self-ratings of academic competence were declining. It seems possible that their increasing awareness of the difference between boys and girls in math achievement was influencing their negative perceptions of their academic competence.

Second, our findings supporting the trajectory hypothesis indicate that preschoolers and kindergartners with negative views of themselves, low academic achievement scores, and internalizing or externalizing problems as their parents and teachers described them, were at risk for behavioral and academic difficulties by the end of first grade (Measelle, chapter 6).

Third, related to the trajectory findings, some children were experiencing difficulties that suggest the need for psychological help, or had already triggered referral to the mental health system by the time they entered kindergarten. Our records from telephone calls and interviews with the parents in kindergarten and first grade indicate that 9 of the 84 first graders had been referred for learning, attention-deficit, or emotional problems (primarily depression) and had been seen by professionals in the mental health system. This figure is supported by our finding reported in chapter 2 that teachers' CABI ratings comparing the target children in our study to their classmates showed that 11.7% of them were in the top 10% of the larger sample in externalizing-aggression and that 14.4% of them were in the top 10% of the population in internalizing-anxiety or depression.

We noted earlier that the literature on this time of life for children suggests that the proportion of kindergarten children potentially needing help is substantial. Alexander and Entwisle (1988) and Lambert (1988) placed the figure at about 20%; what the findings in our study suggest is that half or more of this 20% may come from what have been thought of as low-risk families.

Fourth, we chose two indicators of parents' adaptive functioning, the CES-D scale assessing symptoms of depression, and the Locke-Wallace Marital Adjustment Test, for which previous research with large-sample norms had already established clinical cutoff scores. At one or more assessment periods over the 2 years of our study, 41% of the women and 36% of the men had depression scores of 16 or above, the cutoff at which clinical depression becomes a distinct possibility (Radloff, 1977). In terms of marital distress, 24% of the women and 33% of the men had Locke-Wallace Marital Adjustment Test scores below 90, similar to the scores of couples in therapy (Gottman, 1994). Given that the lifetime divorce rate is close to 50%, and that an estimated 20% of couples have divorced before their children enter kindergarten (Bumpass & Rindfuss, 1979) and were therefore not candidates for enrollment in our study of two-parent families, the Locke-Wallace Marital Adjustment Test scores seem to provide a realistic estimate of the extent of marital distress in our sample.

We also constructed an index of risk associated with experiences in the family of origin. We gave 1-point scores for the presence and 0 points for the absence of six potentially traumatic childhood risk factors and added the risk scores together: a father or mother who was mentally ill, who had substance abuse problems, or who abused the respondent physically. Forty-eight mothers and 40 fathers had experienced at least one of these risks in childhood, and half of the study participants had experienced two or more.

In sum, despite the fact that the fathers, mothers, and children in this study experienced more positive than negative changes, on the average, as the family's first child made the transition to elementary school, a substantial subset of participants started and ended the transition with indicators of individual or relationship distress.

DISCUSSION

Continuity and Discontinuity

Our first questions were concerned with continuity over time. How do families fare, on the average, when the first child enters elementary school? If they change, do they move in a positive or negative direction?

Children.   The children in our study gained significantly in reading, math, and spelling scores when they were compared with the PIAT's normative sample. Of six scales on the BPI, children showed positive changes in three (motivation for achievement, acceptance by peers, and social competence), and no change in two (aggression and depression). Only on self-perceived academic competence was there a negative change as the children entered school, a decline that was significant for girls but not for boys.

By contrast with the data from achievement tests and children's self-reports, parents' perceptions of the children on the six CABI scales (academic and social competence, externalizing-aggressive, externalizing-hyperactive, internalizing-socially-isolated, and internalizing-psychological symptoms) showed no change over the 2 years of this study. Teachers' perceptions of the children's functioning on the same scales also showed continuity over PRE, POST1, and POST2 assessments.

In sum, test scores and children's self-reports predominantly reflected discontinuity in children's group means over time, whereas parents' and teachers' views reflected continuity. That is, the children were viewing themselves differently, but parents and teachers were not. This is one of two important discrepancies in perspective that we discuss further later. It is possible that in the case of the teachers, we missed an important beginning point. Had we been able to obtain teachers' descriptions of the children during the preschool period, we might have been able to construct a more conclusive picture of shifts or continuities in children's behavior once they arrived at school.

Parents.   More than half (55%) of the 40 self-report and observational measures of mothers' and fathers' behavior and adaptation across the five family domains revealed significant change as their first child made the transition to school. Parents' views of themselves, measured by The Pie, suggested that the salience of parenthood and household work were declining whereas the worker aspect of self was increasing. Self-reported symptoms of anxiety were declining, but self-esteem remained stable, and symptoms of depression increased as their child made the transition to school.

Observations of parent–child interaction in our playroom when the child was a preschooler and again in kindergarten, suggested that parents' behavior was becoming more authoritative over time. By contrast, parents' attitudes about parenting were moving in a more authoritarian direction, as they endorsed more items that called for parental control.

In our observations of marital interaction as the parents worked and played with their child, only clarity of communication showed any change (an increase). Although there was no change in parents' reports of their division of household, decision making, and child-related tasks, both fathers and mothers were happier with their division of household and child-related tasks as their child grew from age 5 to 7. Despite these apparently positive changes in the relationship between mothers and fathers, there was a (marginal) increase in marital conflict, a significant increase in the tendency to avoid disagreements or to struggle without resolving them, and a significant decline in overall satisfaction with the marriage.

Fathers' and mothers' perceptions of both past and current relationships in their families of origin showed a great deal of continuity on the Family Relationships questionnaire. Finally, over the 2 years of their child's transition to school, the couples increased their household income, although the rise was statistically significant only for men. An additional positive change was that perceived life stress declined over the same period of time.

The overall picture appears to be one of continuity in a number of aspects of life (space devoted to lover on The Pie, self-esteem, parenting warmth, marital interaction while coparenting, division of labor, perception of relationships in their families of origin), and positive change in others. Only the measures assessing marital quality reflected a shift toward lower levels of adaptation (conflict and power struggles increased, satisfaction decreased).

Why, when a number of aspects of life were either staying the same or improving, did both husbands and wives in this study experience small but significant increases in symptoms of depression and decreases in marital satisfaction while their children were making the transition to school? The changes men and women reported in their self concepts suggested that both parents were investing less in their home and family tasks and more in their work outside the family. This psychological shift may be increasing the distance between mothers and fathers. Some of the findings were consistent with this view, in that parents reported avoiding conflict more and struggling more over disagreements without resolving them during the transition to school period.

In an earlier study of comparable parents, Cowan and Cowan (1988) found significant correlations between sharing of child-related tasks and satisfaction with that division of labor. In an exploratory analysis in this study, we asked whether sharing of tasks, satisfaction with the division of tasks, or change in either of these variables, was related to decline in marital satisfaction over time. We regressed mothers' marital satisfaction when the child was in Grade 1 on their prekindergarten marital satisfaction, their prekindergarten and Grade 1 sharing of child-related tasks, and satisfaction with the division of caring for the children. Results indicated that mothers' dissatisfaction with the couple's division of the care of their first-grade child contributed significant variance to the equation, F-change$(1, 85) = 5.23, p < .05$. Simple correlations revealed that the decline in mothers' satisfaction with marriage during the 2 years of the study was significantly associated with an increase in dissatisfaction with how the couple shared the care of their child. Similar regressions that included sharing of more general household and family tasks and decisions revealed no contribution to variance in mothers' declining satisfaction with marriage.

The story for fathers' growing dissatisfaction with marriage was different. Fathers' descriptions of their relative responsibility for family tasks and care of the child in the prekindergarten period were positively correlated with their marital satisfaction, $r(92) = .21, p < .05$, low, but statistically significant. However, fathers who increased their share of those tasks over the next 2 years as their children made the transition to school were significantly less satisfied with their couple relationship by the time their child entered first grade: family tasks, $F(1, 85) = 9.16, p < .01$; child-care tasks, $F(1, 85) = 3.95, p < .05$. These findings about high child-care involvement and lower levels of marital satisfaction are consistent with earlier findings by Barnett and Baruch (1988).

In other words, wives who wanted husbands to participate more in caring for their child (i.e., they were dissatisfied with current arrangements), and husbands who actually increased their participation in caring for the child, showed declining satisfaction with their overall marriage. This is a dilemma for couples with young children that is not easily resolved. We are concerned not only about the parents' sense of well-being or distress during this period, but also for the children, because, as we show in several other chapters in the volume, parents' conflict and distress as a couple at this stage have implications for the children's subsequent social and academic competence (chapters 6, 7, 8, 11, and 12).

Stability and Instability: The Trajectory Hypothesis

The empirical support for the trajectory hypothesis was very strong. Mothers, fathers, and children—and the quality of their relationships—generally maintain the same rank order relative to one another on measures of adaptation over the first child's transition to school.

Children. Of 59 correlations across time assessing individual differences in children's adaptation to school, 57 or 96.6% were statistically significant. All measures of tested achievement and parents' descriptions of the child on the CABI were highly stable. Academic and social competence as described by teachers and the children themselves were somewhat less stable, but a very high proportion of the measures showed significant correlations across time, with a tendency to show smaller effect sizes in the prekindergarten to kindergarten year and larger effect sizes over the following year.

Five-year-old children with the highest scores on adaptation before school began were likely to be at or near the top of the group in kindergarten. Children who were having more difficulty in the preschool period were at risk for more academic and social difficulty once they entered school, and correlations were slightly stronger from kindergarten to first grade.

Support for the trajectory hypothesis based on correlations from preschool to elementary school does not mean that children's place in the hierarchy of adaptation is fixed for all time. Variation in academic achievement in kindergarten accounted for more than half the variance in first-grade scores, but there was still substantial unexplained variance, signifying that a number of children changed idiosyncratically. Measures from the BPI and the CABI revealed lower stability in children's self-evaluations and teachers' observations of social–emotional competence than in tested achievement.

Parents. Of all 148 correlations of parent measures across time, 87.8% were statistically significant and above .30, Cohen's cutoff for moderate effect sizes. Dividing the results by time periods, we found that in the preschool to kindergarten year, 71.4% of the mothers' measures and 78.6% of the fathers' measures were correlated, with a statistically significant effect size above .30. In the kindergarten to first-grade period, 83.3% of the mothers' measures and 94.4% of the fathers' measures were correlated above the .30 cutoff. Overall, in the 2-year period from prekindergarten to the end of first grade, 93.3% of both mothers' and fathers' measures were correlated above that level.

With the exception of some of the aspects of self described on The Pie, most self-report measures of parents' individual adaptation, relationships in the family of origin, relationships with the child, marital quality, and life stress and social support for the family, were moderately to highly stable in rank order over time. Observational measures across 1 year of parent–child and couple interaction (coparenting) during the whole family's visits to our playroom revealed low to moderate correlations. Despite the small but statistically significant declines in mothers' and fathers' satisfaction with their overall marriage reported earlier, both women and men tended to remain in the same rank order across the 2-year period in their views of their division of family labor, satisfaction with that division, and overall marital quality.

Sex Differences During the Transition to School

Whether we found differences between boys and girls during the elementary school transition depended in part on the source of the data: individually administered achievement tests, interviews with the children using the BPI, and both parents' and teachers' descriptions of the children on the CABI. An interesting pattern emerged in the findings from these independent sources. Scores on achievement tests showed that boys were more accomplished at math than girls in both kindergarten and first grade, and that both boys' and girls' test scores went up over the year. Nevertheless, over the same period, girls saw themselves as increasingly less academically capable than boys, and less competent in first grade than in kindergarten. Another pattern that fits gender stereotypes showed that in kindergarten and first grade, boys described themselves as more aggressive than girls, whereas girls described themselves as more anxious and depressed than boys.

Teachers described girls doing relatively well academically compared with boys, a view at odds with both the test scores and the girls' self-perceptions, but the teachers shared the children's perceptions about boys as more externalizing and girls as more internalizing. By contrast, descriptions of boys and girls by mothers and fathers revealed no sex differences on any of the six major CABI scales. What concerns us here is that gender stereotyped patterns of achievement and behavior, with girls at some disadvantage, are already in place during the children's transition to elementary school. Parents appear to be completely unaware of them. Teachers are aware of sex differences in aggressive and shy, withdrawn, and depressed behavior, but appear to be unaware of girls' actual and self-perceived disadvantage relative to boys in the area of academic achievement.

Sex differences are even more prevalent when we looked at parents. Exactly half of the 40 items we measured showed statistically significant main effect differences between mothers and fathers, and, like their children, parents' self-descriptions tended to be cast in gender stereotypic ways. Mothers were more psychologically and instrumentally involved in child care than fathers and more dissatisfied than their spouses about the division of family labor. Mothers held more authoritative and less authoritarian attitudes about parenting children, were less psychologically and instrumentally involved in work outside the home, and had lower self-esteem than did fathers. In only five measures, widely scattered across domains, were there statistically significant Time × Sex interactions, usually indicating more change in the women than in the men. In most cases, then, differences between men and women grew neither wider nor narrower as their children made the transition to school. This contrasts sharply with earlier findings concerning couples making the transition to parenthood, where over a 2-year period, there were increasing differences between men and women in many domains of life, and these differences accounted for significant variance in marital satisfaction decline (C. P. Cowan et al., 1985).

Reconsidering the Meaning of "Low Risk"

Despite the fact that this is a relatively advantaged sample of families, with two parents and middle-class to upper-middle-class incomes, we found considerable evidence of risk and already-emerging distress both in the children and the parents. This leads us to reconsider the use of the term "low risk." Clearly, low risk does not mean problem-free. Findings that lend strong support for the trajectory hypothesis suggest that, without some kind of intervention, children at the bottom of the achievement or adjustment continuum tend to remain in that position over the early years of elementary school. Other studies that follow children through elementary and high school suggest that these children are more likely to be traveling on the same low end of the trajectory throughout their academic careers (Campbell, 1995; Kellam, Simon, & Ensminger, 1982). The stability findings for the parents in this study also support the trajectory hypothesis, which leads to predictions that individuals will continue to suffer symptoms of depression and perhaps escalating level of marital distress without intervention.

These findings have important implications for both the theory and practice of prevention science. A key step in the establishment of prevention programs is early identification of difficulties, before they have time to become entrenched. It is clear from the data supporting the trajectory hypothesis that it is possible to identify children at risk of problems in academic attainment, peer relationship development, and actual behavior problems at school, based on assessments of children and parents in the year before they enter kindergarten. The pattern of findings can then be used to target specific interventions designed to improve family life and help children to enter school at higher levels of adaptation, which, presumably, would help them to continue on positive academic trajectories over the course of their school careers. We examine the effects of one intervention conducted prior to the children's entrance to kindergarten in chapter 11.

The Child's Entrance to School As a Major Life Transition

In both the Results and Discussion sections so far, we have been describing change during the first child's transition to school as if the transition were causally responsible for the changes. In fact, there are no adequate control or comparison groups that would be required for making such a causal interpretation. Children of the same age cannot be randomly assigned to a kindergarten or "no kindergarten" group. Parents who delay children's school entrance generally do so for reasons having to do with intellectual or emotional maturity and these children cannot serve as a comparison group to assess the impact of schooling.

What about comparing families in states with and without kindergartens? Only 7 of the 50 states in the United States do not require schools to provide kindergartens (Alaska, Colorado, Idaho, Michigan, New Hampshire, North Dakota, West Virginia), although all provide some funds for kindergarten programs. A majority of states, however, do not require kindergarten attendance. The problem in comparing kindergarten and nonkindergarten attendees across states is that there are nonrandom differences between the two groups. We have no way of precisely disambiguating changes that occur naturally over time through biological (Janowsky & Carper, 1996) and social (Ladd, 1996) transformations from those specifically attributable to the school experience.

What we have done in this chapter is to describe what happens to mothers, fathers, and children as the 5- to 7-year-old children in our study entered elementary school. The final question in this chapter is whether the picture of continuity, discontinuity, stability, instability, risk, and outcomes described here represents a major life transition for the child. Do we see alterations in the individual's view of both self and world (including self-concept, values, and affect regulation), of changes in personal competence in response to new challenges, of reorganization of central life roles (adding, subtracting, reorganizing, or shifting the importance of central life roles), and of changes in the quality of significant relationships?

A Transition for the Child.   As observers of the phenomena we have studied, we argued in chapter 1 and at the beginning of this chapter that elementary school presents the child with a new culture, and that meeting the challenges of entering this culture require significant shifts in self-view, competence, roles, and relationships. Taken together, the findings concerning changes in tested academic achievement and self-described academic motivation, achievement, social competence, and peer acceptance, are consistent with the notion that children are in fact making a major transition in their lives.

A Transition for the Parents and the Family As a Whole.   The changes we described in parents also appear to be consistent with the main criteria for life transitions. On the average, both mothers and fathers were changing their views of themselves, their attitudes (about parenting issues), their self-esteem and self-reported symptoms (changing in different directions), family roles, work roles, and life stresses in settings and relationships outside the nuclear family. Observers, too, noted changes, especially in parents' relationships with their elementary school-aged children. Transitions in themselves are neither positive nor negative, and the mixed picture of changes in parents as their children enter elementary school suggests that both occur. Increasing satisfaction with the division of labor in the household occurs at the same time as decreasing psychological investment in the household and more of a turn toward work by the men and women in our sample. Lowered anxiety, perhaps related to their first child getting into the swing of school, seems to go hand in hand with higher depression, increased marital conflict, and lowered satisfaction with the couple relationship.

The data we presented on the differences between the men and women in our sample might have something to do with the mixed picture that we see. Although women are generally not changing in more negative directions than men, they are continuing in what may be a less advantaged position, working for less pay, feeling less like a partner and lover, and experiencing lower self-esteem. These ongoing discrepancies may be taking their toll on both partners as they struggle to balance family and work relationships and demands (Coltrane, 1996).

One possible interpretation of the fact that there was more stability from preschool to first grade assessments across 2 years than there was from preschool to kindergarten across 1 year, is that the disequilibration associated with the child's transition to kindergarten had a somewhat disrupting initial effect that tended to settle down as the child entered first grade. Finally, if mothers, fathers, and their oldest child are all experiencing changes that fit the definition of transition, then the family as a whole is in transition during the 2 years from preschool to the end of first grade.

In this chapter, we have described changes in measures taken in each of the five domains of family life represented in our family systems model. The data help us to locate parenting and the parent–child relationships within a context that includes both continuity and discontinuity in the individual functioning of each family member, relationships among family members, and connections between family members and individuals and institutions in the larger world. So far, we have described what happens to mothers, fathers, and children one domain at a time. The remaining chapters of this volume examine how the interconnection among the five domains of the family system helps to account for individual differences in children's adaptation to school.

III

THE FAMILY CONTEXT
OF PARENTING

4

Authoritative Parenting and the Encouragement of Autonomy

Jonathan F. Mattanah

A substantial proportion of the research on parent–child relationships focuses on the construct of authoritative parenting, a style of behavior that combines two central dimensions found in almost all parenting studies (Maccoby & Martin, 1983)—warmth and responsiveness and optimal control, or limit-setting. The results have consistently revealed correlations between authoritative parenting and both academic and social competence in school-aged children (Baumrind, 1971, 1991; Dornbusch, Ritter, Leiderman, & Roberts, 1987; for extensive reviews, see Maccoby & Martin, 1983; Parke & Buriel, 1998; Steinberg, Elmen, & Mounts, 1989). Other combinations of parental warmth and structure—for example, lack of warmth and structuring behavior as in disengaged parenting, or cold, hostile, controlling behavior as in authoritarian parenting—have been associated with lower levels of social and academic competence and higher levels of problem behavior in the classroom (P. A. Cowan et al., 1994; Deater-Deckard & Dodge, 1997). As we pointed out in chapter 1, studies generally assess parenting styles and children's outcomes at the same point in time. There is surprisingly little information about whether variations in parenting style during the preschool period predict variations in how children meet the early intellectual, social, and emotional challenges of their transition to elementary school. Exploring this question is the first goal of this chapter.

The dimensions of warmth and structure describe parents' level of engagement and connection with the child. Some investigators argue that, although warmth and structure are important aspects of parenting, they may not be sufficient to account for some of the variation in children's competence, especially as it is displayed in settings outside the sphere of home and family (Barber & Olsen, 1997; Darling & Steinberg, 1993; see also Mize & Pettit, 1997, for attempts to identify scaffolding and social coaching, respectively, as uniquely important behaviors engaged in by authoritative parents). Parents' encouragement of their child's autonomy, by "leaving space" for the child to explore, solve problems, and struggle toward solutions, may also help to set the stage for optimal development. Although encouragement of autonomy was originally included in the definition of authoritative parenting by Baumrind (1971), until about a decade ago it was rarely studied in its own right. We do not know whether parents' encouragement of autonomy contributes uniquely to our understanding of variations in children's adaptation, over and above the warmth and structure they provide. Addressing this question is the second goal of chapter 4.

The results that we present here constitute an essential background for the findings reported in subsequent chapters of this volume. That is, we begin with two constructs: authoritative parenting and encouragement of autonomy, both considered central to the study of parenting style, to determine their separate and combined contributions to predicting children's achievement test scores and problem behaviors in the kindergarten classroom. Then, in subsequent chapters, we examine how other aspects of individual, marital, three-generational, and outside the family stress and support provide a context in which parent–child relationships unfold.

AUTHORITATIVE PARENTING DURING THE CHILD'S TRANSITION TO SCHOOL

An authoritative parent is defined as one who "attempts to direct the child's activities in a rational, issue-oriented manner. She . . . affirms the child's present qualities, but also sets standards for future behavior" (Baumrind, 1971, p. 22). Baumrind argued that the balance between reasoned and rational limit-setting and responsiveness to the child's needs would provide optimal conditions for children to internalize parental expectations of individual achievement and socially appropriate behavior. Studies of normally developing preschool and grade school children support this contention, showing that children of authoritative parents are more motivated to achieve academically, more satisfied in the classroom, and show fewer externalizing and internalizing behavior problems than children of nonauthoritative parents (Baumrind, 1967, 1971, 1989; Maccoby & Martin, 1983; Miller et al., 1993). These findings have been extended to studies of clinical populations. For example, parents of children with attention deficit hyperactivity disorder (ADHD), who described themselves as authoritative, had children who demonstrated fewer behavior problems and were more well-liked by their age-mates than children with ADHD who had nonauthoritative parents (Hinshaw et al., 1997).

This chapter examines associations over time between authoritative parenting during the preschool period and children's ability to make the transition to school in an adaptive way. We expected to find that a parent's capacity to set firm limits and have high expectations while remaining warm and responsive to the child's needs during the transition to elementary school would offer the child much-needed stability in the home environment. We expected that this stability would facilitate the child's ability to cope with the academic and social challenges of kindergarten and first grade. Because children are expected to be able to act more autonomously in early elementary school than they had in the preschool period, their parents' encouragement of autonomy before they enter kindergarten seems particularly salient to children's adaptation to the first year of more formal schooling.

AUTONOMY ENCOURAGEMENT DURING THE TRANSITION TO SCHOOL

In her seminal 1971 study, Baumrind labeled one of the two major parenting dimensions of authoritative parenting as the following: "Encourages Independence and Individuality" (the other was called "Firm Enforcement"; Baumrind, 1971, p. 15). Subsumed under this dimension were behaviors such as listening to critical comments from the child, sharing decision making with the child, and giving reasons with directives. Despite the fact that Baumrind included active autonomy encouragement within the authoritative parenting construct, she did not examine its unique value, but rather focused on the construct as a whole. Thus, we cannot tell from her early work whether active autonomy encouragement made its own contribution to the prediction of children's academic and social competence. Consistent with Darling and Steinberg's (1993) useful distinction, we view autonomy encouragement as one example of a parenting practice within the context of parenting style.

A number of studies have examined the importance of autonomy encouragement in predicting children's adaptation in school. A first set of studies focused on third- and fourth-grade children and found that parents who were supportive of autonomy, those who reasoned with their children, encouraged joint decision making, and expressed value for autonomy, had children who were more intrinsically motivated to achieve academically and displayed fewer externalizing behavior problems in the classroom (Grolnick & Ryan, 1989, 1991). A second set of investigations focused on adolescents examined the contribution of three dimensions of authoritative parenting to the prediction of academic achievement in high school: acceptance (comparable to warmth), behavioral control, and psychological autonomy encouragement. Results showed that all three dimensions made unique contributions to the prediction of grade point average over a 1-year period (Steinberg, Elmen, & Mounts, 1989; Steinberg, Lamborn, Dornbusch, & Darling, 1992). One limitation of those studies is that psychological autonomy was defined as the absence of a psychologically intrusive control style (called "psychological control" by Schaefer, 1965), which is characterized by love withdrawal and guilt induction. Because the absence of such control may simply indicate disengagement, it does not necessarily mean that parents actively encourage autonomy in their child.

Following the work of Baumrind (1971) and Grolnick and colleagues (1989), we define active autonomy encouragement as a parent's capacity to allow his or her child a range of autonomous behaviors, such as exploring the environment and taking credit for accomplishments, and to encourage independent behavior more actively. Parents encourage autonomy by recognizing and listening to their children's autonomous assertions and by negotiating with their children when those assertions go against the parent's wishes, rather than giving in to the child entirely or demanding compliance. According to this definition, active autonomy encouragement can require a fairly high degree of parental involvement and should not be confused with a permissive abdication to the child's demands.

We expected that parents' active autonomy encouragement would be especially valuable to children as they coped with the increased demands for independent functioning that are called for in first-grade classrooms. Teachers require them to take responsibility for sitting still at their desks, completing homework assignments on their own, and avoiding peer conflicts on the playground. Accordingly, we expected that for children to negotiate these new demands for independence successfully, their parents would need to accept and actively encourage greater autonomy and independence.

THE BENEFITS OF CONSISTENT PARENTAL AUTONOMY ENCOURAGEMENT

Although we expected active autonomy encouragement to be especially valuable to children's functioning in first grade, we also examined the contribution of parents who consistently encouraged autonomy from the preschool period throughout the transition to kindergarten and first grade. One might expect that the children of parents who encouraged their autonomy prior to their entry to kindergarten would be most prepared to exercise greater independence by first grade. If parents who encourage autonomy throughout the transition to elementary school have children who show higher levels of competence in first grade, that finding would be of importance in teaching parents that it is the continuity of their efforts that best prepares their children for acting independently outside the family environment.

SEX OF CHILD, SEX OF PARENT, AND PARENTING STYLE

We noted in chapter 1 that there has been extensive disagreement over the years about whether mothers and fathers treat sons and daughters differently (Block, 1976; Lytton, 1994; Maccoby, 2000). In an earlier study of a similar population of parents, differences in parenting girls and boys were ubiquitous, more for fathers than for mothers (Cowan et al., 1993). However, in the absence of consistent findings in the literature about sex differences in parent–child relationship patterns, we examined correlations between parenting behavior and children's outcomes separately for mothers and daughters, mothers and sons, fathers and daughters, and fathers and sons.

Hypotheses

In this chapter we tested the following three hypotheses:

1. Authoritative parenting, assessed prior to the child's entry into kindergarten, will account for variance in the child's social and academic competence in kindergarten and first grade.
2. Parents' active autonomy encouragement prior to first grade, a specific behavior used by authoritative parents, will account for additional variance in the child's social and academic competence in first grade.
3. Parents who encouraged autonomy throughout the transition to elementary school will have the most socially and academically competent children.

We also conducted exploratory analyses to determine whether the pattern of correlations between parenting style and children's outcomes differed for boys and girls.

METHODS

Participants

A fuller description of the design, participants, procedures, and measures used in the larger study is documented in chapter 2. The analyses reported here focus on 70 to 80 families for whom complete data were available for the analyses of interest (80 families had complete data sets at prekindergarten, whereas 70 families had complete data sets for the transition to first grade). The sample included 45 families with a first male child and 35 with a first female child; the children's mean age was 4 years and 11.94 months (almost 5 years), with a standard deviation of 6.21 months.

Measures

Authoritative Parenting and Autonomy Encouragement. The primary measures of interest were obtained from observations of parents and children working and playing together during the families' visits to our project playroom prior to the child's entry to kindergarten and first grade. Chapter 2 provides the details of the procedures for the family visits and the observational coding system used to describe mother–child and father–child interaction.

We measured authoritative parenting by focusing on the central ingredients of an authoritative style, as described by many investigators (Baumrind, 1989; Maccoby & Martin, 1983): (a) limit-setting, (b) maturity demands, (c) warmth, and (d) responsiveness. Authoritative parenting represents a style that combines high warmth with high limit-setting (Baumrind, 1989; Hinshaw et al., 1997; Miller et al., 1993). Ratings on each of these dimensions were z scored and added to produce the authoritative parenting index.

Autonomy encouraging behavior was assessed in this observational system with one scale, entitled "parental respect for child autonomy," which is similar to other observational rating scales used to assess parents' encouragement of autonomy in young children (Erickson, Sroufe, & Egeland, 1985; Heinicke & Guthrie, 1992; Van Aken & Riksen-Walraven, 1992). Examples of autonomy encouragement as rated in this system include the parent listening to the child even if the child's desires differ from the parent's, and negotiating with the child when the child's autonomous assertions go against the parent's wishes, rather than demanding compliance with the parent's wishes. More generally, this variable assessed how much the parent encouraged children's mastery by allowing them to claim credit for their accomplishments. Ratings on this scale ranged from 1 to 4, with 1 representing *very low respect for the child's autonomy* (e.g., the parent controls the session and actively discourages the child when he or she makes an autonomous move) and 4 representing *high respect for the child's autonomy* (e.g., the parent generally allows and encourages the child's attempts at autonomy without relinquishing the role as parent).

Children's Adaptation to School. The Peabody Individual Achievement Test (PIAT; Markwardt, 1989) was used as the measure of academic achievement at the end of kindergarten and first grade. To create a single measure of externalizing problem behaviors and a single measure of internalizing problem behaviors, we z scored and summed the two externalizing scales of the Child Adaptive Behavior Inventory (CABI; externalizing-aggressive and externalizing-hyperactive) to create one externalizing problem behavior scale, $\alpha = .77$ in kindergarten; $\alpha = .74$ in first grade, and the two internalizing scales of the inventory (internalizing-socially isolated and internalizing-psychological symptoms) to create one internalizing problem behavior scale, $\alpha = .71$ in kindergarten; $\alpha = .70$ in first grade.

RESULTS

Overview

The warmth and structure aspects of mothers' and fathers' parenting styles, assessed during the preschool period, predicted low to moderate proportions of the variance in different measures of children's social and academic adaptation to kindergarten and first grade. Mothers' autonomy encouragement added significantly to the predictions. Consistency of autonomy encouragement was also important. Mothers' consistent low autonomy encouragement, and fathers' shift from high to low autonomy encouragement between preschool and kindergarten assessments, were associated with their children's lower levels of adaptation to first grade.

Authoritative Parenting Sets the Stage for a Successful School Transition

We began by analyzing the role of authoritative parenting in helping children make the transition to elementary school. We predicted that the parent's level of authoritativeness before the child entered school would explain some of his or her adaptation to kindergarten and first grade, but we also expected that important variance in the child's behavior would remain unaccounted for.

Table 4.1 presents correlations between mothers' or fathers' authoritativeness, assessed prior to children's entry into kindergarten when they were almost 5 years old, and children's social and academic functioning at the end of kindergarten when they were almost 6, first for the whole sample and then for boys and girls separately. Contrary to our expectations, mothers' authoritative parenting (warmth, responsiveness, limit-setting, maturity demands) was not significantly correlated with their children's academic and social functioning at the end of kindergarten. In support of our hypothesis, fathers' authoritative parenting was modestly correlated with their children's overall academic competence, $r(78) = .19, p < .05$; social competence, $r(78) = .30, p < .01$; externalizing behaviors, $r(78) = -.30, p < .01$; and internalizing behaviors, $r(78) = -.19, p < .05$, as observed by teachers using the CABI checklist in the

TABLE 4.1

Correlations Between Authoritative Parenting Assessed Prior to the Child's Entry Into Kindergarten and the Child's Adaptive Functioning at the End of Kindergarten

Authoritative Parenting	Academic Competence	Social Competence	Externalizing Behaviors	Internalizing Behaviors	Math Achievement	Reading Achievement
Whole sample						
Mothers	.16	.07	−.05	.00	.14	.07
Fathers	.19*	.30**	−.30**	−.19*	.09	.09
Girls only						
Mothers	.17	.02	.07	−.09	−.08	−.06
Fathers	.37*	.33*	−.22	−.22	.09	−.04
Boys only						
Mothers	.17	.10	−.16	.04	.19	.11
Fathers	.04	.29*	−.40**	−.21	.06	.15

*$p < .05$. **$p < .01$, one-tailed.

spring of the kindergarten year. Fathers' parenting style was not significantly correlated with the children's math or reading achievement scores on the individually administered PIAT.

We then looked at whether the results differed for boys and girls (Table 4.1). Fathers' authoritative parenting was correlated significantly with social competence for both boys and girls, related to fewer externalizing behaviors in boys only, and related to greater academic competence in girls only. However, none of the father–son and father–daughter correlations differed at a statistically significant level (tested with Fisher's r-to-z transformations; Cohen & Cohen, 1983). Despite these trends, we conclude that there were no sex differences in the results.

Table 4.2 displays correlations between parents' authoritative parenting in the year before the children entered kindergarten and the children's functioning 2 years later at the end of first grade when they were approximately 7. By the end of the 2-year period between the end of the prekindergarten year and the end of the first-grade year, mothers' and fathers' earlier authoritative parenting style predicted higher math and reading achievement. The correlations for mothers were as follows: math $r(68) = .29, p < .01$; reading $r(68) = .19, p < .05$. The correlations for fathers were as follows: math $r(68) = .24, p < .05$; reading $r(68) = .28, p < .01$. An examination of correlations for boys and girls separately showed that mothers' and fathers' authoritative parenting was more strongly associated with boys' achievement than with girls', except for the connection between fathers' authoritative parenting and daughters' reading scores. However, once again, because none of the parent–child outcome correlations for boys and girls differed significantly from each other, we conclude that, in this sample, the patterns of association are similar for families with first girls and first boys.

These results provide some support for the hypothesis that parental authoritativeness in the preschool period helps to set the stage for a more successful transition to elementary school. When we consider the child's behavior in the classroom (academic and social competence, internalizing and externalizing problem behaviors), this conclusion is particularly relevant to fathers' authoritative parenting. The links between parent–child interaction in the preschool period and children's subsequent teacher-rated school adaptation were stronger at the end of kindergarten than at the end of first grade, 2 years later. By contrast, despite the lack of connection between mothers' and fathers' authoritative parenting style in the preschool period and tested achievement in kindergarten, the same measures predicted tested academic achievement in first grade. The low to modest size of the correlations suggests that additional variance in the children's adaptation to school might be accounted for by more specific parenting practices and by other factors both inside and outside the family.

TABLE 4.2

Correlations Between Authoritative Parenting Assessed Prior to the Child's Entry
Into Kindergarten and the Child's Adaptive Functioning at the End of First Grade

Authoritative Parenting	Academic Competence	Social Competence	Externalizing Behaviors	Internalizing Behaviors	Math Achievement	Reading Achievement
Whole sample						
Mothers	.03	-.15	.08	-.16	.29**	.19*
Fathers	.03	-.06	.06	.06	.24*	.28**
Girls only						
Mothers	-.01	-.14	.15	-.41*	.09	.08
Fathers	-.07	-.26	.31*	.03	.09	.36*
Boys only						
Mothers	.01	-.15	.04	-.06	.34**	.23*
Fathers	.10	.10	-.13	.05	.30*	.23*

*$p < .05$. **$p < .01$, one-tailed.

The Role of Parental Autonomy Encouragement During the Transition to First Grade

To test the hypothesis that parents' active encouragement of autonomy would help children particularly in coping with the greater demands of the first-grade environment, we examined correlations between parents' autonomy encouragement and children's social and academic functioning. We found no simple correlation between parental autonomy encouragement, assessed prior to the child's entry into kindergarten, and functioning at the end of kindergarten or first grade (results not tabled). In terms of children's academic and social adjustment and the development of problem behaviors at school, parents' active encouragement of autonomy was particularly important after the child had become an elementary school student.

As shown in Table 4.3, mothers' autonomy encouragement in the spring of the kindergarten year was consistently associated with children's adaptive functioning 1 year later at the end of first grade. Mothers' style of interaction was most strongly linked with children's academic competence, $r(68) = .34$, $p < .01$; social competence, $r(68) = .29$, $p < .01$; and (fewer) externalizing problem behaviors, $r(68) = -.32$, $p < .01$, as perceived by the teachers. Mothers' autonomy encouragement was also linked with children's math achievement scores, $r(68) = .34$, $p < .01$, on the PIAT. Fathers' autonomy encouragement in the spring of the kindergarten year predicted greater teacher-rated academic competence, $r(68) = .21$, $p < .05$, and tested reading achievement, $r(68) = .21$, $p < .05$, but was unrelated to social competence or behavior problems 1 year later at the end of first grade. Looking at boys and girls separately, we found that, although mothers' autonomy encouragement appeared to be more strongly associated with girls' outcomes than with boys' in first grade, the correlations did not differ significantly from each other.

To establish whether parents' autonomy encouragement prior to first grade added to the explanation of children's academic and social functioning, over and above the beneficial effects of an authoritative parenting style, we computed a series of hierarchical multiple regression equations predicting children's first-grade social and academic functioning. In each equation, fathers' or mothers' level of authoritative parenting prior to the child's entry to kindergarten was entered on the first step, and the same parent's autonomy encouragement prior to the child's entry into first grade was entered on the second step.

Mothers' autonomy encouragement added significantly to the prediction of their children's academic competence (12% incremental variance; beta = .35, $p < .01$), social competence (7% incremental variance; beta = .26, $p < .05$), and externalizing behaviors (6% incremental variance; beta = −.26, $p < .05$), as rated by their teachers. Similarly, mothers' encouragement of autonomy added significantly to the prediction of children's math achievement (11% in-

TABLE 4.3

Correlations Between Parental Autonomy Encouragement Assessed Prior to the Child's Entry
Into First Grade and the Child's Adaptive Functioning at the End of First Grade

Autonomy Encouragement	Academic Competence	Social Competence	Externalizing Behaviors	Internalizing Behaviors	Math Achievement	Reading Achievement
Whole sample						
Mothers	.34**	.29**	-.28**	-.15	.32**	.02
Fathers	.21*	.13	.01	-.12	.13	.21*
Girls only						
Mothers	.54**	.45*	-.37*	-.34*	.19	-.07
Fathers	.30	.19	-.01	-.24	.04	.01
Boys only						
Mothers	.26*	.22	-.23	-.02	.36**	.01
Fathers	.09	.07	.08	-.02	.18	.33*

$*p < .05.$ $**p < .01$, one-tailed.

cremental variance; beta = .33, $p < .001$) on the PIAT. Although these regressions suggest that mothers' active autonomy encouragement was incrementally important in the prediction of first-grade competence, we should note, as the simple correlations in Table 4.3 indicate, that mothers' authoritative parenting did not account for significant variance on the first step of these equations, except in the case of math achievement. In sum, these regressions provide evidence that mothers' autonomy encouragement accounts independently for variation in children's school adaptation, specifically in the prediction of math achievement, over and above the effects of their generally authoritative parenting style. Autonomy encouragement by fathers did not add significant variance to the prediction of the children's first-grade outcomes assessed in this study.

The Benefits of Consistent Autonomy Encouragement by Parents

Finally, we tested our third hypothesis, that parents who consistently encouraged autonomy across the whole transition-to-school period would have children who were better able to deal with the academic and social challenges of first grade. We first divided parents into those high or low in autonomy encouragement at the two time points—prior to kindergarten and prior to first grade. Examination of the distribution of scores suggested that a split at the median created two distinct groups with a reasonable number of families in each. We included parents at the median in the high encouragement group. Having created these two dichotomous measures of parents' autonomy encouragement, we then created one variable that captured parental consistency or inconsistency at the two time points. This variable had four categories: (a) parent consistently high on autonomy encouragement at both time points, (b) parent consistently low in autonomy encouragement at both time points, (c) parent who shifted from high autonomy encouragement prior to their child's entry into kindergarten to low autonomy encouragement prior to their child's entry into first grade, and (d) parent who shifted from low autonomy encouragement prior to kindergarten to high autonomy encouragement prior to first grade.

We focused on children's competence at the end of Grade 1 as the outcome variable because we conceptualized this point as the end of the transition to elementary school. Results of a series of one-way analyses of variance with post hoc Tukey tests showed that children of mothers consistently high on autonomy encouragement showed more positive adaptation on a number of outcome measures when compared with children of mothers consistently low on autonomy encouragement. Because this was an exploratory aspect of our investigation, we performed the post hoc tests as long as the probability for the overall F test was $< .10$. As can be seen in Table 4.4, children of the consis-

TABLE 4.4

Means and Standard Deviations of Mothers Consistently High in Autonomy
Encouragement, Consistently Low in Autonomy Encouragement, or Variable
in Autonomy Encouragement From Kindergarten to First Grade

	Consistently High in Autonomy Encouragement (N = 36)	Consistently Low in Autonomy Encouragement (N = 7)	High Prior to Kindergarten and Low Prior to First Grade (N = 10)	Low Prior to Kindergarten and High Prior to First Grade (N = 11)
Academic competence	.52 (2.3)[a]	−2.5 (4.9)[b]	−.57 (3.1)[a]	.76 (1.4)[a]
Social competence	.96 (3.5)[a]	−3.3 (6.8)[b]	−1.3 (4.6)[a]	1.0 (2.9)[a]
Externalizing behavior problems	−.57 (2.2)[a]	2.0 (3.0)[b]	.73 (2.5)[a]	−.47 (2.0)[a]

Note.   Different superscripts indicate significant differences between the groups ($p < .05$).

tently low autonomy encouraging mothers were lower in academic competence, social competence, and externalizing behavior. Overall $Fs(3, 60)$ were significant for academic competence ($2.89, p < .05$) and externalizing problem behaviors ($2.91, p < .05$), and marginal for social competence ($2.73, p < .10$). Tukey tests revealed significant differences between the low autonomy group and all other groups for all three measures. These results support the hypothesis that mothers who were consistently low in autonomy encouragement throughout their child's transition to school had the least competent children, and that those who encouraged their children's autonomy in laboratory sessions at one of the two assessment periods had children who fared relatively well in first grade.

Results with fathers were somewhat different and unexpected. Children of the four groups of fathers showed no significant differences in social or academic competence or achievement in math or reading. Nevertheless, as seen in Table 4.5, children of fathers who shifted from high autonomy encouragement prior to kindergarten to low autonomy encouragement prior to first grade showed more externalizing and internalizing problem behaviors than children in the other three groups. Overall $Fs(3, 58)$ were significant for externalizing ($3.41\ p < .05$) and marginal for internalizing problem behaviors ($2.54,\ p < .10$) whereas Tukey post hoc contrasts revealed significant differences between this condition and the other three autonomy encouragement conditions. Children of fathers who became less autonomy encouraging in the period before first grade had higher levels of psychological symptoms and behavior problems—even higher than children whose fathers were consistently low in encouraging their children's autonomy. Although it is possible

TABLE 4.5
Means and Standard Deviations of Fathers Consistently High in Autonomy
Encouragement, Consistently Low in Autonomy Encouragement, or Variable
in Autonomy Encouragement From Kindergarten to First Grade

	Consistently High in Autonomy Encouragement (N = 28)	Consistently Low in Autonomy Encouragement (N = 13)	High Prior to Kindergarten and Low Prior to First Grade (N = 7)	Low Prior to Kindergarten and High Prior to First Grade (N = 14)
Externalizing behavior problems	−.73 (2.1)[a]	−.20 (2.8)[a]	2.4 (2.6)[b]	−.08 (1.9)[b]
Internalizing behavior problems	−.80 (2.7)[a]	−.35 (2.3)[a]	2.7 (3.5)[b]	−.19 (3.7)[a]

Note. Different superscripts indicate significant differences between the groups ($p < .05$).

that these fathers were less encouraging of autonomy partly in response to their children's emerging problem behaviors, it is also possible that fathers' reactions exacerbated children's early problem behavior and led to even greater problems as they moved from kindergarten to first grade.

DISCUSSION

Parenting Behavior and Children's Adaptation to School

The results provided some support for the three major hypotheses of the study, with similar, though not identical, patterns for boys and girls, and more consistently different findings for fathers and mothers. First, fathers' authoritative parenting in the preschool period was modestly predictive of their children's greater academic and social competence and fewer problem behaviors in kindergarten, and both mothers' and fathers' authoritative parenting of their 5-year-olds was predictive of tested achievement in math and reading 2 years later at the end of first grade. Second, active autonomy encouragement by mothers at the end of the kindergarten year predicted children's academic and social competence 1 year later at the end of first grade. Third, children of mothers who consistently encouraged autonomy across the transition to kindergarten, from before the children entered kindergarten to the end of the kindergarten year, had higher scores in academic and social competence and fewer externalizing problem behaviors, according to their teachers' descriptions at the end of first grade. The data on fathers added an interesting twist: Children of fathers who encouraged less autonomy in their children in kindergarten than they had the year before were perceived by their teachers as higher in externalizing and internalizing behavior problems at the end of first grade (we discuss this finding more fully later).

We raised the issue at the beginning of this chapter about whether authoritative parenting describes a general context, quality, or style of a parent–child relationship (Baumrind, 1973), or whether it is a global summation of a number of specific positive and negative behaviors. What we found here was that, as a specific set of behaviors rated by observers, autonomy encouragement explained variation in children's adaptation to school, over and above the warmth and responsiveness and control- and limit-setting qualities of authoritative parenting.

Overall, our preschool measures of parenting style and autonomy encouragement were correlated with all six measures of children's adaptation either in kindergarten or first grade. However, whether significant links were found between the quality of family relationships and children's adaptation to school depended in part on the measures used and the time of the assessment. This is an often-overlooked point. We generally expect parenting behavior to be associated with children's development, but actual findings depend on what is measured and when it is assessed.

Although there were no statistically significant differences in correlations between parenting style and children's adaptation for mothers or fathers, girls or boys, one pattern emerged that will take on more meaning in subsequent chapters. When the correlations of parenting style were conducted separately by sex of child (Tables 4.1, 4.2, and 4.3), fathers' parenting style was correlated significantly with externalizing behaviors for sons and not for daughters, but fathers' style of interacting with their preschoolers in our project playroom was not linked with internalizing behaviors of sons or daughters at either of the next 2 years' follow-ups. By contrast, mothers' parenting style was correlated with internalizing only for daughters and not for sons. One intriguing difference in these sex-linked patterns is that mothers' autonomy encouragement was correlated significantly with lower levels of externalizing in both daughters and sons.

Similar to the findings in chapter 3 concerning correlations within each domain (individual, marital, etc.), were results revealing that cross-domain correlations (e.g., parenting style and children's adaptation) obtained 2 years apart were not always lower and sometimes higher than those obtained over 1 year. Authoritative parenting in the preschool period was uncorrelated with tested academic achievement in kindergarten, but significantly correlated with achievement at the end of first grade. Two explanations of this finding make sense to us. Because the entrance to kindergarten represents a potentially disequilibrating transition for children, it is possible that pretransition and posttransition measures are more likely to be correlated (for a general argument concerning correlations across life transitions, see Caspi & Roberts, 2001). A second possibility is that the combination of structure and warmth in the parent–child relationship prior to school entry is more relevant to skills demanded by the first-grade curriculum than to those tapped by the kindergarten curriculum.

We acknowledge that associations between specific behaviors of mothers and fathers and specific outcomes for their children were modest at best. Even when authoritative parenting and autonomy encouragement were combined in multiple regressions, they accounted for, at most, 20% of the variance in a given measure of children's adaptation, and usually less than 15%. The quality of the relationship between mother and child or father and child may contribute to our understanding of how children fare in the early years of school, but these relationships must be viewed in the context of other key relationships in the family, and between the family and the outside world (see the following chapters of this volume).

Without the intervention results of this study described in chapter 11, we cannot make causal inferences about whether authoritative parenting and encouragement of autonomy affect children's development, but the longitudinal study design does allow us to rule out one hypothesis about direction of influence. Because the children had not entered the world of kindergarten and first grade when we first assessed them, we know that their parents were not simply responding to their children's academic and social adaptation to elementary school. Nevertheless, we could not rule out the possibility that parents were responding to qualities of their preschoolers that were in evidence at home and in day-care or preschool settings before the transition to kindergarten began.

How Do Authoritative Parenting and Autonomy Encouragement "Work?"

Although causality issues are impossible to resolve with correlational designs, even when studies are longitudinal, the results described earlier are consistent with the widely-held assumption that parenting behaviors influence children's adaptation to school (Steinberg, 2001).[1] Here we present some speculative interpretations of how that influence might occur.

Authoritative Parenting. One possibility is that authoritative parenting provides children predictability and stability during a potentially de-stabilizing transition. Another possibility is that an authoritative style sets up expec-

---

[1]We know that the correlations are also consistent with hypotheses concerning children's influence on parents and hypotheses concerning reciprocal influences. We discuss these later in the volume.

tations in the child about how adults will react to him or her. Darling and Steinberg (1993) contrasted authoritarian parenting styles, in which limit-setting takes place in a cold or harsh context, with authoritative styles, in which limits are set in an atmosphere of warmth and support. Preschool children who experience adults as authoritative in this way may carry those expectations of adults into school classrooms, where new demands are placed on them for socially appropriate behavior and new academic skills. Yet another possibility is that authoritative parenting provides a good model of problem solving, because parents provides support and structure in a way that makes new tasks more easily solvable and children's experience of themselves as competent more likely (Pratt, Kerig, Cowan, & Cowan, 1988).

Autonomy Encouragement. The results reported here are consistent with the hypothesis that active autonomy encouragement, in which the parent allows and encourages the child's attempts at autonomy without relinquishing the parent role, promotes children's competence during the transition from preschool to elementary school. This finding fills in some gaps in a growing body of literature that demonstrates that parents' active encouragement of children's autonomy predicts intrinsic motivation, academic achievement, and social competence in both younger and older children (from 2 to 17 years of age; Allen, Hauser, Bell, & O'Connor, 1994; Allen, Hauser, Eickholt, Bell, & O'Connor, 1994; Crockenberg & Litman, 1990; Geary & Boykin, 1997; Grolnick et al., 1991; Kuczynski, Kochanska, Radke-Yarrow, & Girnius-Brown, 1987; Mattanah, 2001; Steinberg et al., 1989). Whereas mothers' encouragement of autonomy prior to their children's kindergarten year did not explain significant variance in their success in kindergarten, a year with fewer demands for independence, their encouragement of autonomy when their children were in kindergarten was followed by their children doing particularly well in first grade, a year in which increasing independence is typically expected. Parents' encouragement of autonomy may be particularly valuable to children at certain developmental points when they face new challenges and are expected to master new skills and material. That is, the extent of the connection between parenting and children's adaptation to school may depend in part on specific aspects of parenting, the specific contexts in which adaptation is assessed and for which autonomy is called. So far we have focused on cognitive aspects and consequences of parenting styles. Along with Dix (1991) and Gottman (2001), we believe that there is also an important emotional component that is central to authoritative parenting. Parents who provide structure and limits in a context of warmth establish an environment in which children learn how to regulate their emotions in optimal ways. A supportive, structured, predictable, parent–child relationship may facilitate the development of security in the children (Bowlby, 1988; Kochanska & Coy, 2002), which would enhance their willingness to use others as a secure base in times of stress, and to feel free to leave the secure base to explore new things, ideas, and challenges. In other words, children's sense of security resulting from the expectation that they will be supported in their explorations, confusion, or distress, could enable them to turn to adults for help in times of threat, and to feel safe to explore new challenges outside the family. The freedom to explore could play a particularly positive role in exploring new academic material and relationships with new children at school.

Sex Differences. It is not immediately clear why mothers' encouragement of their sons' and daughters' autonomy showed consistent positive correlations with their academic and social competence, whereas fathers' encouragement did not. One highly speculative possibility is that mothers who can hang back to let their children struggle when they are challenged and move in to help only when the child cannot manage (Vygotsky's concept of scaffolding; see Pratt et al., 1988), are less stereotypic in filling the maternal role. It may be this nonstereotyped role that has an impact on children's emerging sense of competence.

The finding that children whose fathers encouraged their autonomy less when their child was in kindergarten than they did in preschool had higher rates of problem behaviors requires further exploration. The problem is one of determining direction of effects. It is not clear whether these children expected or hoped for greater encouragement of their autonomy after they entered elementary school and their failed expectations led to the elevated rates of externalizing or internalizing strategies, or whether fathers were less likely to encourage the autonomy of children who were already demonstrating lower academic and social competence, or higher levels of problem behaviors in their first year of elementary school. Especially with autonomy encouragement, one can imagine a scenario in which children's growing competence and ability to negotiate peer interactions on their own reassures parents that they can support giving even more autonomy to the child. Alternatively, if a child does not appear to be doing especially well at school, a parent might feel the need to step in to take greater control over the child's behavior, thereby appearing to our observers to be less encouraging of autonomy. This scenario would be consistent with our finding that fathers who encouraged less autonomy when their children were in first grade than they had when they were in kindergarten had children with elevated problem behaviors at the end of first grade.

The pattern of links between fathers' parenting and sons' aggression and mothers' parenting and daughters' depression is intriguing. It should not be surprising to find that social gender or biological sex shapes the transmission of gender-stereotypic behavior problems. Fathers may play a more central role in the control and expression of their sons' aggression, and mothers in the control and expression of their daughters' depression through modeling, or through selective reinforcement of gender-stereotyped behavior. Of course, it is always possible that the engine driving the linkage is genetic, or a combination of biological differences and social role stereotypes. We take a more detailed look at sex differences in the links between parenting behavior and children's problem behaviors, with a microanalytic analysis of gender-stereotyped parenting, in the next chapter.

Generalizations about links between the quality of parent–child relationships and children's adaptation to school from the results reported in this chapter are limited in part by the fact that we focused on authoritative parenting and autonomy encouragement, and not on other aspects of parenting style or parenting behavior. Generalizations are also limited by the specific measures of authoritative parenting that we used, and the laboratory playroom context in which they were obtained. One further limitation is that active autonomy encouragement was assessed in this study with a single scale, based on one source of observational data. A more complex assessment would have included separate scales to assess parental autonomy encouragement through reasoning with the child, fostering joint decision making, and encouraging mastery over difficult tasks, as other investigators have done (Allen, Hauser, Eickholt, et al., 1994; Baumrind, 1971; Grolnick et al., 1991).

CONCLUSIONS

The results suggest that during the preschool period, the core elements of authoritative parenting—warmth and control—help to set the stage for children's successful transition to elementary school. An authoritative parenting style appears especially relevant to kindergarten children's ability to establish relationships with peers in ways that lead them to be seen as socially competent, to exhibit few externalizing and internalizing behaviors, and then to do well in first grade in the academic arena in math and reading. In addition, encouragement of autonomy, especially mothers' encouragement when their children are in kindergarten, explains variation in both social and academic competence in their children the next year at the end of first grade. Despite the fact that the aspects of parenting measured here accounted for up to 20% of the variance in children's adaptation to kindergarten and first grade, we move on in the following chapters to examine other family relationship factors that may contribute additionally to our understanding of how children traverse the transition to elementary school.

5

Marital Quality, Sex-Typed Parenting, and Girls' and Boys' Expression of Problem Behaviors

Jeanette Hsu

In chapter 3, we reported group differences between girls' and boys' problem behaviors in kindergarten and first grade, with girls described as showing more internalizing behavior (withdrawn, anxious, depressed) and boys as showing more externalizing behavior (aggressive, hostile, hyperactive). These problem behaviors represent more extreme forms of what can be considered normal sex-stereotyped behavior in which girls are expected to be more emotionally reactive and dependent and boys to be more assertive and aggressive (Leaper, 2002). Our inquiry in this chapter centers on the question of whether variations in family processes that enhance or inhibit sex-typed behavior may help us to understand variations in children's socioemotional adaptation to school.

In chapter 4, we examined correlations between mothers' and fathers' globally assessed parenting styles and internalizing or externalizing behavior. In this chapter, we build a model of family relationships, sex-typing, and children's problem behaviors in two steps. First, we use microanalytic coding to examine how parents responded to their preschool daughters' and sons' feminine- and masculine-stereotyped behaviors during an interaction task in our project playroom. Second, expanding our perspective to a wider family context, we investigate how aspects of the parents' marital relationship and sex-typed interactions with their child combined to predict internalizing and externalizing problem behaviors once the children were in kindergarten.

SEX DIFFERENCES IN PROBLEM BEHAVIOR

Reports of male–female differences in the expression of psychological distress are ubiquitous in the literature. Girls tend toward a pattern of problems with overcontrol and have higher ratings on checklists of internalizing problems, whereas boys tend toward a pattern of problems with undercontrol of aggression and have higher ratings on checklists of externalizing problems, whether or not scores reach clinical cutoff levels (Asher & Cole, 1990; Block, 2002; Deater-Deckard & Dodge, 1997). Adult women more often express distress by directing it inward toward the self (the psychodynamic definition of internalizing; e.g., Kornstein & Clayton, 2002; Weissman & Klerman, 1977), and adult men more often express their distress by directing behavior outward from the self toward others (the psychodynamic definition of externalizing; e.g., Sachs-Ericsson & Ciarlo, 2000).

What family factors are associated with sex-typed patterns of behavior in childhood that are known to predict later problem behaviors or clinical symptomatology? How do these patterns function to increase or decrease the probability of the children's internalizing and externalizing behaviors as children expand their world from their families into the elementary school environment? This chapter explores the possibility that parents' satisfaction with their relationship as a couple, and their sex-typed division of family labor, provide a context for the differential socialization of girls' and boys' sex-typed behavior in the preschool period. In turn, sex-typed parent–child interaction patterns help to explain the contrasting tendencies of girls to display internalizing problems and boys to display externalizing problems (Al-Issa, 1982; Gjerde, Block, & Block, 1988).

Family Factors in Children's Sex-Typed Behavior

Sex-Typed Parenting.   We consider sex-typed those traits and behaviors that show stereotypical sex-linked patterns, and we refer to sex-typing as the societal process "by which children come to adopt the attitudes, feelings, behaviors, and motives that are culturally defined as appropriate for their sex" (Perry & Bussey, 1979, p. 1701). Parental sex-typing includes parents' encouragement of children's gender-appropriate behaviors and discouragement of gender-inappropriate behaviors, with appropriateness defined by society as a whole or by salient subcultures in which the parents and child live. By definition, sex-typed parenting implies differential treatment of boys and girls, with the presumed, not necessarily conscious, aim of encouraging conformity to socially desirable masculine or feminine emotional and behavioral patterns.

We provided a brief summary of some of the issues and current research on sex differences in chapter 1. The questions of whether and how parents socialize daughters and sons differently aroused much controversy in the field of child development several decades ago. Maccoby and Jacklin's (1974) influential text, *The Psychology of Sex Differences*, concluded that very few presumed stereotypic sex-typed parenting behaviors were well-supported in the psychological literature. The evidence, they argued, provided support for the presence of only two differences in the parenting of boys and girls: greater pressure by parents of boys than of girls to conform to appropriate sex-role behavior; and greater use of both praise and punishment by parents of boys. Block (1984) severely criticized Maccoby and Jacklin's summary of the literature on sex differences, basing her analysis on methodological and theoretical considerations that included the young age of children in the studies reviewed, and the reliance on studies that focused on the mother rather than the father as the primary socializing agent. In Block's view, both of these considerations can lead to an underestimation of gender-differentiated socialization practices because such socialization effects increase as children get older, and because fathers may be implicated even more than mothers in the differential treatment of boys and girls.

Despite the fact that a number of studies report that fathers and mothers treat their preschool sons and daughters differently (e.g., P. A. Cowan et al., 1993; Fagot & Leinbach, 1993; Greif, Alvarez, & Ulman, 1981; Huston, 1983), the debate about whether sex-typed socialization is the rule rather than the exception has not been fully resolved (see Fagot, 1995; Leaper, 2002; Maccoby, 2000). Lytton's widely-quoted meta-analyses (Lytton, 1994; Lytton & Romney, 1991) appear to support his conclusion that, except for parents' encouragement of sex-typed play choices, and possibly for the support of autonomy in boys and dependency in girls, there is little evidence supporting the idea that mothers and fathers treat boys and girls differently. However, an unrecognized problem with the meta-analyses is that only the main effects of parents' or children's sex were analyzed and not the possible interaction between the two. A second difficulty is that it is not clear from the account of Lytton's meta-analyses whether both masculine- and feminine-sex-stereotyped behaviors were examined in girls and boys in the same studies. Finally, it is not clear from the meta-analyses whether studies used micro-analytic contingent analysis observation systems. That is, correlations between average or overall parent response to average or overall child sex-typed behavior could obscure possible sex-typed interactions that arise specifically when children behave in a same-sex-stereotyped or opposite-sex-stereotyped way. All of these design features were included in our study.

What seems to be beyond dispute is that many parents tend to encourage sex-typed play choices in their sons and daughters (e.g., dolls versus trucks), and that differential treatment of girls and boys, when it exists, is more likely to be seen in fathers than in mothers (Bem, 1993; Block, 1983; Leaper, 2000; Lytton, 1994; Maccoby, 1980; Parke, 1996). Gjerde (1986) noted that reactions encouraging sex-typed behavior are more likely to occur when fathers are alone with their children—the situation examined in this chapter—than when the whole family is together.

An endemic problem in all of the literature on sex-typed parenting is the difficulty, if not impossibility, of determining direction of effects. Are parents reinforcing their daughter's or son's feminine or masculine behavior, or are they simply responding positively to whatever the child is bringing to the situation? We cannot provide a definitive answer, but the design of our study allows two different perspectives on the question. First, we look at each child—daughter or son—in separate interactions with mother and with father, to see whether the same child is treated differently by mother and father, or whether the pattern of correlations between parental encouragement of sex-typed behavior holds for both parents. That is, if different mother–child and father–child patterns emerge with the same child, it is more difficult, although not impossible, to argue that the child's characteristics are driving the system. Second, because it is so difficult to identify each participant's contribution to the interaction, we created a measure of "parent–child sex-typing" by combining microanalytic assessments of the parent and the child as they worked and played together in our project playroom.

The Marital Relationship.   Our five-domain model of family system factors in children's adaptation (chapter 1, Fig. 1.1 to 1.6) suggests that the couple's relationship provides a context for both sex-typed parenting and children's internalizing and externalizing problem behaviors. First, there is consistent evidence of direct correlations between parents' marital conflict or dissatisfaction and their children's externalizing problems (Cummings & Davies, 1994; Emery & O'Leary, 1984). Second, there is evidence from studies of families with preschool and early school-age children that conflict between parents "spills over" into the parent–child relationship (C. P. Cowan & Cowan, 1997; Katz & Gottman, 1993). Third, marital distress may increase the salience of gendered relationships in the family. For example, Amato (1986) and Kerig, Cowan, and Cowan (1993) found that marital distress is more likely to be associated with negative parent–child relationships between fathers and daughters than between fathers and sons, mothers and sons, or mothers and daughters. There is some evidence from earlier studies that marital distress is associated with internalizing problems in girls and externalizing problems in boys (Block, Block, & Morrison, 1981), possibly due to the effects of modeling and imitation of the same-sex parent (Bandura, 1977).

Parents' sex-typed differentiation of their own household roles may set the stage for children's sex-typed behavior. In more "traditional" families, roles tend to be divided along gender lines (Dempsey, 2002), with women taking primary responsibility for most household and child-care tasks and men taking more responsibility for earning income and typically masculine house-hold tasks (e.g., care of the yard and the car). In families that show a less egal-itarian, more traditional, division of household and child-care responsibili-ties, children are more likely to choose sex-typed toys, activities, and roles (Repetti, 1984; Weisner, Garnier, & Loucky, 1994).

Children's Sex-Typed Behavior and Internalizing or Externalizing Problem Behaviors

A number of political and psychological theories in the latter half of the 20th century assumed that the development of high levels of feminine behavior by girls and masculine behavior by boys, and the taking on of stereotypic sex roles in adulthood, were unnecessarily rigid and likely to be unhealthy, espe-cially for women but also for men (Bem, 1993; Bernard, 1974; Gilligan, 1982). These theorists pointed to three salient facts: young girls and women have of-ten been treated more negatively than men; society tends to reinforce tradi-tional family roles that may restrict both sexes, but hold women back more; and characteristic disorders for each sex have gender-stereotypic associations (depression for women, aggression for men). These facts were linked by causal hypotheses suggesting that sex-typing, societally or biologically con-structed but carried out in the family, could have negative consequences for all. In our search of the literature, we found many studies and summaries of family antecedents of both sex-typing and problem behavior, but none that specifically investigated sex-typing as a link between family relationship qual-ity and problematic outcomes.

Consistent with the tenet of bidirectional causality in family systems theo-ries, we assume that children's sex-typed behaviors are not simply "products" of family forces, but that they affect parents' behaviors and have conse-quences for children's adaptation. In one of the few studies to explore the re-lation between sex-typed behavior and psychological adjustment in children, Sprafkin, Serbin, and Elman (1982) found that preschool-age boys' more fre-quent choice of male-preferred play was associated with greater frequency of angry and defiant behavior and less conformity to rules in the classroom, as reported by their teachers. Boys who participated in female-preferred activi-ties showed greater conformity to rules and compliance with teachers' direc-tions. By contrast, girls' greater frequency of play with male-preferred toys was associated with lower levels of stereotypically feminine behavior prob-lems such as apathy and withdrawal.

The intriguing notion to be extracted from the Sprafkin et al. (1982) study is that higher levels of sex-typed behavior can function as a vulnerability fac-tor that increases the risk of one type of problem behavior (internalizing or externalizing), and as a protective factor that decreases the risk of another type of problem behavior. The issue we are interested in here is not simply that children develop sex-typed behavior, but that this behavior may play a role in whether they behave in the classroom in ways that are identified as problematic. The analyses reported in this chapter examine two possibilities, that (a) when parents, and especially fathers, support and encourage their daughters and sons in non-sex-typed behavior, children might be freer to act and see themselves in less restrictive ways; and (b) parental emphasis on non-sex-typed behavior, by building unexpected strengths that go against social expectations, may have both positive and negative implications for children's psychological health.

Hypotheses

1. Parent and child sex-typed behavior shows main effect sex differences but also sensitivities to context. Girls show more feminine sex-stereotyped behavior than boys, and boys more masculine sex-stereotyped behavior than girls. Mothers and fathers respond more positively to feminine sex-stereo-typed behavior in daughters than in sons, and to masculine sex-stereotyped behavior in sons than in daughters. These predictions appear to imply that sex-typed behavior is trait-like in both parent and child. We investigate the possibility that both sex-typed and non-sex-typed behavior varies with context (mother–daughter, mother–son, father–daughter, father–son).

2. Parents' positive reactions to sex-consistent sex-typed behavior is associated with higher levels of that behavior in the child. A more exploratory analysis investigates whether parents' positive reactions to behavior stereo-typically associated with the opposite sex are associated with higher levels of opposite sex-typed behavior.

3. Couple relationship quality and sex-typed parenting is associated with children's internalizing and externalizing behaviors in kindergarten. Greater marital dissatisfaction, a less egalitarian (more sex-typed) parental division of care of the child, and higher levels of sex-typed parent–child interactions, account for variance in the child's internalizing and externalizing problem behaviors, as described by kindergarten teachers. We expected that high levels of feminine sex-typed behavior in the parent–child relationship would increase the risk for internalizing but decrease the risk for externalizing behaviors, and that high levels of masculine sex-typed behavior in the parent–child relationship would increase the risk for externalizing but decrease the risk for internalizing behaviors, as children make the transition to kindergarten.

METHODS

Participants

Results in this chapter come from 83 families whose oldest child (M age = 5.0, SD = 6.4 months) was preparing to enter kindergarten and who had complete data on the measures of interest. Thirty-three of the children were girls, and 50 were boys.

Measures

As we described in chapter 2, marital satisfaction was assessed by the Short Marital Adjustment Test (Locke & Wallace, 1959). Parents' sharing of child-care tasks was assessed by the Who Does What? questionnaire (P. A. Cowan & Cowan, 1991). Because of the high correlation between mothers' and fathers' views, we used the mean of their combined ratings in both the mothers' models and the fathers' models reported in this chapter.

A Microanalytic Parent–Child Sex-Typed Behavior Coding Scheme. Rothbaum and Weisz (1994) found that links between parent–child interactions and children's problem behavior were strongest when parent–child relationships were assessed by observations or interviews rather than by self-report questionnaires. Because of the nature of the research questions, the global coding scheme used in other chapters in the study was not appropriate here, because it could not reveal contingencies in which specific parental responses were connected with specific instances of children's sex-typed behavior. Therefore, a more microanalytic scheme was developed (Hsu, 1996) to code videotaped sessions of dyadic interactions between the target child and each parent separately during a 40-min visit in which they worked and played together in our project playroom (see chapter 2 for details of the laboratory playroom procedure):

1. Children's sex-typed behaviors—Behaviors described by Block (1983) were grouped on the basis of prior research into those that are stereotypically masculine or stereotypically feminine. Of the behaviors that are stereotypically masculine, three (aggression, noncompliance, large motor movements) have been observed more often in boys than in girls, and self-assertion was identified by Block as a behavior that is more encouraged by parents of sons than by parents of daughters. Of the behaviors that are stereotypically feminine, two are typically associated with femininity (withdrawal, crying), and three (compliance, dependency, introspection) were

identified by Block and others as more encouraged by parents of daughters than by parents of sons.

The coding scheme used here examined the contingent responses of fathers and mothers to the following nine categories of child behavior: (a) self-assertions—the child expresses his or her opinion and will freely; (b) aggression—angry, hostile actions (such as yelling) or other actions or words that express dislike of the parent or the situation; (c) noncompliance—oppositional behavior such as defying or ignoring a parent's direct request; a specific reaction to expectations of the task or the parent; (d) large motor movements—observable physical activity, such as walking around, waving arms, getting up, or kicking feet, that does not specifically express aggression or noncompliance (discussed earlier); (e) compliance—following, conforming with, or agreeing to parent's direct request with little or no struggle; (f) crying—behavior that expresses emotional upset such as whining, pouting, or crying, with no specific or clear goal of requesting assistance, support, or comfort; (g) dependency—behavior that either seeks a parent's approval prior to some action, or requests assistance, comfort, or assurance; (h) self-reflection—verbalizations that indicate introspection, such as commenting on or wondering about self; and (i) withdrawal—passive action expressing disengagement from the task or the parent, with no angry or oppositional qualities.

A procedure for further validation of these behavior categories as stereotypically masculine (a–d) and stereotypically feminine (e–i) was suggested by Kim (1995), who asked psychology undergraduates which of the aforementioned behaviors were more characteristic of boys or girls. Using a scale from 1 (more characteristic of 4- to 6-year-old boys) to 9 (more characteristic of 4- to 6-year-old girls), we recorded in Table 5.1 only those who rated the items

TABLE 5.1
Percentages of Undergraduates Rating Child Behaviors As More
Characteristic of Boys and As More Characteristic of Girls

Child Behavior	Percentage Rating Behavior as More Characteristic of 4- to 6-Year-Old Girls	Percentage Rating Behavior as More Characteristic of 4- to 6-Year-Old Boys
Self-assertion	7%	43%
Aggression	4%	79%
Noncompliance	4%	82%
Large motor movement	7%	71%
Compliance	89%	4%
Crying	50%	18%
Dependency	61%	11%
Self-reflection	36%	11%
Withdrawal	64%	0%

at the extremes (1–2, 8–9) rather than at the middle of the scale. We found that a much larger proportion of these psychology majors ($n = 28$; 18 women, 10 men) rated the behaviors of self-assertion, aggression, noncompliance, and large motor movements, as 1 to 2 on this scale than as 8 to 9, thus agreeing that such behaviors were more characteristic of 4- to 6-year-old boys. Similarly, a greater percentage of the college undergraduates rated the behaviors of compliance, crying, dependency, self-reflection, and withdrawal as 8 to 9 on this scale, indicating that they felt that these behaviors were more characteristic of 4- to 6-year-old girls (Kim, 1995).

2. Parents' responses to children's sex-typed behaviors—We used an event-counting procedure to code parents' sex-typing. All instances of child behavior fitting the nine categories listed earlier were coded, as was each parent's reactions to each behavior. Each child received a score for the total number of stereotypically masculine and feminine behaviors exhibited with each parent, a score used in later analyses as a measure of how much sex-typed or non-sex-typed behavior was observed (e.g., girls' or boys' feminine behaviors with father).

Parental responses to instances of behavior in each of the nine categories were coded on a 3-point scale that denoted valence of affect (positive, neutral, or negative). Positive reactions included enthusiasm, praise, soothing, encouragement, and smiling. Neutral reactions included requests, instructions, and no reaction. Negative reactions included coercion, disapproval, frustration, and anger. Each parent's degree of sex-typing was determined by two composite scores, one indicating the degree of the parent's positive responsiveness to stereotypically masculine child behaviors, the other to stereotypically feminine child behaviors. These composite scores were calculated using the proportion of the total number of each parent's positive responses to stereotypically masculine and feminine child behaviors.

Coding was carried out by five research assistants, two of whom coded mother–child interactions only, without observing father–child interactions, and three of whom coded father–child interactions only, without observing mother–child interactions. Interrater reliabilities (as) for mothers' positive responses to masculine and feminine child behaviors were $\alpha = .71$, $p < .001$, and $\alpha = .69$, $p < .001$, respectively. The correlation coefficients between coders' proportional sex-typing scores for fathers' positive responses to masculine and feminine child behaviors were $\alpha = .70$ and $\alpha = .75$.

Children's Problem Behaviors. As described in chapter 2, children's internalizing behavior (socially isolated, anxious, depressed) and externalizing behavior (aggressive, hyperactive) in kindergarten were assessed using the Child Adaptive Behavior Inventory (CABI) from teacher ratings made in the spring of the kindergarten year.

RESULTS

Overview

Significant differences in children's feminine- and masculine-stereotyped behavior were observed in the playroom session during the preschool period, but only when children were interacting with their fathers. For both boys and girls, there was a consistent association between the level of stereotyped behavior shown by the child and the parent's positive response to that behavior. Marital satisfaction, more egalitarian sharing of child-care tasks, and sex-stereotyped parent–child interactions, were associated with internalizing in models that linked fathers', but not mothers', marital and parenting behavior with daughters' kindergarten outcomes 1 year later. The same set of variables, but with important differences in pattern, was associated with boys' externalizing in father–son models. As we hypothesized, female stereotyped father–child interactions appear to function as a risk for internalizing but as protective against externalizing problem behaviors in kindergarten children, whereas male stereotyped father–child interactions appear to function as a risk for externalizing, but as protective against internalizing behaviors.

Parents' and Children's Sex-Typed Behavior

Main Effect Sex Differences in Sex-Typed Behavior.   We used General Linear Modeling two-way analyses of variance (ANOVAs) (masculine versus feminine sex-stereotyped child behavior, sex of parent) to test the main effect aspect of hypothesis 1—that there would be different levels of children's masculine and feminine behavior with mothers and fathers, and different patterns of positive response to sex-typed behavior by mothers and fathers. Because these measures were obtained prior to the intervention (PRE), we did not need a covariate to control for intervention participation. Analysis of the mean level of feminine- or masculine-stereotyped behavior by children in interaction with fathers and mothers (presented in Table 5.2) indicated that, overall, at 5 years of age, children displayed more stereotypically masculine than feminine behaviors, $F(1, 79) = 4.15, p < .05$, and this was true more with fathers than with mothers, $F(1, 79) = 29.43, p < .001$.

As to the parents' sex-typed behavior, contrary to our hypotheses, three-way ANOVAs (sex of parent, sex of child, masculine versus feminine behavior) revealed no differences between mothers and fathers in the proportion of positive reactions to stereotypically masculine or feminine behavior, either in the whole sample, or in the subgroups of girls and boys (not tabled).

Context Differences in Sex-Typed Behavior.   There was a significant interaction of sex-typed behavior by sex of parent, $F(1, 79) = 4.23, p < .05$. It is clear from Table 5.2 that differences between the amount of masculine-

TABLE 5.2
Mean Child Sex-Typed Behavior and Mean Parent Positive Response

| | Child's Behavior | | | |
| | Mother | | Father | |
	Feminine	Masculine	Feminine	Masculine
Child's sex-typed behavior	25.0	25.1	31.3	38.1
Parent's proportion of positive responses	.26	.24	.26	.25

and feminine-sex-typed behavior shown by children occurred only with fathers. The same children who showed equal amounts of masculine- and feminine-stereotyped behavior during the mother–child visit showed (a) more sex-stereotyped behavior, both masculine and feminine, and (b) more masculine- than feminine-stereotyped behavior when they were interacting with their fathers.

If sex-typed behavior were to be interpreted as a personality trait of the child, then girls' feminine behavior and boys' masculine behavior would show significant correlations across mother and father interactions. In fact, sex-typed behavior in the two contexts was independent (results not tabled). It seems clear that the child's tendency to display sex-typed behavior is influenced by the family interaction context (with mother or father).

Parents' Contingent Reactions to Children's Sex-Typed Behavior

To test hypothesis 2, that the proportion of each parents' positive responses to sex-typed behavior would be associated with the frequency of that behavior by the child, we calculated Pearson correlations between parents' encouragement of sex-typed behavior and children's display of that behavior. We describe the findings, beginning with the parents' positive response, followed by the child's sex-typed behavior, but it is possible that the more the child responds in a sex-consistent-stereotyped way, the more the parents' response is positive. We return to this point in the discussion.

Supporting hypothesis 2, Table 5.3 shows that parents' positive responses to sex-typed behavior by both girls and boys were correlated with the frequency of that behavior during the parent–child interaction session (14 of 16 correlations were statistically significant). When mothers or fathers responded more positively to feminine sex-typed behavior, girls were more likely to behave that way, mothers, $r(31) = .56, p < .001$; fathers, $r(31) = .34, p < .05$, and less likely to show masculine-stereotyped behavior, mothers, $r(31) = -.48, p < .01$; fathers, $r(31) = -.42, p < .05$.

TABLE 5.3
Parents' Positive Responsiveness and Children's Sex-Typed Behavior

| | Child's Behavior | | | |
| | Girls (n = 33) | | Boys (n = 50) | |
Parent's Behavior	Masculine	Feminine	Masculine	Feminine
Mothers				
Positive response to child's masculine behavior	.67***	−.25	.48**	−.48***
Positive response to child's feminine behavior	−.48**	.56***	−.50***	.61***
Fathers				
Positive response to child's masculine behavior	.12	−.65***	.62***	−.27*
Positive response to child's feminine behavior	−.42**	.33*	−.58**	.49***

$*p < .05.$ $**p < .01.$ $***p < .001.$

When mothers responded positively to girls' behavior that went against stereotype (self-assertive, aggressive, or noncompliant behaviors coded as masculine), girls were more likely to behave that way, $r(31) = .67, p < .001$, but not less likely to show feminine-stereotyped behavior. In a second unexpected finding, there was no significant correlation between fathers' positive responses to masculine-stereotyped behavior and their daughters' masculine behavior. By contrast with the mother–daughter pattern, fathers' positive response to daughters' masculine behavior was associated with daughters showing less feminine-stereotyped behavior, $r(33) = −.65, p < .001$.

The story for boys was similar and even more consistent. When mothers or fathers responded more positively to masculine-stereotyped behavior, boys were more likely to show that behavior, mothers, $r(48) = .48, p < .001$; fathers, $r(48) = .62, p < .001$, and less likely to show feminine-stereotyped behavior, mothers, $r(48) = −.48, p < .001$; fathers, $r(48) = −.28, p < .05$. Similarly, boys were more likely to show against-stereotype feminine behavior in the playroom interaction when their parents responded positively to it, mothers, $r(48) = .61, p < .001$; fathers, $r(48) = .49, p < .001$, and less likely to show masculine behavior, mothers, $r(48) = −.50, p < .001$; fathers, $r(48) = −.58, p < .001$.

Are some parents simply more positive and encouraging in their responses? We found that parents who encouraged their child's behavior consistent with one sex-type did not encourage behavior consistent with the other. For mothers, the correlation between positive response to masculine and feminine behavior of their child during the playroom interaction was $r(81) = −.54, p < .001$; for fathers it was $r(81) = −.55, p < .001$. There was very little variation in these associations depending on whether the child was a girl or boy.

In Table 5.3, we presented separate correlations for parents' reactions to masculine-typed and feminine-typed behavior. An exploratory question was whether a combination of parental reinforcement of masculine- and discouragement of feminine-sex-stereotyped behavior could account for the child's sex-typed behavior. Eight hierarchical multiple regressions were performed (mothers' and fathers' positive reactions to feminine and masculine behavior in girls and boys), with children's feminine or masculine behavior as the dependent variables, and mothers' and fathers' reactions as the independent variables. In each regression, parents' positive responses to the stereotyped behavior were entered first (e.g., parents encouragement of feminine behavior when the dependent variable was feminine sex-stereotyped behavior). Responses to the child's behavior that were not consistent with the stereotype were entered on the next step of the equation. Each equation contained three variables (one dependent and two independent). Degrees of freedom for the *F*-change tests were 1 and 30 for girls and 1 and 47 for boys.

Statistical tests for the following conclusions derived from the multiple regressions are presented in Table 5.4. Girls' feminine-stereotyped behavior with their mothers was associated high positive responses to that behavior and low positive responses to masculine stereotyped behavior. The same pattern was found for girls' feminine-stereotyped behavior with their fathers.

Girls' masculine-stereotyped behavior with mothers was associated only with high positive responses by mothers to that behavior, but not with mothers' reaction to feminine behavior. Girls' masculine behavior with fathers' was associated only with fathers' low positive responses to their daughters' feminine behavior.

Boys' masculine behavior with mothers was associated with mothers' high positive reactions to masculine-stereotyped behavior and low positive reactions to feminine-stereotyped behavior. Children's masculine behavior with fathers was associated with that same pattern. Boys' feminine behavior was associated only with mothers' or fathers' positive responses to that behavior. Thus, higher levels of sex-stereotyped behavior in both boys and girls was associated with a differential pattern of higher positive response to it and lower positive response to non-sex-stereotyped behavior. By contrast, higher levels of non-sex-stereotyped behavior in children was associated with reinforcement of that behavior and not with low positive responsiveness to sex-stereotyped behavior by the same-sex parent.

The Family Context of Sex-Typed Behavior and Problem Behaviors at School

We turn now to hypothesis 3 and the question of whether and how preschool family variables combine to predict children's internalizing and externalizing behaviors in the classroom 1 year later. To examine the links among the inde-

TABLE 5.4

Multiple Regressions: Parents' Positive Responses to Masculine and Feminine Stereotyped Behavior and Children's Sex Stereotyped Behavior

Parents' response		R^2	ΔR^2	ΔF	β		R^2	ΔR^2	ΔF	β
		Child Feminine Sex-Stereotyped Behavior					Child Masculine Sex-Stereotyped Behavior			
Girls										
With mothers										
+ to feminine		.32	.32	14.33**	.63	+ to masculine	.44	.44	24.75***	.67
+ to masculine		.33	.01			+ to feminine	.45	.01		
With fathers										
+ to feminine		.11	.11			+ to masculine	.01	.01		
+ to masculine		.43	.32	16.49***	-.69	+ to feminine	.20	.19	6.61*	-.52
Boys										
With mothers										
+ to feminine		.37	.37	27.66	.49	+ to masculine	.24	.24	14.87***	.31
+ to masculine		.41	.04			+ to feminine	.32	.08	5.49*	-.34
With fathers										
+ to feminine		.24	.24	14.86	.48	+ to masculine	.39	.39	29.49***	.44
+ to masculine		.24	.00			+ to feminine	.47	.08	7.27**	-.34

$*p < .05. **p < .01. ***p < .001.$

pendent variables and their connections with the outcomes, we used Latent Variable Path Analysis with Partial Least Squares (LVPLS; Falk & Miller, 1992) to create six latent variables from the manifest variables described in the Method section and in chapter 2. The first latent variable contained two vector variables (dummy coded +1 or –1) differentiating those families with parents who participated in either the maritally-focused or parenting-focused couples group (+1) from families who did not (–1). This latent variable served as a covariate control for the possible impact of the interventions on mean change over time and is not represented in the figures presenting the results. The second latent variable, marital satisfaction, included only one measure— father's or mother's total score from the Marital Adjustment Test (Locke & Wallace, 1959). The third latent variable, sharing of child-care tasks as described by both husbands and wives on Who Does What?, was conceptualized here as a measure of egalitarian parenting roles; higher numbers represented fathers taking relatively more of the responsibility for the daily child-care tasks. These more egalitarian couples shared the tasks more equally than other couples in the study, although in only 10% of the couples (according to the men) or 8% of the couples (according to the women) did men do half or more of the child care.

We have seen that there were substantial correlations between the positive or negative valence of the parents' responses to sex-typed behavior and the frequency of that behavior in the parent–child visits. Because it was impossible to tell whether the parents were responding to the children or the children to the parents, latent variables were created that contained both child behaviors and parents' responses. The fourth latent variable, labeled "parent–child feminine-stereotyped behavior," included six manifest measures: children's compliance, self-reflection, and dependency, and parents' positive responses to each of these behaviors. The fifth latent variable, labeled "parent–child masculine-stereotyped behavior," included six manifest measures: children's aggression, noncompliance, and assertiveness, and parents' positive responses to each. The sixth latent variable, "internalizing behavior as observed by kindergarten teachers on the Child Adaptive Behavior Inventory," contained four manifest variable scales describing the child as depressed, anxious, socially isolated, and withdrawn. The final latent variable was measured by three CABI scales assessing antisocial, oppositional, and hostile behavior.

Four LVPLS models were calculated, each describing paths linking family factors with both externalizing and internalizing behavior in kindergarten (mothers and girls, mothers and boys, fathers and girls, fathers and boys). As we noted in chapter 2, LVPLS models do not yield a test of the overall fit of all paths in the model. However, the amount of explained variance in the dependent latent variable (here internalizing or externalizing behavior) is distributed as a multiple regression coefficient whose statistical significance can be tested with degrees of freedom equal to the following:

latent variable predictors / n -1- # latent variable predictors.

In this case, the test has 5 and 28 degrees of freedom for girls, and 5 and 45 degrees of freedom for boys. Two of the four models, both describing fathers and their children, yielded statistically significant predictions of kindergarten outcomes (see Table 5.5 and Fig. 5.1 and 5.2).

Fathers and Daughters.   Figure 5.1 presents data from the partial least squares (PLS) structural model linking fathers' marital satisfaction, egalitarian sharing of child care, and stereotypically masculine or feminine father–child interaction data with girls' internalizing and externalizing behavior at school 1 year later in kindergarten. The root mean squared index of .08 indicated that the model fit the data relatively well. Overall, the latent variables explain a statistically significant 48% of the variance in girls' internalizing, $F(5, 28) = 6.98$, $p < .001$, but a statistically insignificant 18% of the vari-

TABLE 5.5
Total Variance Explained by Partial Least Squares Models

| | Boys | | Girls | |
	Externalizing	Internalizing	Externalizing	Internalizing
Mothers	.03	.11	.03	.10
Fathers	.40***	.06	.19	.50***

Note. Predictors are marital satisfaction, child-care task sharing, parent–child masculine stereotyped behavior, and parent–child feminine-stereotyped behavior.
***$p < .001$.

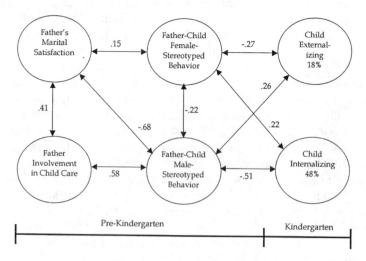

FIG. 5.1.   Fathers and girls.

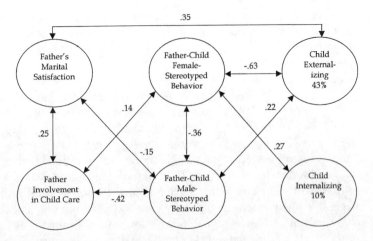

FIG. 5.2. Fathers and boys.

ance in girls' externalizing behavior. It is true that the small sample of girls means that a substantial effect size (18%) was not statistically significant. Nevertheless, what is noteworthy here is the fact that, given the same sample, family variables explained a much larger proportion of the variance in girls' internalizing than their externalizing problem behaviors.

Maritally satisfied fathers of 5-year-old daughters were in couples more likely to share the daily tasks of caring for the daughters (path weight [pw] = .41) before the children entered kindergarten. Although the sharing did not usually approach 50:50, these fathers were more involved in the care of their children than fathers in other families. In the more egalitarian families, observers rated the father–daughter interactions as more masculine-typed (pw = .58). As predicted, greater participation in more masculine-stereotyped father–daughter interactions before the girls entered kindergarten predicted lower levels of internalizing behavior (pw = −.51), but higher levels of externalizing behavior (pw = .26) in kindergarten girls.

Furthermore, as predicted, when father–daughter pairs engaged in higher levels of feminine-stereotyped interaction in the prekindergarten period, the girls were more likely to be viewed by their teachers as showing internalizing behaviors (pw = .22) but less likely to be described as showing externalizing behaviors (pw = −.27) 1 year later.

Fathers and Sons.   Figure 5.2 presents a similar PLS model linking fathers' marital satisfaction, the couple's child-care arrangements, and father–son sex-typed interaction in the prekindergarten period with boys' externalizing and internalizing behavior 1 year later in kindergarten. The root mean squared index of .08 indicates that the data fit the model relatively well. Again, all four independent latent variables appear to be involved in explaining variance in boys' behavior in kindergarten, but this time, the model accounts for a statistically significant 43% of the variance in boys' externalizing, $F(5, 45) = 7.52$, $p < .001$, but not internalizing (10%) problem behaviors.

As with the fathers of girls, fathers of boys who were more maritally satisfied had a higher probability of being in couples with a more egalitarian division of child-care tasks ($pw = .25$). In contrast with the father–daughter model, fathers in more egalitarian couples were less likely to be engaged with their sons in masculine-stereotyped interactions during the playroom visit ($pw = -.42$) and somewhat more likely to be involved in feminine-stereotyped behavior ($pw = .14$). The link with sons' feminine behavior was also indirect. Fathers' greater involvement in the daily care of their sons was associated with lower levels of male-stereotyped interaction, which, in turn, was linked with higher levels of the feminine-stereotyped interaction during the father–son playroom visit ($pw = -.36$).

As predicted by hypothesis 3, when father–son pairs showed higher levels of feminine stereotyped behavior in the preschool period, the sons were described as less externalizing ($pw = -.62$) but more internalizing ($pw = .27$)[1] by their kindergarten teachers. When father–son pairs showed higher levels of masculine behavior, the boys were more likely to be seen as showing externalizing behaviors 1 year later ($pw = .22$). However, there were no meaningful links between masculine-stereotyped behavior and sons' internalizing behaviors. An unexpected path in Fig. 5.2 was the positive direct link between parents' marital satisfaction and boys' externalizing behavior ($pw = .35$). We discuss this further later.

Evidence for the importance of sex-typing in understanding problem behaviors at school comes from a recalculation of the models in which we removed the two latent variables representing sex-typed behavior. Because the models including and excluding the measures of father–child sex-typed behavior contained the same set of marital satisfaction and egalitarian task-sharing data, we can infer an overall statistical effect from the contrast between the two R^2s—in effect a measure of R^2 change. In Fig. 5.1, removing the masculine and feminine sex-typed behavior reduced the amount of variance explained in girl's internalizing from 48% to 25%, F-change (2/26) = 5.75, $p < .01$. In Fig. 5.2, removing the same two latent variables reduced the amount of variance explained in boys' externalizing from 43% to 12%, F-change (2/43) = 11.92, $p < .001$. We can state with some confidence, then, that sex-typed interaction with fathers makes a meaningful contribution to understanding links between fathers' marital satisfaction and involvement in caring

---

[1]We note that the model did not account for a statistically significant proportion of internalizing behavior.

for their children and girls' internalizing behavior and boys' externalizing behavior.

DISCUSSION

Frequency of Sex-Typed Behavior by Children and Their Parents

In this portion of our study, we remedied previous design flaws that might have obscured sex-typed interactions. We analyzed interactions of parent sex by child sex, studied both sex-consistent and sex-inconsistent behavior, and coded contingencies between children's behaviors and parents' responses. We expected, then, to find significant sex differences in sex-typed behavior. However, we found no overall differences between girls and boys, either in feminine or masculine sex-typed behavior, and no overall differences in mothers' or fathers' positive reaction to daughters' or sons' sex-typed or opposite sex-typed behavior.

What we did find were context effects. Sons and daughters showed more sex-typed behaviors during the laboratory playroom visits with their fathers than with their mothers. Furthermore, when girls and boys were working and playing with their fathers, they were more likely to show masculine (noncompliant, self-assertive, aggressive, and engage in getting up, running around, and other large muscle movements) than feminine behaviors (dependent, withdrawn, self-reflective, and crying). This difference between levels of masculine and feminine behavior did not appear in the same children's interactions with their mothers.

The results are mostly consistent with Lytton's findings (1994, 1991) that mothers and fathers tend not to treat children's sex-typed behavior differently, and that daughters and sons tend not to show different levels of sex-typed behavior on the average. These conclusions, of course, are limited to the specific features of this study. We observed parents and their 5-year-olds in a specified set of tasks, and coded specific aspects of feminine and masculine stereotyped behavior. We did not, for example, focus on sex-typed play choices, where the literature has clearly shown differences between girls and boys.

We should also note that the absence of overall difference in masculine- or feminine-stereotyped behavior during playroom assessment during the preschool period is dissimilar from the findings based on teacher's and children's views 1 year later in kindergarten, when girls were described, and described themselves, as more internalizing, and boys were described, and described themselves, as more externalizing, consistent with sex-stereotypes (see chapter 3). It is possible that sex-typing grows stronger over time and is influenced by school as well as family contexts. It is also possible that the kind of sex-typing we measured in the laboratory is different in quality from behavior with peers at school, although the findings here do indicate that the two are correlated. What seems to be emerging from our results is the importance of asking not only about group differences between girls and boys, but about individual and contextual differences in the tendency to display behavior that is consistent with or against stereotype.

Parenting and Children's Sex-Typed Behavior

Our findings with regard to the role of parents in children's sex-typing also emphasize the importance of individual differences rather than group main effects. We found strong support for our prediction in hypothesis 2 that variations in children's sex-typed behavior would be associated with variations in parents' positive or negative responses to that behavior. Microanalytic observational analysis of parents' reactions to specific behaviors showed that children were more likely to show higher levels of masculine- or feminine-stereotyped behavior when parents responded positively to it. Parents' positive responses were also associated with lower levels of positive response to the other stereotype, and with lower levels of children's behavior consistent with the other sex stereotype. Only 2 of 16 correlations revealed results that were inconsistent with this reciprocal system, and both of these exceptions could have been the result of lower statistical power in the smaller sample of girls.

There were interesting sex-linked patterns in the connections between parents' encouragement and discouragement and children's sex-stereotypic behavior. From the regressions summarized in Table 5.4, we concluded that girls who exhibited more feminine sex-typed behavior and boys who exhibited more masculine sex-typed behavior had parents who responded discriminatively with high encouragement and praise of sex-consistent behavior and low encouragement or negative responses to sex-inconsistent behavior. It may be that stereotypic sex-typing emerges when it is supported by clearly differential positive and negative responses by parents in both mother–child and father–child interactions.

Behavior against stereotype was associated with more complex parenting patterns. Girls who were more assertive and aggressive had mothers who responded positively to that behavior and fathers who did not reinforce traditionally feminine behavior. Boys high in feminine sex-typed behavior had mothers and fathers who responded positively to it but did not discourage masculine-typed behavior. Behavior against stereotype, then, was associated with parental encouragement, but not with negative responses to sex-stereotyped behavior when it occurred.

We acknowledge the necessity of caution about inferring the direction of effects. The findings here do not establish definitively whether parents' behavior affects the child's tendency to display sex-typed behavior, whether the child's sex-typed behavior elicits reactions from the parents, or whether the causal forces operate in both directions. Nevertheless, two findings suggest that it is unlikely that the patterns found here were primarily child-driven. If sex-typed behavior were a characteristic of the child's personality, then high levels of masculine behavior should be associated with low levels of feminine behavior, and masculine and feminine sex-typed behavior should be correlated across mother–child and father–child interaction. In fact, masculine and feminine behaviors were uncorrelated within each parent–child interaction, and sex-typed behaviors with mother were not correlated with similar behaviors with father. Furthermore, in the same children, sex-typed behavior was heightened in the presence of fathers, but not mothers. Although it is possible that children believe that fathers expect more sex-typed behavior and shape their behavior to match those expectations, it seems more reasonable to assume that the behaviors emerge from the qualities of the interaction rather than the propensities of the child.

The Family Relationship Context, Sex-Typing, and Internalizing and Externalizing in Kindergarten

Marital Satisfaction and Fathers' Involvement. Most research on sex-typing and socialization focuses on the antecedents or at least the correlates of sex-stereotypic behavior in children. In this chapter, we have been equally interested in the implications of variations in sex-typed interactions during the preschool period for children's internalizing and externalizing behavior early in elementary school. Structural equation models that linked parents' marital satisfaction, egalitarian division of child-care tasks, and sex-typed parent–child interaction with children's problem behaviors as they enter elementary school, showed statistically significant connections for fathers and daughters' internalizing behavior and fathers' and sons' externalizing behavior.

When fathers were more maritally satisfied, they participated more fully in the care of their daughters and sons, but from that point, the paths to children's problem behavior in school were different. We could interpret the higher level of involvement of fathers as nontraditional behavior that contrasts with the traditional male stereotype. Compared with less involved fathers, more involved fathers appeared to reinforce nontraditional behavior in their children; the more involved fathers were engaged in higher levels of masculine-stereotyped interactions with daughters and feminine-stereotyped interactions with sons. We do not know whether personal characteristics or relationship styles of men who choose to do more of the feeding, playing with, and handling their daughters' arrangements were different from those who did the same for sons, or whether girls and boys elicited different sex-typed responses from more involved fathers.

In Fig. 5.2, high levels of marital satisfaction for fathers of preschoolers had a direct, positive link with boys' externalizing behavior. This finding is in apparent contradiction of the chain of associations by which, in the same figure, marital satisfaction and fathers' involvement in child-care tasks were linked with low levels of masculine-stereotyped behavior, which, in turn, was associated with low levels of externalizing problem behavior in kindergarten. How can marital satisfaction have two links in opposite directions? One possibility is that the model includes two kinds of maritally satisfied fathers— those who are more involved in their son's daily care and discourage masculine-stereotyped behavior, and those who are less involved in their son's daily care and engage in the more masculine stereotyped behavior, associated with higher levels of externalizing.

Sex-Typing as Both a Risk and Protective Factor.   In their interactions with fathers, higher levels of sex-typed behavior for boys and girls predicted higher levels of sex-typed problem behaviors in the classroom—internalizing for girls and externalizing for boys. Against-stereotype behavior for father–daughter pairs was associated with lower levels of internalizing in the girls, whereas against-stereotype behavior for father–son pairs was associated with lower levels of externalizing in the boys. That is, when fathers and their preschoolers were involved in less sex-stereotyped behavior, the children resorted less to stereotyped strategies as they met the challenges of making the transition to school.

At first glance, these findings appear to support the argument that conformity to traditional sex-roles and sex-typed parenting are more maladaptive, and the development of behavior against stereotype is more adaptive, for children (Bem, 1993; Block, 1984). However, the fact that parental encouragement of traditional or nontraditional sex-stereotyped behavior has both benefits and risks suggests that there is a delicate balancing act in play in modern families. A high level of father–child emphasis on masculine-stereotyped behavior protects girls against internalizing problems a year later in kindergarten, but too high an emphasis runs the risk of increasing externalizing behavior. Similarly, a high level of father–child emphasis on feminine stereotyped behavior protects boys against developing externalizing problems but too high an emphasis runs the risk of increasing internalizing problems.

The Importance of Fathers in Young Children's Sex-Typed Behavior

Similar to conclusions of other investigators (Block, 1983; Lytton & Romney, 1991; Parke, 1996), fathers in this study appeared to play a more central role in their sons' and daughters' sex-typed behavior than did mothers. One possible explanation of this pattern is that even the most involved fathers spend relatively little direct time with children (Pleck, 1997) and are therefore more prone to act in stereotypic rather than differentiated ways. A second possibility suggested by the structural equation models in Fig. 5.1 and 5.2 is that a combination of marital unhappiness and a relatively low level of involvement in the hands-on care of their children heightens fathers' tendency to treat their children in more stereotypic fashion. By contrast, unhappily married mothers may provide a better buffer than their husbands do between their own marital distress and the quality of relationship they develop with their children (Kerig, Cowan, & Cowan, 1993).

An obvious question is why there are no statistically significant patterns linking mothers' views of their marital relationship and parent–child sex-typing with children's problem behavior. One answer is that children had significantly lower levels of both masculine- and feminine-stereotyped behavior when they worked and played with their mothers, perhaps not enough to produce observable effects on their behavior problems in school. A corollary of this view is that we have not assessed mothers and children using tasks or contexts that would elicit the kind of sex-typed interactions associated with internalizing and externalizing behaviors at school. A second possibility is simply that the effect size is small and would require a larger sample to reveal.

The emphasis on fathers in these findings must be interpreted in light of the fact that this study focused on parents' reactions to gender stereotyped behavior in their firstborn children. Other chapters in this volume, examining other aspects of family dynamics, show that mothers' self-perceptions, marital quality, and parenting behaviors are involved in the emergence of externalizing and internalizing behaviors in their sons and daughters (see chapters 6, 7, 8, and 10).

CONCLUSIONS

The results reported earlier are consistent with the view that sex-typed behavior by both parent and child emerges in the process of relationships between men and women and boys and girls in the family as a system. Despite the fact that there were no overall mean differences in sex-typed behavior shown by male or female children or fathers and mothers, it is clear that sex-typed family interaction plays a role in the tendency of girls and boys to show shy, depressed, withdrawn behavior or aggressive, hostile, noncompliant behavior in kindergarten.

Marital quality and parents' sex-typed division of labor in the daily care of the child also contributed to understanding variations in the sons' and daughters' internalizing and externalizing behaviors at school. When couple relationships are going well and parents have more egalitarian family work arrangements, fathers tend to become more involved with their children, but this appears to have different consequences for girls and boys.

We have argued here that it is necessary to go beyond the usual question of whether there are sex differences in children's and parents' sex-stereotypic behaviors to inquire about the potential risks and benefits associated with more and less sex-typed parent–child interactions. In this study, stereotyped interaction with fathers in the preschool period functioned as a protective factor with respect to nonstereotyped problem behavior, so that masculine-typed interactions with girls were associated with lower levels of aggression in school, whereas feminine-typed interactions with boys were associated with lower levels of aggression in boys. However, the same stereotyped interaction with fathers in the preschool period was a risk factor for sex-stereotyped problem behavior (depression for girls, aggression for boys) in kindergarten 1 year later.

This complex pattern supports a functionalist theoretical interpretation of risk-outcome paradigms. Risk, protection, and vulnerability do not inhere in specific variables, but rather in the network of connections among variables. In this case, during the transition to school period, sex-stereotyped father–child behavior during the preschool period functions as both a protective factor and a buffer with reference to internalizing and externalizing problems, with effects depending on the sex of the child.

6

Children's Self-Perceptions As a Link Between Family Relationship Quality and Social Adaptation to School

Jeffrey R. Measelle

As children enter kindergarten, their social adjustment is partially deter-mined by the degree to which they can negotiate and maintain new relation-ships, become engaged rather than withdrawn from peer-group activities, and behave in prosocial rather than aggressive or antisocial ways (Barth & Parke, 1996; Ladd, 1996). Indeed, the success with which children negotiate the interpersonal challenges associated with school transition will have life-long implications for their mental health (Bagwell, Newcomb, & Bukowski, 1998; Hodges, Boivin, Vitaro, & Bukowski, 1999), scholastic attainments (Alexander, Entwisle, & Dauber, 1993; Wentzel & Caldwell, 1997), and later social relationships (Ladd, Kochenderfer, & Coleman, 1997). Although it is clear that family affective relationship factors provide important contextual influences on children's social adjustment (Goodman, 2002; Sheeber, Hops, Alpert, Davis, & Andrews, 1997), little is known about the specific processes by which problematic or competent outcomes are established. Rather, find-ings show more generally that "bad environments" are associated with "bad outcomes" and "good environments" are associated with "good outcomes."

In this chapter, we focus on links between the emotional quality of multi-ple family relationships and children's social adaptation to kindergarten. Using data collected at two points in time, we examine the predictive power of the positive and negative emotional properties of children's preschool rela-tionships with their mothers, fathers, and siblings in explaining variation in their social adjustment at the end of kindergarten. We pay special attention to how children's perceptions of the relationship between their parents enhance our understanding of these associations. We test the hypotheses that, in addition to their family backgrounds, characteristics of the children also shape their transition to school, and that children's perceptions of themselves as more or less socially competent and likeable individuals play a significant role in enhancing or reducing the likelihood of a successful start to school.

EARLY FAMILY PROCESSES AND CHILDREN'S SOCIAL ADJUSTMENT

We know from the results reported in chapter 4, and from many other studies, that parent–child relationships characterized by high degrees of warmth contribute to children's competent behaviors with peers, whereas interactions defined primarily by negative affect or conflict between mothers and children contribute to children's aggressive or sad-withdrawn behavior at school (Cowan, Cowan, Schulz, & Heming, 1994; Parke & Buriel, 1998; Patterson & Reid, 1984). Children's participation in and feelings about their relationships with siblings also have implications for their early social development. Dunn and her colleagues (Dunn, 1996; Dunn, Slomkowski, & Beardsall, 1994) and Patterson (1986) showed that, when sibling relationships are characterized as amicable, children tend to have close friendships outside of the family (Dunn, 1996), whereas sibling relationships marked by hostility and aggression are associated with antisocial behavior toward peers (Patterson, 1986). Dunn et al. (1994) also found that, although the correlates of social competence change with age, the emotional characteristics of sibling relationships continue to be stable and consistent predictors of adjustment across early to middle childhood. Their conclusion underscores the importance of examining the early contribution of sibling relationships to children's social adjustment.

In addition to considering children's participatory role in parent–child and sibling relationships, it is important for children to take their perceptions of their parents' relationship as a couple into account. As shown by researchers interested in the emotional security hypothesis, it is precisely mother–father transactions in the presence of the child that have been identified as proximal stimuli with the potential to create disequilibrium and distress in the child (Ablow, 1997b; see also Cummings & Davies, 1994; Fincham, 1998). Conflict between parents that is expressed in front of children as they prepare to enter kindergarten may be especially salient to their adjustment in their first year of formal schooling.

Research on emotion in family life suggests that, although positive and negative affectivity in relationships overlap (Fincham, 1998; Watson & Clark, 1997), they appear to be relatively distinct emotional systems, with different implications for children's psychosocial development (Goldsmith & Campos, 1990; Tellegen, 1988; Watson & Clark, 1997). We examined the possibility that the positive and negative emotional qualities of key family relationships in the preschool period make different contributions to understanding variation in children's social adjustment following their entrance to kindergarten.

YOUNG CHILDREN'S SOCIAL SELF-PERCEPTIONS

Increased attention has been paid to children's self-perceptions as markers, if not central determinants, of their school adjustment. Based on studies showing that self-perceptions in school-age children play an important role in the production of competent social behavior (Eccles, Wigfield, Harold, & Blumenfeld, 1993; Harter, 1999), definitions of social adjustment have been expanded to include children's capacity to maintain positive perceptions of themselves (Ladd, 1996; Measelle, Ablow, Cowan, & Cowan, 1998). For example, children who view themselves as socially competent and likeable tend to exhibit greater cooperation, less hostility, and smoother group entry skills than children with negative social self-perceptions (Crick & Ladd, 1993). However, most of the studies investigating links between children's self-perceptions and school adjustment have been conducted with children who have already begun their schooling. The possibility that children's preschool self-perceptions might act as antecedents to a successful transition to school is less well understood.

LINKING PRESCHOOL PROCESSES AND SCHOOL ADJUSTMENT THROUGH CHILDREN'S SOCIAL SELF-PERCEPTIONS

Despite evidence for connections between early family transactions and children's subsequent social adjustment, the process by which these links are created and maintained has not been established. One of the most compelling explanations for behavioral and emotional continuities across relationships comes from attachment theory, which posits that children construct mental representations of themselves as competent and likeable based on experiences in their primary attachment relationship(s), (Bretherton, Ridgeway, & Cassidy, 1990), and that feeling positively about the self as worthy of being loved is a central dimension of attachment (Bartholomew & Horowitz, 1991). Systematic studies reveal that, as their social networks expand, typically in conjunction with school entry, children's perceptions of themselves and others help to shape their interactions in new relationships (Bretherton et al., 1990).

Beyond attachment processes, much less is understood about the extent to which the emotional properties of other family relationships contribute to children's early self-perceptions, in part because assessments of multiple family relationships are rarely conducted within the same study. Yet, evidence that attachment is but one relational context in which children develop socially (Dunn, 1993; Hinde, 1995) suggests that children's early self-perceptions are likely to take shape in multiple family relationships. Indeed, both past (Cooley, 1902; Mead, 1934) and current studies of symbolic interaction (e.g., reflective appraisal processes; Harter, 1999; Kenny, 1996) emphasize the contributions of "important others" (Mead, 1934) to children's perceptions and evaluations of themselves.

In addition to studying the contribution of the positive and negative emotional qualities of mother–child, father–child, coparenting, and sibling relationships to children's school adjustment, we also examined the unique and overlapping associations between children's family relationships and their social self-perceptions prior to the start of kindergarten. We explored the possibility that children's self-perceptions act as mechanisms that link their preschool family environment and later adaptation to school in two conceptually distinct ways. Following procedures recommended by Baron and Kenny (1986), we conducted exploratory analyses to see whether children's self-perceptions operate as mediators or moderators of the family-to-school connection. If they act as mediators, the effects of children's early family environment on their subsequent adjustment to school would be linked through their self-perceptions. For example, it may be that the connection between earlier negative family processes and children's later tendency toward antisocial behavior at school is accounted for by negative self-perceptions that develop within the context of aversive family relationships and are then manifested in other interpersonal situations outside of the family. If children's self-perceptions function as moderators, they might help to explain for whom coercive family environments are most and least disequilibrating. In other words, despite a punitive family environment, a positive self-perception might help keep some children from behaving in socially disruptive ways. Our analyses tested the hypothesis that mediators and moderators represent distinct psychological functions of children's perceptions of their competence and difficulties.

HYPOTHESES

1. We predicted that positive and negative emotional aspects of mother–child, father–child, the couple, and sibling relationships would be correlated with children's self-perceptions in the preschool period. In a more exploratory approach, we investigated whether each of these family relationships explained unique variance in children's self-perceptions.

2. We predicted that family relationship processes and children's self-perceptions in the preschool period would combine to explain variation in teacher-rated social competence, namely, internalizing and externalizing behavior in the classroom. Exploratory analyses investigated whether preschoolers' self-perceptions functioned as mediators or moderators of the links between family processes and their subsequent adaptation to school.

METHOD

Participants

For this study, a total of 71 target children and their families were drawn from the larger Schoolchildren and Their Families (SAF) Project. Because of our interest in measuring the contributions of multiple family relationships, only children with a younger sibling at the time of the preschool home visit were included. Data are presented for 38 boys and 33 girls at the preschool period (M age = 4.9, SD = .36). At the time the target children's self-perceptions were assessed, the mean age of the next youngest sibling was approximately 2.3 years (SD = .31).

Measures

Children's Self-Perceptions. The Berkeley Puppet Interview (BPI; Ablow & Measelle, 1993) was used to measure children's academic and social self-perceptions. Here, we report on two of the original six scales from the BPI: (a) social competence, and (b) acceptance by peers, as characterized by the children. Social competence scores (five items) included the ability to engage effectively in social tasks, such as making friends, asserting oneself in a socially appropriate manner, and seeking engagement more than isolation, α = .65. Peer acceptance scores (eight items) included children's perception of themselves as liked and included by other children, and as not ignored, excluded, or rejected, α = .68. Because the scores on the two scales were correlated, $r(69)$ = .48, $p < .001$, they were averaged to create a single measure of children's perceived social adjustment.

Measures of Relational Affect.

1. Parent–child interactions—In this study, the positive and negative emotional qualities of mother–child and father–child relationships were based on observational ratings of each parent's affect during the separate dyadic parent–child interactions (see chapter 2). A measure of positive paren-

tal affect was created by computing parents' mean scores on three scales: warmth, pleasure, and responsiveness, $\alpha = .84$. A measure of negative parental affect was created by computing parents' mean scores on two scales: anger and coldness, $\alpha = .87$.

2. Coparenting—As described in chapter 2, the behavior of spouses toward each other as coparents was observed during the 40-min family visit to our project playroom. Here we used scales describing coparenting warmth and conflict. These are behaviors observable not only by our project staff but also by the child.

3. Sibling relationships—Two sibling scales from the BPI Family Environment Interview were used to assess children's perceptions of their relationships with siblings. During this phase of the BPI, the oldest child in the family (the target child) was asked questions about his or her next youngest sibling. The BPI's sibling enjoyment scale (6 items, $\alpha = .68$) measures the positive emotional aspects of the sibling relationship. Items in this scale assess children's affection for ("I like my sister") and enjoyment of their sibling ("I like to play with my brother"), as well as their perception that their sibling likes them ("My sister likes me"). The gender reference in each of the BPI question stems was matched to the gender of each child's sibling. The BPI's sibling conflict and hostility scale (six items, $\alpha = .71$) measures the negative emotional aspects of the sibling relationship. Items in this scale assess perceived conflict ("My brother and I fight a lot"), hostility ("I tease my sister" or "I'm mean to my brother"), and dislike ("I don't like my brother") between the siblings.

Teachers' Ratings of Children's Competence and Adjustment. We used the Child Adaptive Behavior Inventory's (CABI) social competence scale, the internalizing-social isolation scale, and, to focus on aggression and not defiant behavior, we used a modification of the CABI's externalizing-aggressive factor, in which only the antisocial and hostile scales were included.

RESULTS

Overview

We found a significant association between preschool family processes and young students' developing sense of competence and acceptance in their relationships with peers. However, the nature of this connection differed, depending on (a) which family relationship was examined (marital, mother–child, father–child, sibling), (b) the specific emotional processes being considered (positive or negative emotion), and (c) whether the analyses adopted a subsystem (i.e., each relationship analyzed separately) or a family-systems perspective (i.e., the overlapping and unique contributions among all relationships analyzed simultaneously).

When each relationship was considered independently, high levels of parental warmth and responsiveness while mothers or fathers worked and played with their children contributed to children's reports of more positive views of their own social adjustment. On the negative side, when mothers (but not fathers) expressed more anger and coldness during the preschool parent–child visit, children tended to describe themselves as less competent and less accepted by peers. It was also the case that, when parents demonstrated high conflict as a couple in front of their children, their sons or daughters held less positive views of their own social adjustment. However, when the emotional quality of each of the specific family relationships was analyzed simultaneously, as advocated by family systems researchers (e.g., Hinde, 1995), only mothers' negative affect, parents' conflict as a couple, and the interaction between conflict and warmth in the couple, emerged as independent predictors of children's perceptions of their own social adjustment before they entered kindergarten.

Descriptive Statistics

A series of two-way multivariate analyses of variance (child sex by sibling status) was conducted to test for differences in the primary measures between children in this subsample who have siblings and children in the larger study who did not have a sibling in the summer prior to kindergarten. Children did not differ on any variables according to their sibling status.

Prior to conducting the study's central analyses, we analyzed the data to see whether boys and girls differed in terms of mean levels or in the pattern of correlations among variables as a function of child sex. Table 6.1 presents the mean levels and standard deviations for the entire sample and for boys and girls separately. With the exception of teachers' ratings of children's antisocial behavior in kindergarten, the means in Table 6.1 were not significantly different. As in the larger sample described in chapters 2 and 3, teachers described boys as showing significantly more antisocial behaviors than girls, $F(1, 69) = 5.31, p < .05$. Using Fisher's r-to-z transformations, the pattern of intercorrelations among the variables in Table 6.1 was also analyzed for sex differences. When comparing the coefficients for boys and girls, the differences appeared neither systematic nor more frequent than would be expected by chance. Accordingly, this study's remaining analyses were conducted on the entire sample of boys and girls. Intercorrelations among the positive and negative aspects of each relationship were examined next to establish their degree of independence. Despite consistently high correlations, $M\ r(71) = -.51$; $range = -.43$ to $-.67$, $ps < .001$, the positive and negative emotional qualities of each relationship demonstrated a fair amount of independence. Within a

TABLE 6.1
Means and Standard Deviations of Study Variables

Variables	Whole Sample[a]		Girls[b]		Boys[c]	
	M	SD	M	SD	M	SD
Mother–Child						
Positive affect	3.69	.32	3.69	.30	3.76	.27
Negative affect	1.52	.49	1.49	.38	1.47	.46
Father–Child						
Positive affect	3.50	.44	3.50	.43	3.54	.44
Negative affect	1.57	.54	1.48	.50	1.58	.51
Coparenting						
Warmth	5.43	.92	5.55	.83	5.35	.98
Conflict	3.59	1.21	3.52	1.19	3.64	1.23
Sibling relationship						
Enjoyment	4.70	.93	4.71	.99	4.69	.90
Hostility	3.78	.94	3.84	1.02	3.74	.89
Child's self-perceived competence	4.78	1.04	4.66	1.13	4.86	1.00
Teacher						
Social competence*	3.09	.65	3.20	.65	3.01	.68
Antisocial behavior	1.50	.64	*1.35*	.51	*1.61*	.72
Sad withdrawn behavior	1.71	.72	1.69	.75	1.76	.69

Note. Despite similarities in the mean and standard deviation values, scores were derived with different measures and scaling. Italicized means indicate that boys and girls differed significantly.
[a]$N = 71$. [b]$n = .38$. [c]$n = 33$.
*$p < .05$.

given relationship (mother–child, father–child, mother–father, or siblings), anywhere from 57% to 77% of the variance in the measure of positive affect was unrelated to the variance in the measure of negative affect.

Correlations across relationships were examined next. Supporting a family-systems view (Hinde & Stevenson-Hinde, 1988) were a number of consistencies in positive or negative behavior across different family relationships, M $r(69) = .25$; *range* = .27 to .47. The question to be explored later in multivariate analyses is whether and how the family relationship variables combine and contribute uniquely to predictions of children's adaptation.

Relational Measures and Children's Social Self-Perceptions During the Preschool Period

Preliminary Correlational Analysis. The data presented in Table 6.2 suggest that there were a number of significant but low to moderate simple correlations between the emotional qualities of specific family relationships and

TABLE 6.2
Preschool Relational Variables and Children's
Perceptions of Their Social Competence

Preschool Variables	Children's Perceived Social Competence During Preschool
Mother–Child	
1. Positive affect	.25*
2. Negative affect	−.33**
Father–Child	
3. Positive affect	.29*
4. Negative affect	−.03
Coparenting	
5. Warmth	.18
6. Conflict	−.37**
Sibling relationship	
7. Enjoyment	.11
8. Hostility	−.22

Note. Within a relationship, underscored coefficients indicate correlations that are significantly different ($p < .05$, two-tailed) when scores are compared using Fisher's r-to-z transformation.

*$p < .05$. **$p < .01$, all correlations are two-tailed.

children's perceptions of their social competence during the preschool period. Mothers' demonstrations of more positive affect and less negative affect toward their children during their dyadic interactions, as we observed them in our project playroom prior to kindergarten, were related to children's tendency to see themselves as more socially skilled 1 year later. Fathers who demonstrated more warmth with their children tended to have preschoolers who perceived themselves as more socially competent, but there was no significant correlation between fathers' negative affect with their children and children's self-perceptions.

Furthermore, only coparenting conflict was associated with children's self-perceptions; when there was greater spousal conflict while working and playing with the child, the child viewed himself or herself as less socially competent prior to kindergarten, whereas warmth in the coparenting pair was not systematically related to children's self-perceptions. Finally, children's perceptions of enjoyment and hostility in their relationships with their siblings were not associated with their perceived social competence before they entered kindergarten.

Multivariate Regressions. The question to be addressed here is whether the separate correlations of positive or negative affect in the parent–child relationship with children's perceived social competence are unique and additive or overlapping (multicollinear). To reduce the potential for collinearity, only family relationship measures that were significantly correlated with children's self-perception at the bivariate level were included in a hierarchical multiple regression. Mothers' positive and negative affect, fathers' positive affect, and coparenting conflict, were entered on Step 1 as a single block. In contrast with the simple correlations' explanation of up to 10% of the variance in children's self-perceptions (in Table 6.2), the combined predictors accounted for 24% of the variance in children's perceptions of their social competence before they entered kindergarten, $F(4, 65) = 4.25, p < .01$. From the significance of the betas, we infer that mothers' negative affect and conflict between the parents in the family interaction session emerged as unique predictors of the preschoolers' self-appraisals.

In a new set of three regression models, interaction terms constructed from the combination of positive and negative affect (e.g., coparenting warmth × coparenting conflict), were each entered on Step 2 to test the hypothesis that positive affect helps to buffer children against the potentially harmful effects of negative interpersonal interactions. That is, if coparenting conflict is associated with negative outcomes only when coparenting warmth is low, but not when it is high, we could say that the warmth between the parents protected the child from the potentially harmful effects of their marital conflict.

Of the three interaction terms tested (fathers', mothers', and couples warmth and conflict), only the interaction between the coparenting warmth and conflict measures accounted for an additional 11% of the variance, $F(1, 64) = 5.09, p < .01$, in children's perceptions of their social adjustment. To determine the meaning of this interaction, we divided children into high and low groups based on a median split of their parents' warmth on the coparenting scales. Children's perceived social competence was then regressed on coparenting conflict. Consistent with a buffering hypothesis, we found that, at high levels of coparenting warmth, children's perception of their social competence remained stable even as coparenting conflict increased. By contrast, at low levels of parenting warmth, children's perception of their social competence was lower when there were high levels of conflict in the coparenting pair during the family visit to our laboratory playroom where the family interaction observations were made.

Relational Measures, Children's Self-Perceptions, and Adaptation to Kindergarten

Preliminary Correlational Analyses of Predictions Across Time. The analyses discussed earlier focused on the family correlates of children's self-perceptions during the preschool period. Here, we examine the extent to which preschool family processes and children's self-perceptions in the preschool period contributed to their social adaptation to school 1 year later, based on their kindergarten teachers' ratings of their social competence, antisocial behavior, and socially withdrawn behavior. As can be seen in Table 6.3, when mothers and fathers exhibited higher levels of positive affect (pleasure, warmth, responsiveness) as they worked and played with their children in the preschool period, and when mothers exhibited lower levels of negative affect (anger and coldness) during that time, kindergarten teachers tended to rate their children as more socially competent (kind, fair, socially skilled, and perceptive) and less antisocial or hostile at the end of kindergarten. The same parent–child measures were not significant predictors of teachers' ratings of internalizing behaviors (sad, socially withdrawn).

Although coparenting warmth was unrelated to all three of the children's adaptation scales, higher coparenting conflict was modestly associated with teachers' views of children as exhibiting less social competence and more antisocial behavior toward peers. Interestingly, of all the family relationship measures, only children's reported level of enjoyment of their siblings was associated with teachers' ratings of sad-withdrawn behavior. Children who reported greater enjoyment of their sibling relationship during the preschool period were viewed by their teachers as exhibiting fewer internalizing problems and less antisocial behavior 1 year later. Children who reported more hostile feelings toward their siblings prior to entering kindergarten were characterized by their teachers as less socially competent and employing more externalizing behaviors at school.

The associations between children's perceived social competence and their teacher's ratings of their behavior were examined next. As predicted, chil-

TABLE 6.3
Preschool Relational Variables, Preschool Children's Perceptions
of Social Competence, and Kindergarten Teacher Ratings of Adjustment

| | Kindergarten Teachers' Spring Ratings | | |
Preschool Variables	Withdrawn Behavior	Social Competence	Antisocial Behavior
Mother–Child			
Positive affect	−.08	.32**	−.30*
Negative affect	.04	−.36**	.26*
Father–Child			
Positive affect	−.15	.27*	−.25*
Negative affect	.12	−.16	.18
Coparenting			
Warmth	−.11	.03	−.04
Conflict	−.10	−.22	−.24*
Sibling relationship			
Enjoyment	−.27*	.16	−.25*
Hostility	.14	−.28*	.24*
Child's perceived social competence	−.32**	.35**	−.24*

*$p < .05$. **$p < .01$, all correlations are two-tailed.

dren's preschool perceptions of their social competence as assessed in the BPI were related to their classroom behavior at the end of kindergarten. Preschoolers who viewed themselves as more socially competent before they entered school were rated by their teachers as more socially competent and less antisocial or sad-withdrawn at the end of kindergarten than preschoolers who had had less positive self-perceptions.

Multivariate Regressions. To examine the joint and unique contributions of the family relationship measures to children's kindergarten adaptation, teachers' CABI ratings of children's social competence, and their externalizing and internalizing behaviors, were regressed separately on the measures with which they had been significantly or moderately associated at the bivariate level in Table 6.3. Statistical interaction terms were also examined in these analyses but were eliminated because they failed to yield significant findings. To predict children's social competence, mothers' positive and negative affect and fathers' positive affect toward the child, conflict between the parents, and hostility between the siblings, were entered simultaneously as a block. Combined, these preschool family predictors accounted for 23% of the variance in teachers' ratings of the children's social competence at the end of kindergarten, $F(5, 64) = 3.84, p < .01$. Only parents' conflict in front of their children emerged as a significant, independent predictor, $\beta = -.26, p < .05$, of children's (lower) social competence scores following their entry to school.

To predict kindergarten teachers' ratings of antisocial behavior, the same five predictors were entered simultaneously as a block. Combined, these predictors accounted for a significant, albeit modest, 18% of the variance in kindergarten teachers' ratings of children's antisocial behavior, $F(5, 64) = 3.34, p < .01$. Again, only conflict between the parents in the presence of their child, $\beta = .25, p < .03$, provided an independent prediction of children's antisocial conduct in kindergarten. Finally, teachers' ratings of children's sad-withdrawn behavior were regressed on children's reports of sibling enjoyment in the preschool period. Lower BPI scores on sibling enjoyment, $\beta = -.27, p < .05$, accounted for a significant 8% of the variance in children's internalizing problems at the end of kindergarten, $F(1, 68) = 5.50, p < .05$.

These multivariate regression results indicate that family processes during the preschool period combine to explain significant portions of the variance in teachers' ratings of children's adjustment to the first year of elementary school. Because children's perceptions of their social adjustment were assessed during the summer prior to kindergarten, this score was entered into these models on a second step. As expected, children's perceptions of their own social competence prior to entering school, combined with the quality of the relationships we observed in their family, predicted aspects of their adjustment to kindergarten. When children's self-perception scores were entered into these equations on the final step, they added unique independent variance to the prediction of teachers' ratings of social competence, $\Delta R^2 = 12\%$, $\beta = .37$, $p < .01$, and internalizing behaviors at the end of kindergarten, $\Delta R^2 = 10\%$, $\beta = -.32$, $p < .01$. By contrast, children's perceptions of their social competence did not significantly improve the predictability of externalizing behaviors in kindergarten.

Are Children's Self-Perceptions Mediators or Moderators of Preschool Family Environment to School Adaptation Linkages?

Thus far, these data describe connections across time between the emotional qualities of children's family relationships prior to making the transition to elementary school and their social adjustment in the first year of school. They also revealed links between children's self-perceptions and their social adjustment once in school. Is it possible that children's appraisals of their competence and acceptance by peers help to explain how preschool family processes predict school adaptation? That is, do children's self-perceptions function as mediators or moderators of the statistical association?

Mediation Effects. As recommended by Baron and Kenny (1986), we conducted tests of mediation through a series of regressions. Mediation is demonstrated when the variance in the dependent variable explained by the independent variable (the A-C correlation) is reduced after the mediator B, reflecting the B-C correlation, has been added as a control. First, the measure of children's preschool self-perceptions—the hypothesized mediator (B)—was regressed on each of the family relationship (A) variables in separate models (no. 1 equations in Table 6.4). Second, teachers' ratings of children's social adjustment to school—the outcome variables (C)—were regressed on the relational measures in separate equations (no. 2 equations in Table 6.4). Finally, in number 3 equations, each outcome variable (C) was regressed on the independent variable (A) and mediator (B). Prior to testing for mediation, a relation must be demonstrated among all three variables (Baron & Kenny, 1986). Accordingly, tests for mediation were restricted to the significant simple associations reported in Tables 6.2 and 6.3.

Of the mediation analyses conducted with the coparenting or sibling measures, none proved significant. However, when the maternal and paternal affect measures were examined in relation to children's social competence and antisocial behavior, a different picture emerged. These results are presented in Table 6.4. The first set of equations (no. 1 equations) confirmed that children's self-perceptions of social competence were associated with mothers' and fathers' positive affect and mothers' negative affect (A-B). The second set of equations (no. 2 equations) confirmed that teachers' ratings of children's

TABLE 6.4
Multiple Regression Tests for Mediation

Equation	Dependent Variable for Each Equation	Predictor(s) Entered	R^2	β
Mother–Child models				
1.	BPI-social competence	Mother-positive affect	.07*	.25*
2.	Teacher-social competence	Mother-positive affect	.08*	.28*
3.	Teacher-social competence	Mother-positive affect	.03	.18
		BPI-social competence		.42***
2.	Teacher-antisocial	Mother-positive affect	.09*	−.31*
3.	Teacher-antisocial	Mother-positive affect	.05*	−.26*
		BPI-social competence		−.18
Mother–Child models				
1.	BPI-social competence	Mother-negative affect	.11**	−.33**
2.	Teacher-social competence	Mother-negative affect	.13**	−.36**
3.	Teacher-social competence	Mother-negative affect	.04*	−.22*
		BPI-social competence		.39***
2.	Teacher-antisocial	Mother-negative affect	.07*	.26*
3.	Teacher-antisocial	Mother-negative affect	.03	.20
		BPI-social competence		−.19
Father–Child models				
1.	BPI-social competence	Father-positive affect	.06*	.23*
2.	Teacher-social competence	Father-positive affect	.07*	.27*
3.	Teacher-social competence	Father-positive affect	.02	.16
		BPI-social competence		.40***
2.	Teacher-antisocial	Father-positive affect	.06*	−.25*
3.	Teacher-antisocial	Father-positive affect	.03	−.20
		BPI-social competence		−.19

Note. $N = 69$. BPI = Berkeley Puppet Interview.
*$p < .05$. **$p < .01$. ***$p < .001$.

social competence and antisocial behavior were also predicted by mothers' and fathers' positive affect and mothers' negative affect (A-C). As shown in Table 6.4, the third set of equations (no. 3 equations) provided evidence that controlling for children's self-perceptions (B-C) led to a decrease in the portion of variance in the teachers' ratings accounted for by the relational measures (the A-C correlations). A mediation test created by entering the BPI measure of children's self-reported social competence into the regression on teacher ratings of social competence resulted in a decline from .08 to .03 (nonsignificant) of the R^2 explained by mothers' positive affect in the number 2 equations. Entering the BPI measure of social competence into the regression on teachers' ratings of antisocial behavior also resulted in a lowering of the R^2 explained by mothers' positive affect in the number 2 equations. Similarly, children's self-reports of social competence on the BPI mediated the connection between mothers' negative affect and teachers' ratings of social competence, and between fathers' positive affect and teachers' ratings of both social competence and antisocial behavior.

In some cases, entering the hypothesized mediator reduced the strength of the connection between parents' behavior and children's outcome to nonsignificance; in other cases, the reduction was substantial, but parents' behavior remained a significant predictor. Over all, there was some reduction in variance explained by the hypothesized mediator in all seven statistical tests. These results suggest that children's perceptions of their own competence and difficulty at least partially mediated the links between the emotional quality of the parent–child relationship and children's social competence or antisocial tendencies at school. Mediation effects are consistent with the hypothesis that there may be a causal connection, with family processes affecting how children see themselves, and children's self-views functioning as one mechanism affecting how they approach peers in school.

Moderation Effects. Moderator effects examine whether a given variable (B) reduces or increases the connections between risks (A) and outcomes (C). To examine the possibility that children's self-perceptions moderate the family-to-school link, a series of hierarchical regressions was performed, following Baron and Kenny's recommendations (1986). All three kindergarten teacher-rated outcomes served as the dependent variable in separate regression models. In each model, a single relational measure (predictor) was entered in the equation first, followed by children's self-perceptions (moderator) on Step 2, and a two-way interaction term between the predictor and moderator on Step 3.

None of the models constructed to examine the potential role of children's self-perceptions as moderators of links between teachers' ratings and mother–child affect, father–child affect, or sibling affect, was significant. However, as shown in Table 6.5, children's self-perceptions during the preschool period moderated the relation between coparenting conflict and kindergarten teachers' ratings of social competence and antisocial behavior. The F-change resulting from adding the interaction between coparenting conflict and BPI social competence to the equation on Step 3 was statistically significant, $\Delta R^2 = 4\%$, F-change$(1, 68) = 3.65$, $p < .05$. As shown in Fig. 6.1, children in the high positive self-perception group (median split) exhibited greater social competence than children in the low positive self-perception group, regardless of the level of conflict we observed between their parents. The moderating effect was that in contrast to the association between high levels of parents' conflict in the preschool period and low social competence in kindergarten when children had more negative self-perceptions, there was no such association in the high-positive self-perception group. That is, positive self-perceptions may buffer children's competence in getting along with peers against the risks associated with parents' marital conflict.

TABLE 6.5
Hierarchical Multiple Regressions: Tests of Moderation

Step	Independent Variable Entered	R^2	$R^2\Delta$	$F\Delta$	β	F Equation
Dependent variable: Teacher-rated social competence						
1.	Coparent conflict	.04	.04	2.46+	−.23+	
2.	BPI-social competence	.28	.22	15.16***	.49***	
3.	Coparent conflict × BPI-social competence	.32	.04	3.65*	−25*	9.83***
Dependent variable: Teacher-rated antisocial behavior						
1.	Coparent conflict	.05	.05	3.32+	.28+	
2.	BPI-social competence	.12	.07	5.69*	−.35*	
3.	Coparent conflict × BPI-social competence	.17	.05	3.20*	.25*	3.11*

Note. $N = 69$. BPI = Berkeley Puppet Interview.
*$p < .05$. **$p < .01$. ***$p < .001$.

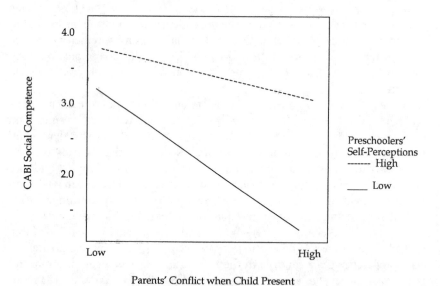

FIG. 6.1. Preschoolers' self-perceptions as a moderator of the relation between exposure to parents' conflict and classroom social competence as rated by kindergarten teachers.

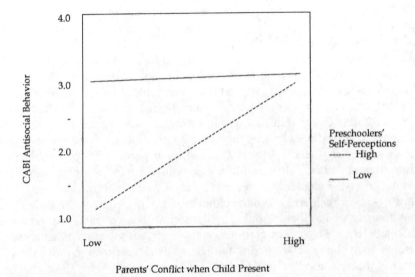

FIG. 6.2. Preschoolers' self-perceptions as a moderator of the relation between exposure to parents' conflict and classroom antisocial behavior as rated by kindergarten teachers.

It was more difficult to interpret children's self-perceptions as moderators of antisocial behavior. As illustrated in Fig. 6.2, at most levels of coparenting conflict, children with less positive self-perceptions exhibited more antisocial behavior than children with more positive views of themselves. However, in families with high coparenting conflict, children in both the high and low self-perception groups exhibited increasing levels of antisocial behavior until there were no differences between the groups of children. That is, high levels of conflict between the parents overrides the buffering effect of positive self-perceptions on children's antisocial behavior in kindergarten.

DISCUSSION

Family Processes and Children's Self-Perceptions in the Preschool Period

Mothers and Fathers. Why would mothers' negative affect but not their positive affect contribute uniquely to explaining variance in preschoolers' perceptions of their social adjustment? It could be that this is part of a general phenomenon in which negative emotion plays a greater role than positive emotion in affecting relationship quality and personal adaptation (Gottman,

1994). It could also be, of course, that the findings have something specific to do with mothers and preschool-age children. Typically, preschoolers' views of themselves are quite positive (Stipek, Recchia, & McClintic, 1992); processes like self–other comparison that can lead to normative declines in self-appraisal begin to appear later in middle childhood (Harter, 1999). The results we have presented here suggest that preschoolers' sense of themselves as competent social beings may be vulnerable to high levels of negativity from their mothers. Given that mothers in this study were observed as they attempted to guide their children through cognitively challenging tasks, it may be that some mothers' cold and angry affect is particularly palpable when they attempt to teach their children new skills. Perhaps, when preschoolers do not meet the challenge as quickly as their mothers' hope they will, and mothers show their irritation, the children sense this, conclude that they are not doing as well as they "should," and suffer the consequences in their sense of competence. This interpretation is consistent with social referencing studies, in which young children look to their mothers' reactions to judge the valence of their efforts (Campos, Campos, & Barrett, 1989). Even somewhat benign reactions such as a maternal frown have been shown to produce self-evaluative emotions such as shame in young children (Lewis, 1987; Stipek et al., 1992).

Still to be explained is why mothers' and not fathers' affective parenting was related uniquely to their children's early social self-perceptions. Typically, mothers are the parent figures who orchestrate preschoolers' peer relationships by arranging "play dates" and other social activities before their children become elementary school students (Ladd, 1996). If mother–child relationships are characterized by more negative affect, children could be deprived of the emotional support they need to feel competent in the face of new and challenging situations. The unique link between mothers' affect and children's perceived social competence may also reflect the fact that women tend to focus on interpersonal processes, whereas men appear to emphasize self-sufficiency and achievement over social dynamics (Cross & Madson, 1997). Fathers do make contributions to their preschoolers' social self-perceptions and other measures of adaptation as we have seen in chapters 4 and 5, and will see in other chapters of this volume.

Couples. Variation in children's perceptions of their competence with peers was also accounted for in part by the conflict parents engaged in with one another while they worked and played with their child. Numerous other studies have documented the adverse effects of conflict between the parents on children's adaptation (Cummings & Davies, 1994). The data here suggest that marital anger and competition may have an impact beyond the couple relationship and beyond the home by coloring children's views of themselves with peers. Parents who clash while trying to parent together are more likely to implicate children in their verbal and nonverbal communication (McHale, 1997). Furthermore, if parents' disagreements are about the child, this might increase the probability that the child will extract negative information about himself or herself from the strain between the parents.

The significant moderating effect of coparenting warmth on coparenting conflict supports other research that suggests that not all interparental conflict is necessarily harmful to children (cf. Ablow, 1997a; Fincham, 1998; Gottman & Katz, 1989). Regardless of whether the parents' conflict was classified as high or low in intensity, children of parents who were warmer toward one another in their presence reported positive self-perceptions. By contrast, children of parents who exhibited high levels of conflict and showed little or no warmth tended to perceive themselves as less accepted by their peers and less socially competent overall.

Siblings.   Contrary to expectation, sibling relationship quality, at least as reported by the first child in the family, was not significantly related to that child's perceptions of competence or acceptance by peers before they entered elementary school. This lack of association was somewhat surprising given that children's perceptions of their sibling relationships and their own strengths and weaknesses were both assessed with the BPI. Even at 4½ to 5½ years of age, children appeared to maintain relatively independent views of their sibling relationships and their competence with and acceptance by peers. The lack of association may be due to the fact that the participants in this study were the oldest children in their families, with siblings who were typically 2 to 3 years younger, many still babies or toddlers. Perhaps it is not until younger siblings develop greater behavioral and sociocognitive competencies of their own that they contribute significantly to the variance in their older brothers' and sisters' sense of themselves. These results are consistent with work by Dunn and her colleagues (Dunn, 1996; Dunn et al., 1994), who found that children's self-esteem is not related to sibling relationship qualities until after 10 years of age.

Preschool Predictors of Children's Social Adaptation to School

Family Relationships.   As we expected, variations in the tone of children's family relationships prior to their entry to school contributed to explanations of variance in children's adaptation to the social demands of kindergarten. In this chapter, we focused on children's initial school adjustment according to kindergarten teachers' ratings of their social behaviors at school in the spring—namely their overall social competence, antisocial behavior, and socially withdrawn behavior.

Similar to the pattern with children's self-perceptions, each family rela-tionship contributed differently to explaining variation in teachers' views of the children's social competence and adjustment, depending on the specific relationship and emotional process considered. When our staff observed mothers' and fathers' parenting as warm and positive in their separate inter-actions with the children prior to kindergarten, teachers rated the children as having higher levels of social competence and fewer signs of antisocial prob-lem behaviors the next year in kindergarten. When mothers' parenting was characterized as negative and angry in the last preschool year, teachers rated the children as lower on social competence and higher on antisocial behaviors the next year. These findings are consistent with evidence indicating that dur-ing the transition to school, the emotional quality of parent–child relation-ships functions as support, stressor, or both, thereby exerting a positive or negative influence on children's capacity to adapt to school (Cowan et al., 1994; Ladd, 1996). This fits with Ladd's (1996) reasoning that early par-ent–child relationships that are more supportive than punitive enhance the likelihood that children will employ prosocial rather than antisocial behav-iors when forming new peer relationships.

Contrary to expectation, the simple correlations in Table 6.3 revealed that warmth between the parents as they worked and played with their child was not directly related to children's self-reported social adjustment. Higher con-flict between the parents was only modestly associated with lower levels of so-cial competence and higher levels of antisocial behavior in kindergarten. These modest associations were surprising, given evidence documenting links between marital difficulties and children's maladjustment in older children (Fincham, 1998). Nevertheless, when each of the preschool dyadic par-ent–child and sibling relationship measures was entered simultaneously in multivariate regressions with coparenting affect, and all of the overlapping variance among these measures was statistically controlled, coparenting con-flict was the only unique predictor of children's social competence and anti-social behavior 1 year later. It should be noted that our measures of co-parenting affect were obtained while parents and children were involved in triadic interactions. It seems plausible that the effects of spouses' couple in-teraction processes on children are best detected in analytic strategies that simulate family-systems contexts (see chapter 10).

This finding illustrates another theme of the chapters in this volume. There are important links between method and substance in our field. What we find depends a great deal on how we measure constructs and especially how we think about and analyze the data. The reporting of simple correlations often obscures an underlying pattern that can only be revealed when we combine data from multiple domains. Almost every chapter in this volume finds asso-ciations between marital quality and children's outcomes, but they are not al-ways simple and direct.

In contrast with the lack of association between children's self-assessments of their social competence and the emotional quality of their relationships with siblings in the preschool period (discussed earlier), their reports of the early quality of sibling relationships predicted the quality of their peer relationships 1 year later in kindergarten. Consistent with evidence that children's sibling relationships help to shape their behavior with peers (Dunn, 1996; Patterson, 1986), children who described their earlier sibling relationships as more enjoyable and less hostile were rated by their teachers as making a more successful adjustment to peers in kindergarten. Of particular interest was the fact that, of all of the family relationships examined in the analyses presented here, only children's reports of sibling enjoyment were predictive of less socially withdrawn behavior in the classroom. Thus, children's capacity to derive pleasure from their relationship with a younger brother or sister—and possibly the practice siblings afford in negotiating an ongoing relationship with another child—may contribute to their desire to play with and meet other children, and act as a buffer against being shy or withdrawn once they enter the larger world of school. Alternatively, according to a social information model, a history of positive sibling interactions is likely to shape children's expectations that other children will be enjoyable and fun to play with (Crick & Dodge, 1994).

Children's Self-Perceptions.   In this investigation, children's perceptions of their social competence and acceptance by peers, as assessed with the BPI, were combined to create a single measure of self-perceived social adjustment. A unique aspect of this measure was that it was assessed during the preschool period, a relatively understudied period of self development. As expected, children's earlier self-perceptions of their social abilities were significantly correlated with their kindergarten teachers' ratings of their social competence, antisocial behavior, and sad-withdrawn behavior with peers at school. Moreover, when entered into a multivariate equation with the family relationship measures, children's self-perceptions added significant, unique variance to the prediction of their socioemotional behavior in kindergarten.

Although similar associations have been reported for older school-age children (Eccles et al., 1993), evidence for the relevance of preschoolers' self-perceptions to their school adaptation is relatively new. Other investigators have argued that children's behavior patterns, especially those in the peer domain, are among the best predictors of long-term psychosocial adjustment (Kupersmidt, Coie, & Dodge, 1990; Ladd, 1990). Further, systematic studies of social-cognition suggest that children's self-perception processes play central roles in their interpretation of social cues and the production of the interpersonal behaviors that shape their socioemotional adjustment at school (Crick & Dodge, 1994). To date, most studies showing a positive link between perceived social competence and social adjustment have been limited to children between the ages of 8 and 14 (Crick & Dodge, 1994). These findings extend this general connection downward to 4- to 5-year-old children.

In sum, these data are consistent with results of previous investigations that suggest that older children's negative social self-perceptions forecast, and may function as risk factors for, social maladjustment during elementary school. Data from this study suggest that children's negative views of self may be detectable as early as 4½ years old, before they embark on their school careers, a view that may be reflected in their teachers' assessments of their earliest school adaptation.

Children's Self-Perceptions as Mediators and Moderators of the Family-School Connection

The results of the analyses guided by Baron and Kenny's formulation (1986) provided evidence consistent with the hypothesis that children's self-perceptions function as mediators of relationships in which they are participants (parent–child), and as moderators of relationships in which they are primarily observers (the couple). Specifically, children's preschool self-perceptions acted as partial mediators of the links between the emotional qualities of their relationships with mothers and fathers and their social competence and antisocial behavior at school. Although coparenting and sibling relationships were also correlated with children's adaptation to kindergarten, only in the case of parent–child relationships did these self-perceptions link family processes with school outcomes. To the extent that we can interpret the connections as causal, the emotional quality of parent–child relationships may be affecting children's adaptation to school because they affect children's views of themselves, which, in turn, shape the way they approach other children in their classroom and on the playground.

By contrast, children's preschool social self-perceptions emerged as moderators of links between the parents' conflict with each other and children's actual social competence and antisocial behavior a year later in kindergarten. Graphs of these moderation effects suggest that children's positive social self-perceptions can protect them against the negative effects of conflict that children observe between their parents. It is also possible that children with more negative self-concepts are more vulnerable to their parents' conflict. In both cases, we can conclude that whether the parents' marital relationship affects the child depends in part on how the child evaluates his or her own characteristics.

How might we explain this differing role for children's self-perceptions, depending on whether they are participants in or observers of these key family relationships? As suggested earlier, children appear to extract information about themselves from direct interactions with their parents (see also Stipek et al., 1992). Mothers' and fathers' emotional expressions may be particularly laden with judgments about the child during interactions that challenge both children's talents and parents' competency to guide and support them. The primacy of these relationships, as well as children's reliance on their parents for evaluative feedback, make the parent–child relationship a particularly salient context for the children's development of a sense of self. By contrast, the parents' relationship with each other, even if it involves conflict while they are interacting with their children, may not hold quite the same meaning for the children's appraisals of themselves.

That children's self-perceptions played a moderating role in the links between family factors and school outcomes is consistent with evidence that children's appraisals of their parents' conflict (e.g., perceived conflict intensity, threat, self-blame) help to specify its level of impact on their adaptation (Ablow, 1997a; Grych & Fincham, 1990; Kerig, 1998). Children with less positive perceptions of themselves might be at increased risk of blaming themselves or feeling threatened by their parents' conflict. Their low self-esteem may leave them vulnerable to insecure working models of attachment, and the fear that they may lose their fighting parents through separation or divorce (Davies & Cummings, 1998). By contrast, children with more positive self-concepts may have the internal resources needed to discern that their parents' conflict is not necessarily about them.

The results from the mediation and moderation analyses must be viewed cautiously for several reasons. First, mediation requires that the independent variable be temporally and causally antecedent to the mediator, so that in this case, the relationship measures precede the children's self-perceptions. As mentioned, these conditions were assumed but could not be verified with these data. Second, when testing for moderation, Baron and Kenny (1986, p. 1176) suggested that it is "desirable that the moderator variable be uncorrelated with both the predictor and criterion to provide a clearly interpretable interaction term." In this case, as a moderator of the link between coparenting conflict and social adjustment, children's self-perceptions were associated with both variables. Finally, the use of a nonzero interaction term to detect moderation is problematic. Not only does the scaling of the independent and moderator variable affect the size of the interaction term (Aiken & West, 1991), but the use of different statistical methods on the same data (e.g., liner versus logistic versus log-linear models) can produce a significant interaction term with one but not another model. In other words, until replicated, reports of interactions should be viewed with caution.

The Lack of Connection With Internalizing Behavior

There was a surprising lack of connection of family relationship measures and self-perception measures with internalizing behavior. Simple correlations did show that children's self-perceptions and their perception of their relationship with their siblings showed low to moderate correlations with teachers' descriptions of shy, withdrawn, depressed behavior in the classroom. However, none of the mother–child, father–child, or coparenting variables assessed in the preschool period was directly connected with internalizing behavior at school 1 year later. Several possibilities require further investigation. First, it is possible that connections between these measures and internalizing emerge over time. Second, it may be, as we find in other chapters, that more global measures of parenting style that include both warmth and structure are needed to account for variations in shy, withdrawn, and sad behavior in school. Third, we return to the strategic decision to combine girls' and boys' subsamples because there were no significant differences in means or correlational patterns between them. Although the correlations did not occur more frequently than one would expect by chance, there is substantial evidence throughout this volume that there are some unique connections between family processes, especially the quality of mother–child relationships, and internalizing for girls. The sample of girls was too small to do the kind of mediator and moderator analyses reported here, so this issue needs to be resolved by replication studies with larger samples of girls.

CONCLUSIONS

Information from multiple family relationships can help to improve our understanding of the links between early family processes and children's early social adaptation to elementary school, especially their social competence and antisocial behavior. Different family relationships serve different functions in children's development, and unique contributions to understanding variations in adaptation to school come from the assessment of different family relationships within subsystem and family-systems analytical frameworks. Indeed, at the subsystem level, the affective qualities of the mother–child, father–child, sibling, and marital relationships each contributed differently to specific aspects of children's socioemotional development prior to and following their transition to elementary school. However, when these relationships were analyzed simultaneously, only the marital or coparenting relationship accounted for individual differences in children's social competence and externalizing behaviors at school, and only the sibling relationship accounted for variation in children's internalizing behaviors.

What is unique about this study is its inclusion of children's perceptions of their competence with and acceptance by peers before they enter elementary school. Two buffering effects were noteworthy. First, warmth between parents protected their children from the negative effects of marital conflict on the children's self-perceptions. And, children's positive self-perceptions pro-

tected them against the negative effects of marital conflict on social competence in the kindergarten classroom.

On the whole, the findings presented here offer a different view of young
children's social self-perceptions than has been offered previously (see review
by Harter, 1999). Rather than depicting young children's self-perceptions as
uniformly positive and therefore less relevant to their behavioral adjustment,
these results suggest that individual differences in the social self-perceptions
children possess before they enter elementary school are linked to socially
adaptive and maladaptive behaviors by the end of their first school year.
Even preschoolers know something about themselves that seems to shape
and predict their early development as students.

7

When Parents Conflict or Disengage: Children's Perceptions of Parents' Marital Distress Predict School Adaptation

Jennifer C. Ablow

During the past decade, research on the links between parents' marital conflict and children's outcomes has moved from demonstrating that marital conflict is a general risk factor for both internalizing behaviors (Johnston, Gonzalez, & Campbell, 1987; Peterson & Zill, 1986) and externalizing behaviors (Jenkins & Smith, 1991; Miller et al., 1993) to investigating specific aspects of marital conflict that may prove problematic for children (Cummings & Davies, 1994; Grych & Fincham, 1993; Jenkins & Smith, 1991; McHale, Freitag, Crouter, & Bartko, 1991). Two defining themes have emerged from these studies: (a) Not all parents express conflict in the same way, and (b) not all children react to marital distress in the same way.

This chapter focuses on some of the mechanisms that underlie the association between different types of marital conflict between parents and young children's socioemotional adjustment in kindergarten. In chapter 5, we examined the quality of the marriage as measured by parents' own reports of their marital satisfaction or adjustment and their division of labor in the daily care of their child. In chapter 6, we included our observers' perceptions of the couples as they worked and played with their children in our laboratory playroom. Here we add children's perceptions of conflict between their parents. We shall see, as we did in chapter 6, that young children's social cognitions—in this case their perceptions of their parents' relationship—add to our understanding of the links between familial dynamics and children's psychosocial adjustment as they enter elementary school.

The links between family processes and children's adaptation seem especially salient as children confront the academic and interpersonal challenges that accompany their initial adjustment to elementary school. We expected that family environments characterized by high levels of ineffectively negotiated marital tension might leave young children vulnerable to developing problematic ways of relating to others. Using structural equation modeling, we examined the overarching hypothesis that parents' overt and covert styles of handling marital conflict would be related to their children's perceptions of, and style of making sense of, their parents' conflict. In turn, we expected that the children's perceptions would be related to individual differences in their internalizing and externalizing symptomatology as they faced the challenges of starting school.

THE MULTIDIMENSIONAL NATURE
OF MARITAL CONFLICT

Researchers have begun to acknowledge that marital conflict is not unidimensional and that not all marital conflict is expressed overtly through shouting or fighting (Cummings & Davies, 1994; Fincham, 1998; Grych & Fincham, 1990; Katz & Woodin, 2002). In fact, disengagement from conflict has been identified by some marital investigators as one of the best predictors of marital distress and dissolution (Bradbury & Karney, 1993; Gottman, 1993; Levenson & Gottman, 1983). Disengagement has been identified as a style of handling conflict that may also reflect parents' attempts to manage their negative affect when their children are present or can overhear them. Some parents who hope to protect their children from their conflict by delaying their attempts to deal with their impasses "for the sake of the children" are curt, short, or silent with one another, at least when their children are present. We thought it possible that disengagement or conflict avoidance might lead to generalized tension in the family environment, which could contribute as much to children's distress or troubling behavior as overt, unrelieved bickering and shouting.

Children notice more about their parents' relationship than whether parents fight overtly. Several studies reveal that nonverbal expressions of anger are as distressing to children as verbally expressed anger (Ballard & Cummings, 1990; Cummings, Ballard, & El-Sheikh, 1991). However, we know little about how children make sense of hostility between their parents when it is not articulated or expressed directly. Because chronic, nonverbal anger between parents is difficult to identify or label, it may be a source of ongoing stress for children, but the effect of this stress requires further exploration. In this report, distinctions were made between strategies for handling marital conflict by overt disagreement, shouting, or hostility, and strategies that involved disengagement and withdrawal when the parents experienced tension between them. We hypothesized that overt and covert conflict strategies would be associated in different ways with children's expression of internalizing and externalizing symptomatology during their first year of school.

YOUNG CHILDREN'S PERCEPTIONS OF MARITAL CONFLICT

Young children have been a relatively neglected group in examinations of the effects of marital conflict on children's perceptions. Clearly, developmental age and ability play a role in how children make sense of and are affected by their parents' distress. Despite the fact that preschoolers are able to make inferences about why events happen, the sophistication of their causal reasoning is limited (Miller & Aloise, 1989). Older children are more likely to understand that a variety of factors might lead to their parents' conflict and be more adept at making appropriate causal attributions about conflict between their parents. Children who are at an egocentric level of thought (Piaget, 1967) may not understand that their parents' conflict may have little to do with them. Thus, children who are approaching the transition to school when they are between 4 and 6 years of age may be at heightened risk for blaming themselves and assuming that they created the difficulty between their parents, even if they actually play little or no role in their parents' distress. This vulnerability may be especially pronounced when parents' style of conflict is taken into consideration, with covert marital conflict strategies associated with young children's increased confusion as to who is responsible for the tension they perceive. Children entering kindergarten may be particularly vulnerable to family relationship problems as they make the transition from home to elementary school. As they enter kindergarten and face new and challenging social situations, they often call on the coping strategies they have witnessed at home or in their preschool environments. Thus, some children may be able to negotiate conflict successfully as they form new peer relationships, others may withdraw or disengage, whereas others still may resort to more antisocial, aggressive strategies.

To date, most researchers have relied on at least one parent's report to assess how much their children are exposed to or are aware of the parents' conflict as a couple (for exceptions, see Grych et al., 1992). Parents' reports may not provide the most accurate account of their children's awareness of conflict because some parents overestimate and others underestimate their children's exposure to, or awareness of, conflict between them. Although stress and coping theorists emphasize the mediating role of an individual's appraisal of stressful events in the genesis of emotional responses (Lazarus, 1992), there are surprisingly few empirical studies of children's interpretations of their parents' conflict as a couple.

Most hypotheses advanced to explain the relation between parents' marital conflict and children's adjustment assume that marital conflict affects children negatively. Lazarus (1992) suggested that stress responses must be viewed in terms of a transaction between the individual and the environment, and that the meaning, appraisal, and ultimate impact of the event are intrinsic to its significance. Accordingly, the same event may be perceived differently by different individuals. For example, some children may perceive their parents' conflict as benign and not relevant to them, whereas others may experience it as threatening and potentially harmful.

Grych and Fincham (1990) emphasized the central role of children's cognitive appraisal in shaping their response to, or interpretation of, their parents' marital conflict. In their investigations, Grych and his colleagues (1992) suggested that several kinds of appraisals, such as the perceived threat posed by parental conflict, the efficacy of the child's coping and the child's causal attributions concerning the source of the conflict and ascription of blame, may be particularly salient in the impact of marital conflict on children, their response to the conflict, and the risk for developing behavioral or emotional problems. Questionnaire measures that assess how children appraise marital conflict in these studies of older children were not appropriate for children below the age of about 8. In this study, we used the Berkeley Puppet Interview (BPI; see also chapter 6, this volume; Ablow & Measelle, 1993; Measelle, Ablow, Cowan, & Cowan, 1998)—a method developed to assess younger children's perceptions of their parents' marriage—to evaluate whether kindergarten children's perceptions were associated not only with their parents' particular styles of handling marital conflict but also with specific forms of adaptation or difficulty in adjusting to the first year of elementary school.

GIRLS VERSUS BOYS

In addition to considering individual children's appraisals of their parents' marital conflict, we explored the possibility that marital conflict may affect girls and boys differently (Kerig, Cowan, & Cowan, 1993; Osborne & Fincham, 1996). Not only is there evidence that mothers and fathers argue differently depending on whether they are in the presence of sons or daughters (Ablow & Suh, 1997; Hetherington, 1993), but some studies suggest that boys and girls have different ways of processing and responding to marital conflict (Cummings & Davies, 1994; Osborne & Fincham, 1996). To examine sex-specific associations between marital conflict and young children's internalizing and externalizing behaviors following entry into school, we tested separate structural models for sons and daughters.

INTERNALIZING AND EXTERNALIZING

Reviews of research on factors involved in children's mental health outcomes point to marital processes as significant predictors of behavior problems (Gotlib & Goodman, 1999; Sheeber et al., 1997). Although marital discord has been linked to academic difficulties, children from high conflict homes are particularly vulnerable to both internalizing and externalizing problems (Davies & Forman, 2002; Goodman, 2002; Ingoldsby, Shaw, Owens, & Winslow, 1999). Many children will outgrow early mood dysregulation and problem behaviors arising in high conflict homes, but the presence of these behaviors around the transition to school is a strong predictor of mental health trajectories that reflect chronic maladaptation. The analyses in this chapter focus on explicating some of the marital and familial processes that might function as early antecedents or risk factors that predict difficulties in children's initial adjustment to school in typically developing children.

HYPOTHESES

1. With the use of structural equation models, we expected to find that high levels of overt and covert marital conflict combine with data on children's reports of parental fighting, and whether they blame themselves for the fights, to predict internalizing and externalizing behavior in kindergarten. Although structural models cannot establish the direction of effects, we expected that models consistent with a family socialization perspective (marital interaction → child perception → child adaptation) would be more useful than alternative models that give primacy to children's adaptation as the engine driving the system.

2. We predicted that overt and covert parental fighting during a family interaction task would have different path links to children's perceptions and kindergarten outcomes.

3. Without being able to make specific predictions, we explored the possibility that there would be different pathways for girls and boys linking marital conflict, children's perceptions, and adaptation to school.

METHOD

Participants

Because one of the central constructs in this investigation—children's perceptions of their parents' conflict—was not assessed at prekindergarten (PRE) for children in the first of the three waves of families in the larger study, data for the 80 families (46 boys and 34 girls) included in this report were drawn from the kindergarten (POST 1) assessments. In the context of this study, it would have been preferable to obtain children's perceptions of their parents' marriage before they entered school, but the BPI items on the family were not created in time to be administered to the whole sample, resulting in the present shorter-term longitudinal design (fall kindergarten family observations to spring kindergarten teacher reports of children's internalizing and externalizing symptomatology). It seems unlikely that children's experiences in school could color their perceptions of their parents' marriage, but because this possibility exists, it would be helpful to replicate the findings within a longitudinal design and reexamine the hypotheses to test for more complex models of mediation or moderation.

Children's mean age was 5.9 ($SD = .38$) at the time of the kindergarten teachers' spring assessments of them. Both children and parents in this subsample were similar in age, income, and ethnicity to those in the larger study (see chapter 2 for recruitment procedures and demographic details), and the parents did not differ in level of marital satisfaction.

Measures

Marital Interaction.   At the conclusion of the family visit in the fall of the kindergarten year, trained observers provided global ratings of husbands' and wives' behavior toward one another as they worked and played with their child in a number of structured and open-ended tasks (chapter 2 provides a detailed description of the tasks and the global rating system). The fall ratings of the couple during the whole family visit were used as an index of the marital tension to which children were exposed during their first year of elementary school. Because we were interested in both overt and covert conflict for this chapter, we combined the ratings of marital tension in a slightly different way than that described in chapter 2, by using two conceptually distinct aspects of conflict expression. The first, overt conflict expressed between the parents through the direct exchange of anger, included measures of competition, anger, disagreement, coldness, and displeasure. The second, disengaged conflict, reflected covert tension expressed between the parents through behaviors such as withdrawing from interaction or not responding to one another; this factor included reverse scored measures of pleasure, warmth, interactiveness, and responsiveness.

A Principal Components Factor Analysis was conducted next to test the degree to which overt and disengaged forms of conflict were identifiable and separable. When rotated to a varimax solution, the results yielded clearly identifiable overt and disengaged factors that together accounted for 73.1%

of the total variance in the factor structure (46.0% and 27.1%, respectively). As an additional test, separate overt and disengaged scale scores were computed by taking the average of each factor's respective subscale scores. The correlation between the overt and disengaged scales was considerable, $r(78) =$ .56, $p < .001$, but the two were not redundant.

Children's Perceptions and Processing of Marital Conflict. The BPI (Ablow & Measelle, 1993) was used to measure children's perceptions of their parents' relationship during a home visit in the summer before they entered kindergarten. Here, we report on two BPI parent relationship scales: (a) children's perceptions of marital conflict scale, and (b) children's self-blame scale. The children's perception of marital conflict scale was selected to provide an index of the degree of conflict children perceive and acknowledge to occur between their parents. The scale is comprised of three items from the BPI: (a) "My parents have fights"/"My parents don't have fights," (b) "My parents fight a lot."/"My parents don't fight a lot," and (c) "When my parents have a fight, they stay mad for a long time"/"When my parents have a fight, they don't stay mad for a long time," $\alpha = .55$. The children's self-blame scale, designed to assess children's tendency to blame themselves for the conflict they perceive between their parents, was included to assess one way that children process their parents' fights (e.g., "It's my fault when my parents have a fight"/"It isn't my fault when my parents have a fight"). Because young children are particularly vulnerable to blaming themselves for family tensions, it was thought that this measure of cognitive processing might be particularly salient for most children in this 5- to 6-year-old age group. Four items from the BPI address children's tendency to blame themselves for their parents' conflict, $\alpha = .69$. Despite the relatively low alpha of the children's perceptions of marital conflict scale, earlier studies using the BPI showed consistent patterns of association between children's perceptions of parents' fighting and ratings of the marital interaction by adult observers (Ablow, 1997b). Furthermore, the items from this scale loaded highly when included in the larger structural equation measurement model as manifest variables (see Table 7.2).

The Child's Adaptation to School. We used kindergarten teachers' ratings of the children's behavior during the spring semester on the Child Adaptive Behavior Inventory (CABI) as measures of children's adjustment to the first year of school. The latent variable representing depressed, anxious, internalizing behavior included scales assessing depression, anxiety, and somatization. The latent variable representing aggressive externalizing behavior included scales assessing antisocial, oppositional, and hostile behavior.

RESULTS

Overview

Results of path models examining both observers' and children's reports of parents' styles of handling marital conflict were consistent with a socialization hypothesis: how parents expressed their conflict as a couple was related to children's perceptions of their parents' conflict, which, in turn, was linked to internalizing and externalizing behavior at the end of the kindergarten year. The models suggested that overt and covert marital conflict have differential links with children's perceptions of conflict, and that perceptions of conflict have different connections with internalizing and externalizing for girls and boys.

Descriptive Statistics

Table 7.1 presents the means, standard deviations, and *t* tests for differences between boys' and girls' manifest variables in the various models. There were no statistically significant mean differences between mothers and fathers of 5- to 6-year-old boys and girls in terms of observed marital conflict or between daughters' and sons' perceptions of their parents' marital conflict, and no differences in teachers' perceptions of the degree to which boys and girls expressed anxious and depressed behavior in kindergarten (see also chapter 3). Nevertheless, as was the case for externalizing scores reported in chapter 3 (analyses based on the same data), kindergarten teachers rated boys as exhibiting higher mean levels of aggressive externalizing and hostile behavior than girls. There were no differences in teachers' ratings of boys' and girls' oppositionality. Separate models for boys and girls were run to determine whether the patterns of associations among the tested constructs varied with the sex of the child.

Analytic Strategy

Latent Variable Path Analysis with Partial Least Squares estimation (LVPLS; Falk & Miller, 1992; Lohmoeller, 1989; Wold, 1982) was used to examine the relations among observers' ratings of parents' conflict resolution strategies as a couple, children's perceptions and processing of their parents' conflict as a couple, and children's problem behaviors during their first year of elementary school. By using this analytic technique (see chapter 2 for detailed discussion of LVPLS), we were able to explore the hypothesis that parents' marital conflict and children's behavioral adjustment are linked through children's per-

TABLE 7.1
Descriptive Statistics and Results of *t* Tests of Differences Between Girls'
and Boys' Manifest Variables

Variable	Range	Girls		Boys		
		M	SD	M	SD	t
Overt marital conflict						
Competition	1–4.5	1.94	.81	1.93	.80	−.05
Disagreement	1–4.5	1.82	.80	1.81	.84	−.06
Coldness	1–4.5	2.24	1.01	2.21	.78	−.17
Displeasure						
Covert marital conflict						
Pleasure (reverse scored)	2–6	3.24	.84	3.42	.90	.91
Warmth (reverse scored)	2–6	3.57	.92	3.55	.94	.12
Interactiveness (reverse scored)	1–4	2.13	.77	2.38	.63	1.59
Responsiveness (reverse scored)	1–4	2.17	.75	2.24	.57	.43
Children's perceived marital conflict						
Parents have fights	1–6	3.46	1.56	3.12	1.51	−1.07
Parents fight a lot	1–6	2.45	1.25	2.47	1.26	.09
Parents stay mad for a long time	1–6.5	2.94	1.58	2.95	1.67	.05
Children's perceived self-blame						
My fault	1.5–5.75	2.53	1.03	2.27	.67	−1.39
Mad at me	1.75–6	2.88	1.18	2.62	1.00	−1.11
Anxious and depressed behavior						
Depressed	1–3.83	1.55	.67	1.67	.72	.80
Anxious	1–3.60	1.83	.67	1.94	.78	.68
Somatic complaints	1–3.40	1.74	.70	1.56	.59	−1.31
Aggressive externalizing behavior						
Antisocial	1–3.0	1.26	.39	1.61	.64	3.18**
Oppositional	1–3.17	1.58	.57	1.80	.57	1.65
Hostile	1–3.75	1.40	.54	1.71	.71	2.35*

Note. $N = 80$. $n = 34$ (girls). $n = 46$ (boys).
*$p < .05$. **$p < .01$.

ceptions of their parents' conflict, and to describe the potentially different patterns of connections among these constructs for girls and boys.

Testing Four LVPLS Models

LVPLS models were used to examine the linkages among five latent constructs created from 16 manifest variables selected for each structural equation (see Table 7.2): (a) overt marital conflict, (b) covert marital conflict, (c) children's perceptions of how much their parents fight, (d) children's tendency to blame themselves for parents' fighting, and (e) teachers' ratings of children's adaptation. Four models were constructed to predict girls' and

TABLE 7.2
Latent Variable Path Analysis With Partial Least Squares:
Loadings on Manifest Variables

| | Outcome | | | |
| | Anxious and Depressed | | Aggressive Externalizing | |
Latent Variable (LV)	Girls	Boys	Girls	Boys
LV1: Overt marital conflict				
Competition	.85	.91	.86	.89
Disagreement	.80	.87	.80	.85
Coldness	.89	.91	.89	.92
Displeasure	.90	.89	.89	.91
LV2: Covert marital conflict				
Pleasure (reverse scored)	.86	.65	.86	.60
Warmth (reverse scored)	.90	.91	.90	.91
Interactiveness (reverse scored)	.90	.93	.89	.93
Responsiveness (reverse scored)	.84	.91	.84	.91
LV3: Children's perceived marital conflict				
Parents have fights	.80	.87	.80	.90
Parents fight a lot	.74	.65	.74	.61
Parents stay mad for a long time	.98	.99	.99	.99
LV4: Children's perceived self-blame				
My fault	.99	.98	.98	.94
Mad at me	.60	.73	.60	.77
LV5: Anxious and depressed behavior				
Depressed	.77	.82		
Anxious	.87	.74		
Somatic complaints	.68	.77		
LV6: Aggressive externalizing behavior				
Antisocial			.90	.85
Oppositional			.88	.93
Hostile			.93	.92

boys' internalizing and externalizing in kindergarten (see Fig. 7.1, 7.2, 7.3, and 7.4).

The Measurement Models. Each latent variable comprised a minimum of two measures from the same source, with three different sources included in each model (staff observers, the child, the teacher). Correlations among couple interaction, children's perceptions, and teachers' ratings of classroom behavior were not inflated by coming from the same source.

Examination of the measurement model revealed that the manifest variables in all four models were reasonable indicators of their latent constructs. The mean communality index in both boys' and girls' models ranged from .70

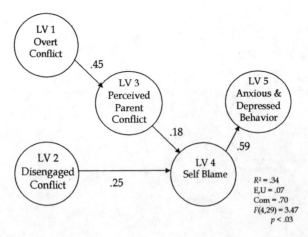

FIG. 7.1.   Path model with girls' anxious and depressed (internalizing) behavior as outcome.

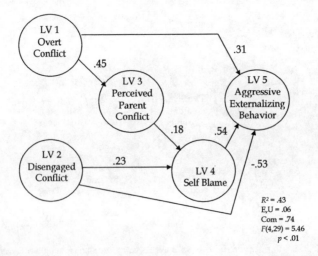

FIG. 7.2.   Path model with girls' aggressive externalizing behavior as outcome.

to .76, indicating adequately derived latent constructs (Falk & Miller, 1992). The manifest loadings for each of the child gender and outcome models are presented in Table 7.2. All path models in this study yielded Root Mean Square Covariance (RMS COV [E,U]) coefficients from .06 to .07, indicating a good fit between model and data.

The Structural Models.   For girls, the models accounted for a statistically significant 34% of the variance in internalizing behavior, $F(4, 29) = 3.73$, $p < .05$, and a statistically significant 43% of the variance in externalizing be-

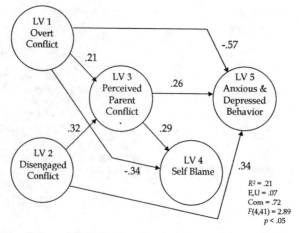

FIG. 7.3.   Path model with boys' anxious and depressed (internalizing) behavior as outcome.

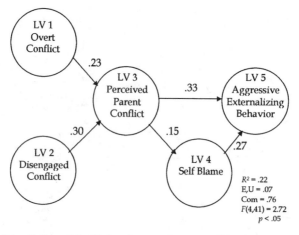

FIG. 7.4.   Path model with boys' aggressive externalizing behavior as outcome.

haviors, $F(4, 29) = 5.46$, $p < .01$, as reported by kindergarten teachers. For boys, the models accounted for a statistically significant 22% of the variance in externalizing behavior, $F(4, 41) = 2.89$, $p < .05$, and a statistically significant 21% of the variance in internalizing behaviors, $F(4, 41) = 2.72$, $p < .05$. In other words, as hypothesis 1 suggested, a combination of observations of the parents' interactions as a couple while they worked with their children on challenging tasks during the preschool visit to our laboratory, and their daughters' or sons' perceptions of the parents' patterns of handling conflict, accounted for moderate to high proportions of the variance in children's anxious, depressed or angry, aggressive behavior at the end of the kindergarten year.

Comparison of the Socialization Perspective With Other Approaches.
Although we recognize that children can contribute to both the frequency and content of their parents' conflict, the arrangement of the latent variables in Fig. 7.1 to 7.4 is consistent with theories of socialization in which parents' characteristics and behaviors (overt and disengaged conflict) predict outcomes in their young children (perceptions of parent conflict, self-blame, and behavioral adjustment in school).[1]

Because other processes might provide competing explanations for the associations among the variables presented in Fig. 7.1, two alternative models were tested and compared to the socialization model. In the first comparison model, we reasoned that marital conflict could explain variance in children's behavior, which, in turn, would contribute to children's perceptions. Because children's developing social perceptions and self-related appraisals may be abstracted from actual experience, it is plausible that both marital conflict and children's actual classroom behaviors might shape their perceptions of themselves and their parents. The second competing model tested a child-effects hypothesis in which children's behavior contributes to marital conflict and to children's perceptions. Child temperament research (e.g., Bates, 2001) provides support for the notion that hard-to-manage children can contribute to marital discord. Despite the theoretical plausibility of these competing models, neither the models' fit indexes (total variance explained and root mean squared) nor the path weights provided stronger explanations of the data than the socialization models depicted in Fig. 7.1 to 7.4.

Overt and Covert Couple Conflict and Children's Perceptions

The pattern of results supports hypothesis 2, that there are different pathways between the two styles of handling couple conflict and children's perceptions. Furthermore, the patterns differed for girls and boys. When parents engaged in higher levels of overt conflict with each other during the family interaction with their daughters in our playroom, as observers described it (Fig. 7.1 and 7.2), the daughters reported that their parents had higher levels of marital conflict and they tended to blame themselves for their parents' fights. When parents engaged in higher levels of disengagement or covert conflict, daughters did not report that their parents fought a lot, but the girls were more likely to blame themselves for any parental conflict that did occur.

---

[1]In chapter 11, we demonstrate that the quality of parents' marital interaction does indeed affect the school outcomes under discussion here.

By contrast, boys' reports of higher levels of fighting between parents were associated with both overt and covert couple conflict observed during the family interaction with their sons in our playroom (Fig. 7.3 and 7.4). Although the effect sizes[2] were small, it was the case in all four structural equations that, the more children described their parents as fighting a lot, the more they tended to blame themselves for their parents' conflict.

Sex Differences in Pathways Linking Marital Conflict, Children's Perceptions, and Children's Adaptation to School

Now, we turn to similarities and differences among the models connecting couple conflict, 6-year-old children's perceptions of that conflict, and children's behavior in the classroom at the end of the kindergarten year. As expected, girls' and boys' models revealed different pathways from parents' marital conflict to daughters' and sons' problem behaviors at school. Pathways reflect path weights (PW; standardized beta weight between variables) that met criteria specified in chapter 2.

Girls' Anxious and Depressed Behavior. In Fig. 7.1, different pathways linked observers' ratings of parents' overt and covert marital conflict with girls' tendency to blame themselves, but regardless of its source, self-blame assessed in the fall of the kindergarten year predicted anxious, depressed, internalizing behaviors 6 months later. Higher overt marital conflict during the family interaction tasks was associated with girls' perceptions that their parents fought a lot ($pw = .45$). In turn, girls' perceptions of higher levels of conflict between their parents were associated with their tendency to blame themselves for their parents' arguments ($pw = .18$). We reported earlier that parents who were disengaged were not seen by their daughters as having high conflict, but the girls tended to blame themselves for any conflict their parents displayed ($pw = .25$). Finally, girls' tendency to feel responsible for their parents' fighting was linked with their teachers' views of them as exhibiting higher levels of anxious and depressed behavior in the spring of the kindergarten year ($pw = .59$).

Girls' Aggressive Externalizing Behavior. Similar to the path model for girls' depressed and anxious behavior, Fig. 7.2 showed that marital conflict was indirectly connected to aggressive externalizing behavior through links with the girls' perceptions of their parents' marriage. However, in this case, there were also direct links from the couples' marital conflict to their daugh-

---

[2]The effect size—amount of variance explained—is the product of the path weight times the correlation between the two latent variables.

ters' aggressive externalizing behavior in kindergarten. As hypothesized, a higher level of overt conflict between the parents during the playroom visit was related to a higher level of aggressive externalizing behavior in kindergarten ($pw = .31$). Unexpectedly, high ratings of withdrawn and disengaged behavior between parents were associated with lower levels of externalizing behavior in kindergarten girls ($pw = -.53$).

Boys' Anxious and Depressed Behavior. Paths linking observers' and sons' reports of marital conflict with teachers' ratings of boys' anxious and depressed behavior in kindergarten are presented in Fig. 7.3. As in the models for girls, when parents of boys engaged in more overt marital conflict in our project playroom, their sons reported more conflict between their parents ($pw = .21$) and their teachers were more likely to report that the boys showed anxious and depressed behaviors at the end of kindergarten year ($pw = .26$). However, contrary to expectations, observations of overt conflict between parents in front of their sons in our project playroom were linked directly with teachers' descriptions of boys as less anxious and depressed in kindergarten ($pw = -.57$). Also unexpected was the fact that parents' high overt conflict was associated with sons' reports of less self-blaming ($pw = -.34$). Boys' self-blame concerning their parents' conflict was not associated with teachers' ratings of internalizing behavior as it was for girls.

The paths from more covert or disengaged conflict between parents of boys provided a contrasting pattern with overt conflict and with the models for parents of girls. First, as hypothesized, parents' disengaged style of handling conflict was associated directly with boys showing more anxious and depressed behavior at school according to their teachers' descriptions on the CABI ($pw = .34$). The second pathway revealed an indirect connection. When observers noted parents' tendency to disengage from conflict as a couple, their sons were more likely to report higher levels of conflict between the parents ($pw = .32$) and that, in turn, was related to teachers' reports of more internalizing behavior in the spring of the kindergarten year ($pw = .26$).

Boys' Aggressive Externalizing Behavior. The path model linking observers' and sons' reports of marital conflict with teachers' ratings of aggressive externalizing behavior was different from the model of boys' depressed and anxious behaviors. As shown in Fig. 7.4, observers' reports of marital conflict behaviors were not associated directly with boys' externalizing classroom behaviors. Rather, observers' ratings of spouses' overt and disengaged conflict styles were linked to sons' perceptions of more conflict between their parents ($pw = .30$), which, in turn, were associated with their teachers' reports of higher levels of aggressive externalizing behavior in kindergarten ($pw = .23$).

The second major difference between boys' internalizing and externalizing models occurred in relation to boys' perceptions of their parents' conflict.

Boys' tendency to blame themselves for their parents' conflict was not related to their internalizing behavior in kindergarten. However, perceptions of conflict between their parents were linked both directly ($pw = .33$) and indirectly to sons' externalizing behavior. When boys perceived higher conflict between their parents, they were more likely to blame themselves for these problems ($pw = .18$) and to engage in more externalizing behaviors at school later that year ($pw = .27$).

DISCUSSION

Explaining Variance in Internalizing and Externalizing Behavior

Hypothesis 1, that staff-observed marital conflict and children's perceptions of it would combine to explain variance in kindergarten adaptation, was supported. The four Latent Variable Partial Least Squares (LVPLS) models presented in Fig. 7.1 to 7.4 yielded statistically significant regression coefficients that accounted for 21% to 43% of the variance in children's internalizing and externalizing behavior. Furthermore, although we could not test the statistical significance of the differences, models that assumed a socialization perspective in which parents' conflict was the independent variable and children's behavior in kindergarten was the dependent variable fit the data better than models that posited children's problem behavior as the independent variable affecting parents' level of conflict.

The general pattern of results linking parents' styles of handling conflict and their young children's perceptions of those patterns is consistent with findings of connections between parents' marital conflict and older children's behavior outside the family (see Cummings & Davies, 1994). In this study, we found such links in families with 5- to 6-year-olds setting out on their school careers. Consistent with a family systems orientation to children's development, the findings highlight the importance of the parents' marital atmosphere—and their children's appraisal of it—to the children's development of relationships with others during their early days at school. The main focus of the analyses was on how this linkage occurs.

Children's Perceptions of Marital Conflict in Couples With Overt and Disengaged Patterns

Across all models, observers' ratings of the parents as argumentative and angry with one another during the family's visit to our project were consistently related to children's perceptions that their parents fight or have arguments. Just as trained observers who were unfamiliar with the family noticed overt conflict between parents when they were working and playing with their children, children as young as 5 to 6 years old were aware of their parents' conflict and described it to the puppets during the BPI. With parents who disengaged or withdrew, boys reported that they fought a lot, but girls did not. That is, if we can assume that the differences lie in perceptions and not in willingness to report, we could conclude from these data that boys may be more sensitive to the unspoken tensions between their parents than are girls. Of course, such a conclusion requires further exploration and replication.

Regardless of the parents' style of handling conflict during the laboratory visit, higher levels of perceived conflict between parents were associated with higher levels of self-blame for both girls and boys about to enter kindergarten. In only one of the four analyses was there a direct link between observed conflict and self-blame, and that was in a direction opposite to the general trends (high overt conflict, low self-blame for boys). Perhaps parents' open expression of their conflict may lead some boys to conclude that the conflict between their parents is a "parent" problem that has nothing to do with them; for these boys, overt conflict appears to be associated with lower levels of self-blame and lower levels of internalizing problems. The results provide some support for Lazarus's (1999) conclusion that it is not only whether parents actually fight, but whether children appraise their behavior as fighting, that plays a role in whether children feel responsible for their parents' marital distress.

Pathways to Aggressive and Depressed Behaviors in Kindergarten

Direct Connections: Marital Conflict and Kindergarten Adjustment. Parents' overt and covert styles of handling conflict were directly linked with teachers' ratings of girls' aggressive externalizing behavior but not their anxious and depressed behavior. Overt marital conflict, as we observed it in the fall of the kindergarten year, was associated with higher aggression shown by the girls in the spring of that year, but covert conflict predicted lower aggression. In brief, parents with high levels of overt fighting during a family interaction task tended to have girls who fought with others in kindergarten.

By contrast, covert and overt marital conflict were directly linked with teachers' ratings of boys' anxious and depressed behavior, but not their externalizing, aggressive behavior. Parents who were more disengaged had sons who were more anxious and depressed in the classroom 6 months later, whereas boys whose parents fought overtly were less anxious and depressed. In brief, parents with high levels of covert fighting had sons who were likely to be more withdrawn in the classroom.

Social learning theory would suggest that the direct link between children's tendency to be disobedient, uncooperative, and argumentative in the classroom is based on imitation. The children may be employing tactics learned from their parents to get something that they want to play with, to get others to do something for them, or to resolve problems with peers or teachers. From the point of view of emotion regulation dynamics, direct links between ratings of parents' overt handling of conflict and their children's aggressive behavior support the "spill-over" hypothesis, in which conflict in the marital system spills over and acts as a palpable stressor for the child. Children experiencing stress in their key family relationships may begin to rely on dominant, well-learned coping responses that are less mature or adaptive (Spielberger, 1979). Exposure to their parents' anger may be experienced as internally disequilibrating, leading children to act out in more oppositional, hostile ways or to hesitate to form new relationships, which could result in social isolation and signs of depression.

Indirect Connections: Marital Conflict, Self-Blame, and Children's Adaptation. There were different links between girls' and boys' tendency to blame themselves for their parents' conflict as a couple and their own problem behaviors in kindergarten. When parents tended to fight overtly, daughters reported higher levels of marital conflict, tended to blame themselves for it, and were more likely to show anxious and aggressive externalizing behavior in the first year of elementary school. When the parents had more disengaged ways of handling the conflict between them, their daughters tended to blame themselves and show more anxious or antisocial behavior at school. Thus, young daughters appeared to feel responsible for conflict between their parents regardless of how their parents handled it, and those perceptions were associated with more troubling behavior in their first year of school. This suggests that daughters' intrapsychic processing of their parents' conflict may serve as a critical link between parents' withdrawal or disengagement and their daughters' symptoms of anxiety or depression as they begin their schooling.

An unexpected finding was that, despite the fact that most theories tend to associate self-blame with depression (e.g., Beck, 1963), children in this study who blamed themselves for their parents' fighting were as likely to be aggressive as they were to be anxious or depressed at the beginning of their school careers. This finding is counter to results from studies of older children (e.g., Grych et al., 2000), but we could not find studies of this issue in girls in the early years of elementary school. It is possible that the link between self-blame for parents' distress and children's depression becomes solidified only after the children develop the self-consciousness associated with adolescence (Elkind, 1985). Before that time, blaming oneself for parents' fighting may be equally likely to lead to social withdrawal or anger and peer aggression, or both.

Sex Differences in Patterns.   Self-blame for their parents' fights played a different role in explaining boys' externalizing and internalizing behaviors than it did in girls' problem behavior in the kindergarten classroom. When parents handled their conflict overtly, their sons were less likely to feel responsible for the parents' problems and less likely to be anxious or depressed at school. But, when parents avoided engaging directly in their marital differences in the presence of their sons, the boys were more likely to report that their parents had a good deal of conflict and more likely to blame themselves for the difficulties. Their teachers, in turn, were more likely to describe them as anxious or depressed at school. Despite parents' attempts to hide their conflict when the child was present, it is possible that the boys especially were preoccupied with their parents' struggles.

CONCLUSIONS

Whatever the explanation of the linking mechanisms, there are implications for parents and for intervention in these results. It appears that parents' withdrawal or disengagement from conflict in front of their young children does not protect them from the negative effects of parents' troubling differences. Parents' withdrawal or disengagement from conflict was associated with sons' tendency to be anxious and depressed and daughters' tendency to blame themselves and show signs of depression or aggressive behavior at school. These findings suggest that parents' conflict strategies would be a fruitful family arena to target in preschool interventions so that girls and boys can enter school with less vulnerability to problems in relating to others. Chapter 11 describes the results of such an intervention offered to some of the parents in the larger study.

The PLS models in this chapter explained between 21% and 43% of the variance in the children's outcome variables, but a substantial portion of the variance in their kindergarten adaptation remained unexplained. Some of the limitations in explanatory power may have been due to the measures used here. Although the study employed multiple informants and multiple measures of marital conflict, only single scales were used here to define the child's perception of parents' conflict and their tendency to blame themselves for its occurrence. Observers were used to rate parents' interaction as a couple, but the rating scales were global in nature and did not allow us to assess microanalytic sequences such as patterns of escalating negative conflict that have been shown to be detrimental to couples and to their children (Katz & Gottman, 1993).

In this investigation, the scores reflecting parents' interaction as a couple were scores for the couple. Future investigations might fruitfully consider ratings of each partner's behavior toward his or her spouse, rather than rely-ing solely on ratings of the parents' behavior as a couple. Independent scores for husbands and wives could make a significant contribution to our under-standing of the role of gender in parents' management of conflict and their children's experience of it. Those data would allow us to examine whether mothers and fathers express conflict in front of their children differently, and whether those differences have differential effects on sons' and daughters' perceptions, behavior, or overall adaptation. Observations of each parent separately would also further our understanding of whether the same sex or opposite sex parent's approach to conflict explains additional variance in children's experience of conflict—between their parents and in their own rela-tionships with others.

We draw several conclusions from the present findings in the context of previous chapters. The general topic is understanding the links between par-ents' marital quality and children's emotional and social adaptation to kin-dergarten. The results in chapter 5 suggest that sex-stereotyped parenting that follows from an unsatisfying marriage plays a role in understanding vari-ations in children's internalizing and externalizing. Chapter 6 focuses on ob-served coparenting during a family interaction task and the ways in which parent–child relationships and children's self-perceptions predict adaptation to kindergarten. Here in chapter 7, we considered the possibility that chil-dren's perceptions of their parents' conflict and their attributions about the source of this conflict also account for variation in children's adaptation to kindergarten. Perhaps the most significant implication of the findings in this chapter is that young children appear to be keenly aware of conflict between their parents, and more specifically, that they are actively working to make sense of the conflict they perceive; both are related to their behavioral adjust-ment as they make their transition to elementary school.

The results also emphasize the need to take different aspects of marital conflict into account rather than treat all conflict alike. Despite the fact that marital researchers have identified the tactics of disengagement from conflict and "stonewalling" as serious predictors of marital distress, most investiga-tors of child development have focused solely on parents' overt marital con-flict. By including observational ratings of couples' level of both overt and disengaged styles of handling marital conflict, this study helped elucidate re-lationships among parents' marital conflict, their children's perceptions of it, and the children's subsequent adjustment to school.

8

Parents' Working Models of Attachment: The Intergenerational Context of Parenting and Children's Adaptation to School

Philip A. Cowan, Isabel Bradburn,
and Carolyn Pape Cowan

This chapter adds an intergenerational dimension to our examination of parent–child and marital relationships as they predict children's adaptation to elementary school. A common belief, buttressed by empirical data, is that patterns of parenting tend to be repeated from one generation to another (Smith & Drew, 2002; Van IJzendoorn, 1992). To examine this belief, we did not have an opportunity to meet the parents of the parents in our study (the children's grandparents) or to observe the interactions among grandparents, parents, and children, although the grandparents often seemed psychologically present in the interviews we conducted with the children's parents at each follow-up. Instead, we obtained information about the parent participants' early and current relationships with their parents using a partially-structured 90-min Adult Attachment Interview (AAI) created by George et al. (1985). We found that AAI codes representing qualities of the early and current relationships between parents and grandparents added significantly to our ability to predict early school outcomes for children, over and above our observations of the parents' marital interaction and parenting style as they worked and played with their child in our project playroom.

A growing body of research demonstrates that parents' narrative accounts of relationships with their parents are highly correlated with the observed quality of relationships they have with their children. For example, studies find relatively high concordance between mothers' working models of attachment, based on their responses to the AAI about relationships in their families of origin, and their infant's security of attachment after a brief separation

(Ainsworth et al., 1978; Steele, Steele, & Fonagy, 1996; van IJzendoorn, 1995). In turn, children's attachment status in infancy predicts their attachment status and the quality of relationships they have with their parents and peers in early and middle childhood (Sroufe, Carlson, & Shulman, 1993). These findings have been used to support hypotheses about the continuity of parent–child relationship quality across the generations. In this chapter, we examine the possibility that one of the mechanisms involved in this transmission is the quality of the marital relationship between the parents.

STATES OF MIND REGARDING ATTACHMENT

Within attachment theory, the psychological constructs used to explain intergenerational links between parents' mental models of attachment and their children's adaptation or dysfunction are drawn from Bowlby's conception of "working models" (1988) and Main et al.'s (1985) related construct of "state of mind with reference to attachment." The data on working models and states of mind in adults and children come from different sources, but descriptions of the major attachment styles or categories are quite similar. Both Bowlby and Main and her colleagues characterized a working model or state of mind regarding parent–child relationships as secure when adults or children are able to think about or use their parents as a secure base (Bowlby, 1988)—a source of comfort, to whom they can turn under conditions of heightened stress, and from whom they can venture to explore their surroundings when stress is at manageable levels. A secure state of mind implies not only that the person can expect help from parents, but also that the self is worthy of support and being taken care of, especially when an important relationship is threatened (Bartholomew & Horowitz, 1991).

Attachments characterized as insecure generally take one of three forms for both adults and children: (a) the adult seems to dismiss the importance of relationships with attachment figures, whereas the child avoids the attachment figure; (b) the adult is preoccupied, sometimes angrily, with details about attachment experiences, whereas the young child behaves in an angry, clinging, ambivalent manner when the parent returns from an absence; or (c) the adult makes linguistic slips suggestive of failure to monitor the discourse, whereas the child becomes disorganized around issues of separation and loss (Hesse, 1999).

How does a secure or insecure working model of parent–child relationships develop? "Since there is evidence that the pattern of attachment a child ... develops with his mother is the product of how his mother has treated him (Ainsworth et al., 1978), it is more than likely that, in a similar way, the pattern he develops with his father is the product of how his father has treated him" (Bowlby, 1988, p. 10). That is, attachment patterns evolve in the course of early experience with key attachment figures. Although working models can shift from secure to insecure or vice versa if the young child's relationship with his or her parent changes (Vaughn, Egeland, Sroufe, & Waters, 1978), Bowlby (1988) assumed that "once built, evidence suggests, these models of the parent and self in interaction tend to persist and are so taken for granted that they come to operate at an unconscious level" (p. 130). Working models of attachment to parents are usually conceptualized as templates, governing children's expectations and interactions in other close relationships, especially with peers and with romantic partners in adolescence and adulthood (Hazan & Shaver, 1994). The assumption is that these templates help to maintain continuities across different close relationships by shaping both expectations for what can happen in intimate relationships and behavior toward potential attachment figures.

ATTACHMENT ACROSS GENERATIONS AND FAMILY DOMAINS

The high degree of concordance among parents' schemas or working models of attachment with their own parents, their children's behavior in relationship to them, and the children's relationships with their peers (Berlin & Cassidy, 1999), is especially impressive because these links have been established using different methods (adult narratives, observations of parent–child interaction, peer reports), across measurement contexts (interview, laboratory, school), and across time. And yet, we know surprisingly little about the mechanisms that underlie this strong tendency to repeat relationship patterns from one generation to another and from one relationship context to another.

The research so far tends to examine connections between mental representations of attachment to parents in the family of origin and one domain at a time in the family of procreation—attachment and parent–child relationships, marital relationships, or children's outcomes. Despite the fact that a family systems perspective on attachment theory would suggest that parents' working models of attachment affect their children through their impact on the quality of both parent–child and marital relationships (cf. Marvin & Stewart, 1990), this hypothesis has not been tested empirically with the exception of an earlier exploratory study (P. A. Cowan, Cohn, et al., 1996).

Adult Attachment and Parent–Child Relationships

Investigators have examined the association between mothers' internal working models of attachment to their parents and their style of parenting their young children (see Hesse, 1999; Van IJzendoorn, 1992, for reviews of research). In two studies with different samples, mothers who provided coherent narratives describing relationships in their families of origin, and were therefore classified as having secure working models of attachment, had more positive interactions with their infants (Haft & Slade, 1989) and toddlers (Crowell & Feldman, 1989). By contrast, mothers who were classified as having insecure working models of attachment were less attuned to their own infants' or preschoolers' emotional expressions or needs (Crowell & Feldman, 1989; Haft & Slade, 1989).

Although most of the early studies of attachment relationships were of mother–child relationships, more recent studies show that fathers' representations of relationships based on their experiences in their families of origin are also connected to the quality of the relationship they have with their children (P. A. Cowan et al., 1996; Grossmann et al., 2002; Steele et al., 1996). Using data from fathers' AAI interviews and observations of their style when they worked and played with their children, Cohn, Cowan, Cowan, and Pearson (1992) found that fathers who gave coherent narratives of their early family relationships provided more warmth and structure to their preschoolers during challenging tasks than fathers whose narratives were not coherent.

Adult Attachment and Marital Interaction[1]

In the last decade, information has emerged about links between adults' state of mind regarding attachment to parents, assessed with the AAI, and their quality of interaction with a married partner. For example, Bradburn (1997), Cohn, Silver, Cowan, Cowan, and Pearson (1992), Creasey (2002), Kobak, Ruckdeschel, and Hazan (1994), Pianta, Morog, and Marvin (1995), and Paley, Cox, Harter, and Margand (2002), reported significant correlations between adults' insecure state of mind with reference to relationships with their parents (AAI) and expressed negative emotion, conflict, or ineffective problem solving during a marital or family interaction task (see Mikulincer, Florian, Cowan, & Cowan, 2002, for a review). In sum, support has been emerging for the hypothesis that security of attachment in individual adult

---

[1]We are omitting from this summary the large body of research within the field of social and personality psychology on the connection between how young adults' describe their attachment style, using questionnaires or interviews, and the quality of their romantic or marital relationships (Bartholomew & Shaver, 1998; Collins & Read, 1990; Shaver, Belsky, & Brennan, 2000). Although significant correlations have been found between self-described attachment styles and the relationship with a partner, it is not clear how these findings apply to this study because almost all the data have been obtained from college students in short-term relationships, and rarely have the self-report data been validated by observation of interactions (for an exception, see Kobak & Sceery, 1988). Furthermore, it is not clear whether adult attachment measured within this paradigm and attachment measured with the intensive Adult Attachment Interview is similar. Preliminary indications suggest that the correlation between the two approaches may be low or absent (Bartholomew & Shaver, 1998; Owens et al., 1995).

partners, as assessed by narratives about parent–child relationships, is corre-lated with observable qualities of both emotional aspects (conflict resolution style) and instrumental aspects (problem-solving efficacy) of their relation-ships as couples.

Adult Attachment and Children's Adaptation

As far as we know, researchers studying attachment have not examined at-tachment patterns in relation to children's school achievement in the first year or two of elementary school, choosing to focus instead on links with socioemotional aspects of children's behavior. For example, studies of clini-cal samples consistently find links between mothers' attachment status and their children's problematic behaviors or diagnostic status (Crowell & Feld-man, 1989; Greenberg, Speltz, & DeKlyen, 1993; Lyons-Ruth, 1996). The role of fathers' working models of attachment in samples of clinical families has yet to be examined. Studies of the association between parents' attach-ment status and their children's behavior problems in nonclinical samples are rare. One small exploratory study of a nonclinical sample of 27 families found that attachment data from both parents' AAIs in the preschool period predicted teachers' ratings of the children's internalizing and externalizing behavior in the kindergarten classroom (P. A. Cowan et al., 1996). The find-ings supported the hypothesis that the connection was a product of interme-diate family relationship mechanisms: Parents' narratives about their family of origin relationships were associated with the quality of their relationships with their spouses and their children. In turn, the quality of those two central family relationships (marital and parent–child) in the preschool period were significant predictors of the children's problem behaviors in the first year of elementary school. Structural equation models with latent variables repre-senting adult attachment, marital quality, parenting quality, and children's kindergarten outcomes predicted between 39% and 69% of the variance in their children's externalizing and internalizing behaviors as observed by kin-dergarten teachers.

Variations in the quality of the parents' marital interaction, as the parents described it and as observers rated it during a visit with the whole family, added significantly to predictions of children's problem behaviors at school, over and above that predicted by the parents' attachment status or parenting style alone. The patterns in the Cowan et al. (1996) study suggested that mothers' working models of attachment played a stronger role in children's internalizing behaviors than did fathers' working models, but that fathers' at-tachment played more of a role in their children's externalizing behaviors than did mothers' attachment. The sample was too small to determine whether there were differences in patterns for parents of girls and boys.

This report extends the Cowan et al. (1996) study in several respects. Because the earlier study was an exploratory investigation, no specific a priori hypotheses about linking mechanisms were proposed. The relatively small sample size precluded separate analyses of patterns for parents of boys and parents of girls. In this larger sample, we were able to construct sex-specific models and test specific hypotheses. Another limitation of the earlier study was that the latent variable measuring marital quality was constructed from ratings of the couple working and playing with their child (see Cohn, Cowan, et al., 1992; P. A. Cowan et al., 1996, for details). The coding system did not indicate the separate contributions of husband and wife to the interaction. As a result, it was not possible to determine whether the individual parents' state of mind regarding attachment in their families of origin functioned as a template for their reactions to one another as partners. In this study, husbands' and wives' behavior was measured separately while the couple tried to resolve a conflict when their child was not present. This allowed us to examine the contribution of each partner's interaction in the couple, independent of the quality of that parent's interaction with the child. Finally, by including a brief look at the children's academic and socioemotional outcomes, we begin to expand the network of potential linkages between parents' state of mind with respect to attachment and their children's adaptation to school.

Hypotheses

We tested three sets of hypotheses using four Latent Variable Path Analyses with Partial Least Squares (PLS) structural equation models of mother–daughter and father–daughter, mother–son and father–son linkages across relationship domains:

1. Measures of parents' working models of parent–child attachment based on coding AAI narratives, and measures of observed marital and parent–child interaction, all obtained when the preschool child is 5, will combine to predict internalizing and externalizing behavior in the kindergarten classroom 1 year later at age 6.
    1a. The latent variables assessing past and current aspects of the parent–child relationship in the family of origin will add unique variance to the predictions.
    1b. Structural equation path models will show that measures of parents' attachment to their parents in the family of origin are linked with their current marital quality, which, in turn, is linked with the quality of the parent's relationship with his or her child, which, in turn, predicts children's kindergarten outcomes. This pattern would be consistent with the

hypothesis that marital relationships are centrally involved in the intergenerational transmission of parenting patterns.

2. Sex of parent, sex of child, and type of problem behavior will all affect the links between family process and children's school adaptation. We made two kinds of predictions about sex differences, each of which could be tested only in exploratory fashion.

2a. Guided by previous research, we focused on the amount of variance in internalizing and externalizing explained by PLS models containing data from families with daughters compared with models for families with sons, and by models comparing information about mothers' attachment with information about fathers' attachment. We also predicted that statistical models containing data from mothers' attachment would explain more of the variance in daughters' internalizing behaviors than models containing data from fathers, and that statistical models containing data from fathers would explain more of the variance in their sons' externalizing behaviors than would mothers' models.

2b. Without previous research to guide us, we explored mother–daughter, mother–son, father–daughter, and father–son differences in the pathways linking adult attachment, marital interaction, authoritative parenting, and children's adaptation to school.

3. Our main focus in this chapter is on the contribution of intergenerational relationships to the prediction of children's relationships with peers. However, in light of our concern with children's early academic competence, we examined the unique contribution of parents' attachment to predictions of their children's tested academic achievement in kindergarten on the Peabody Individual Achievement Test (PIAT; Markwardt, 1991).

METHODS

Participants

Of the 84 families who completed Phase 2 of the study (prekindergarten through the first grade follow-up), 73 had complete data required for this chapter's analyses, 46 families with a firstborn son, 27 with a firstborn daughter. The attachment interviews and the assessment of both marital and parent–child interaction took place before the group interventions for parents began. Because the children's kindergarten behaviors were assessed after the end of the intervention, we included two vectors representing intervention and control contrasts as covariates in the structural equation models (discussed later).

Measures

Adult Attachment.   In visits during the spring of the child's prekindergarten year, each parent was interviewed individually with the AAI by a member of the project staff. An initial set of 17 continuous scales represent the rater's view of various aspects of the interviewee's "probable experience" with mother and father (e.g., whether the mother or father is described convincingly as loving or rejecting), and the interviewee's state of mind regarding attachment (including involving anger at the parent and coherence of the narrative). These scales are characterized as representing probable experience because they reflect the rater's impression that the interviewee is describing his or her relationships with parents in a convincing and coherent way. Based on the pattern of codes on these scales, the coder then assigned the protocol to one primary attachment category—secure, dismissing, preoccupied, unresolved, and cannot classify (see chapter 2 for more detail).

The AAI has demonstrated impressive reliability and validity in cross-cultural samples (van IJzendoorn & Bakermans-Kranenburg, 1996), using a category system of assessing adults' working models of attachment. Nevertheless, this approach potentially misses information contained in the scales themselves (Fraley & Waller, 1998). For studies of children, Fraley and Spieker (2003) provided evidence that attachment data are more consistent with the assumption that the construct is continuous. A similar argument has been made for data from the AAI (Fife, 1997). For example, some adults who generally present their experiences coherently (and would be categorized as securely attached) may have aspects of their discussion that are more angry or idealizing and therefore function differently than other individuals in the secure category who do not show these traces of insecure working models. Because we intended to use the data from the attachment interview in structural models and to correlate them with continuous outcome measures of children's problem behaviors, we chose to use a subset of the AAI continuous codes in our analyses.

Our choice of attachment measures was based on the fact that we were most interested in predicting emotionally-laden problem behavior of children in the classroom (withdrawn, depressed, internalizing behavior and aggressive, acting out, externalizing behavior). We selected two continuous rating scales that reflect emotional qualities of the parents' early relationships with their parents: one continuous rating scale selected from the 5 probable quality of experience scales and one continuous rating scale selected from the 12 state of mind scales. Each scale was used to form separate ratings of the interviewee's relationship with his or her mother and with father.

From the five experience scales, we selected father loving or mother loving, reflecting the rater's estimate of whether the respondent provided a convincing description of mother or father as loving in the relationship with him or her. Ratings of loving ranged from 1 (*very lacking in love—no evidence of real affection*) to 9 (*very loving—believable evidence of the parent as loving, accepting, and dedicated to the child and his or her development*). Interrater reliabilities were high (Pearson correlations, all $df = 71$; loving in the relationship with mother: Interrater $r_{\text{Project Mothers}} = .84$; $r_{\text{Project Fathers}} = .87$; loving in the relationship with father: $r_{\text{Project Mothers}} = .89$; $r_{\text{Project Fathers}} = .87$). The two ratings of the parents' father and mother as loving were incorporated in one latent variable in the path model.

Still with an eye to predicting emotional problem behavior in the children, we selected the scales assessing current involving anger toward mother and father from the 12 state of mind scales on the AAI. This scale represents a quality of the discourse during the interview—the degree to which the respondent spoke about his or her parents with current, involving anger. Ratings ranged from 1 (*no direct expression of current anger*) to 9 (*current involving anger toward a parent comes close to being the dominant theme of the interview*). Interrater reliabilities ranged from acceptable to high (current anger at mother: $r_{\text{Project Mothers}} = .86$, $r_{\text{Project Fathers}} = .97$; current anger at father: $r_{\text{Project Mothers}} = .83$, $r_{\text{Project Fathers}} = .72$). The two anger scales (toward mother and father) constituted the second latent variable in the statistical models for fathers and mothers.

We selected the loving and anger scales, rather than scales rating the level of parental rejection, neglect, or the interviewee's metacognitive processes, or derogation of attachment, because we believed that the quality and regulation of both positive and negative emotion in these central family relationships would play a central role in the transmission of behavior patterns across the generations (cf. Caspi & Elder, 1988; Gottman, Katz, & Hooven, 1997). We made this choice based on the assumption that these scales most succinctly captured salient aspects of positive and negative emotional quality in the relationship. In preliminary analyses, we considered including derogation, but anger seemed closer to our emphasis on the direct expression of negative emotion. The loving scores represent (perceived) positive emotion from the grandparent to the parent as a child, and the anger scores represent negative emotion conveyed by parents in our study about earlier relationships with their parents.

In an exploratory study by P. A. Cowan, Cohn, et al. (1996) that used a similar measurement strategy and analytic approach, a third latent variable assessing coherence of transcript was included in the path models. In this study, we found that men's and women's descriptions of their mothers and fathers as loving were significantly correlated with the ratings of coherence of transcript: for men, correlations of coherence with loving mother, $r(71) = .55$, with loving father, $r(71) = .43$; for women, correlations of coherence with loving mother, $r(71) = .44$, with loving father, $r(71) = .39$; all $ps < .01$. When the models in this study were run with coherence included as a latent variable, there was no significant addition in the predictive power of the two models.

Resolution of Marital Conflict. Data concerning marital interaction were drawn from the 10-min dyadic discussion of a marital conflict or disagreement between the parents as described in chapter 2. From the nine scales based on attachment-derived codes, we created two aggregate scales: positive (supportive, constructive problem solving, collaborative) and negative (avoidant, minimizing, rejecting, blaming, ruminating, controlling). The positive and negative scale scores for each spouse's behavior were included in the path models as one latent variable reflecting the quality of that partner's contribution to the interaction as the couple discussed a troubling problem.

Authoritative Parenting Style. We have described our observational measures of parenting style from warmth, structure, and respect for autonomy scales in chapters 2 and 4.

The Child's Adaptation to School. When the children were in kindergarten, we collected reports from their teachers in the spring using the Child Adaptive Behavior Inventory (CABI; see chapter 2) scales describing internalizing (depression, social isolation, and anxiety) and externalizing (antisocial, oppositional, and hostile) behaviors. In a home visit during the summer following the kindergarten year, our staff also administered a PIAT (Markwardt, 1991) to each child.

Constructing the Structural Equation Model

To examine the direct and indirect links among parents' attachment histories, marital quality, parenting quality, and children's externalizing and internalizing behaviors at school, we employed LVPLS estimation procedure (Falk & Miller, 1992; Lohmoeller, 1989; Wold, 1982). In this case, nine latent variables with an $n = 46$ for parent–son models and $n = 27$ for parent–daughter models were created from the manifest variables described earlier. Although these numbers are small, this is precisely the situation for which the LVPLS approach was created:

LV (Latent variable) 1. Intervention effects—This is maritally-focused intervention versus controls and parenting-focused intervention versus controls. As in chapter 5, because the research design contained three conditions (maritally-focused intervention, parenting-focused intervention, and consultation [low-dose controls]), two binary covariates were needed to control for the fact that the child's adaptation to school was assessed at the end of kindergarten, after parents participated in the couples groups or control condition. The covariates were treated as manifest variables represented by two dummy-coded vectors (controls = 0; intervention = 1). The third contrast (marital versus parenting) would be redundant as a control variable. We included a path from each of the two vectors to all of the succeeding latent variables in each structural equation model, to remove any direct effect of the intervention before we considered links among all other independent variables and the latent variables representing children's behavior in the kindergarten classroom. Although the intervention vectors were included in each analysis, we did not represent them in Figs. 8.1 to 8.4 to reduce the complexity of the already complex diagrams.

LV 2. The participant's mother and father are characterized as loving on the AAI.

LV 3. This is the participant's current anger toward his or her mother and father on the AAI.

LV 4. This is the father's conflict resolution style (laboratory observation of his positive and negative [reverse scored] behavior during the couple problem discussion).

LV 6. This is the mother's conflict resolution style (laboratory observation of her positive and negative [reverse scored] behavior during the couple problem discussion).

LV 7. This is the mother's or father's authoritative parenting style (laboratory observation of parent's warmth, structure, and autonomy encouragement during the separate parent–child interactions).

LV 8. This is the children's internalizing behavior (depression, social isolation, and anxiety).

LV 9. This is the children's externalizing behavior (antisocial, oppositional, and hostile).

In exploratory analyses, we substituted children's PIAT achievement scores (reading, math, spelling) as the latent variable predicted by the first six latent variables described earlier.

RESULTS

Overview

The results supported most of our specific hypotheses concerning links among parents' attachment representations, family processes, and children's problematic behavior outcomes. Parents' working models of attachment assessed in an interview, and both marital and parent–child relationship qualities assessed in laboratory playroom observations, combined to predict the

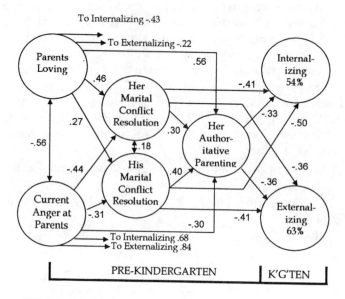

FIG. 8.1. Mothers' attachment and daughters' adaptation to school.

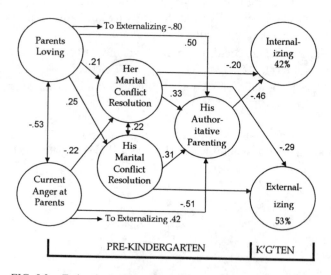

FIG. 8.2. Fathers' attachment and daughters' adaptation to school.

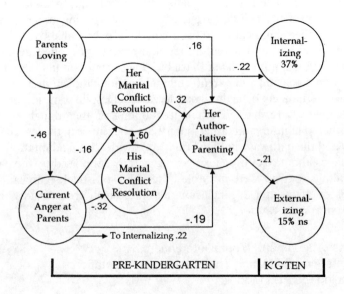

FIG. 8.3. Mothers' attachment and sons' adaptation to school.

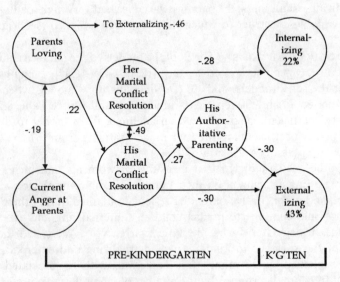

FIG. 8.4. Fathers' attachment and sons' adaptation to school.

children's internalizing and externalizing behavior and, to some extent, academic achievement in kindergarten. Measures of working models of adult attachment added significantly to the predictions, over and above the information about marital and parenting relationships. Path models demonstrated meaningful links among latent variables measuring parents' attachment to their parents, marital and parent–child interaction, and children's internalizing and externalizing behavior in kindergarten. Despite some important similarities, there were marked differences among mother–daughter, mother–son, father–daughter, and father–son PLS models in both the level of predictability and the pathways linking family data with school adaptation. Specific hypotheses about sex differences were generally supported by the pattern of the findings, but we were not able to test the statistical significance of the moderator effects and so conclusions about these differences must be treated with appropriate caution.

Parents' Attachment, Marital Interaction, and Parenting Style, and Their Children's Adaptation: Examining the PLS Models

The Measurement Models. The eight latent variables included in the PLS models (see the Method section) were constructed from 19 manifest variables. In almost all cases, the manifest variables had very high loadings on the latent variable construct to which they had been assigned (see Table 8.1).

The Structural Models. The fit of the models to the data was quite good, with the root mean square covariance (RMS COV [E,U]) ranging between .07 (for the sons' models) and .10 (for the daughters' models when 0 represents a perfect fit and .20 represents an unacceptable fit; see Table 8.2). Communality coefficients also reflected an adequate fit of model to data, with communality coefficients in the four models ranging from .67 to .73 (lower level of acceptability was set at .50).

Hypothesis 1a predicted that measures of women's and men's state of mind regarding attachment in their families of origin, resolution of marital conflict, and authoritative parenting style, all obtained during the preschool period, would combine to predict children's internalizing and externalizing behaviors 1 year later during the kindergarten year. We tested the significance of the variance in kindergarten internalizing and externalizing outcomes explained by the models (see Table 8.2), with Fs associated with degrees of freedom determined by the number of latent variable predictors and by the number of participants minus the number of predictors minus 1 (Falk & Miller, 1992). Although the results are reported separately for different parent by child sex combinations, we are focusing in this section on the overall predictive power of the models.

TABLE 8.1
Latent Variable Path Analysis With Partial Least Squares:
Loadings on Manifest Variables

Latent Variable (LV)	Mothers		Fathers	
	Daughters	Sons	Daughters	Sons
LV1. Intervention				
Parenting versus control	.94	.90	.86	.94
Marital versus control	.40	.89	.94	.87
LV2. Participant's parent as loving				
Mother loving	.87	.89	.81	.90
Father loving	.94	.82	.53	.71
LV3. Participant's current anger at parent				
Anger at mother	.91	.90	.92	.85
Anger at father	.95	.96	.10	.79
LV4. Wife's marital conflict resolution				
Positive behavior	.96	.96	.95	.97
Negative behavior	.96	.76	.97	.86
LV5. Husband's marital conflict resolution				
Positive behavior	.93	.91	.95	.93
Negative behavior	.91	.88	.83	.93
LV6. Authoritative parenting				
Warm and responsive	.96	.98	.74	.89
Structure and limits	.50	.37	.58	.59
Respect for autonomy	.17	.22	.61	.85
LV7. Child's internalizing behavior in kindergarten				
Depression	.90	.76	.93	.79
Isolation	.90	.65	.89	.65
Anxiety	.92	.82	.63	.80
LV8. Child's externalizing behavior in kindergarten				
Antisocial	.95	.88	.92	.87
Oppositional or defiant	.93	.90	.94	.92
Hostile	.94	.92	.91	.92

Of the eight predictions from preschool family data to kindergarten outcomes (four models, each with two outcomes), five overall multiple regressions were statistically significant, explaining between 37% and 63% of the variance in children's internalizing and externalizing behavior at school. In mother–daughter pairs, mothers' AAI state of mind scores (loving and current anger), the couple's positive conflict resolution behaviors, and mothers' authoritative parenting in the preschool year, accounted for 54% of the variance in daughters' internalizing, $F(6, 19) = 3.19$, $p < .05$, and 63% of the vari-

TABLE 8.2

Intervention Vectors As Covariates, Adult Attachment, Marital Quality, Parenting Quality, and Children's Outcomes

	Internalizing			Externalizing				
	R^2	F	$F(R^2$ change)	R^2	F	$F(R^2$ change)	Fit	Communality
Mothers and daughters								
Full model (6, 19)	.54	3.72*		.63	5.44**		.10	.73
without AAI	.34	ns	4.13* (.20)	.11	ns	13.33** (.52)		
Mothers and sons								
Full model (6, 38)	.37	3.83**		.15	ns		.07	.66
without AAI	.33	4.94**	ns (.04)	.13	ns	ns .02		
Fathers and daughters								
Full model (6, 19)	.42	2.29		.53	4.83***		.10	.67
without AAI	.40	3.50*	ns (.02)	.16	ns	7.49** (.37)		
Fathers and sons								
Full model (6, 38)	.22	Ns		.43	4.83**		.07	.72
without AAI	.22	2.82*	ns (.00)	.24	3.16*	6.33** .19		

Note. AAI = Adult Attachment Interview.
*p < .05. **p < .01.

ance in daughters' externalizing behaviors as reported by their teachers in the spring of the kindergarten year, $F(6, 19) = 5.53$, $p < .01$. The same variables assessed in mother–son pairs accounted for a statistically significant 37% of the variance in sons' internalizing behavior, $F(6, 38) = 3.72$, $p < .01$. The fathers' model explained 53% of daughters' externalizing behaviors, $F(6, 19) = 3.57$, $p < .05$, and 43% of the variance in sons' externalizing behavior, $F(6, 38) = 4.77$, $p < .001$, at the end of the kindergarten year.

The fathers' models did not account for statistically significant variance in internalizing behavior, either for daughters (42%), $F(6, 19) = 2.22$, ns, or sons (22%), $F(6, 38) = 1.78$, ns. The fact that the father–daughter internalizing model was not statistically significant despite explaining 42% of the variance, whereas the mother–son internalizing model was statistically significant in explaining 37% of the variance, is attributable to the fact that there were fewer families with daughters ($n = 27$) than with sons ($n = 46$). Finally, the mother–son model explained a nonsignificant 15% of the variance in sons' externalizing behavior in kindergarten. It is important to note that the pattern of nonsignificant findings occurred in parent–child combinations expected to yield low correlations (mother–son externalizing; father–son and father–daughter internalizing).

Unique Contributions of the Latent Variables

Hypothesis 1a stated our expectation that mothers' and fathers' working models of their relationship with their own parents would explain unique variation, over and above marital and parent–child relationship quality, in children's problem behaviors as they adapted to elementary school. To test this hypothesis, we compared the results from the full path model regressions in Table 8.2 with path model regressions that removed the two latent variables measuring parents as loving and current preoccupied anger. This strategy, similar to a backward elimination technique in multiple regression analysis, evaluates the significance of the R^2 change between the full model and a model omitting one domain from the equation. To provide a clearer account, we report the data in terms of how adult attachment data added to the predictive power of the equations.

Table 8.2 shows that including the AAI data in the structural equations significantly increased the power of half of the eight models to explain variance in the children's behavior at school. Adding the latent variables measuring mothers' working models of attachment to the marital and parenting observations resulted in significant increases in the amount of variance explained in daughters' internalizing behavior (from .34 to .54) and externalizing behavior (from .11 to .63). Similarly, adding data from the father's description of his parents as loving and his current anger at his parents resulted in significant increases in R^2 in fathers' models predicting sons' and daughters' externalizing behaviors (father–daughter from .16 to .53; father–son from .24 to .43). The unique variance contributed to these equations by data from the AAI was substantial, ranging from 19% to 52%.

Table 8.2 shows that four of eight models were statistically significant after removing the AAI data—mother–son, father–daughter, and father–son models accounting for variance in internalizing, and the father–son model accounting for variance in externalizing. That is, over and above variations in working models of attachment, there was unique variance in children's internalizing and externalizing behavior in kindergarten explained by marital and parenting behavior.

Multiple Pathways From Parents' Attachment to Children's Problem Behaviors

Here we explore our expectation in hypothesis 1b that there would be pathways through current family functioning that link parents' attachment to their parents with their children's problem behaviors in kindergarten (i.e., that connect recalled information about grandparent–parent relationships with the grandchild's adaptation to school). We want to underline the fact that in these models, each domain of functioning is assessed independently in different contexts using different sources of information (attachment interview, marital observations, parenting observations, and children's teacher-rated outcomes). Figures 8.1 to 8.4 present four PLS models calculated separately for each pairing of sex of parent and sex of child. Following P. A. Cowan, Cowan, et al. (1996), path weights that did not meet the guideline level of 5% of the variance explained were eliminated. In this section, we describe the patterns of connection. In the following section, we focus on issues of sex differences in these patterns.

Mothers and Daughters.   When mothers described their parents as loving in a clear and convincing way, there was a direct link with daughters' lower levels of internalizing behavior (*pw* [path weight] = −.43) and externalizing behavior (*pw* = −.22) the next year in kindergarten. When mothers displayed current anger at their parents as coded from AAI transcripts, their daughters showed higher levels of both internalizing (*pw* = .68) and externalizing behaviors (*pw* = .84) in kindergarten. All of the remaining links to school outcomes were indirect, suggesting that working models of adult attachment accounted for variance in daughters' outcomes by virtue of the connections with the quality of the couple's marital interaction and the parent's relationship with the child.

Mothers with parents described as more loving were likely to show more positive behavior (supportive, constructive problem solving, collaborative) toward their husbands during the conflict discussion (*pw* = .46) and toward their children in the parent–child interaction (pw = .56). Husbands were also more likely to show positive behavior toward these wives (pw = .27). Not surprisingly, mothers' lower level of current anger at their parents was linked with more positive behaviors toward their husbands as they tried to resolve a marital conflict (pw = −.31) and a more authoritative parenting style (pw = −.30) with their daughters.

The paths linking husbands' and wives' marital conflict behavior and their daughters' behavior at school were quite similar. Mothers' positive responses in the marital discussion predicted daughters' lower level of internalizing (pw = −.41) and externalizing behaviors (pw = −.36). There was also an indirect path; mothers who treated their husbands more positively in a marital discussion were warmer and more structuring with their daughters (pw = .30), who, a year later, showed less internalizing (pw = −.33) and externalizing in the kindergarten classroom (pw = −.36).

Still another indirect path can be seen in the fact that when mothers' behavior was more positive in the marital discussion, this behavior was more likely to be reciprocated by fathers (pw = .18). When the fathers were more positive toward their spouses, daughters displayed less externalizing behavior at school (pw = −.41). Furthermore, the wives of husbands with more positive behavior during marital problem solving were more likely to be authoritative with their daughters (pw = .30), which, as we have seen, predicted lower levels of the children's internalizing and externalizing behavior at school.

Fathers and Daughters. We found direct links between fathers' adult attachment responses and daughters' outcomes. Daughters had higher scores in externalizing as described by their kindergarten teachers when their fathers described their relationships with their parents as low in loving (pw = −.80) or conveyed more current anger at their parents during the AAI interview (pw = .42).

As in the mother–daughter model, when fathers described their parents as loving, independent observers rated the men as behaving more positively— toward their wives during the conflict resolution discussion (pw = .25) and toward their daughters in the parent–child interaction task (pw = .50). Wives of these men were more supportive and constructive during the conflict discussion (pw = .21). Similarly, when husbands' anger at their parents was low or contained in the AAI, their wives showed more positive behavior toward them during the marital discussion (pw = −.22).

Husbands' positive behavior in the marital interaction task directly predicted lower levels of externalizing problems in their daughters' school behavior (pw = −.51), with an indirect linkage as well. Men who showed more positive behavior when they worked with their wives on an unresolved marital problem showed similar positive parenting qualities when they worked with their daughters on difficult tasks (pw = .31). In turn, fathers' authoritative parenting behavior during the preschool period was linked with daughters displaying fewer internalizing behaviors ($pw = -.46$) a year later in kindergarten.

Wives' positive behavior in the marital interaction predicted lower levels of internalizing ($pw = -.20$) and externalizing ($pw = -.29$) for daughters. An indirect path suggested that, when wives' reactions to their husbands were positive during the conflict discussion, husbands showed more warmth, limit-setting, and respect for their daughters' autonomy ($pw = .33$) in the separate father–daughter visit. As we have noted, fathers' parenting style in the year before their children entered elementary school was linked with girls showing fewer internalizing behaviors in kindergarten.

Mothers and Sons. The mother–son model showed a direct link between mothers' attachment measures and children's internalizing ($pw = .22$), but all of the remaining connections were indirect, following a path from attachment to marital interaction to parent–child interaction to child outcomes. As in the mother–daughter model, mothers rated as preoccupied with anger at their parents acted less collaboratively with their husbands during the conflict discussion ($pw = -.16$) and were less effective in helping their preschool sons with difficult tasks during the family visit ($pw = -.19$). There was a direct link between mothers' higher negative and less positive behavior with their husbands, and their sons showing more internalizing behaviors at school 1 year later ($pw = .22$). Unlike the mother–daughter model, none of the variables in the mother–son model explained a significant proportion of the variance in sons' externalizing behavior in kindergarten.

Fathers and Sons. Of all four models, the links in the father–son models were simplest and clearest. Fathers' working models of attachment assessed during the preschool period when children were age 5 were related directly to the marital quality we observed, and to sons' externalizing behavior that kindergarten teachers reported 1 year later when the children were 6. Fathers' working models were also related indirectly to their parenting style. When fathers' described their parents in a convincing way as loving their sons were less likely to be angry, oppositional, and hostile in kindergarten 1 year later, according to their teachers ($pw = -.46$). By contrast, fathers' current anger at their parents, as rated by coders of the AAI, was not a significant, direct predictor of sons' internalizing or externalizing behaviors at school.

As we have seen in the father–daughter model, fathers who had sons and viewed their own parents as loving were more generally supportive, constructive, and collaborative with their wives ($pw = .22$). The wives' positive style of working on marital conflicts, in turn, was associated with their sons' lower levels of internalizing 1 year later at the end of kindergarten ($pw = -.28$). In contrast with the father–daughter model, there were no meaningful links between any of the fathers' latent variables and son's internalizing behavior.

However, fathers' positive style of working with their wives was directly associated with their sons' exhibiting fewer externalizing behaviors at school (pw = −.30). In addition to this direct link, we found that husbands' positive behavior with their wives was associated with their greater warmth, limit-setting, and respect for their preschool sons' autonomy (pw = .27), which, in turn, predicted fewer externalizing behaviors in the boys the next year at school (pw = −.30).

The visual arrays of the path models in Fig. 8.1 to 8.4 demonstrate that there are important similarities in patterns of linkage between mothers' and fathers' responses to the AAI and their daughters' and sons' level of internalizing and externalizing problem behaviors as they make their transition to school. Taken together, the father–daughter and mother–daughter models suggest that, when mothers and fathers have a more positive view of their relationships with their parents, and are less angry when they talk about their parents, they tend to behave more positively and supportively with their spouses during the discussion of a disagreement. They are also warmer, more limit-setting, and more granting of autonomy with their daughters when their daughters confront challenging tasks. The daughters, in turn, are less likely to be shy, withdrawn, or depressed, or aggressive and hostile, as they make their transition to elementary school.

Sex Differences in Explaining Variance in Kindergarten Outcomes

In hypothesis 2a, we predicted that there would be differences in accounting for variation in internalizing and externalizing behavior, depending on the sex of child and sex of parent. The pattern of results from all four models allows us to draw some tentative conclusions about the predicted sex differences. The conclusions are tentative especially because we cannot evaluate the significance of the difference between the models in amount of variance explained.

Our prediction that mothers' models would explain more of the variance in children's internalizing than fathers' models held true for both girls (55% of the variance predicted by the mothers' model compared with 42% for the fathers' model) and boys (37% of the variance in sons' internalizing predicted by the mothers model, compared with 22% for the fathers' model). This is not to say that internalizing behavior in daughters is associated only with their mothers' characteristics. The PLS model for fathers and daughters also explained a substantial proportion of the variance in girls' internalizing behavior in the kindergarten classroom.

We had predicted that fathers' path models would predict more variance in children's externalizing than would mothers' models. This prediction was confirmed only for fathers and sons (43% of the variance compared with 15% for the mother–son model). We were surprised to find that fathers' data from the preschool period predicted daughters' externalizing behavior in kindergarten as well or better than did mothers' (53% of the variance predicted by the fathers' model, 47% by the mothers' model).

There were different patterns of connection between parents' working models of attachment and parenting style in each of the four models. In the mother–son and father–daughter models, both the loving and the anger latent variables from the AAI were directly linked with authoritative parenting. In the mother–daughter model, only the description of parents as loving was linked with mothers' parenting style. In the father–daughter model, the only connection was indirect, through fathers' behavior in the husband–wife conflict discussion task.

Predicting Academic Achievement

We calculated PLS structural equation models for the four pairings (mother–daughter, mother–son, father–daughter, and father–son) with children's academic achievement measured by the PIAT as the dependent variable. Only the mother–daughter equation explained a significant amount of variance in kindergarten achievement (58%), $F(6, 19) = 4.43$, $p < .05$. Using the removal procedure, we found that the attachment data explained a unique 25% of the variance, $F(2, 19) = 5.07$, $p < .05$, over and above the 33% explained by marital and parenting observations. Here again, we face problems associated with sample size and power. However, we should note that in the same samples, family-to-child outcome linkages were shown for externalizing and internalizing, and that for academic achievement, the one significant PLS equation was found for girls, the smaller sample.

DISCUSSION

In analyses of data from recalled relationships between parents and their own parents, the couple's marital relationship, and the parent–child relationship observed in our project playroom, five of the eight PLS regressions accounted for significant amounts of variance in children's adaptation to kindergarten 1 year later. In addition, one of four models that examined links with academic achievement, the mother–daughter pairing, also showed significant connections between family relationships and daughters' adaptation to school. A latent variable describing the parents' parents as loving, and another describing the level of current anger at parents (the grandparents of the children), added significantly to the predictions of both internalizing and externalizing for mothers and daughters, and of externalizing for fathers of both daughters and sons.

It seems clear that parents' emotional memories of early relationships with their parents provide a significant context for understanding how children cope with the challenges of beginning school. The key question, of course, is how this context operates.

The Parenting Template Hypothesis Requires Revision

As noted earlier, the frequent finding that working models of mothers' and fathers' attachment to their parents show continuity with their children's attachment to them has given rise to a template theory of intergenerational transmission that focuses entirely on parent–child relationships. Working models of parent–child relationships in one generation are somehow "stamped in" through the early experience of parenting in ways that are replicated in the relationships between parents and children in the next generation (Bowlby, 1988).

A number of findings reported in this chapter cause us to question the simple notion of a template-like transmission of parenting relationships through inner dynamic cognitive–emotional schema. We must first consider the fact that although the representations of parenting from the AAI contribute uniquely to the prediction of their children's adaptation to kindergarten, so do measures of the quality of their marital and parent–child transactions. Second, the path models indicate that there are both direct and indirect links between working models of attachment and the other major domains of interest in this study—marital problem solving, parenting style, and children's outcomes.

We must be cautious about what is meant by the idea of intergenerational transmission. We have no evidence in this study that the similarities in perceived positivity and negativity of grandparent–parent, parent–parent, and parent–child relationships result from a transmission process in which early relationships in the family of origin function as templates that mold or determine the quality of subsequent intimate family relationships. Neither do we have direct evidence that the AAI narratives provide a veridical picture of the quality of the relationship between grandparent and parent, as it would have been coded by an independent observer watching that earlier family engaged in interaction. However, from the AAI we do have a well-validated measure of what Reiss (1989) has called the "representational family," a set of working models, scripts, or narratives that influence but do not determine patterns of interaction in what Reiss called the "practicing family." Strictly speaking, our investigation focuses on the continuity between measures of the represented family of origin (adult attachment narratives) and the practicing family of procreation (the couple and parent–child dyads as we observe them). The template derived from working models of parent–child attachment, then, may be more of a potential action system than a mold that shapes marital and parent–child relationships within the family.

We speculate that the links between parents' working models and their children's outcomes occur as inner meanings about close relationships (the representational family) begin to be reflected in overt behavior in close relationships of both adults and children (the practicing family). It may be that fathers and mothers who recall their own parents as unloving and continue to express unresolved anger at them expect family relationships to be disappointing and unfulfilling—expectations that may contribute, in turn, to irritability and anger with spouse and children, particularly when those relationships are stressed and elicit "attachment behavior." If parents are preoccupied with frustrations or hurts from past relationships, they may not feel confident about their ability to resolve difficulties and this may hamper their ability to create a more positive relationship atmosphere, particularly when their close relationships are vulnerable.

THE MARITAL RELATIONSHIP AS A LINK BETWEEN ADULT ATTACHMENT AND PARENTING STYLE

The path models presented in Fig. 8.1 to 8.4 are consistent with clinical family systems theorists who emphasize the role of the parents' marriage as an amplifier or reducer of stresses in all domains of the family system (cf. Wagner & Reiss, 1995) and with a recent study of marital function and children's attachment (Frosch, Mangelsdorf, & McHale, 2000). We are saying "consistent with" rather than "supports the hypothesis" because LVPLS models do not provide tests of specific path arrangements (Falk & Miller, 1987). The results do suggest the possibility that there is a spillover or cascade of effects from parents' mental models of their early relationships, to the quality of their relationships as a couple and with their child, to the child's style of coping when the world presents challenges (Mikulincer et al., 2002). That is, adults' recollections of negative experiences in the family of origin are more likely to be replicated in their families of procreation when their marriages are stressful. In cases where parents recall early negative experiences but have current marital relationships in which they can negotiate conflict effectively, there may be less likelihood that their early negative experiences will be reproduced with their children. A hypothesis for further testing, then, is that the commonly found connection between adults' attachment to their parents and their children's attachment to them is not simply a replication of parenting patterns, but rather a process in which the quality of adults' earlier parenting affects the quality of their marital relationship, which affects parenting in the next generation—just the pattern that Caspi and Elder (1988) found using very different measures and methods in a large longitudinal study.

The Central Role of Affect Regulation in Intergenerational Relationships

Although this correlational study cannot determine how states of mind as revealed in an interview affect the quality of marital and parenting relationships, one possible candidate for a mechanism that drives the system is "emotion regulation." A number of authors have suggested that the central defining attribute of the attachment system is a set of strategies for coping with upset that is elicited when there is a threat to the relationship (Dozier & Kobak, 1992; Mikulincer & Florian, 1998; Shaver, Belsky, & Brennan, 2000). P. A. Cowan, Cohn, and colleagues (1996) have argued that the AAI provides a context in which high scores for coherence are attained if an individual is able to think about and recount difficult or painful family experiences in a balanced way that is understandable to the interviewer. Zimmermann (1999) showed in a correlational study of adolescents that their security of attachment as measured by the AAI was significantly correlated with a measure of their emotion regulation in response to social rejection in a story. In a new theoretical analysis of the ecology of attachment in the family, Hill, Fonagy, Safier, and Sargent (2003) and Steele and Steele (2003) also make a persuasive case that affect regulation is a key component of the attachment process. The AAI challenges the interviewee both to pay attention to his or her inner distress and to monitor the interpersonal transaction with the interviewer so that the story makes sense. This is exactly the kind of dual strategy that can facilitate the discussion of a troubling marital problem or a parent's interaction with a child who is having trouble completing a difficult task.

In the AAI coding system (Hesse, 1999), high ratings of current involving anger do not simply reflect whether the respondent expresses anger at parents, but rather the degree to which the anger is uncontained and "takes over" the quality of the discourse. That is, affect regulation is not only a matter of controlling negative emotion, but of expressing it in productive ways. In the analyses reported here, fathers' current anger at their parents was unrelated to their behavior with their wives during the marital conflict resolution task. By contrast, mothers who were rated as still angry at their parents were more blaming or controlling of their husbands during the discussion of a marital disagreement, which may suggest that they have difficulty regulating negative emotions with important attachment figures.

We know from the work of Gottman, Katz, and Hooven (1997) that parents who are able to regulate their own emotions provide examples of how to avoid escalating negative affect during a disagreement. Gottman and colleagues showed that when parents help their children to express difficult or negative feelings without escalating out of control, their children are better able to regulate their own emotions when faced with challenging academic or social situations by resorting less to extremes of acting out aggressive, or shy withdrawn reactions in elementary school.

An Interpersonal Task Analysis Perspective

Our analysis so far suggests that continuities of behavior across relationships are carried primarily by the individual—either in terms of representations of attachment relationship or style of regulating emotion during stressful exchanges. Another possible contributor to the correlations between grandparent–parent, marital, and parent–child relationships may be the similarities in what it takes to maintain intimate relationships regardless of the age of the participants. Hazan and Zeifman (1999) noted that the four defining features of attachment relationships between parents and infants—maintaining proximity, dealing with separation, use of the relationship as a safe haven, and use of the attachment figure as a secure base when the relationship is threatened—all apply directly to adult pair bonds. To these features we would add the necessity of balancing the expression of both positive and negative emotions as a basic requirement for parent–child and marital relationships that are both satisfying and growth-enhancing. Evidence supporting the general importance of emotion regulation in family processes associated with children's adaptation to school also comes from chapter 7, where we saw that boys' and girls' perceptions of marital conflict play out differently in predicting both internalizing and externalizing behavior in kindergarten.

Sex Differences and Intergenerational Transmission

What the separate analyses by sex of parent and child revealed clearly is that intergenerational transmission may have different dynamics, depending on whether we are focusing on the mother line (Lowinsky, 1992) or the father line, and whether the transmission concerns a son or a daughter. Mothers were less strongly implicated in their sons' antisocial, hostile, and oppositional behaviors and more powerfully in their daughters' and sons' depressed, anxious, and withdrawn behavior in kindergarten. Fathers were more strongly implicated in their sons' and daughters' externalizing behavior and less strongly implicated in their sons' depressed, anxious, and socially isolated behaviors at school. However, data from fathers were strongly predictive of internalizing in their daughters. The role of fathers in their daughters' internalizing and their sons' externalizing behavior is similar to that found by Hsu in chapter 5. We need to treat these interesting patterns as tentative ones, because we cannot test the significance of the differences between the arrangement of the paths in each PLS model. They must be replicated and explored further in other studies.

If we accept the continuous scores in the latent variables assessing current anger and parents as loving as indexes of parents' attachment security or insecurity, we can speculate about how insecurity about parent–child relationships plays out in the relationships that each adult then establishes in the new families they create. It may be that insecure attachments in women and men get expressed in different ways, with more withdrawn, depressed behavior more characteristic of women, and more angry and hostile behavior more characteristic of men. Future research could profitably examine this possibility in more microanalytic observational studies of both marital and parent–child relationships.

It is not clear to us why mothers' working models of attachment and their behavior in the marital problem solving and parent–child interactions predicted angry aggressive behavior in their daughters but not in their sons. Here is where it could be helpful to incorporate the children's views of their parents into more complex intergenerational models as we did in chapter 7, but this would require a larger sample than is available in this study.

Note that the father–son model is the only one of the four in which current anger at parents is not related either to family processes or children's outcomes. It appears that fathers find ways to avoid having the anger at their parents spill over into their relationships with their sons. In future studies, it will be important to explore parents' attachments to their mothers and fathers separately. Based on what fathers reported in an earlier investigation (C. P. Cowan & Cowan, 1992), it may that be some men make conscious efforts to avoid repeating with their sons the negative experiences they had with their fathers.

Further research should investigate the possibility that the sex of the parent toward whom the anger is expressed may play a role in the intergenerational transmission of relationships. A hint from the current data set can be found in the fact that in the father–daughter model, the father's anger at his mother has very high loadings on the latent variable assessing current anger (.92), whereas anger at his father has very low loadings (.10). We interpret this to mean that the fathers' anger at his mother plays more of a role in his treatment of his daughter—a trend not present in the father–son models. Especially because of the small sample size, acceptance of this finding awaits further replication studies.

CONCLUSIONS

When AAIs elicit convincing accounts of parents' experiences of little loving in childhood or uncontained anger at their parents, those parents' working models of attachment appear to function as risks for their children adopting internalizing or externalizing behavior strategies as they face the challenges of beginning elementary school. The accuracy of the prediction depends on the gender of the parent being interviewed, the gender of the child, the qualities of the other key relationships in the family, and the particular outcome used as a measure of the child's adaptation to school. The results suggest that our understanding of the generational transmission of attachment patterns can profit from looking at the interactions among the subsystems of a family. It is also clear that mental representations of growing up in one's family or the quality of parents' current relationships with their parents do not determine their behavior with spouse or child, and in that sense, the "template" is more of a potential action system within the family than a mold that shapes parents' behavior with their children.

9

Parents' Work Experiences and Children's Adaptation to School

Marc S. Schulz

In this chapter, we continue our emphasis on family processes, moving for the first time outside the zone of intimate family life to examine associations between parents' outlook on their work lives and their children's adaptation to elementary school. Employed work is a pervasive presence in the daily life of most families in our society. Rapid social changes in workforce participation for women and continually evolving cultural values about work and family roles have created uncertainty about the most optimal balance between work and family life for men, for women, and for couples (Hochschild, 1989, 1997; Zimmerman, Haddock, Current, & Ziemba, 2003). This uncertainty is particularly salient during the early years of family development when children are babies, and again when they are making transitions into day care, preschool, and elementary school (C. P. Cowan & Cowan, 2000). Because these are periods filled with many family responsibilities, the risk of conflict between work demands and family needs is high (S. M. McHale & Crouter, 1992; Repetti & Wood, 1997; Thompson, 1997). Work routines, particularly for mothers, often change in important ways from the birth of a first child through that child's entry into school. Working parents are well aware of the impact that work can have on family life. Fifty-nine percent of men and 61% of women indicated in one national survey that the reason they had taken their current job was its "effect on family life" (Diamant, 1993). That is, choices about where to work and how long to work were affected by the extent to which the job facilitated or complicated workers' efforts to support and enjoy their family lives.

THREE DIMENSIONS OF WORK

Research on work–family connections tends to focus on whether both partners are working outside the home, how many hours each partner works, and the relative earnings of each spouse (Stebbins, 2001). This chapter examines a multidimensional model of the influence of parents' work on family life and on their children's initial social and academic adjustment to kindergarten. Moving beyond the consideration of number of hours worked or income earned, it seeks to articulate ways in which psychologically significant aspects of parents' work experiences reverberate within the family, and to provide evidence concerning how these work-related reverberations might be linked with children's functioning.

The work-related variables that we examined here build on the multidomain model articulated in this volume. To tap individual-level aspects of work, in addition to weekly work hours we examine each partner's psychological investment in his or her work. Second, at the couple relationship level, we examine satisfaction with partners' support for decisions about working outside the home. Third, we assess variables that are part of the workplace context outside of the family—the degree of autonomy men and women have in carrying out their jobs, and their control over their work schedules. Taken together, autonomy and control represent the degree of flexibility and personal control that each partner has at work. Continuing with the theme of gender differences in family patterns, we examine differences and similarities between mothers and fathers in how these work-related factors are connected to their children's adaptation to the first year of elementary school.

Psychological Investment in Work

Individuals working at the same job may experience their work in very different ways because they are not invested in this aspect of their life in the same way. Past research suggests that parents' psychological investment in their work roles is associated with their well-being (Greenberger & O'Neil, 1993). Investment in work has been conceptualized and measured in two primary ways. The first treats the number of hours engaged in work as a marker of the degree of investment one has in work. The second approach focuses more directly on the degree of psychological engagement in work. In this approach, the significance of work to each person's daily life is the critical construct. Although hours worked and psychological investment in work may be related, these constructs are clearly not equivalent. For example, some individuals may work long hours based on financial necessity but not feel a particularly strong connection to their work.

Work and Marital Relationships

The influence of parents' work experience on children's functioning may depend in part on its impact on the couple relationship and on the way in which work outside the home is supported within a marriage (Repetti, 1989; Rogers & May, 2003; Schulz, 1997; Schulz, Cowan, Cowan, & Brennan, 2004). Despite the contemporary increase in employment of mothers of young children, important differences persist in expectations about the "proper" roles for men and women in the family and in the workplace. For married men with young children, the role of breadwinner continues to be highly valued and encouraged in our society. Married women with young children face a less clear set of expectations regarding their role. Because of this ambiguity in role expectations, women's work experiences and their impact on the family and children may be particularly influenced by their partners' supportiveness of their work (Gray, Lovejoy, Piotrkowski, & Bond, 1990; Parcel & Menaghan, 1990; Sears & Galambos, 1992; Vannoy & Philliber, 1992). In our review of this literature, we found that researchers often inquire about the role of husbands' support for wives' work in explaining variations in family relationships and children's adaptation, but not about the role of wives' support for husbands' work. In this chapter, we investigate each partner's perceptions of the spouses' support for decisions about work. A partner's psychological sanctioning of a job outside the family, and emotional support for the daily challenges and pleasures associated with that job, might reduce the strain associated with trying to balance work with family role expectations and responsibilities.

Disagreement over a partner's work investment (psychological and actual time invested) could lead to friction in the couple relationship and individual adjustment difficulties (Greenberger & O'Neil, 1993), which are risk factors for children's development (P. A. Cowan, Cowan, Schulz, & Heming, 1994; Cummings & Davies, 1994), as we have seen in this and other studies. Moreover, a lack of support for working from one's partner, or high levels of unresolved marital conflict, are likely to amplify the difficulties associated with balancing work and family roles and managing work stress in general (Repetti, 1989).

Flexibility and Personal Control

Variations in the degree of general autonomy one has at work and in whether one has control over the scheduling of work hours are also likely to influence both parents' experience of their jobs and the options they have to balance work and family demands. Having greater autonomy at work might provide parents with psychological benefits such as a sense of control, a feeling of independence, and opportunities for the development of new skills (Kohn &

Schooler, 1973). Having control over scheduling work hours, which is likely to be more common in jobs that have greater overall autonomy, might benefit working parents and their children by giving parents flexibility to respond to family needs as required. Both the psychological benefits of autonomy to the worker and the family benefits associated with control over one's work schedule could carry over to facilitate children's development in positive ways. To begin to understand which of these potential benefits may be operative, we have included measures of both autonomy over the way in which work is carried out and of control over the scheduling of work.

Hypotheses

1. We hypothesized that psychological work investment, support from a spouse for decisions about work, and autonomy and control over work, would all be positively linked with children's social and academic functioning in kindergarten. We sought to establish the utility of applying a multidimensional model of the influence of parents' work on children's functioning by delineating the connections among these work-related variables and simultaneously considering their unique association with children's adaptation to school.

2. We expected that mothers' and fathers' experiences of work outside the family would have different links with their children's adjustment to school.

METHOD

Participants

Fifty-nine dual worker families from the Schoolchildren and their Families Project were included in this analysis, selected from the larger sample (chapter 2) if both parents worked at least 20 hours per week in the months before their first child entered kindergarten.[1] The men and women in the study worked in a variety of jobs characteristic of a middle- to upper-middle-class sample, such as administrative or sales positions in commercial settings, nurses, doctors and other health professionals, attorneys, civil service workers, and small business owners. Women were employed an average of 34.6 hr (SD = 10.4 hr) per week. The mean annual income for the women in this subsample was \$38,487 (SD =

---

[1]All families in which both partners worked at least 20 hours per week were included in analyses if teacher observational ratings on the child in the family were available. This resulted in a sample of 59 families. Data were missing on aspects of the work or family life of one of the women and six of the men in the sample resulting in a slightly reduced sample size for particular pairings of variables.

$31,069). The men worked an average of 43.5 hr (SD = 8.1 hr) per week, and their mean annual income was $59,366 ($SD$ = $46,937). The large standard deviations result primarily from the fact that about 10% of the sample earned extremely high incomes, whereas the remaining income levels are normally distributed. In the 59 families considered here, 34 of the couples' first children were boys, and 25 were girls.

Measures

The data concerning work were obtained from the prekindergarten assessments of the parents. The school outcome data were from teachers' descriptions of the children in the fall of the kindergarten year.

Work. A detailed description of the items in each of the work scales can be found in chapter 2:

1. Investment in work—In addition to work hours and income, a three-item Work Investment scale adapted from previous studies (Ladewig & White, 1984; Lodahl & Kejner, 1965) measured the degree of psychological investment each participant had in his or her work.

2. Marital support of work—Satisfaction with the partner's support of decisions made about work outside the home was assessed in a single item with a 4-point Likert-type scale.

3. Flexibility and personal control—Work autonomy was assessed with a three-item self-report scale measuring the degree to which participants believe their job provided independence, discretion, and freedom in determining how to carry out the work. To distinguish general autonomy over the way one works from control over the hours worked, participants were also asked whether they had control over the hours they worked (Schedule Control: *no* = 0; *yes* = 1).

Children's Social and Academic Functioning. Teachers rated children's adjustment to kindergarten during the fall using the Child Adaptive Behavior Inventory (CABI). The two summary scales of academic competence and social competence were used in the analyses. In the sample of families examined in this chapter, teachers' ratings of children's social and academic competence were correlated highly, $r(57)$ = .68, $p < .001$.[2]

---

[2]In the spring, the Child Adaptive Behavior Inventory academic and social competence scales were less highly correlated. Because the academic and social competence scales are conceptually interesting to consider separately and there is evidence that they become more independent over time, they were not aggregated for the analyses in this chapter despite their high degree of overlap.

Ratings completed by kindergarten teachers during the fall were used for two reasons. First, we were interested in capturing children's initial school readiness and adaptation to kindergarten. Second, the fall ratings were closest in time to the parents' reports of their work lives. Shifting patterns in work during this time of family life, particularly for mothers, necessitated caution about generalizing across time about participants' psychological investment in work, spousal support for work, and the stability of work conditions.

RESULTS

Overview

All three types of work variables (investment in work, support from spouse, and flexibility and personal control of working conditions) assessed during the preschool period were correlated with each other and with children's social and academic competence in the fall of the kindergarten year. Over and above hours worked, each of the three sets of work variables (psychological investment, support from spouse, flexibility and personal control) contributed unique variance to the prediction of children's adaptation to school.

Descriptive Statistics

Table 9.1 summarizes the means and standard deviations of the measures. The means for fathers and mothers on each of the predictor variables other than income and hours worked were highly similar (paired t tests were nonsignificant). As noted here and in chapter 3, fathers worked more hours per week and earned more income per year than did mothers.

The participants generally viewed the nature and context of their work in a positive light. On a 4-point scale, both partners rated support from their spouse for work decisions as just above 3. In addition, a large majority (74%) of both husbands and wives were employed in jobs in which they felt they had some control over the hours they worked. The positive evaluations of spousal support and job flexibility are not surprising for this sample for two reasons. First, the sample is generally well educated and well compensated. Both of these factors are usually associated with jobs that have greater autonomy and schedule control. Second, the parents in this sample all had at least one child under the age of 6 at home at the time the work data were collected. Flexibility in work arrangements is a great advantage for parents with young children, and they might have been motivated to seek and remain in jobs with this characteristic.

TABLE 9.1
Children's Academic and Social Adjustment and Parental Work Variables

	M	SD		
Children				
Academic competence	−.01	3.40		
Social competence	−.63	4.36		

	Mothers		Fathers	
	M	SD	M	SD
Work hours	34.64	10.36	43.47	8.05
Income	38,487	31,069	59,366	46,937
Work investment	2.46	.50	2.39	.62
SPSW	3.08	.71	3.09	.56
Work autonomy	5.88	1.01	5.78	.95
Schedule control	.74	.44	.74	.45

Note. $n = 53$ to 59. SPSW = Satisfaction with Partner Support for Work Outside the Home.

Correlational Analyses

Associations Among Work Variables. The results of correlational analyses examining linkages among all the variables are presented in Table 9.2. As anticipated, a number of the work-related variables were significantly interrelated, although generally at a low to barely moderate level. The overall patterns for men and women are consistent with the notion that these variables measure important subcomponents or dimensions of parents' work experience. Mothers' and fathers' self-investment in paid work was related to the number of hours they worked and, for fathers, to their salaries. More hours of work and a higher income were associated with participants reporting that work was more personally significant for them. For women, but not for men, there was a connection between how satisfied they were with their partner's support for their decisions about work and their level of income: Women who earned more money were more satisfied with their husbands' support of their work. Parents who reported that they had control over their work hours also reported that their jobs provided more autonomy than parents who had no control over their work hours.

Parents' Work-Related Variables and Children's Adaptation to School. The correlational analyses presented in Table 9.2 also provided initial evidence of links between parental work-related variables and children's functioning in kindergarten. The linkages that were present were generally weak to moderate in strength, with the largest correlation (mothers' autonomy at

TABLE 9.2

Correlations Among Work-Related Variables and Children's Social and Academic Functioning in Kindergarten

	Work Hours	Income	Work Investment	SPSW	Autonomy	Schedule Control	Academic Comp.	Social Comp.
Mothers								
Work hours	—	.64**	.31*	-.02	.04	-.22	-.24	-.12
Income		—	.22	.30*	.14	.03	-.18	-.04
Work investment			—	.02	.29*	-.10	-.02	.01
SPSW				—	.23	.31*	.17	.25
Autonomy					—	.29*	.26*	.39*
Schedule control						—	.29*	.11
Academic competence							—	.68*
Social competence								—
Fathers								
Work hours	—	.33*	.39*	-.14	.14	-.08	-.14	-.03
Income		—	.33*	-.06	.18	.11	-.07	.12
Work investment			—	-.15	.26	.30*	.31*	.26
SPSW				—	.23	.05	.04	.02
Autonomy					—	.23	-.04	-.06
Schedule control						—	-.02	-.19
Academic competence							—	.68*
Social competence								—

Note. SPSW = Satisfaction with Partner Support for Work Outside the Home.

*p ≤ .05. **p ≤ .01 (two-tailed).

work and children's social competence) accounting for 15% of the total variance in children's social competence.

Within the middle-class range of incomes reported by the participants in this study, neither mothers' nor fathers' income level was related to teachers' ratings of the children's social or academic competence. There was no link between mothers' work investment and their children's competence. The children of fathers who reported that work was of greater personal significance were rated by teachers as more academically competent than children of fathers who reported that work was of less personal significance.

Children of mothers who reported greater autonomy in their work situation were seen by teachers as more socially and academically competent than children of mothers with less autonomy. The children of mothers with control over their work hours were rated by teachers as more academically competent than children whose mothers had no control over their work hours.

Combined Contributions of Parents' Work-Related Variables

Hierarchical multiple regression analyses were conducted to determine the unique and additive contributions of parents' work-related variables to their children's social and academic functioning in kindergarten. The order of entry of variables in the model was guided by the multidomain ecological model emphasized throughout this volume. Hours worked and income were entered first so that the potential influence of more psychologically meaningful work-related variables on children's school functioning could be examined after accounting for the indicators of work status. In the second step, an individual-psychological work variable, work investment, was entered. The two more contextually-based types of work variables were entered in the final two steps. In the third step, satisfaction with partner's support for work was entered. In the final step, two variables indexing perceptions of work conditions were entered together: work autonomy and control over work schedule. Simultaneous entry of autonomy and schedule control in one step allowed for consideration of their joint contribution (by examination of the ΔR^2 for that step) as well as the independent contribution of each variable over and above the other variable (by examination of the individual regression coefficients for each variable in the final model). The results of these regression analyses are presented in Table 9.3.

Mothers' Work Experience and Children's School Adaptation. In contrast with the weak to moderate effect sizes of the individual correlations, the combined models examining mothers' work-related variables explained a higher proportion of the variance in their children's academic and social competence—21% of the variance in academic functioning, $p = .06$, and 22%,

TABLE 9.3
Hierarchical Multiple Regression Linking Work-Related Variables
to Children's Social and Academic Functioning in Kindergarten

Measure	Academic Competence		Social Competence	
	β	ΔR²	β	ΔR²
Mothers				
Step 1		.06		.02
Hours per week	−.10		−.04	
Income	−.19		−.11	
Step 2				
Work investment	−.03	.00	−.14	.00
Step 3				
SPSW	.16	.04	.23†	.07*
Step 4		.10*		.14*
Autonomy	.23		.41*	
Schedule control	.21		−.03	
Total R²		.21†		.22*
Fathers				
Step 1		.02		.02
Hours per week	−.30†		−.23	
Income	−.13		.09	
Step 2				
Work investment	.52**	.17**	.40*	.07*
Step 3				
SPSW	.07	.00	.05	.00
Step 4		.03		.09†
Autonomy	−.06		−.08	
Schedule control	−.15		−.29*	
Total R²		.22†		.18

Note. The β values reported are standardized betas from the final regression model with all variables entered. SPSW = Satisfaction with Partner Support for Work Outside the Home.
†p ≤ .1. *p ≤ .05. **p ≤ .01.

$p < .05$, of the variance in social functioning. In three important respects, the results of the regression analyses clarify and extend the correlational analyses. First, the zero-order correlational analyses indicated a marginally significant negative association, $r = −.22, p < .1$, between the number of hours mothers worked and children's academic competence. When this association was considered simultaneously with the other work-related variables in the regression analyses, it was substantially diminished ($\beta = −.10, p = .54$). These results, consistent with Baron and Kenny's (1986) definition of mediation, indicate that a portion of the shared variance between the hours mothers worked and children's academic competence is accounted for by the quality and context of women's work experiences. Once these dimensions of work experience were accounted for, any link between mothers' work hours and children's academic competence was largely eliminated.

Second, mothers' satisfaction with their husbands' support for their decisions about working accounted for a significant increment in variance (7%) in their children's social competence, over and above any influence of income, hours worked, and degree of investment in work. The contribution of mothers' satisfaction with their husbands' support remained marginally significant in the model when the contextual variables of control over work schedule and job autonomy were added to the model.

Third, the unique contributions of mothers' job autonomy and control over work hours to their children's early school functioning were clarified. Together as a block, both autonomy and control over work schedule for mothers explained significant variance in their children's academic and social competence (10% for academic competence, 14% for social competence), over and above the influence of all the other work-related variables considered. In the case of children's social competence, mothers' job autonomy accounted for significant variance in children's success at school, over and above the influence of their control over work hours and all other work-related variables. As in the correlational analyses, mothers' control over work hours was not a significant independent predictor in the children's social competence model. This result suggests that, independent of their control over the hours they work, mothers' sense of autonomy at work has beneficial effects for their family lives, and ultimately for the social competence of their children as they begin their school careers.

Consideration of the regression coefficients in the academic competence model indicate that neither schedule control nor work autonomy of mothers made significant independent contributions to predicting children's academic functioning. However, together as a block they contribute significantly to the model, over and above the influence of all other work-related variables. Mothers who reported having control over their work schedule and more autonomy at work had children who were seen as more academically competent by their kindergarten teachers.

Fathers' Work Experience and Children's School Adaptation. Important similarities and differences between the sexes in the pattern of correlational findings presented earlier became clearer with the regression analyses presented in Table 9.3. In contrast to the importance of satisfaction with the spouse's support and work autonomy in the mothers' models, fathers' psychological investment in work and, to a lesser extent, aspects of work conditions such as control over work schedule and hours worked, emerged as predictors of children's early school adaptation.

For children's early academic functioning, 22% ($p < .10$) of the variance was explained by fathers' work-related variables. The strongest predictor in the regression model was fathers' psychological investment in their work, which accounted for a substantial and statistically significant portion (17%, p

< .01) of the variance, over and above the influence of fathers' income and hours worked. The more fathers were psychologically invested in their work, the more likely their children were to be viewed by their teachers as academically high functioning. The implications of this positive link are particularly intriguing when contrasted with the negative but nonsignificant association that emerged between fathers' work hours and children's level of academic achievement. Despite a moderate positive correlation between work investment and hours worked, these variables have distinct associations with children's academic functioning. Regardless of the number of hours fathers work outside the home, their psychological investment in their work may have potential benefits for their children's development and their life as a family.

The importance of fathers' psychological investment in work for children's social adaptation as they made the transition to school received further support in the regression examining fathers' work-related variables and children's social functioning. Although the overall regression was not statistically significant, we can see in Table 9.3 that fathers' work investment was a significant predictor and accounted for 7% ($p < .05$) of the variance in their children's social competence, over and above the influence of income and hours worked. The children of fathers who reported being more psychologically engaged in their work were rated as more socially competent than were children of fathers who were less invested in their work. Fathers' control over work hours emerged as another significant predictor of children's social functioning. In contrast to the absence of a link between mothers' control over work and children's social competence, and opposite to our expectations, fathers who had job flexibility and control over their work hours had children who were seen as less socially competent by their kindergarten teachers. Because work flexibility and the number of hours men worked were uncorrelated, this finding cannot be explained simply by the fact that men who had jobs with higher levels of personal control worked more hours (and were therefore away from home more).

DISCUSSION

Beyond Hours Worked

Large-scale studies tend to use employment status (yes–no) or number of hours worked as the main indicator of men's and women's involvement and investment in the workplace, and as a consequence, their lack of involvement in home and family life (e.g., Brooks-Gunn, Han, & Waldfogel, 2002). The findings in this study suggest that the hours parents work need to be considered in concert with more psychologically-oriented measures of parents' work experience to understand their association with children's functioning.

The findings indicate that multiple dimensions of parents' work-related experiences are associated with their children's adaptation over and above the influence of hours worked. Each of the three aspects of parents' work that we examined (work investment, support from spouse, and perceived job flexibility) predicted unique variance in children's academic and social adjustment to kindergarten. For mothers, the context in which work occurred—indexed here by satisfaction with partners' support for decisions about work, control over work schedule, and autonomy at work—was associated with their children's more successful adaptation in the first year of elementary school. For fathers, a more individually-based aspect of work—their level of psychological engagement or investment in work—had the strongest and most consistent implications for their children's adjustment to early elementary school. The effect sizes of the significant predictions ranged from 7% to 22% of the variance in children's academic and social adaptation to school. The higher end of these effect sizes for work predictors is similar to the predictive power of other aspects of family life, described in the preceding chapters, in accounting for variations in children's adaptation to school.

Context of Employment and Mothers' Work Experience

Two contextual factors, work-friendly spouses and family-friendly jobs, may be particularly important in understanding the connections between mothers' work and children's academic and social competence in kindergarten. First, the results point to wives' perceptions of their husbands' support for their decisions to work outside the family as an important contextual factor of parents' work that has implications for children's functioning. Perhaps, because women typically experience higher levels of strain between their work and family roles than do men (Hochschild, 1989), and because there is less cultural consensus regarding the desirability of employment for mothers with young children (Parcel & Menaghan, 1990), husbands' support for their wives' work decisions is particularly important for the well-being of mothers of young children.

Second, previous studies suggest that when work settings are supportive of family life, working parents benefit (e.g., Galinsky, Bond, & Friedman, 1996). Flexibility in scheduling of work may be of particular benefit to working mothers because they are more likely than working fathers to shoulder most of the responsibility for the care of young children (Hochschild, 1989). Having control over their work hours and greater autonomy over how they accomplish that work might make it easier for mothers to balance the competing demands of work and family, and ultimately to meet their young children's needs.

Over and above the importance of being able to control one's work schedule, autonomy at work may be associated with other psychological processes that facilitate working mothers' adaptation and the quality of their parenting. Autonomy may offer opportunities for self-direction and growth that foster the development of new skills. Either directly because of these new skills, or indirectly because of the sense of mastery and accomplishment that often accompanies the acquisition of new skills, workers with greater autonomy may be more effective in domains outside of work, including parenting (Greenberger, O'Neil, & Nagel, 1994). A socialization perspective (e.g., Kohn & Schooler, 1973) suggests that parents may learn to value self-direction and responsibility when they have jobs with greater autonomy, and they may then encourage similar behaviors in their children. Children entering kindergarten with more self-direction and initiative are likely to be seen as more socially competent by their teachers, although this would not necessarily be related to their academic competence. The results are consistent with this perspective.

It is important to acknowledge that the correlational nature of this study limits our ability to identify the direction of influence among the variables and to rule out potential confounds. The positive association between mothers' work autonomy and their children's functioning in kindergarten may reflect the fact that mothers who are generally higher functioning, or who have children who are generally higher functioning, are able to seek and obtain jobs that provide more autonomy. Even without untangling the direction of effects, these results suggest that there may be continuity of approaches to relationships in the workplace and the family; autonomy fostered in one setting may lead to autonomy being fostered in the other.

Fathers' Investment in Their Work

Although fathers' greater psychological investment in work could imply increased psychological absence, we found that, over and above the hours worked, this variable was linked positively with their kindergartners' academic and social adjustment. Previous research has revealed both positive and negative implications of parents' psychological investment in work (Greenberger & O'Neil, 1993; Pleck, 1985). One potential reason for these apparently conflicting results is the possibility that previous measures of work investment or the related construct of work commitment may have unknowingly captured both a positive dimension reflecting strong engagement in work and a negative dimension reflecting overabsorption in work (Goldberg, Greenberger, & Nagel, 1996; Greenberger & O'Neil, 1993). The overabsorption dimension may be more reflective of what others have called role overload (Gutek, Repetti, & Silver, 1988). The number of hours that fathers worked, which had a marginally negative association with children's academic functioning in this study, may capture part of this overabsorption dimension. Previous studies have found associations between parents' work hours and poorer social and academic adjustment in their children (Goldberg et al., 1996). Accounting for the hours men work without considering their actual psychological investment in work may lead researchers to miss the positive implications of men's work commitment.

The negative association between fathers' control over work hours and children's social competence may also reflect a kind of overabsorption by fathers in their work lives. Although there was no connection between how many hours fathers generally worked each week and whether they had control over their work schedule, it is possible that fathers with control over their schedule tended to occupy jobs with greater responsibility, which might make it difficult to disengage from work for family needs. Control over their work schedule may have its greatest impact for these men in allowing them to meet increased demands at work as they occur. Fathers in these circumstances may need or feel compelled to focus their energies on work activities during busy stretches, with the result that they are not as available to their families and children as one might expect. This possibility suggests that having control over work may serve different functions for working mothers and fathers, and points to the importance, in future research, of identifying factors that influence the weekly work schedule of those who have control over their hours (Hochschild, 1997). For example, do mothers and fathers typically decrease their work hours in response to family demands? Or do they typically increase their work hours to respond to work demands?

Differences Between Mothers and Fathers

The differences between mothers and fathers in the overall pattern of linkages between work and children's adaptation are consistent with beliefs concerning men's and women's general orientation to the world (Gilligan, 1982; Tannen, 1990). Although these differences may reflect, in part, personality characteristics of each sex, they are also likely to be shaped by a social structure that still treats men's and women's work outside the home differently (Hochschild, 1989). It may be that only when the family and work context is supportive for women can they fill their family roles in ways that are satisfying and beneficial to them, their spouses, and their children. By contrast, benefits from work for men may depend more directly on their psychological investment in their jobs rather than the degree of support they get from their partner or the flexibility of their jobs.

CONCLUSIONS

Although the theoretical focus of this chapter has primarily been on the ways in which work-related experiences predict children's adaptation to school, it is likely that the findings reflect reciprocal influences between work and family life. Family processes and characteristics of the child may influence whether life at work seems manageable. Husbands may be less supportive of wives working outside the home when family relationships at home are strained. A particularly promising methodology for investigating mediating processes that explain how work conditions affect family life at home, and vice versa, is the use of intensive daily data collections to provide repeated measures of important aspects of daily work and family experience (e.g., Crouter, Perry-Jenkins, Huston, & Crawford, 1989; Repetti, 1989; Repetti & Wood, 1997). A subset of 42 couples from the Schoolchildren and their Families Project completed such daily measures over the course of 3 days. Analyses focused on the spillover of negative emotional arousal from the parents' workday indicated that end-of-the-workday feeling states predicted the quality of subsequent family interactions at home (Schulz, 1997; Schulz et al., 2004). These influences of parents' daily work lives on their life at home could certainly have a direct impact on children's adaptation to school. It is also the case that children's successes and failures in meeting the daily challenges of making the transition to kindergarten could affect family interactions at home, with subsequent spillover to the parents' next day at work.

The findings here provide a base for speculations about how aspects of parents' work experiences could affect children's adaptation. These ideas follow the outline of the multidomain family systems model that we have been exploring throughout the volume. First, there are individual considerations. Fathers who are psychologically invested in their jobs (but are not always at work), and mothers who have autonomy and control over their work circumstances, may have the psychological freedom, strength, and confidence to be effective parents at home. Conversely, the repeated experience of arriving home from work stressed, overloaded, and feeling badly about oneself is likely to affect individual adjustment and family life in significant ways and provide a negative model for coping with stress that children may emulate (Repetti, 1989; Repetti & Wood, 1997; Schulz, 1997; Schulz et al., 2004).

Second are considerations on the couple level; a husband's support for his wife's work outside the family is an important part of their partnership. Earlier research suggests that a supportive spouse helps men cope with their work demands (Repetti, 1989), and that support from a spouse is even more important to women's well-being than to men's (Greenberger & O'Neil, 1993). Conversely, lack of support from the spouse about work can spill over into the marriage in ways that can be debilitating for children, as we have shown.

Third, parent–child relationships are part of the mix. An important series of studies has explored work–family connections utilizing a socialization model to explain how parents' work experiences influence their family values, childrearing practices and skills, and ultimately their children's social functioning (e.g., Greenberger et al., 1994; Kohn, 1969, 1979, 1983). In this model, parents' values about children's behavior (e.g., the importance of children's self-direction vs. obedience to authority) and their parenting behaviors are shaped by the demands and experiences they encounter in their daily jobs. The model has been invoked to explain social class-based differences in parenting practices and children's social behavior, as well as to examine within-class differences in childrearing practices that might be linked to differences in work conditions (e.g., Greenberger et al., 1994). A central focus of research within the socialization model has been on the degree of autonomy or self-direction a worker has on the job (Hulin, 2002) and how that is related to his or her behavior in the family.

Finally, although not part of the investigation here, the intergenerational history of work patterns may provide a context for understanding parents' current investment in work and their support for their spouses' involvement in work. For example, younger generations may make choices and evaluate their own work trajectories in reaction to their parents' work patterns ("My mother never worked after I was born, but she was unhappy and so I'm going to do things differently" or "My father was never home, and so I'm determined to be home more with my children"). These patterns, and the judgments that follow from them, may have a combined impact on how young children set a course for their own school careers.

10

Family Process and Family Structure in Children's Adaptation to School

Vanessa K. Johnson

In most family studies, certainly including this one, descriptions of family functioning have been guided by clinically-based theories that argue for the importance of considering the family as a system when we try to understand adaptation and dysfunction in children's development (Minuchin, 1974). In this chapter, we present one approach to a family-level analysis (see Wagner & Reiss, 1995) of links among family process, family structure, and children's school outcomes, using measures that attempt to characterize the family as a whole rather than assessing one or more of the relationship pairs in the family (mother–father, mother–child, father–child, sibling–sibling).

Specifically, this chapter explores connections between mothers' and fathers' perceptions of their family environment on the Family Environment Scale (FES; Moos & Moos, 1976) in the prekindergarten year and teachers' reports of the children's academic competence, internalizing, and externalizing in the early months of kindergarten. The FES describes three dimensions of the family environment: (a) the relationship dimension, focusing on family members' feelings of belonging to, and pride in, their family, and the degree to which open expression and conflictual interactions are characteristic of the family climate; (b) the system maintenance dimension, which assesses the organization within the family (e.g., highly structured and rule-oriented versus a more laissez-faire organization) and the degree of control usually exerted by family members over one another; and (c) the personal growth dimension, which emphasizes the family's encouragement of autonomy and its emphasis on academic concerns and getting ahead in life. The first two of these dimensions are familiar to clinical family system theorists (e.g., Minuchin, 1974), who tend to pay attention to the quality of family transactions or processes and levels of family structure and organization rather than to the adaptation of specific individuals or dyads.

PROCESS AND STRUCTURE

As dimensions of family life, family process and family structure can be thought of as two conceptually-distinct lenses applied to the same set of phenomena (Demo & Acock, 1996; Schoppe, Mangelsdorf, & Frosch, 2001). The process dimension is concerned with the quality of interaction among members and the valence of that interaction, typically measured in positive or negative scales such as warmth or conflict. The family structure dimension is more difficult to define. It refers to formal characteristics of systems that describe a pattern of connection or disconnection among the parts. Families with parents that are married, separated, or divorced have different structures, but the aspect of structure we are concerned with here involves organization (rigid versus chaotic), control (the family enforces rules for all members versus little emphasis on rules), and value orientation (the family emphasizes or does not emphasize achievement and getting ahead). These are all descriptors of the system as a whole that do not portray specific patterns of interaction among family members (e.g., this dimension does not tell us how the family enforces the rules, or whether rule-enforcement transactions occur with warmth or hostility).

Process and structure are conceptualized as orthogonal dimensions of family life, and there is some evidence to support this assumption (Olson & Gorall, 2003). Families can be warm and cohesive in their relationships and either highly structured and rule-following or chaotic and anarchic. Families high in conflict or with no conflict can be described as high or low in structure and organization.

DYADIC VERSUS WHOLE-FAMILY
LEVELS OF ANALYSIS

A growing body of family research documents meaningful differences between dyadic and whole family assessments of family functioning. Both marital interaction and parenting behavior may be qualitatively and quantitatively different when observed in family dyads or when the entire family is together (Johnson, Silverman, Compton, & Leon, 1998). For example, many couples behave differently when talking alone or with their child. One study found that when husband–wife discussions were examined when the couple was alone and again while working with the child, the presence of the child resulted in lower levels of hostility, warmth, assertiveness, coercion, communication, and self-disclosure between the parents (Deal, Hagan, Bass, Hetherington, & Clingempeel, 1999). Parent–child relationships also vary across dyadic and whole-family contexts. Gjerde (1986) found that the presence of the spouse influenced the extent to which parents treated girls and boys differently; mothers differentiated more between girls and boys when their spouse was present, whereas fathers differentiated more between girls and boys when their spouse was absent.

There is evidence that, over and above variation in marital conflict and parenting styles as assessed in dyads, family-level functioning assessed when all members are present contributes uniquely to the prediction of children's externalizing behavior (Johnson et al., 1999; J. P. McHale & Rasmussen, 1998). Furthermore, studies examining affective processes and structural aspects of families find that both are related to the quality of marital and parent–child relationships (Christensen & Margolin, 1988; Johnson et al., 1999; J. P. McHale, 1995). For example, families characterized as less cohesive (lower levels of emotional bonding of family members toward one another) and less organized (lower levels of parental leadership, connection, and interaction among family members) are more likely than non-distressed family systems to contain maritally distressed couples (Christensen & Margolin, 1988; J. P. McHale, 1995) and negative father–child relationships (Johnson et al., 1999). These findings suggest that assessments of marital quality and parenting in isolation from the rest of the family (i.e., in dyads) may not fully capture the family dynamics that result from the interplay among the family dyads when all family members are together.

FAMILY-LEVEL ANALYSIS
AND CHILDREN'S ADJUSTMENT

A few studies have begun to move beyond the dyad to examine the connection between family process at the level of the whole-family and children's academic competence (Brody & Flor, 1996; Nelson, 1984) and emotional adjustment (Brage & Meredith, 1994; Cumsille & Epstein, 1994; Feldman, Rubenstein, & Rubin, 1988; Kashani, Allan, Dahlmeier, & Rezvani, 1995; Messer & Gross, 1995; Westerman & Schonholtz, 1988). Studies of early childhood reveal that family cohesion (the warmth and relatedness dimension) is associated with both parents' and teachers' reports of fewer internalizing and externalizing behavior problems in the children. Similarly, family cohesion is linked to lower levels of depression in middle childhood and adolescence: Six to 12-year-old children diagnosed with depression describe their families as less cohesive than nondepressed children (Kashani et al., 1995). Depressed adolescents report having less cohesive (Cumsille & Epstein, 1994; Feldman et al., 1988) and less adaptive (Brage & Meredith, 1994) families than nondepressed adolescents. Cole and McPherson (1993) found that depression is more closely associated with cohesion in the father–adolescent relationship than in the mother–child relationship.

With a few exceptions (e.g., Brody & Flor, 1996; Johnson et al., 1999; J. P. McHale & Rasmussen, 1998; Westerman & Schonholtz, 1988), studies have primarily assessed family characteristics and child outcomes on the basis of information obtained from the child or adolescent. Furthermore, most studies examining the role of family level processes in children's adjustment focus on a single dimension of the family environment, typically the dimension of relatedness (cohesion), neglecting other more structural aspects of the whole family context such as the system maintenance and personal growth dimensions. Moos and Moos (1976) reported that all three dimensions (relatedness, system maintenance, and personal growth) differentiate functional and dysfunctional family systems. Finally, studies of family process and structure tend to examine adaptation outcomes using concurrent measures. This chapter takes a prospective approach to investigating the connection between parents' perceptions of both relatedness and structure in the family before their oldest child entered elementary school, and the children's academic competence, internalizing behavior, and externalizing behavior during the first months of kindergarten.

BETWEEN-PARENT DIFFERENCES
IN PERCEPTIONS OF FAMILY LIFE

If we ask different family members to describe their family, it should come as no surprise that they often disagree about what they see or report. Using the Family Environment Scale, Feiring and Lewis (1998) found that families with differing perceptions had adolescents with poorer school outcomes (Fiese, 1992). In a longitudinal study of parents' declines in marital satisfaction after the birth of a first child, the major predictor of the decline was differences between husbands and wives in their perceptions of life in their family (C. P. Cowan et al., 1985). Furthermore, in an earlier study, parents' lower marital satisfaction in the preschool period predicted more academic, internalizing, and externalizing difficulties in the children once they entered kindergarten (P. A. Cowan et al., 1994). Here, we expected that husband–wife differences in perceptions of whole-family process and structure would similarly be associated with lower levels of children's adaptation to kindergarten.

PROCESS AND STRUCTURE DIMENSIONS:
LINEAR OR CURVILINEAR RELATIONS
WITH ADAPTATION?

In studies of family dimensions using bipolar family scales, it is not always clear whether the scales are linear, with optimal functioning at one of the extremes (e.g., high organization), or curvilinear, with optimal functioning somewhere in the middle, represented by a balance of opposites. Moderate levels of each family environment dimension should be optimal according to Olson (1993), who reported curvilinear relations between family level processes (e.g., family cohesion and adaptation) and adolescent psychopathology. Too little warmth and sense of belonging are detrimental to the functioning of a family, but too much could reflect tangled and enmeshed relationships. Too little organization can be associated with chaos, but too much organization can be a sign of rigidity and rule-boundedness. Here we examine the case for both linear and curvilinear assumptions about family functioning and its relation to children's outcomes in the first year of elementary school.

HYPOTHESES

We tested three specific hypotheses and explored an additional question:

1. We expected that parents' perceptions of their family process (the affective, related, aspect of their relationships) and of how their families are structured and organized (system organization and personal growth values) would yield independent assessments of whole family functioning that would be differentially related to children's academic competence, and their internalizing and externalizing behaviors in the early months of kindergarten.

2. To examine whether optimal levels of relatedness and structure lie at the extremes or the middle of the range, we tested the hypothesis that children in families with moderate rather than very high or very low ratings on each family environment dimension would be seen by their teachers as more academically competent and as having fewer internalizing and externalizing problem behaviors than their peers as they made their transition to school.

3. Although we were not in a position to predict whether there would be mean differences between mothers' and fathers' perceptions of their family environment, we expected that larger discrepancies between the parents would be followed by lower levels of achievement and higher levels of internalizing and externalizing behaviors in their kindergarten children. In statistical terms, interactions between mothers' and fathers' views of the family

would add to explanations of variance in the children's early adaptation to school.

4. Based on previous findings that the connection between whole family functioning and children's behavior problems differ for families with sons and daughters (J. P. McHale, 1995), we also explored whether the links between parents' perceptions of the family environment and children's classroom behavior differ as a function of the child's sex.

METHOD

Participants

Participants were 86 families from the Schoolchildren and their Families Project who had completed each of the measures and tasks described later. Fifty of the target children in the participant families were boys, and 36 were girls.

Measures

Prior to their eldest child's entry into kindergarten, mothers and fathers completed the FES independently (Moos & Moos, 1976), as described in chapter 2. As in previous chapters, intervention participation was treated as a covariate in the analyses that follow. In the fall of the kindergarten year, teachers completed ratings of the study children and their classmates' academic and social competence using the Child Adaptive Behavior Inventory (CABI), as described in chapter 2.

Family Environment. This study used an adapted version of the FES that included 7 of the original 10 FES subscales (see chapter 2), divided among three dimensions: family relatedness (cohesion, expressiveness, conflict), system maintenance (organization, control), and personal growth (independence, achievement orientation). Each of the items describes the family as a whole rather than the individuals or pairs within it (e.g., "Family members really help and support each other," "Rules are pretty inflexible in our household," and "We feel that it is important to be the best at whatever you do"). The system maintenance and personal growth factors described by Moos and Moos (1976) were combined to create a family structure variable that described the system as a whole, but not the quality of the interactions within it. High ratings on family structure were indicative of families in which members have a strong emphasis on following rules and feel it is important to achieve relative to others.

To facilitate examination of the curvilinear relations between parents' perceptions of their families and their children's school adjustment, each composite variable was divided into thirds representing the third of the sample reporting the lowest ratings, the third reporting moderate ratings, and the third reporting the highest ratings on each factor.

Children's Adjustment to Kindergarten. Teachers' perceptions of children's initial academic and emotional adjustment to kindergarten relative to the other same-sex children in their class were assessed using three composite variables from the CABI. Children's academic competence in the fall of the kindergarten year was assessed using the three-scale factor described in chapter 2 (intelligent, creative, and task-oriented). Children's internalizing behavior was assessed using a similar type of composite variable that averaged teachers' reports of children's depressed and anxious behavior and social isolation ($\alpha = .74$). High scores on this internalizing scale were indicative of children who were seen by their teachers as socially isolated, sad, and anxious in the fall of the kindergarten year. Children's externalizing behavior was assessed using a composite variable averaging two factors described in chapter 2: children's aggression and hyperactivity ($\alpha = .85$). High scores on this externalizing scale were indicative of children who had difficulty relating to peers and were seen by teachers as either aggressive or restless, whereas low scores were indicative of children who exhibited few problem behaviors.

RESULTS

Overview

The findings are consistent with a family systems perspective, which suggests that the quality of the family environment as a whole can help us to understand variations in children's academic and emotional adaptation as they make the transition to elementary school. Both mothers' and fathers' perceptions of their family environment before the children entered elementary school were predictive of their children's early success and troubling behaviors in kindergarten. Few differences overall were found between mothers' and fathers' perceptions of the family environment. Nevertheless, as hypothesized, children of mothers and fathers who differed most in the way they viewed family structure and relatedness had a more difficult time negotiating the transition to kindergarten. Support was also found for the hypothesis that children in families with moderate rather than very high or very low family relatedness and family structure would be seen by their teachers as more academically competent and as having fewer internalizing problem behaviors than their peers. The connection between family relatedness and children's externalizing behavior, as seen by kindergarten teachers, appeared to be more linear than curvilinear. Finally, the connection between whole family functioning and children's adjustment to kindergarten differed for families with sons and daughters, but only when predicting children's academic competence and internalizing behavior, not when predicting aggression and inattention in kindergarten.

Descriptive Statistics

Table 10.1 lists the means and standard deviations for each family environment factor. Table 10.2 lists the means and standard deviations of the kindergarten teachers' ratings of the children's academic competence, and their internalizing and externalizing behavior in the classroom.

Family Relatedness and Family Structure: Independent Dimensions

The data for the relatedness and structure dimensions were continuous scores that we categorized into three levels: low, medium, and high. Because we as-

TABLE 10.1
Family Environment Factors

	Fathers' Reports		Mothers' Reports	
	M	SD	M	SD
Family relatedness				
Low	6.84	2.11	6.51	2.22
Mid	11.13	0.84	11.18	0.77
High	14.28	1.10	14.44	1.26
Family structure				
Low	14.40	2.22	15.17	2.01
Mid	19.42	1.21	19.30	1.18
High	25.17	2.46	24.56	2.44

TABLE 10.2
Means and Standard Deviations of Kindergarten
Teachers' Ratings of Children's Classroom Behavior

	Boys		Girls	
Variables	M	SD	M	SD
Academic competence	0.18	2.62	−0.55	3.01
Internalizing behavior	−0.01	2.14	0.21	2.20
Externalizing behavior	−0.23	1.95	0.79	3.31

sumed that optimal would be defined by a range rather than a specific point on a curve, we preferred to use the categorical scores in our analysis. A potential problem with this approach is that it eliminates much of the variability in the dimensions. Analyses that we conducted using both correlations and continuous scores yielded identical patterns of connection or lack of connection between parents' perceptions of their family and children's adaptation to school, and so we present the categorical scores in the following results.

First, we examined the data relevant to hypothesis 1—that the dimensions of family relatedness and structure were independent. Consistent with this hypothesis, neither correlations nor chi-square analyses yielded significant associations between the two dimensions in mothers' or fathers' responses to the FES.

Mothers' and Fathers' Perceptions of Their Family Environment

To test for mean differences between mothers and fathers, we used mixed, two-way analyses of variance (ANOVAs). The between-subjects effect was sex of child and the within-subject effect was family environment ratings made by mothers and fathers. ANOVAs were performed separately for family relatedness and family structure. No significant mean differences were found between mothers' and fathers' perceptions of family relatedness or family structure. There were no significant main effects of child sex, and there were no significant interactions between the sex of the child and parents' perceptions of either of these overall dimensions of the family environment.

Chi-square analyses indicated significant agreement between partners in the low, medium, and high ratings of both family relatedness, $X^2(4) = 13.72$, $p < .01$, and family structure, $X^2(4) = 26.48$, $p < .001$.[1] Despite the similarities between parents as a group (no average difference), and agreement between parents within families, the far from perfect associations indicated that parents in some families showed marked discrepancies in their perceptions of relatedness and structure. We examine what follows from this disagreement in the interaction terms included in the ANOVAs in the next section.

Family Environment and Children's Adaptation to Kindergarten

To test the hypothesis that parents' ratings of family process and structure would be associated with children's adaptation to school, and that optimal levels of the two dimensions would be somewhere in the midrange on each di-

---

[1]Correlations indicated that mothers' and fathers' ratings shared 9% of the variance in family relatedness and 21% of the variance in family structure.

mension, we examined kindergarten teachers' ratings of children's classroom behavior in the fall using a 2 (child sex) × 3 (low, medium, high mothers' perceptions of family environment) × 3 (low, medium, high fathers' perceptions of family environment) × 3 (academic competence, externalizing, internalizing) multivariate analyses of covariance (MANCOVA), with treatment condition (intervention, no intervention) as a covariate. Separate MANCOVAs were calculated for parents' reports of family relatedness and family structure as dependent variables. Eta^2 statistics (based on univariate tests) were calculated to determine the amount of variance in dependent variables accounted for by parents' perceptions of family relatedness and family structure. Planned comparisons were used to test the specific hypothesis that moderate levels of family relatedness and family structure would be characteristic of families with children seen by their teachers as more academically competent and as having fewer externalizing and internalizing problem behaviors.

Our analytic strategy was to examine the multivariate F tests and when they were significant, to follow up with univariate tests and planned comparisons. The multivariate main effect of family relatedness ratings by mothers and fathers on children's outcomes, the interaction between mothers' ratings of family relatedness and child sex, and the interaction between mothers' and fathers' ratings of family relatedness, all showed statistical significance. The multivariate effect of parents' perceptions of family structure was not statistically significant, but the interaction between fathers' ratings of family structure and child sex, and the interaction between mothers' and fathers' ratings of family structure, were also significant. We were justified, then, in pursuing the univariate tests reported later. Note that the means describing academic competence, externalizing behavior, and internalizing behavior in Tables 10.3 and 10.4 are z scores with a mean of 0 and a standard deviation of ± 1.

Academic Competence. We found support for hypothesis 2 in fathers' but not mothers' family environment ratings. Perceptions of both relatedness, $F(2, 52) = 4.26, p < .05, eta^2 = .14$, and structure, $F(2, 51) = 4.62, p < .01, eta^2 = .15$, by fathers, were associated with children's academic competence. Furthermore midrange ratings of the relationship dimension appeared to be optimal. Planned comparisons indicated that children whose fathers viewed their family members as midrange in relatedness (cohesion, expressiveness, conflict) were rated by their kindergarten teachers as being more academically competent ($M = .70$) than children in families rated by fathers as either low ($M = -.68$) or high ($M = -.41$) in family relatedness, $F(1, 52) = 5.00, p < .05$ (see Table 10.3).

The pattern of findings for relatedness was similar for parents of girls and parents of boys. By contrast, the pattern linking fathers' perceptions of family structure and the child's academic competence 1 year later differed by sex of child. No significant effect was found for girls. However, the association

TABLE 10.3
Means and (Standard Deviations) of Kindergarten Teachers' Ratings of Children's Classroom Behavior for Children in Families Rated by Parents as Low, Moderate, and High in Family Relatedness

		Mothers' Perceptions of Family Relatedness			Fathers' Perceptions of Family Relatedness		
		Low	Mid	High	Low	Mid	High
Academic competence	Girls	−1.61	1.20	−.58	−1.43	.85	−1.13
		(3.13)	(2.08)	(1.34)	(3.08)	(1.57)	(2.07)
	Boys	−.53	−.10	.72	−.94	.64	.50
		(2.22)	(2.04)	(3.40)	(1.46)	(3.56)	(2.40)
Internalizing behavior	Girls	.29	−1.70	1.33	.55	−.58	.84
		(2.07)	(1.63)	(2.16)	(2.96)	(1.22)	(2.13)
	Boys	1.24	.16	−.85	.96	.07	−.84
		(1.52)	(2.51)	(2.16)	(1.64)	(2.78)	(1.66)
Externalizing behavior	Girls	2.24	−.47	.30	.97	−.75	2.33
		(4.87)	(1.37)	(1.91)	(2.30)	(.83)	(5.02)
	Boys	.89	−.32	−.68	.16	.23	−.91
		(2.37)	(1.94)	(1.72)	(1.98)	(2.43)	(1.40)

TABLE 10.4
Means and (Standard Deviations) of Kindergarten Teachers' Ratings of Children's Classroom Behavior for Children in Families Rated by Parents as Low, Moderate, and High in Family Structure

		Mothers' Perceptions of Family Structure			Fathers' Perceptions of Family Structure		
		Low	Mid	High	Low	Mid	High
Academic competence	Girls	−.43	.34	−1.23	.29	−.94	−.70
		(2.07)	(.78)	(3.54)	(1.98)	(3.28)	(2.15)
	Boys	−1.02	.82	.69	−1.03	.67	1.32
		(1.70)	(3.48)	(2.39)	(1.90)	(4.07)	(1.80)
Internalizing behavior	Girls	.31	.01	−.23	−.01	.70	−.56
		(1.52)	(1.90)	(2.34)	(1.51)	(2.54)	(1.70)
	Boys	.83	−.50	−.48	.57	.25	−1.06
		(2.74)	(1.87)	(1.69)	(2.54)	(1.99)	(1.49)
Externalizing behavior	Girls	1.09	−.90	2.39	.05	.58	1.74
		(2.76)	(.82)	(4.57)	(2.60)	(3.03)	(4.24)
	Boys	.44	−.96	−.49	.13	−.16	−1.07
		(2.11)	(1.25)	(2.04)	(2.08)	(2.15)	(1.23)

between fathers' perceptions of family structure and teachers' reports of sons' academic competence in kindergarten was linear, rather than curvilinear as had been for perceptions of family relatedness (see Fig. 10.1). That is, fathers who perceived their families to be highly structured had sons with fewer academic difficulties adjusting to kindergarten ($M = 1.32$) than sons in moderately structuring families ($M = .67$); sons with the lowest academic competence scores had fathers who described the family as low in structure ($M = -1.03$). Exploratory post hoc follow-up analyses of sex differences at low, medium, and high father-perceived structure indicated a significant effect of sex of child for families described as high in structure, $F(1, 52) = 6.11$, $p < .05$. Compared to girls, boys were seen by their kindergarten teachers as more academically competent ($M = -.70$ for girls and $M = 1.32$ for boys). This finding is especially interesting in light of our finding in chapter 3 that, overall, boys in kindergarten and first grade were described by their teachers as less academically competent than girls. This subset of boys with fathers who see the family as organized and rule-following is an exception.

Although mothers' perceptions of family life were not directly associated with children's academic competence in kindergarten, they were important in cases where parents' perceptions were discrepant. We found a significant two-way interaction effect of mothers' and fathers' perceptions of family structure, $F(2, 51) = 4.21$, $p < .01$, $eta^2 = .25$ (see Fig. 10.2). Planned comparisons indicated that children whose parents agreed in their perceptions of the family as moderate in family structure were rated by their kindergarten teachers as more academically competent ($M = 1.79$) than children in families rated by mothers as moderate in family structure and by fathers as either low

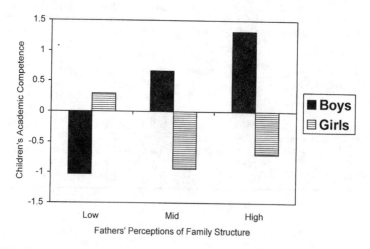

FIG. 10.1.   Fathers' reports of family structure and kindergarten teachers' fall ratings of children's academic competence for boys and girls.

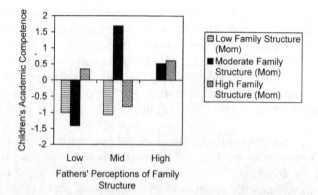

FIG. 10.2.   Mothers' and fathers' reports of family structure and kindergarten teachers' fall ratings of children's academic competence.

($M = -1.38$) or high in family structure ($M = .77$), $F(1, 51) = 5.69$, $p < .05$. No other significant effects of parents' perceptions of family structure were found.

Internalizing Behavior.   In the analysis of internalizing behavior, there were no significant main effects for mothers' or fathers' perceptions of family relatedness, but for mothers there was a significant interaction between family relatedness and sex of child, $F(2, 52) = 4.77$, $p < .01$, $eta^2 = .16$ (see Fig. 10.3). Follow-up analyses indicated that there was a significant effect of mothers' perceptions of family relatedness, although only for daughters' in-

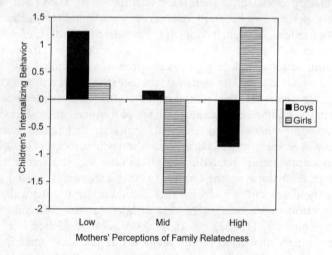

FIG. 10.3.   Mothers' reports of family relatedness and kindergarten teachers' fall ratings of children's internalizing behavior for boys and girls.

ternalizing, $F(2, 52) = 3.71, p < .05$. The planned comparison testing the specific hypothesis that moderate levels of family relatedness are characteristic of families with children seen by teachers as more withdrawn was statistically significant, $F(1, 52) = 8.89, p < .05$. When mothers perceived family members as moderate in family relatedness ($M = -1.70$), kindergarten teachers described the daughters as showing more internalizing problem behaviors than girls in families rated as low ($M = .28$) or high ($M = 1.11$) in family relatedness.

Fathers' perceptions of family structure but not mothers' were also associated with kindergarten teachers' fall ratings of children's internalizing behavior problems, $F(2, 52) = 3.64, p < .05$. Contradicting our hypothesis about midrange as optimal, the association between fathers' views of family structure and teachers' perceptions of children's internalizing behavior in their kindergarten classrooms appeared to be linear, with no differences found in this trend between girls and boys. On average, children in families rated by fathers as less organized with little structure were perceived by their teachers as the most socially isolated, depressed, or anxious ($M = 1.53$) in the fall of the kindergarten year, followed by children in families rated by fathers as having moderate ($M = 0.37$) and high ($M = -0.03$) structure (no figure included).

We found no significant interaction effects of mothers' and fathers' evaluations of their family environments. Thus, contrary to hypothesis 3, discrepancies between mothers' and fathers' perceptions of family process or structure were not linked with children's internalizing behavior.

Externalizing Behavior.   Significant univariate effects of both mothers' and fathers' perceptions of family relatedness were found for teacher reports of children's externalizing behavior, $F(2, 52) = 10.51, p < .001, eta^2 = .29$ for mothers, and $F(2, 52) = 5.89, p < .01, eta^2 = .19$ for fathers. Overall, externalizing behavior in kindergarten children was associated with low levels of family relatedness. The evidence was less strong but still present in favor of the hypothesis that the optimal region on the family relatedness dimension was in the midrange. Separate analyses of mothers' and fathers' ratings in planned comparisons failed to reveal significant differences in externalizing behavior in kindergarten between children whose mothers or fathers described moderate family relatedness and children whose parents described low or high relatedness in the family. Further analyses suggested that the midrange trend was obscured by the fact that there was a statistically significant interaction between mothers' and fathers' ratings and children's externalizing behavior, $F(2, 52) = 6.96, p < .001, eta^2 = .35$ (see Fig. 10.4).

When mothers' perceived family members as relatively unconnected to one another (low on family relatedness), and fathers rated the family as moderate in family relatedness, their children were seen by their teachers as dis-

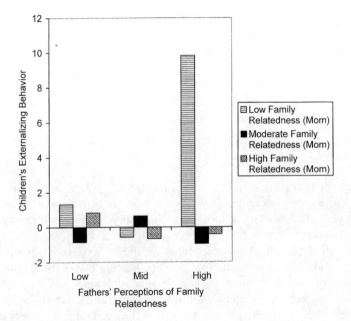

FIG. 10.4.   Mothers' and fathers' reports of family relatedness and kindergarten teachers' fall ratings of children's externalizing behavior.

playing significantly fewer externalizing behaviors ($M = -.57$) than children in families rated by fathers as low ($M = 1.33$) or high ($M = 9.83$) in family relatedness. That is, fathers' perceptions of midrange relatedness provided something of a buffering effect. However, when parents were at the two extremes in their perceptions of relatedness (mothers rated family relatedness low and fathers rated it high), the children were seen by their teachers as the most aggressive, noncompliant, distractible, and inattentive, consistent with hypothesis 3.

We also found a significant effect of mothers' perceptions of family relatedness in families rated by fathers as high in relatedness, $F(2, 52) = 7.14, p < .01$. The planned comparison testing the specific hypothesis that moderate levels of family relatedness are characteristic of families with children seen by their teachers as less aggressive and hyperactive was statistically significant, $F(1, 52) = 17.43, p < .01$. When fathers viewed their families as very cohesive (family members are connected to one another, high on family relatedness), and mothers rated moderate levels of family relatedness, teachers perceived the children as displaying fewer aggressive and inattentive externalizing behaviors ($M = -.96$) than children in families rated by mothers as low ($M = -.40$) or high in family relatedness ($M = 9.83$).

There were no other significant main effects or interactions of mothers' and fathers' perceptions of their family environment with respect to children's aggressive, hostile, and oppositional behavior in the early months of kindergarten. Externalizing behavior, then, was related to perceptions of family relatedness but not family structure.

DISCUSSION

A Whole-Family Perspective: Process and Structure Are Different

This chapter takes a family-level, multi-informant, prospective approach to linking dimensions of children's family environments to their adaptation to the first year of elementary school. Extending the work of previous studies in which adolescents' perceptions of their family environments were related to their clinical disturbance (Brage & Meredith, 1994; Cumsille & Epstein, 1994; Feldman et al., 1988), we found that parents' perceptions of family functioning before the children entered elementary school were predictive of their children's academic competence and internalizing and externalizing behaviors as described by teachers 6 months later at the beginning of kindergarten.

Taken together, the results are consistent with Moos and Moos's (1976) conceptualization of the importance of looking at multiple dimensions of the family environment (family relatedness and family structure). Similar to recent findings using observational methods to assess family functioning (cf. Johnson et al., 1999), these data offer empirical support for the theoretical argument that there are two conceptually distinct, at least partially independent, components of family environments: (a) process, having to do with the quality of the interactions among family members; and (b) structure, having to do with the organizational properties of the family as a unit (Minuchin, 1974). Results from this study support the hypothesis that both affective (relatedness) and structural (system maintenance and personal growth) dimensions of the family environment provide information for understanding children's adjustment to school. Beyond this generalization, it is difficult to draw a single overall conclusion because important differences emerged in the patterns of associations, depending on which parent was the reporter, which dimension of family life was being described, and which child outcome was being considered.

Children's academic competence in kindergarten was predicted by both family relatedness and structure dimensions as described by fathers but not mothers. Girls' but not boys' internalizing was predicted by mothers' perceptions of family structure. Only the process dimension of the whole family environment (family relatedness) was linked with children's aggressive and inattentive behavior early in their transition to school. Recall that the descriptions of the family environment in this chapter were based on parents' reports. In an earlier report of observational measures of triadic interaction in the families in this sample at the kindergarten period, both structural and process aspects of the family environment provided nonredundant information to explain variation in children's externalizing problems the next year in first grade (Johnson et al., 1999). Only future studies of prekindergarten observations and both kindergarten and first-grade outcomes can reveal whether the lack of association between family structure and externalizing in this study is a function of measurement method (self-report, observation) or time of assessment (prekindergarten to kindergarten or concurrent measures of family and child in first grade).

Are High or Moderate Ratings of Family Relatedness and Structure Associated With More Optimal Outcomes for Children?

The findings here offer partial support for Olson's (1993) position that family relatedness or cohesion is optimal in the midrange with respect to children's adaptation, with very high cohesion in families promoting overidentification or enmeshment among family members and very low cohesion promoting limited connection and intimacy among family members. Several statistically significant differences were found between children in families seen by parents as moderate in family relatedness and children in other families. For example, children in families whose fathers perceived family members as moderately "related" were described as more academically competent in kindergarten. A similar curvilinear relation was found between mothers' perceptions of family relatedness and daughters' internalizing behavior. We interpret the midrange category of relatedness to describe families who have moderate levels of warmth, are not afraid to express emotion, and manage conflict in ways that do not let it escalate to extremes. These families, in contrast to those who minimize or maximize the expression of emotion and conflict, would seem to foster the development of children who do well during their transition to school.

The hypothesis that midrange on the family structure dimension constitutes optimal family functioning was not supported. Instead, we found a linear association between fathers' descriptions of family structure in the preschool period and boys' academic competence, and both boys' and girls' internalizing behaviors in kindergarten. Most notably, boys whose fathers perceived the family as highly structured were perceived by their kindergarten teachers as more academically competent, and both girls and boys were less socially isolated, depressed, and anxious than children whose fathers described their families as having little structure. One possible explanation of these findings is that the items on the FES that describe structure, organization, and rules do not tap the extreme end of the dimension in which the structure becomes rigid and insensitive to shifting circumstances and changing times. A different hypothesis that could explain the same result is that families on the extremes of the structure dimension were not adequately represented in this sample.

Discrepancies Between Mothers and Fathers

Although parents tended to agree in their perceptions of family relatedness and structure, discrepancies between the parents in their perceptions of structure predicted children's lower academic competence scores, and discrepancies in parents' perceptions of relatedness predicted children's higher externalizing behavior scores in the fall of the kindergarten year. Perhaps differences between parents in how they see rules in the family are more relevant to task-focused contexts that have a bearing on children's achievement, whereas differences concerning the more affective, emotional aspects of family relationships lead to tensions or arguments between the parents, which are more likely to be associated with the children acting out. The findings are consistent with earlier studies indicating that disagreement between mothers and fathers in regard to parenting practices are predictive of marital difficulties (Block et al., 1981). It may not be the actual level of relatedness in the family that is most predictive of children's behavior problems, but the fact that parents' perceptions of their family environment are discrepant to the point that overt or covert conflict is generated.

What are we to make of the fact that, despite substantial agreement, children's outcomes varied somewhat depending on whether the mother or father was the reporter on structure or process dimensions? Men and women could have somewhat different sensitivities to organization and process dimensions in the family, but without observational data on the family environment from a similar whole-family perspective, it is not possible to determine whether one parent is a more "accurate" reporter of each of these dimensions. We are currently at work on creating observational ratings from this perspective.

This discussion leads to a speculative picture of how parents' perceptions are linked with children's adaptation to school. One possibility is that at least one of the parents is describing the "reality" of family processes that affect children's development. A second possibility, not mutually exclusive with the first, is that each parent's perceptions, regardless of their veridicality, lead to behavior with his or her partner and child that ultimately affects both academic and social competence in the early school years.

Sex Differences

Whereas links between parents' perceptions of their family environment and children's externalizing behavior did not appear to differ for families with kindergarten sons and daughters, the pattern of links between family environment and children's academic competence or internalizing behavior did vary depending on the sex of the child. That is, when fathers viewed their families as highly structured, their sons appeared to manage the academic challenges of the transition to kindergarten relatively well, according to their teachers, whereas daughters in highly structured families seemed to be struggling more academically. When mothers viewed family members as highly related to one another, daughters were seen by their kindergarten teachers as more anxious, depressed, and socially withdrawn, but this was not true for families with sons. These findings are consistent with Minuchin's (1974) family systems view that high degrees of family relatedness can result in enmeshed relationships and internalizing problems for the children, particularly for girls.

CONCLUSIONS

In summary, by looking at the system as a whole, we have shown that aspects of family process (cohesion) and family structure (personal growth and system maintenance) are connected in complex ways to three major indexes of children's adaptation to kindergarten: academic achievement, externalizing behaviors, and internalizing behaviors.

We have been very careful to describe the results in terms of parents' perceptions of the family and their links with children's outcomes. Future research might profitably compare the inner view or represented family (Reiss, 1989) with observations of the practicing family (see chapter 8) to determine how these two perspectives on the family as a whole combine to help us understand variations in children's adaptation to school. We do not mean to imply that the FES yields representations that are far from the practicing reality. It is possible that both parents, or at least one of the parents, is reporting accurately on family life, and that the findings here reflect real differences in family relatedness and structure that are associated with children's adaptation to kindergarten. However, the represented family may have its own contribution to make in explaining how children fare as they set out on their school careers. For example, when fathers or mothers view the family as warm and supportive or structured and organized, they may behave in more positive ways toward each other and toward the children. Why these perceptions or beliefs of the parents would have different associations with different outcomes for their children is not clear, but a running theme of this volume is that the pathways linking family functioning with children's adaptation to school vary with the source of information we use, the aspect of the family we assess, and the index of child adaptation we consider.

IV

INTERVENTIONS AS TESTS OF CAUSAL MODELS OF FAMILY INFLUENCE ON CHILDREN'S ADAPTATION TO SCHOOL

11

Two Variations of a Preventive Intervention for Couples: Effects on Parents and Children During the Transition to School

Carolyn Pape Cowan, Philip A. Cowan,
and Gertrude Heming

In chapters 3 through 10, we demonstrated that when we combined data from key aspects of parenting, marital, and three-generational relationships, or examined workplace conditions along with spouses' support in the prekindergarten period, we could predict statistically significant proportions of the variance of children's academic competence, social competence, and problem behaviors in kindergarten and first grade. The family–school connections obtained in this study, along with correlational research from other investigators cited in previous chapters, all point to a general, but unsurprising conclusion: When family relationships are positive and satisfying, children are better able to meet the challenges of early elementary school. This study has assessed these connections in a longitudinal context, and shown that specific aspects of family function, especially in combination, have rather substantial predictive power over a 1- and 2-year period. The consistency and strength of the associations suggest that if we can find ways to improve family relationships during the preschool period, children might be able to enter elementary school with more resources to meet the challenges of this transition. Of course, this hypothesis is based on the supposition that family relationship variables play a causal role in shaping children's development.

As we have noted throughout this volume, correlations, no matter how strong, do not provide proof of causality or the direction of effects. It is always possible that the engine driving the family system is located in the child

(Bell, 1968) and that the child's cognitive difficulties, social rejection, and aggressive or depressed behavior, lead to negative effects on relationships in the family. Before this study began, we searched the literature on intervention studies to determine whether experimentally-induced changes in family relationships were causally linked with children's adaptation. A number of therapeutic intervention programs have findings that fit this model (see P. A. Cowan et al., 1998, for a review). Heinicke and his colleagues (Heinicke et al., 1999) have provided this kind of evidence in a preventive intervention study of nonclinical, low-income families during the transition to first-time parenthood. However, we found no school interventions around the child's entrance to elementary school with randomized control designs or with any type of systematic evaluation. As far as we know, the efficacy of a family-based intervention focused on children's transition to school has yet to be tested. This is the central goal of this chapter.

The primary preventive interventions that we offered to mothers and fathers of prekindergartners (5-year-olds) took the form of couples groups. The groups were further subdivided to test the effects of two variations of the intervention and to test our theories about how key family relationships might play out in children's school adjustment. We discuss the rationale for this approach by responding to a set of questions about key elements of the intervention design.

WHY AN INTERVENTION FOCUSED
ON A NORMATIVE LIFE TRANSITION?

According to a meta-analysis of preventive intervention studies by Durlak and Wells (1997), there are three ways to think about selecting a target population. A universal intervention is directed toward all members of a designated category, regardless of their specific characteristics (e.g., all families with 5-year-olds). A targeted risk intervention is offered to those more likely to have psychological or social problems, such as children of depressed parents. A third strategy involves reaching out to people about to experience a similar, potentially stressful, life transition. We selected the third strategy based on the notion that transitions typically introduce the kind of disequilibrium that challenges family members' usual coping strategies (P. A. Cowan, 1991). When people feel vulnerable as they attempt to cope with unfamiliar challenges, they may be more open to intervention and to trying new strategies (Caplan, 1964; Rapaport, Rapaport, & Streilitz, 1977). The fact that the family system is already in the process of change in anticipation of the transition should amplify the potential impact of intervention.

WHY FOCUS ON THE TRANSITION TO SCHOOL?

We had developed a couples group intervention for an earlier study in which we worked with couples making the transition to first-time parenthood over a period of 6 months (C. P. Cowan & Cowan, 2000) and compared their adaptation over time with a set of randomly selected no-treatment control couples. In the first 2 years of parenthood, couples who had participated in the group intervention before and immediately after they had their babies reported less decline in marital satisfaction than the controls, bucking a trend found in almost every transition to parenthood study (cf. Belsky & Pensky, 1988; Cox, Owen, Lewis, & Henderson, 1989; Heinicke, Beckwith, & Thompson, 1988; Osofsky & Osofsky, 1984). At 3 years postpartum, we found further evidence of the impact of the couples groups in the fact that there were no separations or divorces in the couples who had participated in a couples group, whereas 15% of the comparison couples with a child had already separated or divorced. Then, by the time the children made their transition to kindergarten, we found significant effects of the early intervention on the parents' trajectories of marital satisfaction and adjustment from pregnancy to almost 6 years later (Schulz & Cowan, 2001). Couples who had participated in the couples group intervention maintained their level of marital adjustment and satisfaction, whereas the comparison couples with children showed a slow but steady decline in satisfaction with their marriage.

Despite the early signs of positive intervention effects on the parents in that study, kindergarten teachers' descriptions of the children's adaptation to school 6 years after the couples groups ended showed no direct effects of the earlier intervention with the parents on their children's academic competence or problem behaviors at school. Yet, overall, the parents' well-being or distress as individuals, as couples, and as parents when the children were 3½ to 4 years old, predicted substantial variance in their sons' and daughters' kindergarten adjustment—almost 2 years after we observed their relationship quality. We reasoned that an intervention focused on the parents' relationships as couples and with their children, and offered closer to the children's entrance to school, might increase the chance of enhancing the parents' effectiveness as partners and as parents and increase the likelihood of subsequent benefits for their children's adaptation.

We noted in chapter 1 and showed in subsequent chapters that there is evidence to support the trajectory hypothesis: As children enter elementary school, they move along trajectories in which they tend to remain in the same rank order over time (Alexander & Entwisle, 1988). We reasoned that if we designed an intervention for parents that resulted in their children entering elementary school at a higher point on the adaptation continuum than children whose parents had no intervention, the forces that maintain developmental trajectories over time might preserve and possibly enhance the initial benefits of the intervention.

WHY A PREVENTIVE INTERVENTION
FOR APPARENTLY "LOW-RISK" FAMILIES?

Because of severe limitations on public and private funding for family services, most therapeutic and prevention programs target families at high risk for distress. We have argued elsewhere (C. P. Cowan & Cowan, 1995, 1997) that, just as the selection of families from a high-risk population does not guarantee that all will be in need of psychosocial services, the selection of a sample from a low-risk population does not guarantee that all will be problem free. On the contrary, there are clear indications from studies of nonclinical families that parents' depression (Nolen-Hoeksema, Wolfson, Mumme, & Guskin, 1995) and marital distress (Cummings & Davies, 1994) constitute risk factors for their children developing both academic problems and internalizing and externalizing styles of coping with challenge. We described in chapter 3 that from one third to one half of the apparently "low-risk" parents in this study showed signs of individual or marital distress. Furthermore, by the time their children reached first grade, 10% of them had been identified by teachers, medical doctors, or mental health professionals as showing diagnosable levels of psychopathology—primarily ADHD and depression. In other words, if we consider parental depression and marital distress as risk factors for children's development, and diagnosed difficulty in young children as an indicator of problems in development, there is cause for concern even in families generally considered at low risk. We expected that preventive interventions addressed to the parents' strain and distress early in the family development period would provide a buffer to reduce the probability that these family risks would result in distress or full-blown clinical diagnoses as children began their academic and social careers.

WHY INTERVENE WITH COUPLES?

There is now a burgeoning literature that shows links between children's peer relationships and their adjustment (e.g., Asher & Coie, 1990), which suggests that peer group interventions might improve children's adaptation to school. Studies of children's academic and social competence at school indicate that providing classroom- or school-based interventions can enhance children's school success (Perry & Weinstein, 1998). Our choice of a couples group intervention format was based in part on our desire to focus on the parents' marital and parent–child relationships as contexts for the development of coping strategies in their children, and in part to test hypotheses about the central role of marital and parenting quality in children's early development and adaptation.

The choice of a family-based intervention rests on a substantial body of research that links family processes, particularly the quality of parent–child relationships, with children's academic and social outcomes (e.g., Wagner & Reiss, 1995). Although fathers' participation in preventive interventions or therapy has been sought slightly more often during recent decades (C. P. Cowan, 1988; Dadds, Schwartz, & Sanders, 1987; Levant, 1988), the inclusion of fathers in intervention or nonintervention studies remains the exception rather than the rule. For example, the one report that we found of a preventive intervention for parents around the child's transition to school included only mothers (Signell, 1972). This state of affairs is puzzling in light of compelling evidence that fathers make significant and unique contributions to their children's developmental successes and difficulties (see Parke, 1996; Pruett, 2000) and that recent family systems treatment approaches clearly advocate the inclusion of fathers if they are available (see Goldenberg & Goldenberg, 1996; Heinicke, 1991).

Evidence that parents' marital quality is a factor in the children's adjustment in both intact and divorced families has been summarized in chapters 1, 5, 6, 7, 8, and 10 and will be included in the summary model examined in chapter 12. Empirically-based justification for interventions that focus on the relationship between the parents comes from Brody and Forehand's work (1985), in which the investigators searched for factors that interfered with therapeutic success in the treatment of mothers whose children were having behavior problems. When they found that the interventions were not as effective for mothers in high-conflict marriages, Brody and Forehand added a new intervention strategy for mothers and fathers, with a specific emphasis on coparenting and marital issues. Results of this modification revealed that the combined marital and parenting emphasis was more successful in reducing sons' problem behavior than a traditional parenting skills approach with mothers only (Dadds et al., 1987). Webster-Stratton (1994) showed similar results in her recent work with couples whose children had behavior problems. These findings provide support for creating interventions to strengthen the relationship between the parents to provide a more solid foundation for the relationships between each parent and the child.

Two contradictory hypotheses emerge from family systems theory:

Hypothesis A

According to Satir (1972), couples are the "architects of the family." If the relationship between the parents sets the tone for other family relationships, then intervention with a marital emphasis ought to affect both the marital and parent–child relationships, thereby having a stronger impact on children's adaptation than an intervention focused on parenting alone.

Hypothesis B

Family systems theories (Wagner & Reiss, 1995) assume that causality is circular rather than linear, and that change anywhere in the system will have reverberating effects on other parts of the family. A corollary of this assumption is that the marital and parenting emphases ought to produce comparable results, and that change in one of those domains ought to be accompanied by a shift in the other.

To test these two competing hypotheses, we designed two variations of our couples group intervention—one that would place more emphasis on the relationship between each parent and their child and one that would focus more on the relationships between the parents.

WHY A GROUP INTERVENTION?

Three bodies of clinical theory and some empirical research indicate that group interventions can be helpful: (a) Group therapy for individuals (Lieberman, Yalom, & Miles, 1973) and for couples (Coche, 1995) has been shown to be effective; (b) psychoeducational groups that provide a combined didactic and open-ended opportunity to learn new coping strategies have produced change in individuals and families who share a particular problem or life circumstance (Burnette, 1998; Helgeson, Cohen, Schulz, & Yasko, 1999); and (c) self-help groups, either leaderless or with lay leaders, in which individuals meet regularly to support each other in dealing with a specific problem such as the death of a child (Huss & Ritchie, 1999), have had positive effects. There is also evidence that adults' social support, defined in various ways by different investigators (Crockenberg, 1981; Cutrona & Troutman, 1986; Gottlieb, 1988), is an important ingredient of well-being and adaptability in coping with stressful events.

We reasoned that at this time in history, when many American parents rear children far from their families of origin and friends from earlier years, a group format with clinically trained leaders would offer a temporary safe setting in which men and women could explore their key family decisions and concerns with others while they were occurring. A regular time in which couples could have ongoing discussions about important family issues would also have the advantage of providing a normalizing experience for partners in which some of their anxiety and disappointment could be allayed (Caplan, 1964; C. P. Cowan & Cowan, 1997, 2000; Rapaport et al., 1977; Yalom, 1995). Finally, we believe that a group format suggests a more collaborative atmosphere among contemporaries rather than a therapy experience in which parents are characterized as "troubled" and staff members are seen as "experts." We hoped that the collaborative setting might make a group intervention more attractive to potential participants.

Hypotheses

In two related articles, West, Sandler, Pillow, Baca, and Gersten (1991) and Wolchik and her colleagues (1993) argued that in establishing the effectiveness of an intervention, it is necessary to go beyond an examination of main effects to determine whether the outcomes are tied to change in the variables that the theory specifies as accounting for the intervention effects. An answer to this question requires an assessment of both direct and indirect effects of the intervention. Using structural equation models (Falk & Miller, 1992) and regression analyses, we tested two hypotheses and explored an unresolved issue:

1. Participation in a couples group with a marital or parenting emphasis would lead to more positive interaction between the intervention parents, and between the parents and their child, than that found in the comparison families. These more positive interactions would constitute the direct effects referred to by West et al. (1991) and by Wolchik et al. (1993). Because we were not prepared to predict whether the variations of the couples groups with a marital or parenting emphasis would lead to differential direct effects, we treated this as a question to be explored.

2. We proposed marital and parent–child relationships as two mechanisms that are causally related to children's academic and social adaptation. We predicted that change in the quality of these relationships would be associated with children's enhanced academic, social, and emotional adaptation to kindergarten and first grade. We would then interpret this pattern as representing indirect effects of the intervention.

METHODS

Participants

Recruitment. Chapter 2 summarized our two-phase selection strategy. The sample began with 300 couples who made initial inquiries after hearing about the study, of which 192 met the initial selection criteria: a family with a first child entering kindergarten the next fall and two parents willing to complete an initial four-page questionnaire booklet. All 192 couples were then interviewed individually by one of four staff couples, all of whom were licensed mental health professionals: psychologists, social workers, or marriage and family counselors. By the time the staff arrived to conduct the initial interview, the couples had been randomly allocated to one of three conditions:

1. A couples group with a marital focus—These groups of four to five couples met weekly with a staff couple for 16 weeks prior to the children's entrance to kindergarten (see the following for a more detailed description of the group structure and process).

2. A couples group with a parenting focus—These groups of four to five couples met weekly with a staff couple for 16 weeks prior to the children's transition to school.

3. A low dose consultation—Because the intervention in our earlier study of couples making the transition to parenthood was helpful to men and women's relationships as partners (C. P. Cowan, 1988, 1992), ethical considerations argued against a true no-treatment control condition in the Schoolchildren and Their Families Project. Thus, the final one third of the couples were assigned to a comparison condition in which parents could request one consultation meeting per year in the prekindergarten, kindergarten, and first-grade years with the staff couple who conducted their initial interview. Parents were told that these three meetings with staff could be used for consultation about any family issue or problem that arose during the transition to school period.

In both the maritally-focused and parenting-focused conditions, 40% of those invited agreed to participate in a couples group, and 36% actually attended at least one group meeting. In the consultation condition, in which much less was asked of the participants, 64% of those invited agreed to participate. Because of the lack of comparable data from other studies, we have little way of evaluating the magnitude of the acceptance rate of 40% by parents offered a couples group. We suggest two other preventive intervention studies as a reference point. In Markman et al.'s study of the PREP program for engaged couples (Markman, Renick, Floyd, & Stanley, 1993), 50% accepted an invitation to participate in a 5-week program after an extensive two-session assessment. When Vinokur (1998) and his colleagues offered couples an intervention when one partner had lost a job, 40% agreed to take part. Based on these guides, we believe that 4 in 10 couples willing to sign up for the 16-week couples group intervention after an initial interview would compare well with the rates of acceptance into any community-based prevention program, especially because we required the agreement of both partners to participate in the intervention.

Families entered the study in 1990, 1991, or 1992. Over those years, we conducted eight maritally-focused groups with a total of 28 couples, and seven parenting-focused groups with a total of 27 couples. Each of the four coleader teams conducted some marital-emphasis and some parenting-emphasis groups and several brief consultations with individual couples in the control condition if they requested them.

Selection Bias.   Although we focus in this chapter on the random assignment design (marital, parenting, control), there were actually five experimental conditions, including the participants in a self-selected no-treatment condition and a set of couples who refused further participation after filling out the initial questionnaires. As we reported in chapter 2, there were no statistically significant differences among parents in the five study conditions on any of the initial questionnaire measures: marital adjustment (Locke & Wallace, 1959), symptoms of depression (Radloff, 1977), parenting stress (Abidin, 1980), negative experiences in parents' families of origin (C. P. Cowan & Cowan, 1992), or concerns about their child starting school. It is true that the power to detect small differences is low, but we can conclude from this analysis that on the measures tested, the families in different conditions were not markedly dissimilar.

Furthermore, the self-selected no-treatment parents (intervention refusers) did not differ from the intervention participants or the random controls on any measure of observed parenting or marital interaction, or on any parent self-report measure used in the prekindergarten phase of the study. Finally, there were no significant differences among the children in any of the study conditions in terms of positive engagement or oppositional behavior while the child was tested by a project experimenter in a half-hour laboratory visit (discussed later). In sum, despite differences in acceptance rates across conditions, there were no significant pretest differences among families who participated in the group intervention, families who refused the invitation to a couples group but agreed to be assessed further, and families in the brief consultation condition.

Retention.   Once couples agreed to participate in the study, most continued over the transition to school period—84% of the intervention couples, 80% of the consultation couples, and 90% of the self-selected control couples. In the randomized clinical trial design, then, there were 46 intervention families and 20 randomly assigned controls. In this subset of participating families, the first child was a girl in 28 families and a boy in 38 families.

The Interventions

The overarching aim of the couples groups was consistent with the goals of any family-based primary preventive intervention—to recruit families not yet identified as having major mental health or psychological problems and to reduce family risks and enhance family protective factors known to be related to children's adaptation (Coie et al., 1993).

General Principles. The couples groups were similar in format, content, and process to those in our earlier transition to parenthood study (C. P. Cowan, 1988, 1992). Four or five participant couples and a staff couple met for 2 hr every week for 4 months. The format was semistructured, which combined (a) an ongoing stated agenda formed collaboratively by participants and leaders, and (b) an open-ended check-in during which couples could raise any current family issue or problem for discussion. In the structured portion of the 16 meetings, leaders raised topics from the five domains of our conceptual model and helped parents focus their attention on their own ideas and experiences, in part by revisiting issues covered in the questionnaires that each of the participants had completed prior to the intervention.

In all three intervention conditions (marital focus, parenting focus, consultation), the staff couples attempted to help partners tackle their problems and unresolved conflicts and work on the troubling or confusing parts of their relationships with each other and with their child(ren). They did this in two ways. When group leaders or participants raised general issues or questions about any aspect of family life (individual, marital, parenting, three-generational, or outside the family), the leaders encouraged the parents to consider how those issues might be affecting them or their children during the transition-to-school period. With the help of the coleaders, it often became apparent that one issue was related to other parts of life the group had discussed. For example, the group might be asked to think about how their stress as individuals or as couples might be affecting their reactions to their children. The leaders encouraged parents to modify processes known to be associated with risk and vulnerability and to adopt patterns that are known to protect against risks and optimize resilience. From our perspective, the leaders were focusing on men and women as individuals, as couples, and as parents, by addressing their (a) cognitive appraisals (Bradbury & Fincham, 1992), (b) patterns of regulating emotions (Gottman, 1993; Markman et al., 1993), (c) styles of solving problems (C. P. Cowan & Cowan, 1992; Markman et al., 1993), and (d) social support from others (Crockenberg, 1981).

The leaders also used techniques that are common to psychodynamic therapies for individuals and groups (e.g., Jones, 2000; Clulow, Cleavely, Coussell, & Dearnley, 1982) to help participants explore their past and present relationships with their parents, as well as their changing identities as parents, workers, lovers, and friends. Our reluctance to focus solely on cognitive-behavioral techniques stems in part from our theoretical family model, which suggests that partners' attributions and communication styles represent only two aspects of effective and satisfying family functioning.

The format of the groups lies midway on a continuum in which one end represents open-ended therapy with topics dealt with as they arise from the participants and the other end represents a didactic workshop with a specified curriculum, in which the issues to be discussed and the proposed approach to addressing them are presented by the leaders to the couples in the audience. In the interventions described here, we think of the groups as semistructured; there was a structured part of each evening, and a theoretical model guiding what should be covered over the 4 months, but the couples were free to bring their own issues to the group. The leaders and other participants helped partners make headway in the group, try things out in the week in between meetings, and return for further discussion at the next meeting.

The Distinction Between Groups With a Marital or Parenting Focus. When a group member raised a problem for discussion in the open-ended part of the evening, leaders of the maritally-focused groups highlighted the effect of the problem on the partners' relationship as a couple, in which, for example, tension from unresolved disagreements can lead partners to feel more distant or unsupported. Leaders of these groups also focused on characteristics of the couple's relationship that might be affecting their ability to solve the problem, such as a tendency to ignore or avoid a problem to minimize open conflict. By contrast, leaders of the parenting-focused groups highlighted the implications of whatever problem was raised for the parents' relationships with their child(ren). For example, in discussing parents' work stress, leaders in the parenting-focused groups worked with mothers and fathers to deal with the potential for spillover of work stress to the tone of their relationships with their child at home (see also chapter 9). In a comparable discussion of work stress in the maritally-focused groups, leaders encouraged couples to talk about and deal more productively with the spillover of strain at work to arguments they might have as a couple at home.

The first two authors met with the intervention staff every 2 weeks in a group that provided consultation and supervision to clarify and reinforce the separate group orientations. Using a manual designed to specify the focus on aspects of our conceptual model,[1] we discussed examples that the staff couples brought from their work with the couples groups. In this way, we translated the general principles into action, heightened the distinctions between the maritally-focused and parenting-focused interventions, and worked on any relationship issues that arose—between the participating husbands and wives, between each pair of coleaders, and between the staff and the study participants.

---

[1]This manual is available from Philip A. Cowan and Carolyn Pape Cowan at the Department of Psychology, 3210 Tolman Hall—1650, University of California, Berkeley, CA 94720–1650.

Measures

The Use of LVPLS Models to Assess Intervention Effects.   Given the fact that this study contains a large number of measures from a relatively small number of families (66 in the randomized clinical trial design), and that we wanted to examine connections among a number of constructs, choices had to be made in constructing the data analytic strategy. We used structural equation models (Falk & Miller, 1992) as our major analytic tool so that we could present a dynamic picture of how the marital and parenting interventions shaped the patterns of linkage among marital quality, parenting quality, and children's subsequent adjustment to school. Because of the limited size of the sample and the complexity of interpreting the results, we were not able to use the structural modeling approach to examine intervention effects on multiple measures from all five domains of family functioning. We focused on data from the marital and parenting domains because these were the most direct targets of the group interventions.

To provide a rigorous test of our theoretical model, we selected observational rather than self-report measures of marital and parent–child interaction, and independently-gathered measures of children's outcomes based on teachers' checklist descriptions (externalizing and internalizing behaviors), academic achievement tests administered individually to each child by our project staff, and children's descriptions of themselves on the Berkeley Puppet Interview (BPI; Ablow & Measelle, 1993, and chapters 6 and 7). We examined links among parents' participation in the intervention, changes in marital and parent–child relationships (the hypothesized mediators), and variations in children's subsequent adaptation to school.

Four structural equation models were tested, each examining pathways linking family functioning to different latent variables measuring children's adaptation in kindergarten and first grade (internalizing behaviors, externalizing behaviors, academic achievement, and children's perceptions of their adjustment to school). Each structural equation model contained 11 latent variables composed of a total of 29 manifest variables. Of course, this is a large number of variables for a data set of 66 families. However, as we discussed in chapter 2, LVPLS models are constructed for the purpose of handling what are sometimes called "thick" data sets (multiple measures and perspectives on a relatively small number of participants, in contrast with thin data sets such as survey research studies with few measures of many participants; Rosenbaum & Silber, 2001).[2] There were other reasons for using LVPLS: We wanted to take advantage of the power of structural equation models to provide more solid measures of our constructs through the creation of latent variables, and we hoped to take advantage of this method to

---

[2]For a more detailed discussion of the variables-to-subjects ratio, see chapter 12.

chart pathways among the independent variables to assess indirect as well as direct effects of the intervention. Nevertheless, because of traditional concerns about variables-to-subjects ratios, we performed a check on the LVPLS analyses by conducting regression analyses that essentially replicated the findings concerning the direct effects of the intervention.

Measures of Manifest and Latent Variables.   The measures used to assess families at prekindergarten, kindergarten (Post 1), and Grade 1 (Post 2), are described in detail in chapter 2, and mentioned only briefly here as the "ingredients" of the latent variables in the PLS models.

LV 1 (latent variable).   Child sex—The first latent variable was child sex (boys = 0, girls = 1). Although we have been interested in differences between boys and girls throughout this volume, there were several reasons to treat sex as a covariate rather than to construct separate models. First, although a plausible rationale could probably be created, we had no reason to believe that couples groups would have different effects on parents of boys or girls. Second, concerns about the number of variables in the analysis would be increased if we created models of 38 families (boys) and 28 families (girls) rather than the full sample of 66 families in the randomized clinical trial design.

LV 2.   Observed marital conflict at pretest—This latent variable included observations of couple conflict during the whole-family interaction. The manifest variables were two factor scores: negative emotion and conflict. Note that these measures describe the tone of the parents' interaction as a couple (cold, angry), not the behavior of each marital partner separately. Our emphasis on negative emotions expressed between the parents was based on the fact that the literature emphasizes negative emotion between parents as a risk factor for children and does not seem to find positive emotion as a protective factor (Gottman & Katz, 1989). Our exploratory path models that included positive indicators of interaction between the parents (warmth, responsiveness) were consistent with this finding, as they did not add to explanations of variance in children's outcomes.

LV 3 and LV 4.   Observed parenting style at pretest (mothers' and fathers')—This latent variable included four composite measures based on observations of parent–child interaction during the dyadic visits to our project playroom. Taken together, they represented a measure of authoritarian parenting style—low scores on warmth and respect for the child's autonomy, and high scores on cold, nonresponsive, structure, and limit-setting. One latent variable for fathers and one for mothers were included in the PLS model.

LV 5 and LV 6.   Marital and parenting intervention vectors—In studies using structural equation modeling to examine intervention effects (Forgatch & DeGarmo, 1999; Wolchick et al., 1993), a single contrast between intervention and control groups is represented by a dummy variable or vector. Because we have a three-group design that includes two intervention conditions, we entered two vectors as latent variables in each structural equation model. In the first vector, marital group participants were dummy-coded as +1, parenting group members as 0, and consultation parents as −1. In essence, the marital vector examined the contrast between marital group couples and controls, holding the parenting group couples constant. Similarly, the second vector contrasted parenting group couples and controls, using dummy codes for parenting group participants as +1, marital group members as 0, and consultation parents as −1. Any two of the three possible contrast vectors define a main effect and the third (marital vs. parenting) is redundant, although that comparison can be tested in a new equation (Keppel & Zedeck, 1989), and we do so later.

LV 7.   Observed marital conflict at POST1—The same two manifest variables as in LV2, assessed 1 year later by a different research team, were included in this latent variable.

LV 8 and LV9.   Observed parenting style at POST1—The same manifest variables as in LV3 and LV4 for mothers and fathers, assessed 1 year later by a different research team, were included in this latent variable.

LV 10.   Fall kindergarten outcomes—Latent variables representing two of the child outcomes were derived from teachers' responses to the Child Adaptive Behavior Inventory (CABI) in the spring of the kindergarten and first-grade years. Internalizing included as manifest variables multi-item scales describing extraversion (reversed), introversion, social isolation, and depression. Externalizing included multi-item scales describing antisocial, oppositional, and hostile behavior. Academic achievement was measured by reading, math, and spelling scales from the individually administered Peabody Individual Achievement Test (Markwardt, 1989). Children's perceptions of their adaptation to school were assessed by four multi-item scales from the BPI that capture academic motivation and achievement, acceptance by peers, feelings of hostility regarding peers, and feelings of depression and rejection.

The placement of latent variables in the model was determined in part by time sequence (preintervention to postintervention), with one-way arrows linking earlier to later measures. Because observed authoritarian parenting and marital conflict were rated on the same day in different sessions (dyads vs. whole family), it was not immediately clear how to determine the direction of arrows in paths linking the marital and parenting latent variables. For this reason, the arrows are presented as bidirectional, suggesting a reciprocal or circular effect. Note that the marital conflict latent variables refer to the quality of interaction observed between fathers and mothers in front of their child when they worked together in the triad, whereas the parenting style variables refer to observations of the separate mother–child and father–child dyads. Because the latent variables measuring marital conflict and authoritarian parenting at time 1 (prekindergarten and preintervention) had identical components to those variables at time 2 (kindergarten and postintervention), we interpret the time 2 variables as measures of change in marital and parent–child interaction. The position of these intervention vectors in the model allows a test of whether they account for preintervention-to-postintervention change in both marital and parenting behavior.

RESULTS

Overview

The interventions with a marital and parenting emphasis were causally implicated in positive change in family relationships and in children's adaptation to elementary school. Four LVPLS structural equation models indicated that, in comparison with children of consultation control families, children of couples participating in the interventions had higher tested academic achievement scores and more positive self-reports of adaptation in kindergarten. In first grade, they were seen by their teachers as showing fewer internalizing and externalizing problems. There was some indication of a crossover effect in which the maritally-focused intervention also increased the probability of a positive change in parenting style. There was no comparable probability of a positive change in marital interaction for parents in the parenting-focused intervention.

We also used multiple regression tests that, in essence, replicated the major results of the structural equation modeling, supporting our hypothesis that the couples groups had positive effects on the parents and on their children's adaptation to school. Finally, a number of analyses provided support for the putative mediator hypothesis that intervention-induced change in marital and parent–child interaction accounted for significant proportions of variance in children's adaptation to school.

Assessing Model Fit

In chapter 2, we described how the adequacy of fit between LVPLS models and the data is calculated in terms of a fit index (RMS COV [E,U]; the proportion of variation not accounted for by the statistical model), and by overall F tests of the R^2 accounted for by predictor variables in the model. Table 11.1 shows that the fit index for the full models varied between .08 and .10, which indicates an adequate fit between the data and the models. Table 11.1

TABLE 11.1
PLS Models: Child Sex, Marital Quality, Parenting Quality, Interventions, and Children's Outcomes

Model	Externalizing			Internalizing			Academic Achievement			Self-Reported Adaptation		
	R^2	F	Fit	R^2	F	Fit	R^2	F	Fit	R^2	F	Fit
Kg. with intervention	.23			.13			.40	3.67**	.08	.28	2.41*	.08
Kg. without intervention	.13			.13			.28	3.23**	.08	.07		
Kg. ITT	.15			.11			.38			.09		
F (diff) w-w/o							5.50**			8.02***		
F (diff) ITT							8.17***			ns		
Grade 1 with intervention	.54	6.51***	.08	.36	3.10*	.08	.80	22.22***	.08	.47	4.90***	.08
Grade 1 without intervention	.23	2.13*	.08	.24	2.26*	.10	.79	26.70***	.08	.45	5.85***	.08
Grade 1 ITT	.54	6.42***	.09	.31	3.15*	.09	.80	28.14***	.08	.45	5.63***	.08
F (diff) w-w/o	19.38***			5.04**			ns			ns		
F (diff) ITT	34.41***			5.11**			ns			ns		

Note. PLS = ; Kg. = ; ITT = ; diff = ; w-w/o = .
*p < .05. **p < .01. ***p < .001.

292

also includes the R^2 in the kindergarten and first-grade outcomes explained by the latent variables measuring child sex, marital conflict, authoritarian parenting, and participation in the intervention. In kindergarten, the models accounted for significant variance in two of the outcomes—academic achievement (40%) and children's perceptions of their own adaptation to school (28%)—but not teachers' descriptions of externalizing and internalizing behaviors. In first grade, the models accounted for significant variance in all four latent outcome variables: academic achievement (80%), children's perceptions of their adaptation to school (38%), externalizing behaviors (54%), and internalizing behaviors (36%).

An Overall Test of Intervention Effects

To evaluate the overall impact of the interventions, we calculated the R^2 in the kindergarten and first-grade outcome variables that were accounted for by the latent variables measured preintervention and postintervention. We did this for identical models in which the vector for maritally-focused intervention versus controls and the vector for parenting-focused intervention versus controls were included, and models in which the intervention vectors were removed. Because the models including and excluding the intervention vectors contained the same set of marital, parenting, and outcome variables, we can infer an overall intervention effect from the contrast between the two R^2s—in effect a measure of R^2 change.[3]

The full statistical models did not predict a statistically significant amount of variance over and above the marital and parenting measures in children's kindergarten externalizing and internalizing behaviors. Therefore, we did not test for the contribution of the intervention vectors to those emotional adaptation outcomes.

Table 11.1 shows the F tests of the significance of the difference between the pairs of models. Academic achievement and children's perceptions of their own adjustment to kindergarten were influenced by parents' participation in the group interventions. The R^2 of .40 in the kindergarten academic achievement model that included the intervention vectors was significantly larger than the R^2 of .28 in the model with the intervention vectors removed, $F(2, 55) = 5.50$, $p < .01$. Similarly, the R^2 of .28 in children's perceptions of their school adjustment in kindergarten was significantly larger than the

---

[3]The F-test for the difference between two nested multiple regressions is as follows:

$$\frac{(R^2 \text{ explained by equation 1}) - (R^2 \text{ explained by equation 2})/ \text{ number of variables in larger } R^2 - \text{ number of variables in the smaller } R^2}{(1 - R^2 \text{ equation 1})/ N(\text{number of subjects}) - k(\text{number of variables in equation 1}) - 1}$$

The F is tested with the degrees of freedom in the numerator divided by the degrees of freedom in the denominator.

nonsignificant R^2 of .07 in the model with the intervention vectors removed, $F(2, 55) = 8.02, p < .001$.

At the first-grade follow-up, models that included the intervention vectors explained significantly more variance in children's externalizing behavior (.54 vs. .23), $F(2, 54) = 19.38, p < .001$, and internalizing behavior (.36 vs. .24), $F(2, 54) = 5.04, p < .01$, than models with the intervention vectors removed. Because these models contained both kindergarten and first-grade outcomes, we interpret the findings as showing intervention effects on the children's change between kindergarten and first grade. There was no significant contribution of the intervention to change in academic achievement from kindergarten to first grade. Because 79% of the variance in the model for first-grade academic achievement was accounted for by variables representing family interaction and kindergarten achievement scores, there was little variance left to be accounted for by intervention effects.

The R^2 change comparing regressions with and without intervention vectors yields a measure of effect size. Table 11.1 shows that, over and above the quality of marital and parenting relationships, the interventions with parents accounted for (a) 12% of the variance in children's academic achievement scores as tested in kindergarten, (b) 21% of the variance in children's perceptions of their adjustment to kindergarten, (c) 31% of the variance in reductions in externalizing behaviors between kindergarten and first grade, and (d) 12% of the variance in reductions in their internalizing behaviors over the same period of time. Taken together, these results indicate that parents' participation in 16-week couples groups with a marital or parenting emphasis played a causal role in their children's achievement in the first year of elementary school, and in the reduction of the children's problem behaviors between the first and second years of school.

Comparing the Marital and Parenting Interventions

Did the marital- and parenting-focused group interventions have different effects? To compare the overall effect of the two different emphases in the couples groups, we reran the models in Figs. 11.1, 11.2, 11.3, and 11.4, by including as a latent variable only the vector that compared the two group interventions (marital = +1, consultation = 0, parenting = −1). Children of parents in the parenting intervention described themselves more positively in terms of their adaptation to kindergarten, R^2 change = .14, $F(1, 56) = 9.74, p < .01$, and their teachers saw them as using fewer internalizing behaviors, R^2 change = .12, $F(1, 56) = 8.62, p < .01$. By contrast, children of parents in the marital intervention obtained significantly higher academic achievement scores, R^2 change = .10, $F(1, 56) = 8.06, p < .01$, and significantly lower ratings of externalizing behavior from their first-grade teachers, R^2 change =

.31, $F(1, 55) = 34.44$, $p < .001$. These results are consistent with Figs. 11.1 through 11.4, in which there was a direct link between the parenting intervention vector and children's internalizing behaviors and self-perceived adaptation and a direct link between the marital intervention vector and children's externalizing behavior.

More Stringent Intervention Tests

Intention to Treat Analyses.   Contemporary approaches to the analysis of preventive and therapeutic interventions argue that random assignment to conditions may not result in truly random samples if there are systematic differences in characteristics between those accepting intervention participation and those accepting participation in a control group (Little, 1996). Although there were no differences between parents offered the different conditions in their preintervention measures of marital satisfaction, depression, parenting stress, or concerns about their child's entrance to kindergarten, the rates of acceptance to participate in the longitudinal study differed for parents in intervention and control conditions (40% vs. 64%).

For the intention to treat analysis, the 20 couples who refused participation in a group intervention but agreed to be followed over time (these couples were not used in the analyses discussed earlier) were reassigned to the intervention conditions they were offered initially (9 to the marital-emphasis couples groups and 11 to the parenting-emphasis couples groups). We then reanalyzed the differences among marital, parenting, and consultation conditions using contrasting structural equation models, as described earlier. These analyses showed that adding couples who had been offered but did not accept the intensive group intervention reduced the size of the effects of the intervention in all but one case (the impact on externalizing behavior in first-grade children). Nevertheless, the impact of the intervention remained statistically significant on children's tested academic achievement in kindergarten, R^2 change $= .10$, $F(2, 74) = 8.17$, $p < .05$, and on first-grade teachers' descriptions of externalizing, R^2 change $= .31$, $F(2, 76) = 34.41$, $p < .001$, and internalizing behaviors, R^2 change $= .07$, $F(2, 74) = 5.11$, $p < .01$. Only in the case of children's perceptions of their adjustment to kindergarten (BPI) was the intervention effect no longer statistically significant. Intention to treat analyses, then, also support the conclusion that our interventions had a significant impact on the couples group participants as compared with the consultation controls.

Ruling Out the Impact of Preexisting Differences in Children.   Because we did not have preintervention descriptions of the children from teachers (the children had not yet entered elementary school, not all were in preschools, and they lived in more than 20 different communities), the results reported so far are open to the challenge that posttest differences favoring the intervention children were attributable to some preexisting prekindergarten differences in the children's behavior. To address this concern, we examined project staff observers' reports of the children's behavior during the preschool preintervention playroom visits to our project, in which children worked with each parent separately for 40 min on challenging tasks. One-way analyses of variance comparing the preschool reactions of children of parents in the marital groups, parenting groups, and consultation controls (not tabled), revealed no significant differences on any of the 17 scales describing the children's interactions with either of their parents (e.g., cooperative, defiant, warm, sad, engaged). This gives some support to the hypothesis that, overall, children in intervention and control groups, who later showed significantly different outcomes at school in first grade, had not been different in terms of their typical interactions with their parents before they participated in the couples group interventions.

General Trends Across the Path Models

Despite some important differences in detail, the models revealed a reassuringly consistent picture (see Figs. 11.1, 11.2, 11.3, 11.4). All four showed meaningful paths linking parents' participation in the maritally-focused groups (top center of the models) with less conflict between the parents after the intervention. In three of the four models, parents who showed lower postintervention marital conflict observed in the presence of their children had children who showed more successful adaptation to kindergarten, in terms of fewer externalizing and internalizing behaviors and higher academic achievement. Furthermore, a reduction in parents' conflict as a couple (the postintervention latent variable can be interpreted as a measure of change) was associated with children showing greater improvement in terms of academic achievement and greater reductions in externalizing and internalizing behaviors between kindergarten and first grade—that is, between the first and second years after the couples group intervention ended.

All four statistical models also showed a meaningful path linking participation in the parenting-focused groups (bottom center of the models) and a reduction in fathers' or mothers' authoritarian parenting style from preintervention to postintervention (less cold, angry, and limit setting, and more respect for the child's autonomy). All four models linked reductions in authoritarian parenting style directly with positive outcomes for the children in kindergarten and first grade. In the models for internalizing behavior, academic achievement, and children's self-perceptions of adaptation, we found a "cross-over" effect: Parents' participation in the groups with a marital emphasis was also associated with a reduction in mothers' authoritarian parenting style when they worked alone with the child. By contrast, none of the models showed a cross-over effect in which participation in the groups with a parenting emphasis directly affected the quality of the parents' interaction as a couple in the presence of their child.

In all four models, reductions in parents' marital conflict between the pre-school and kindergarten years for the couples in the maritally-focused groups were associated directly with reductions in authoritarian parenting for fathers, although not for mothers. This pattern is consistent with findings from our earlier transition-to-parenthood intervention study in which the links between marital distress and parenting quality were stronger for fathers than for mothers (Kerig, Cowan, & Cowan, 1993).

Multiple Regression Tests of the Impact of the Intervention: A Converging Alternative Analysis

Given the relative novelty of testing for intervention effects using structural equation models, we hoped to be able to demonstrate that a more traditional statistical analysis would lead to the same conclusions.

Direct Intervention Effects on Children's Adaptation. Using multiple regression analyses, we tested for simple direct effects of the group interventions on the manifest variables measuring child outcomes (the components of latent measures of externalizing, internalizing, academic achievement, and self-perceived school adjustment). Although some of the tests revealed marginally significant effects, none reached the $p < .05$ level. Guided by the fact that the path models revealed significant effects of the intervention when we used latent variables that combined three or four measures, we tested for main effects on child outcomes using factor-based composites from the BPI and the CABI.

As in the path models, there were no simple main effects of the intervention on kindergarten teachers' descriptions of children's internalizing and externalizing behavior, but there were consistent intervention effects the next year on first-grade teachers' reports. On each first-grade outcome, we regressed child sex, the kindergarten outcome, and the intervention vectors. Compared with children of consultation parents, children of parents from the marital-emphasis groups were judged by their first-grade teachers as more academically competent, R^2 change $= .09$, $F(1, 60) = 4.13$, $p < .05$, and less hyperactive, R^2 change $= .13$, $F(1, 60) = 7.06$, $p < .05$, than they had been in kindergarten. In a similar contrast with controls, children of parents from the parenting-emphasis groups were seen by their first-grade teachers as less socially withdrawn or isolated, R^2 change $= .13$, $F(1, 60) = 7.31$, $p < .01$, and less depressed and anxious than they had been in kindergarten, R^2 change $= .11$, $F(1, 60) = 5.08$, $p < .05$.

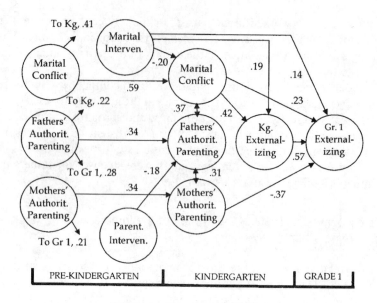

FIG. 11.1.   Externalizing behavior.

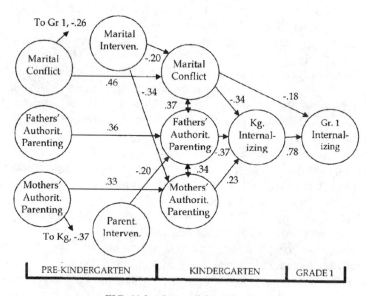

FIG. 11.2.   Internalizing behavior.

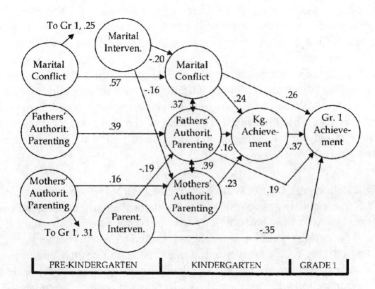

FIG. 11.3. Academic achievement.

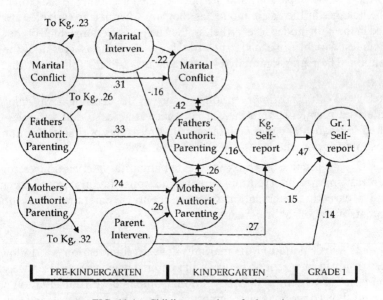

FIG. 11.4. Child's perception of adaptation.

299

These findings, too, reinforce the results of comparing LVPLS structural equation models with and without the intervention: The groups with a marital focus had a positive impact on children's academic competence and externalizing, and the groups that emphasized parenting had a positive impact on children's internalizing, and a tendency to affect the children's own views of their adjustment to kindergarten. The path models add the information that some of the impact appears to be indirect, especially on externalizing behaviors—attributable to the effect of the marital intervention in reducing conflict between the parents in front of their children (see the next section).

Direct Intervention Effects on Couple and Parent–Child Interaction. In LVPLS models, it is possible to test the statistical significance of the overall equation but not of the paths linking the intervention vectors to marital conflict and parenting style. For example, we wanted to know whether participating in a maritally-focused intervention might have had positive effects on parents' conflict and negative emotion in their interaction as a couple or on their style of interaction with their child. Again we used multiple regressions. The analyses are not exactly parallel to the path models because they examine the manifest variables separately and are not weighted according to the pattern of all the linkages in the entire model, as they are when latent variables are included in the path models. Nevertheless, they help to ascertain which of the single manifest variables in each latent variable are changing as a result of the intervention. The regression analyses were conducted in the following way:

Step 1.   With a postintervention measure as the dependent variable, we entered a preintervention measure of that variable, so that variables entered subsequently could be interpreted as measures of preintervention to postintervention change (Cohen & Cohen, 1983).

Step 2.   As discussed earlier, we created a marital intervention vector to contrast marital intervention parents and consultation control parents, and a parenting intervention vector to contrast parenting intervention parents with consultation controls.

Parents' participation in the maritally-focused intervention was followed by less troubled interactions between the parents when the children were in kindergarten, 1 year after the intervention. Compared with consultation parents, who showed more negative emotion and conflict as a couple in front of their children than they had before the children entered kindergarten, parents from the maritally-focused groups showed stable levels of negative emotion, $F(1, 62) = 4.26, p < .05$, and significantly less conflict as a couple while working with their child in the project playroom, $F(1, 62) = 4.11, p < .05$.

Two of the four observation-based manifest measures of parenting style showed evidence of significant effects of the parenting-focused intervention. In the first year after the intervention ended, when the children were in kindergarten, fathers who had been offered the consultation were less warm and responsive to their children than they had been before the children entered school, whereas fathers from the parenting-focused couples groups showed greater warmth and responsiveness than they had 1 year earlier, $F(1, 62) = 5.59, p < .01$. Compared with mothers offered the consultation, mothers from the parenting groups provided more structure for their children than they had in the preschool period, $F(1, 62) = 5.04, p < .05$. There were no statistically significant simple effects or interaction effects of the parenting intervention on marital conflict or on negative emotion between the parents.

Testing the Putative Mediator Hypothesis. Using the results of both LVPLS and regression models, we can conclude that the group interventions with couples (A) stimulated improvement in family relationships (A→B) and children's outcomes (A→C). To strengthen the argument that the intervention was causally related to children's adaptation to school, the final step in this analysis is to determine whether the intervention-induced changes in the putative mediators—marital and parenting relationships—were associated with positive outcomes in terms of the children's adjustment to elementary school.

According to the LVPLS models, family relationship improvement was also associated with positive outcomes for the children (B→C). Therefore, we have the appropriate pattern of results to test for mediation effects—to ask whether family process changes induced by the intervention (A) were responsible for some of the positive effects on children's adaptation (C). Traditional tests of mediation use Baron and Kenny's (1986) strategy of examining whether the addition of measures of family relationship quality (B) to a multiple regression equation lowers the A–C correlation.

According to Kraemer, Stice, Kazdin, Offord, and Kupfer (1999), mediators are factors that affect patterns of change after assignment to intervention conditions. Within intervention designs, mediators can be tested by determining whether there is a significant interaction between treatment (A) and change in the hypothesized mediator (B)—in this case marital or parenting quality—as they combine to predict variance in children's outcomes (C). In other words, it is not just that treatment produces change in parents, and change in parents is associated with variance in children's outcomes, but that parents' relationship changes in the marital or parenting intervention groups accounted for a significant proportion of the variance in the children's ability to cope with the challenges of making the transition to school.

Following a strategy used by Hinshaw et al. (2000), we created a score representing decline in marital conflict and decline in authoritarian parenting by subtracting algebraically the posttest observational measures from the pre-test measures. We then created an interaction term by multiplying the marital or parenting vectors by the change scores. This variable estimates the impact of the intervention on the participants. Because interaction effects are usually discussed as moderators, we want to emphasize the fact that the interaction term discussed here represents an effect that occurs after assignment to inter-vention. The regression analysis tests whether this effect is linked with the outcome and can be interpreted as a putative mediator of the pretest-to-posttest change in the parents.

In separate equations, we created regressions to predict kindergarten aca-demic achievement and children's perception of their own school adjustment (the two outcomes that revealed significant intervention effects), followed by regressions on all eight outcome composites in first grade (academic achieve-ment on test scores, children's perception of school adjustment on the BPI, and teacher-rated externalizing-aggressive, externalizing-hyperactive, inter-nalizing-socially withdrawn, internalizing-depressed, socially competent, and academically competent on the CABI). Because there were three equations for each outcome measure, one including decline in marital conflict, one in-cluding decline in fathers' authoritarian parenting, and one including decline in mothers' authoritarian parenting, there were 6 equations predicting kin-dergarten outcomes, and 24 equations predicting first-grade outcomes. In 12 of these 30 equations, the intervention $\times$ change interaction variable added significant variance over and above the intervention in accounting for vari-ance in the outcome (see Table 11.2). Based on the fact that it is difficult to obtain statistically significant interaction effects using multiple regressions (McClelland & Judd, 1993), we believe that this represents substantial sup-port for our hypothesis that the couples group intervention effects on the children's school adaptation were mediated by intervention-induced changes in their parents. In this case, significant effects ranged in size from explaining an additional 4% to 16% of the variance in children's adaptation to the first 2 years of elementary school.

Preschool to Kindergarten Putative Mediator Effects.   Over and above the effect of participation in a maritally-focused group, the interac-tion of marital treatment $\times$ decline in mothers' and fathers' authoritarian parenting accounted for significant improvement, $F(1, 62) = 4.26$ and 4.79, $p < .05$, in children's perceptions of their academic and social competence between prekindergarten and kindergarten assessments. Furthermore, the interaction between a marital intervention and decline in fathers' authori-tarian parenting accounted for significant variance in children's academic achievement on the Peabody Individual Achievement Test, $F(1, 62) = 5.13$, $p < .05$. Regressions calculated separately by intervention condition re-vealed that a decline in parents' authoritarian parenting was more strongly

TABLE 11.2
Increase in R^2 for the Intervention

| | Kindergarten | | | | | | Improvement Between Kindergarten and First Grade | | | | | |
| | Marital Conflict | | Mothers' Parenting | | Fathers' Parenting | | Marital Conflict | | Mothers' Parenting | | Fathers' Parenting | |
	R^2	F	R^2	F	R^2	F	R^2	F	R^2	F	R^2	F
Achievement (PIAT)	—	—	.08	4.26[a]M	.09	5.13[a]M			.04	4.26[a]M	.07	4.79[a]P
Child's perception of school adjustment	—	—	—	—	.07	4.79[a]M			.06	4.47[a]M	.09	4.88[a]P
Externalizing-aggressive	—	—	—	—	—	—						
Externalizing-hyperactive	—	—	—	—	—	—				ns	.12	5.76[a]P
Internalizing-social isolation	—	—	—	—	—	—				ns	.04	4.02[a]P
Internalizing-depression	—	—	—	—	—	—						
Social competence	—	—	—	—	—	—				ns	.16	7.72[a]M
Teacher-perceived academic competence	—	—	—	—	—	—	.15	6.15[a]M				

Note. PIAT = Peabody Individual Achievement Test.
[a]Marital (M) or parenting (P) change interaction term.

associated with children's positive perceptions of their own competence and academic achievement in families in the marital intervention than in families in the consultation control. Note that this is one of the cross-over effects in which significant effects on parenting behavior occurred following the maritally-focused interventions.

Kindergarten to First-Grade Putative Mediator Effects. For parents who participated in a maritally-focused group, a reduction in marital conflict from pretest to kindergarten was associated with an increase in teacher-perceived academic competence the next year as the children progressed from kindergarten to first grade, $F(1, 63) = 6.15, p < .05$. A reduction in the authoritarian parenting of fathers who had participated in a marital group was more strongly related to their children's improvement in social competence over the kindergarten to first-grade year than was a reduction in the authoritarian parenting of fathers from the consultation controls, $F(1, 63) = 7.72, p < .01$. Compared with mothers in the consultation condition, mothers in the marital groups who reduced their authoritarian parenting after the intervention had children with more positive perceptions of their own competence, $F(1, 63) = 4.47, p < .05$, and greater increases in the Peabody Individual Achievement Test scores between kindergarten and first grade, $F(1, 63) = 4.21, p < .05$.

The treatment × change interaction effects on internalizing and externalizing all involved a reduction in authoritarian parenting by fathers who participated in the parenting interventions. An interaction of parenting treatment × decline in fathers' authoritarian parenting accounted for significant reductions in children's externalizing-aggressive behavior, $F(1, 63) = 4.88, p < .05$, between kindergarten and first grade, and a reduction in internalizing-social isolation, $F(1, 63), p < .05$, and internalizing-depression, $F(1, 63), p < .05$, over the same period. Again, simple correlations revealed that fathers' shifts to more effective parenting between the preschool and kindergarten years accounted for significantly greater reductions in their children's externalizing and internalizing behaviors for families in the parenting intervention than for those in the consultation controls.

In sum, consistent with our second hypothesis, not only did parents' experience in the maritally-focused and parenting-focused groups make a difference to the quality of their subsequent interactions as couples or with their children, but intervention parents' positive changes were more likely to be linked with benefits for the children than were parents' changes in the consultation controls. That is, even when staff observations of consultation parents suggested some positive changes in the quality of their interactions between pretest and the next year, those shifts were not systematically linked with positive shifts in their children.

DISCUSSION

Couples Groups Affected Both Parents and Children

Our rationale for providing interventions for parents as their children embark on the transition to elementary school was based on the hypothesis that, because the quality of family relationships accounts for substantial variance in children's school successes and failures, interventions that enhance both marital and parent–child relationship quality should foster more optimal school adaptation for the children. The results provided encouraging support for this hypothesis. The parenting-focused groups appeared to encourage fathers and mothers to develop those aspects of parenting that go against gender-stereotyped behavior: Fathers became warmer, and mothers became more structuring and inclined to set limits with their children when they were involved in challenging tasks. Because both of these central qualities of parenting have been implicated in the development of children's intellectual and social competence (Baumrind, 1973; Maccoby & Martin, 1983), these effects may have important consequences for the children in the longer run as well.

Over and above the data on marital and parenting quality, vectors representing the maritally- and parenting-focused interventions explained 31% additional variance in the reduction of externalizing behaviors, 21% additional variance in the children's own perceptions of their adaptation to kindergarten, 12% additional variance in children's achievement scores, and 12% additional variance in reductions of internalizing behaviors according to their teachers, as the children moved from kindergarten to first grade.

Testing the Theory Behind the Intervention: Putative Mediators. The path models and the mediation analyses lent support to a "putative mediator" hypothesis of the kind proposed by West et al. (1991) and Wolchick et al. (1993). Just as Wolchick and her colleagues found that a preventive intervention with divorced parents resulted in increases in effective parenting, which, in turn, predicted reductions in behavior problems in their children, we found that a group intervention with parents as couples produced positive changes in our intervention's main targets—marital and parenting quality. Significant interactions between treatment and parents' change provided support for the hypothesis that the targeted family processes could be interpreted as mediating mechanisms that account for links between interventions for parents and their children's subsequent school adaptation. Reductions in marital conflict and authoritarian parenting strategies in intervention participants between the last preschool year and kindergarten year were more likely to be followed by improvement in their children's adaptation in the following year between kindergarten and first grade. These links were not found in the consultation control families.

The Relative Impact of Marital Versus Parenting Groups. The fact that there was also some evidence for positive effects of the maritally-focused groups on parenting but no evidence for any impact of the parenting-focused groups on marriage seems to suggest that the marital intervention has superior preventive force. We suggest that the story is more complex, especially when we examine the outcomes for the children. In comparison with families in the control condition, parents' participation in groups that emphasized marital issues was associated with their children's enhanced academic competence and fewer problematic externalizing behaviors, whereas participation in the groups that emphasized parenting issues was associated with lower levels of social withdrawal and depression in the children—as observed by teachers and as reported by the children themselves during the BPI. Thus, each couples group focus had different, positive effects on the children whose parents participated.

The Importance of Including Fathers. Although we did not compare these interventions for couples with interventions for mothers only—a more typical intervention approach—the results underline the importance of including fathers from two-parent families in preventive interventions designed to foster children's adaptation. First, we saw from observations and self-reports that the significant intervention effects were on fathers' behavior with their children (decreases in authoritarian parenting) or on reduced conflict and volatility between the fathers and mothers. It is difficult to imagine how interventions with mothers alone would be more effective in achieving these effects than work with both partners. Second, in analyses not reported here, we ran separate path models for fathers and mothers. The path models that included fathers' parenting explained as much or more of the variance in children's outcomes than the models that included mothers' parenting. As we argue later, including fathers in the groups, especially when the discussions pay attention to couple relationship issues, increases the possibility of affecting both of the major relationships in the nuclear family that affect children's well-being.

"Sleeper Effects." The fact that there were stronger effects 2 years after the intervention than 1 year after for both variations of the group intervention is consistent with the results of our earlier couples group intervention during the transition to parenthood study (C. P. Cowan & Cowan, 1992), in which the strongest intervention effects occurred 15 months after the intervention ended, not shortly after at the 6-month postpartum follow-ups. Increased effects at later assessment points are consistent with results of a study

of group therapy in which Burlingame and Barlow (1996) found that the group members' improvement was greater after group therapy ended than it had been while the group was ongoing. The fact that positive, developmental "sleeper effects" emerge after these intensive interventions end suggests that the work in the groups may create the kind of disequilibration for participants that triggers processes of disorganization and reorganization—processes that ultimately lead to adaptive individual and relationship change. This is consistent with comments from a number of the parents in both of our intervention studies who reflected in follow-up interviews that it had taken time to incorporate the new ideas and reactions they had had during the groups into their day-to-day interactions as partners and as parents.

The preventive approach described in this chapter capitalizes on the fact that two seemingly contradictory forces are at play during the child's transition to school. First, the age 5 to 7 shift (Sameroff & Haith, 1996) is a time of rapid physiological, psychological, and social change for children, with abundant opportunities to develop new and more sophisticated coping skills. Second, Alexander and Entwisle's (1988) trajectory hypothesis suggests a stability-maintaining process that, without intervention, tends to maintain children's place on the adaptation trajectory over the course of their school careers. We reasoned that if we could help parents foster a family environment more conducive to helping children develop adaptive responses to their earliest academic and social challenges, the stability-maintaining forces of the family and school systems should help them maintain those initial gains over the course of their school careers.

Interventions As Tests of Family Systems Theory. A few years ago, a flurry of controversy arose when Harris (1997, 1998) claimed that parents had little influence on their children's personality development (see W. A. Collins et al., 2000, for a thoughtful response). Harris's argument was based on a review of research that curiously omitted intervention studies. This study provides a clear example of a case in which parents have significant and meaningful effects on their children's academic and socioemotional adaptation.

Although the evidence supporting the directional impact of the maritally focused intervention on parenting was not strong, we should note that in no analyses did we find that the parenting focused groups had a statistically significant impact on the couple's relationship. We conclude tentatively, then, that it may be necessary to be more differentiated about the family systems notion that perturbations in any part of the system have ripple effects (spillover) throughout the system. In our study, changes in parenting were not necessarily accompanied by improvements in the marital relationship. Especially if only one spouse attends (the usual case), parenting classes may be helpful for at least one of the parents' relationships with their children, but they may not help to address or resolve conflicts between the parents that can cloud the atmosphere at home and carry over into the child's school day.

Speculations About How the Groups Produce Positive Effects

Why would the links between quality of family interaction and children's adaptation to school be stronger in the intervention groups than in the controls? This study did not allow systematic tests of hypotheses about the active ingredients of the intervention, but we have a number of speculative hypotheses. In contrast with "psychoeducational groups" that rely on a structured curriculum and a skills-teaching approach, the leaders of our groups drew the content of most of the discussion from the participants themselves and they collaborated with the group members in a process of active problem solving.

Impact on the Parents' Family Schemas. It is possible that ongoing conversations in the couples groups, in which the staff drew attention to connections among key family relationship experiences, helped create stronger links in the parents' minds as well. That is, the psychoeducational function of these groups is not primarily to impart a set of skills to the participants, but rather to foster an appreciation of the interconnectedness of central aspects of family functioning. This conception is consistent with our family systems model, in which the quality of one family relationship affects the tone in other relationships, and ultimately in combination, these relationship qualities exert their effects on children's adaptation or distress.

Impact on Emotion Regulation in the Couple. Regardless of the focus of the intervention on parenting or couple relationships, both kinds of groups were attended by mothers and fathers, which is unusual in itself, and both interventions produced some significant positive effects on the family. To explain how this impact occurred, concepts derived from research and clinical work with troubled couples seem useful. In a series of longitudinal studies of couples, Gottman and Levenson demonstrated that the regulation of negative affect is a central aspect of marital satisfaction and a buffer against marital dissolution (Gottman, 1993; Gottman & Levenson, 1999). By regulating negative affect, we do not mean suppressing it completely. In both laboratory observations of couples and experimental studies of individuals (Gross & Levenson, 1997), investigators have found that there is a physiological cost of suppression to both the individual and the relationship: When one partner "stonewalls" or shows no emotion, his or her arousal system becomes elevated and remains elevated long after the nonstonewalling partner's system has returned to baseline. A more adaptive pattern seems to involve expressing negative feelings in a controlled way that is direct, but does not contribute to out-of-control escalation of conflict between the partners. Helping parents do this on a regular basis was one goal of our couples group leaders.

In his book on couples therapy, Wile (1981) suggested that the therapist's task is to "get couples on a platform" from which they can take a look at their relationship, stop acting as antagonists, start collaborating on making sense of their painful interactions, and work together to produce small but meaningful changes. The metaphoric platform provides a safe environment in which problems can be discussed and negative feelings expressed in ways that promote the expression and regulation of both positive and negative affect. The leaders of the couples intervention groups in the study described here worked to help both partners gain this kind of perspective to take a look at and work more productively on potentially "hot" issues in their relationships. Because the couples had the regular guidance of staff members who were supportive and clinically trained, potentially negative interchanges could usually be tolerated, contained, and kept from escalating out of control. Couples could then be encouraged to experiment with small changes that felt more rewarding and less disturbing and to evaluate the success of those attempts in follow-up discussions over the 4 months of the groups. The ideal of helping parents to get on the platform to solve problems and resolve differences is equally relevant to interventions with a marital or parenting focus. In both cases, the goal is to provide an environment in which the couple can work together as intimate partners and as coparents to meet the inevitable challenges of shepherding young children as they begin their academic and social careers.

Impact on Emotion Regulation in Parent–Child Relationships. Gottman and his colleagues (1997) described parents who are able to function as effective "meta-emotion coaches" for their children. When their children are upset, the parents acknowledge their children's emotions, help them to cope with their disturbing feelings, and pursue the discussion to encourage the children toward the next step. In the Gottman et al. study, 5-year-old children whose parents coached them about emotional matters in this way were more likely to show physiological self-soothing, higher levels of academic competence, and greater skill in managing their relationships with peers 3 years later in third grade when they were 8 years old than were children of parents who dismissed or otherwise disparaged their children's fear or anger. We believe that the group leaders in this study were functioning as meta-emotion coaches for parents of preschoolers. Regardless of the problem parents brought for discussion, and whatever the level of intensity, the staff attempted to help both fathers and mothers explore their feelings and pursue a discussion of them in a productive or at least nondestructive manner. In subsequent interviews after the couples groups had ended, many couples in both of our intervention studies reported that because the group leaders helped them pursue emotionally-laden discussions farther than they would have on their own, they were later able to handle their own and their children's upsets more effectively (C. P. Cowan & Cowan, 2000).

Fonagy (1996, 1998) has suggested that an essential ingredient of parenting that leads to children's adaptation is the ability of parents to "mentalize" or engage in reflective functioning. He views this ability as a central component of secure working models of attachment. In our view, this idea converges with Gottman's (1997) focus on meta-emotion coaching and Wile's (1981) emphasis on helping couples to take a collaborative perspective from the vantage point of the platform.

The Unexamined Role of Intergenerational Issues. The focus in this chapter has been on the impact of the intervention on marital and parenting relationships. In this study, we administered the Adult Attachment Interview during the pretest assessment, but for reasons of both time and expense, did not administer it again after the intervention. Thus, we do not know whether the frequent discussions of whether to repeat patterns from their families of origin resulted in any modification of their working models of attachment, and if so, whether that modification contributed to improvements in marital and parenting relationships, as the correlational models in chapters 8 and 12 would suggest.

Impact on the Family As a Secure Base. Having identified marital and parent–child interactions as mechanisms of change in children's adaptation, we can ask how these mechanisms have their effects. The most parsimonious assumption is that reduced conflict or increased warmth and structure are sufficient to account for children's more positive self-evaluations and their ability to manage the academic and social demands of the early elementary school grades. A more elaborate hypothesis draws on one of the constructs central to this volume but not directly assessed in this study. It is possible that the intervention affects the family environment in ways that create a more "secure family base" (Byng-Hall, 1999). Extrapolating from dyadic constructs to the family system as a whole, Byng-Hall (1999) defined a secure family base as one in which there is a reliable and readily available network of relationships so that family members can expect that caregivers will be present and willing to meet their central needs. In such a family, the members typically feel sufficiently secure that they are free to explore their potential. For children, enhanced expectations of security within the family could also foster the development of positive working models of relationships outside the family. In other words, children's optimistic working models of relationships could facilitate autonomy, curiosity, willingness to explore, and collaborativeness, which would increase their ability to concentrate on new academic content, enhance their expectations of positive relationships with others in the school environment, and possibly lead to a reduced tendency to resort to externalizing or internalizing strategies when confronted with new challenges. This is an admittedly speculative leap from our findings. The kernel of the argument that bears further testing is that it is the system of relationships as a whole (see Johnson, chapter 10), and not just the connections between each pair of family members, that provides an emotion context that facilitates or interferes with children's adaptation to school.

The Group Context of the Intervention.   All of the mechanisms we have discussed so far could be included in an intervention in which one or two mental health professionals work with one couple at a time. We argue for the merits of a couples group intervention for three reasons. Groups that include both mothers and fathers can provide the following: (a) social support to reduce isolation and a tendency to normalize parents' challenges as partners and as parents; (b) a range of ideas, behaviors, and styles as models for mothers and fathers to consider; and (c) a safe setting for couples' exploration and trial of more effective problem-solving and conflict management strategies (see Gottlieb, 1988). Adequate social support and strategies to manage conflict more effectively can reduce individual isolation and marital tension, thereby helping couples to regulate negative affect and prevent the escalating negative patterns that are harmful to both marital (Gottman & Levenson, 1988) and parent–child relationships (Crockenberg, 1981; Patterson & Capaldi, 1991). Only with a design that contrasts group interventions with interventions for individual couples can we determine whether a group format contributes "added value" to the intervention. Even if there were no significant differences in outcome between group and individual couple interventions, the economic savings of working with more couples at the same time might argue for a group intervention approach.

Clinically-Trained Group Leaders.   In a review of interventions with families with young children, Heinicke et al. (1988) observed that the clinical experience of the intervenors makes a positive difference to the program. We do not have data on this point in our own study, but we believe strongly that although the parents were not recruited because they were in need of immediate psychological help, the couples intervention we have described requires staff with substantial training and expertise. As we noted, on entering the study, some participants were already experiencing significant distress as individuals, as couples, and as parents. Furthermore, the issues discussed in the group were often fraught with emotion and reflected problems that some group members had been struggling with for years but never discussed. The staff's clinical training prepared them to handle high levels of emotion sensitively and tactfully, to regulate the level of tension in individuals and in the group, and to recognize mental health problems that require further assessment or referral for treatment outside of the group setting.

CONCLUSIONS

Using both LVPLS and regression analyses of a randomized clinical trial design, we have established that the preventive interventions in this nonclinical sample have positive effects on the couples and their children, and (the putative mediator) that these effects are interconnected. It is a truism of intervention research that research-based answers raise more questions. Most importantly, we do not yet know for whom these interventions work best, whether modifications in the interventions would serve some families more effectively, whether more focus on intergenerational issues would be helpful to the participants, and whether this approach can be generalized to quite different populations, especially to low-income couples, or couples from a variety of ethnic groups. Still, the news from this study is encouraging, and we hope to report on beginning extensions of this intervention model to less advantaged populations in future research.

V

INTEGRATIONS

12

Five-Domain Models: Putting It All Together

Philip A. Cowan and Carolyn Pape Cowan

The previous chapters revealed how information from different selections of two or three of the five family domains that we believe affect children (individual, marital, parenting, three-generational, outside-the-family) combined to predict substantial amounts of variance in children's early adaptation to school. In each chapter, preschool measures of family functioning from one to three family domains accounted for from 12% to 57% of the variance in children's kindergarten and first-grade outcomes, depending on the sample size (full sample or boys and girls separately), the specific independent variables in the regressions or path models, which outcomes we examined (e.g., problem behaviors or achievement), and which family members we assessed (mothers, fathers, sons, or daughters). Parenting style, an important ingredient in children's functioning, represents only one of many factors that contribute to children's earliest adjustment to school.

In this chapter, we come back full circle to the five-domain model presented in chapter 1, to examine how information from all of these domains in combination, gathered before the child enters elementary school, can help us to predict which children will adapt relatively well to the transition, whereas others will have a hard time of it. In trying to calculate the combined contribution of various aspects of family life to predictions of children's adaptation, we do not believe that it is possible to simply add up the variance explained in each chapter. Clearly, this would total more than 100%. Predictor variables that are markers of the quality of family processes are correlated with each other, and they often account for the same or similar portions of how well or how inadequately children meet the challenges of the early years of their academic careers. Nevertheless, as one way to evaluate the schematic model in Fig. 1.5 (chapter 1), in this chapter we present an exploratory examination of the combined predictive power of data from all five domains: the three-generational legacy, each family member's adaptation, outside-the-family stressors and social supports, marital quality, and parent–child relationship quality at the same time. Our goal is not simply to learn whether children's school adaptation can be predicted, but to identify potential mechanisms or processes by which various aspects of family functioning are associated with children's academic, social, and emotional adaptation in their first years of elementary school.

A RETURN TO THE ISSUE OF THE SUBJECTS-TO-VARIABLES RATIO

The task of testing hypotheses about how variables combine to predict a given outcome is usually accomplished with multiple regression equations. Rules of thumb concerning the minimum "allowable" subjects to variables ratio range from a low of 2:1 to a high of about 100:1, with most statisticians settling on a ratio of about 10:1 (Bryant & Yarnold, 1995; Ferguson & Cox, 1993). We have followed the consensus guideline in our use of multiple regressions throughout this volume. However, we have obviously come close to the low end of this ratio in our use of Latent Variable Analysis with Partial Least Squares (LVPLS) structural equation models, for example, in chapter 11, with 66 families and 29 manifest variables, and in this chapter, with 80 families and 26 manifest variables.

In our view, there are several central issues and controversies in the field of research design and statistics that bear on our approach. First, it seems to us that there is a bimodal distribution of styles in the family research field. Some investigators analyze a few bits of information from hundreds or even thousands of participants (e.g., Udry & Chantala, 2002, using data from the Add Health study). Other investigators analyze a large quantity of information in a study of more than 150 families (Collins, 1997), and still others attempt to integrate multimeasure, multimethod, multidomain measures from a relatively small number of families as in Cox et al. (1989). We are clearly in the third group, attempting to paint a complex picture of family relationships with many measures and many analyses, but running into issues of sample size, power, and capitalizing on chance findings.

A second issue focuses more directly on statistical inference. In large-sample structural equation modeling, the statistical significance of the model is assessed by a chi-squared goodness-of-fit index, which is very sensitive to low sample size. Some authors point out that models with good fit indexes may still be considered inadequate or not useful because they do not account for much variance in the dependent variables (Chin, 1998). This argument can be viewed in the context of current concerns about overvaluing statistical significance and ignoring measures of effect size (Capraro & Capraro, 2003; Kirk, 2003).

Falk and Miller (1992) added two comments specific to LVPLS. They pointed out that the least squares estimates in LVPLS make few assumptions about the nature of the data (in contrast with LISREL), and that the procedure is analogous to a data reduction technique in which factor scores are obtained through principal component analysis and used in subsequent analyses. Their argument is that PLS models are less likely to provide biased estimates of relationships than other structural equation model programs.

OUR APPROACH

We believe that there are trade-offs involved in either the large-sample or small-sample approaches to analyzing data, and that caution must be exercised in making inferences using either alternative. We regard the structural equation models presented in this chapter that include latent variables assessing five domains of family life as a hypothesis-generating rather than hypothesis-testing enterprise. In this chapter, we examine four models: separate ones for fathers and mothers, and separate ones for predictions of kindergarten or first-grade outcomes. Each model includes the same set of independent variables from preschool assessments of the family. Our first goal was to determine whether information from the five family domains combines to predict significant amounts of variation in academic achievement, as well as externalizing and internalizing behavior in school. The second central question addressed in this chapter is whether information from each of the family domains assessed during the preschool period adds unique predictive power to variations in children's early school adaptation.

METHODS

Participants

A complete longitudinal data set containing the key variables from preschool through the kindergarten and first-grade years was available for 80 families.

Measures

As measures of adaptation to school, we selected the same latent constructs that we used in chapter 11, created from Child Adaptive Behavior Inventory scales (CABI), completed by classroom teachers, to reflect the children's internalizing (depression, anxiety, social isolation, and social withdrawal scales) and externalizing (aggression, hostility, and oppositional scales). Also, as in chapter 11, we used three scales from the Peabody Individual Achievement Test (PIAT) to create a latent variable measuring academic achievement. To represent preschool family predictors, we chose one or two sets of measures of parents' functioning from each of the five family domains.

In a process similar to that of a hierarchical multiple regression, we began by entering three covariates into four LVPLS structural equation models.

LV 1 (latent variable). Sex of the child (dummy coded 0 or 1)—Although we would have preferred to run separate models for boys and girls, the size of the sample relative to the number of manifest and latent variables in these equations precluded that possibility.

LV 2 and 3. Two vectors assessing intervention versus control group (a maritally-focused group versus control contrast, and a parenting-focused group versus a control contrast) to eliminate direct effects of the interventions on the outcomes—Participants included the self-selected controls used in the Intention to Treat analyses (see chapter 11).

Following the three latent variables as covariates, we entered data from the family domains in an order determined mostly by the developmental trajectory of family life. We assumed that participants' descriptions of relationships in their family of origin logically preceded measures of relationship quality in their current family. Assuming that spouses bring relatively stable characteristics to their relationship as a couple, we then entered measures of individual well-being and life stress events. Next, we entered observational assessments of marital interaction and parenting style. We are aware that the theoretical order that we imposed on the data did not necessarily represent a true temporal ordering, especially because all of these measures were obtained contemporaneously. However, it represented a theory-driven way of bringing order to the large array of constructs.

LV 4 and 5. Coders' ratings (see chapter 8) of mothers' or fathers' descriptions of their parents as loving (LV 4) and ratings of their current anger at parents expressed during the interview in ways that disrupted the coherence of the narrative (LV 5).

LV 6. Two psychological symptom scales (see chapter 2), the Center for Epidemiological Depression Scale (CES-D; Radloff, 1977), and the Anxiety scale from the Brief Symptom Inventory (BSI; Derogatis & Melisaratos, 1983).

LV 7. Life stress outside the family, including work stress, using scores on the Recent Life Events scale assessing life changes over the past 2 years, weighted for both recency and level of stress (Horowitz et al., 1977, chapter 2).

LV 8 and LV 9.   Marital quality measured in two contexts: LV 8 included observations of husbands' and wives' negative behavior from the couple problem-solving discussion (chapter 7), and LV 9 included measures of conflict and negative emotion between the parents when the child was present during the whole family visit (chapters 7, 8, and 11).

LV 10.   Observers' ratings of authoritarian parenting style (chapters 4, 6, 8, and 11; low warmth, high structure, low respect for autonomy).

LV 11 and LV 12.   Children's perceptions—To address the point made in several chapters that children's self-perceptions as well as adult self-perceptions are important predictors of children's adaptation to school, we included measures from the Berkeley Puppet Interview of children's perceptions of their own adaptation (chapter 6, LV 11) and their perceptions of whether their parents fight a lot (chapter 7, LV 12). These variables were included last because we wanted to test the hypothesis that the child's perspective would add significant predictive power, over and above parents' reports and our observations of their behavior.

LV 13, 14, and 15.   The three dependent variables were academic achievement, internalizing, and externalizing assessed in kindergarten (mothers' and fathers' models) or first grade (mothers' and fathers' models).

In sum, each of the four structural equation models included 26 manifest variables arranged in 15 latent variables: 3 covariates, 9 predictors, and 3 dependent variables. There were fewer manifest variables (26 vs. 29), more latent variables (15 vs. 11), and more participants (80 vs. 66) than the models in chapter 11. Variables assessing the marriage and the child's perceptions were identical in mothers' and fathers' models. The differences between models lay in each mother's and father's information about their own early attachment, depressive symptoms, life stress, and preschool parenting style. It would have been more ideal to include information from both parents in the same statistical models, but even with 80 families, the models will not run with that many manifest variables.

In multiple regressions, no matter what the order of variables, it is possible to determine whether each independent variable makes a unique contribution to explaining variance in the dependent variable. Here we could determine a significant increase in R^2 only in successive tests comparing a partial with a full structural model. We constructed a set of nested PLS equations, starting with the full model, and removed one additional latent variable in each subsequent equation. This allowed us to test for the significance of the difference in variance accounted for between two "adjacent" equations, in essence producing a measure of R^2 change. For example, if the full model contains measures from each of the five domains as they predict children's externalizing behaviors and we remove the measure of marital conflict from the equation, we can test the difference between the full model and the partial model to determine whether removing the marital conflict data makes a significant reduction in explaining the outcome. If it does, then we can conclude that variation in marital conflict adds uniquely and significantly to the predictive power of the equation. The procedure is analogous to a backward multiple regression in which the reduction in explained variance when a variable is removed from the equation is treated as a measure of its contribution, over and above the variables remaining in the equation. In addition to taking advantage of the improved measurement characteristics of latent variables, this procedure allowed us to specify a theoretically-determined order in which to remove variables from the equation. By deconstructing the full model, the nested models allowed us to test our hypothesis that a combination of family factors from multiple domains provides the best explanation of variation in children's school adaptation.

RESULTS AND DISCUSSION

Family Predictors of Children's Adaptation to School

Figures 12.1 through 12.4 present four separate five-domain LVPLS models illustrating the links among measures of family adaptation in the preschool period and how children fare in kindergarten (top) and first grade (bottom). We adopted two strategies to simplify the task of understanding the complex links among the variables in these models. First, although the covariates were included in the statistical analyses, we have not included them in the figures or tables (child sex, intervention participation by parents). We were thinking of them as "control" variables and trying to assess the contribution of the other variables over and above the effects of the sex of the child and the intervention with the parents. Second, given the large number of meaningful paths, we did not include the numerical weights on each path in the figures. We were not focused here on the specific pathways, but rather on the gestalt, to demonstrate the fact that there is a dense network of connections among the family predictor variables, and between the predictor variables and each school outcome. Thus, in these figures, the presence of a path line signifies a link between two latent variables (that explains more than 5% of the variance) and the absence of a path means that the amount of overlapping variance in the two was too small to be interpreted meaningfully.

Amount of Variance Explained.   In each model in Figs. 12.1 through 12.4, the circles representing the latent variable measures of children's outcomes (externalizing, internalizing, academic achievement) also display the total amount of variance explained by the two covariates and all of the latent variables to the left of the outcomes. The fathers' model explained from 35% to 47% of the variance in kindergarten outcomes, and from 54% to 61% of the variance in children's adaptation to first grade. The mothers' model explained from 37% to 41% of the variance in kindergarten outcomes and from 38% to 65% of the variance in children's adaptation to first grade. The root-mean-squared covariance indexes varied between .06 and .09, describing the average correlation between the residuals on the manifest and latent variables that is not accounted for by the model relations (Falk & Miller, 1992), indicating that the data fit the model quite well. Thus, over and above the sex of the child and the parents' participation in the intervention, fathers' and mothers' working models of attachment, symptoms, life stress, and parenting style, the couple's marital interaction, and the children's perception of self and their parents' marriage, together predicted substantial proportions of the variation in teachers' descriptions of children's kindergarten and first-grade academic, social, and emotional adjustment.

Statistical tests of the overall explanatory power of the equation (Falk & Miller, 1992) revealed that all the Fs associated with total variance explained were statistically significant (see Table 12.1; the degrees of freedom for the F tests were 11/54). By contrast, in each of the previous chapters, some regressions or structural models relating preschool family functioning to kindergarten or first-grade adaptation were statistically significant, whereas others were not. This is not simply an artifact of including more variables in the equations in this chapter. Although the amount of explained variance always increased as more variables were added to the equation, this increase did not guarantee that the final model would account for a statistically significant amount of variance.

These findings indicate that it is possible to make statistically significant predictions about how children adapt to early elementary school with structural equation models that include preschool data from all five domains of family life in our conceptual model. In 5 of the 12 prediction-outcome tests, the models accounted for more than half of the variation in children's aggressive behavior, depressed, anxious behavior, and academic achievement. It is always possible that the amount of variance explained results from misspecification of the latent variables in the model, but the root-mean-square-covariance indexes give us some assurance that our conceptual grouping of the manifest variables into the latent variables fits the data. Still, the precise specification of predictability and effect size can be determined only through replications with different samples.

Another way of interpreting the meaning of the path models in Fig. 12.1 is simply to look at the spaghetti-like arrangement created by the fact that so many of the potential paths showed meaningful connections. For the nine la-

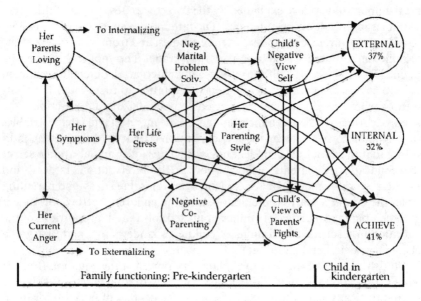

FIG. 12.1.   Mother's model; child in kindergarten.

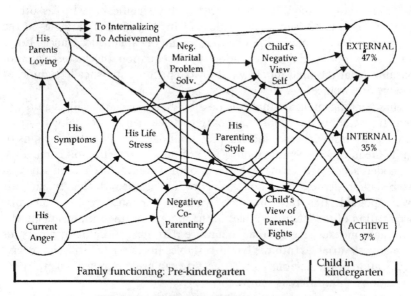

FIG. 12.2.   Fathers' model; child in kindergarten.

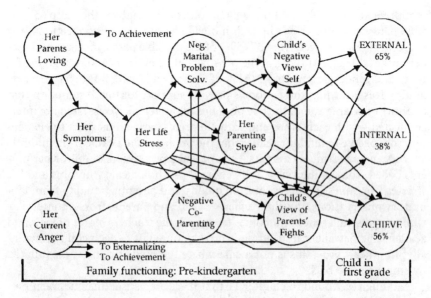

FIG. 12.3. Mothers' model; child in first grade.

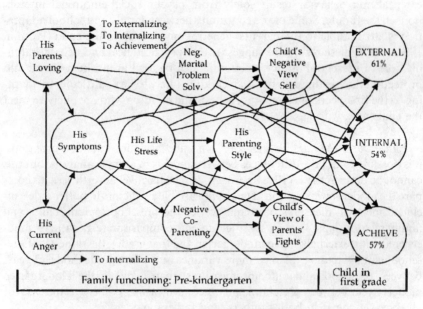

FIG. 12.4. Fathers' model; child in first grade.

tent predictor variables and three latent outcome variables, there are 63 possible pair-wise connections in each model. The number of connections that met the criterion ranged from 37 (59% of the possible paths; mothers and kindergarten) through 41 (65% of the possible paths; mothers and first grade, fathers and kindergarten) to 42 (67% of the possible paths; fathers and first grade). It is clear that these models provide support for our assumption that qualities of adaptation in the five domains of family life we assessed are interconnected—with each other and with children's early adjustment to elementary school. We remind the reader that the predictor data came from multiple sources and assessment contexts: each parent's perceptions of his or her parents coded from an interview, self-reported psychological symptoms and life stresses from questionnaires, marital quality and parenting quality from laboratory observations, the child's views of self and parents from an interview with puppets, and school outcomes from both the teachers' point of view and academic achievement tests administered by our staff to each child individually. In other words, this is not a case where the predictive power is inflated by single source bias.

Although we found in chapter 11 that there are causal links between preschool family functioning and the child's adaptation to school, we do not assume that variations in academic achievement and internalizing and externalizing behavior result solely from psycho-social-emotional interactions in the family. Some of the continuity between family and school adaptation is attributable to the parents' genetic contribution to the child (Plomin, 1994). What these results do suggest is that psychological and behavioral indicators of preschool family functioning can be used as markers of risk and protection that distinguish between children likely to have difficulty in adapting to the first years of elementary school and children who are likely to meet the challenges with ease.

Kindergarten Versus First Grade.   In some structural equation programs, it is possible to test the differences between models in a single analysis, but this cannot be done in the LVPLS approach. It is instructive, nevertheless, to compare the models by inspection. The latent variable predictors in both models included identical measures of adaptation of the preschool parent, child, and family relationships. In each specific outcome comparison (e.g., fathers' models predicting externalizing in kindergarten and first grade), the same set of preschool family factors explained more variance in the first-grade model (2 years between preschool and outcome measures) than it did in the kindergarten model (1 year between preschool and outcome measures). This was the case for all three outcomes in both mothers' and fathers' models.

It is common to find that predictive power of any assessment decays over time. In this study, the same preschool variables were stronger predictors of the children's subsequent adaptation 2 years later than they were 1 year later. There are at least three possible explanations of this finding. First, it may be that kindergarten measures of children's adaptation are less reliable or less valid than measures obtained in first grade. Second, as we speculated in chapter 1, it may also be that the child's initial transition to kindergarten is more disequilibrating, and consistency is reestablished only as the children work to adapt and settle into their second year of school. Third, the data may reflect "sleeper" effects, in which the impact of the transition to school only emerges after a period of disorganization and reorganization.

Trends Across the Models. In all four models shown in Figs. 12.1–12.4, when mothers and fathers of the children in our study described early relationships with their parents (the children's grandparents) as low in loving or currently angry at their parents, they were more likely to report that they were experiencing psychological symptoms and higher life stress. It may be that individuals with less secure working models are more anxious, depressed, and subject to stressors in their current lives, or that current anxieties and stress color mothers' and fathers' accounts of relationships in their families of origin.

Compared with those reporting low life stress, fathers and mothers reporting high life stress were more likely to show negative behavior during the problem-solving discussion with their partners, more authoritarian behavior while working with their child on challenging tasks, and, usually, more negative coparenting that is high in conflict as they worked together with their child. It seems reasonable to assume that, when men and women are attempting to cope with inner distress or outside-the-family stressors, they will be more irritable and less tolerant or patient when their relationships with their partners or children feel strained (e.g., Conger et al., 1992).

As we move to the children, we see that in three of the four models, children's negative views of themselves were associated with an authoritarian parenting style. Certainly, harsh or angry messages from parents could reinforce a child's negative self-perceptions. Furthermore, because authoritarian parenting style was consistently associated with negative interaction between the parents, it makes sense that it was also associated with the children's perceptions that their parents fought a lot.

Completing the chain of associations, we see that both children's views of themselves and their parents' marriage and parenting style were associated with three of the outcomes representing school adaptation. Children's negative self-descriptions during the preschool period were consistently linked with subsequent descriptions from their teachers of more internalizing behavior in kindergarten and first grade. In three of the four models, children's reports of high levels of fighting between their parents in the year before they entered kindergarten were associated with more externalizing behavior 1 and 2 years later.

Note that the links between marital quality and parenting style occurred only for parents' relationships as coparents in the presence of their child, not for their style of resolving problems as a couple when their child was not present. This kind of specificity in the models is reassuring. It tells us that the paths do not simply reflect the fact that negative aspects of family life tend to be correlated; it reveals the possibility that specific mechanisms, such as conflict over parenting issues rather than all conflict as a couple, may be responsible for the links between the marital and parent–child domains.

As we continue with our speculations about possible causal forces behind the correlations, we note that a negative quality of family life, with depressed, anxious, or highly stressed parents who fight with each other and the child, is associated with worrisome family and self-perceptions in the child that hinder the child's ability to meet the academic and social challenges of early elementary school. Even within a population of supposedly "low-risk" families, then, we can see how risks occurring in one family domain during the preschool period tend to reverberate throughout the family system and pose further risks for the children as they face the challenge of becoming competent students and peers.

Differences Among the Models.   Although the models in Figs. 12.1 through 12.4 are similar, they are not identical. Even so, at this point, we are reluctant to make too much of what may be chance variations between them. For example mothers' symptoms are linked with negative marital problem solving only in the model with kindergarten outcomes, whereas fathers' symptoms are linked with negative interaction in the coparenting relationship. We can construct a plausible post hoc explanation of such differences, but we prefer to leave that task to further research. We are taking this tack in part to avoid overinterpreting random fluctuation, but also because the numbers precluded an analysis of the boys' and girls' data separately. Based on data from our earlier longitudinal study (Kerig, Cowan, & Cowan, 1993), we expect that gender-specific models might show clearer links between fathers' symptoms and the quality of marital interaction in families whose first child is a girl.

We acknowledge, as we have throughout the volume, that this study contains a relatively small sample of families. It is possible that the strength of association among specific domains in this study capitalizes on chance. However, the consistency of the connections between family and school and the coherence of the data leave us with the working hypothesis that future studies will replicate the overall conclusion about the strong predictive linkage among family relationships and children's academic competence and problem behaviors, and the fact that parent–child relationships constitute only one important link in a complex systemic chain.

Why did so many paths in each model show meaningful connections? Is it that we are simply assessing and reassessing the same family dysfunction with different measures so that wherever we apply the thermometer we obtain the same temperature reading? For example, the correlations could represent overlapping indicators of emotion regulation processes that are in or out of control in both individual and relationship domains of family life. Or, could the plethora of correlations have resulted from the fact that each family domain contributes something unique to children's adjustment to school? The data in the section that follows support the second alternative.

Unique Contributions of Family Domains to Predicting Children's Adaptation

Table 12.1 presents the total proportion of variance explained by each LVPLS model, and the reduction in explained variance created by the removal of a specific latent variable or variables. The nine latent variable predictors representing measures of the preschool family were removed in the order that they were entered into the equation, based on the rationale described earlier: (a) three-generational attachment (two latent variables), (b) psychological symptoms, (c) life stress, (d) marital conflict during a couple problem-solving discussion, (e) marital conflict during a whole-family laboratory interaction, (f) parenting style, (g) children's negative views of themselves, and (h) children's perceptions that their parents fight a lot. The covariates were left in each equation at all times, whereas the latent variables were removed in eight successive steps. The proportion of variance in the outcome explained by a predictor is presented in the table only when the F-change between two steps was statistically significant ($df = 1/54, p < .05$). If we start at the top of each column in Table 12.1 and read down, we get a sense of how successive steps of the LVPLS equation contribute to understanding variance in the outcome in question.

Note the fundamental difference between this table and the models presented in Figs. 12.1 to 12.4. The figures include the presence or absence of links among the independent variables, whereas this table presents the additive contribution of each independent variable to the explanation of variance in one of the dependent variable outcomes.

In all, there were 96 tests of F-change (4 models × 3 outcomes × 8 steps) to determine whether removing that variable from the equation resulted in a significant decrement in the equation's ability to predict an outcome. Of these tests, 53 (55%) were statistically significant at the $p < .05$ level. In general,

TABLE 12.1

Predicting School Outcomes From Family Domain Data: Significant R^2 Change in Successive Steps

	Kindergarten						Grade 1					
	Mothers' Model			Fathers' Model			Mothers' Model			Fathers' Model		
Variance explained	External	Internal	Academic	External	Internal	Academic	External	Internal	Academic	External	Internal	Academic
Total R^2 (%)	37	32	41	47	35	37	65	38	56	61	54	57
$F(11, 54)$	2.90**	2.31*	3.42**	4.36**	2.65**	2.90**	9.09***	3.00**	6.28***	7.71***	5.78***	6.48***
Decrease in R^2												
Three-generation attachment		5		5	7	15	13		22	12	7	8
Parents' symptoms			3		5		11		8	9	14	3
Life stress	5		4	3			4	3			4	23
Couple problem solving	11	8	5	13								
Coparenting	5	3			3		4	5			3	4
Parenting style	3		9	8				4	14	8		
Child's view of self	7	12		13	12							8
Child's view of marriage	6		9			8	20	3	7	19		7

*$p < .05.$ **$p < .01.$ ***$p < .001.$

then, latent variable measures of family functioning from the five domains were not redundant. Adaptation in each domain played its own unique role in predicting, and perhaps affecting, different measures of children's adaptation in the first two years of elementary school. To increase clarity in the following sections, instead of reporting the decrement in explained variance resulting from eliminating a variable from the model, we describe the results in terms of the more familiar concept of an increase in R^2 when the variable is added. The statistical calculations are exactly the same either way.

Kindergarten Adaptation: Mothers' Model. The mothers' five-domain model explained 37% of the variance in their children's externalizing behavior, 32% of the variance in their internalizing behavior, and 41% of the variance in their tested academic achievement in the first year of elementary school.

The preschool family predictors of each outcome are presented in order of the effect size of their unique contribution to explaining variance in school adaptation, despite the fact that this effect size was obtained in a predetermined order of model testing. Conflict between the parents appeared to be an important predictor of children's externalizing in terms of negative scores for problem solving between the parents (11%), the child's negative view of himself or herself (7%), the child's view that the parents fight a lot (6%), negative scores on observed coparenting (5%), and, in addition, life stress (5%) and authoritarian parenting style (3%) also contributed to predictions of aggressive and oppositional behavior in kindergarten.

As might be expected, children's negative descriptions of themselves during the preschool period contributed unique variance to the prediction of their internalizing in the mothers' model (12%), as in the fathers' model described in the following section. This statement may appear to be "obvious" because the latent variable measuring children's self-descriptions was identical in the two models. However, LVPLS models present the optimal weighting of all latent variable predictors, so it is possible to have substantial variation across models, even when some of the measures are identical. Unique variance was also predicted by conflict during the couple problem-solving interaction (8%), low loving and high current anger scores on the Adult Attachment Interview (5%), and conflict during the whole-family laboratory interaction session (3%).

The pattern predicting academic achievement in the mothers' model was quite different from that for the social–emotional behaviors summarized in the externalizing and internalizing dimensions. Mothers' authoritarian parenting style (9%), the child's view of the marriage (9%), coparenting conflict (5%), life stress (4%), and psychological symptoms (3%), all provided nonoverlapping contributions to difficulties in children's academic achievement.

Kindergarten Adaptation: Fathers' Model. The fathers' five-domain model explained 47% of the variance in children's externalizing, 35% of the variance in internalizing, and 37% of the variance in academic achievement test scores in kindergarten. Parents' high marital conflict in the problem-solving discussion (13%), the child's negative view of anticipated adaptation to school (13%), and fathers' authoritarian parenting style (8%), all contributed significant variance to the prediction of externalizing behavior 1 year later at the end of kindergarten, as did fathers' responses to the Adult Attachment Interview (5%). Fathers' life stress explained an additional 3% of the variance.

The pattern relating family functioning to internalizing is both similar and different from that for externalizing. Again, the child's negative self-description of anticipated school adjustment (12%), and fathers' working models of attachment (7%), were implicated in children's internalizing, but this time, fathers' psychological symptoms (5%) and the couple's negative quality of coparenting (3%) also contributed significantly to the prediction of internalizing. One way of summarizing these trends is that both externalizing and internalizing in these 5½- to 6-year-old kindergarten children were connected to fathers' working models of relationships. Whether the child showed externalizing or internalizing behavior depended on whether the couples were high in negative behavior and fathers were authoritarian, in which case the children were more likely to use externalizing strategies, or whether the parents were anxious and depressed, in which case the children were more likely to use internalizing behaviors.

Data from only two of the family domains contributed to predictions of children's academic achievement in kindergarten. When fathers were coded as low in loving relationships with their parents and high in current anger toward them (15%), their children had lower academic achievement scores. An additional 8% of the variance was accounted for by children's perceptions of their parents as fighting a lot.

First Grade Adaptation: Mothers' Model. The mothers' five-domain model accounted for a very high 65% of the variance in children's externalizing, 38% of the variance in internalizing, and 56% of the variance in academic achievement in first grade. Unique predictors of externalizing in the first graders were children's views of the parents' fighting as a couple (20%), current anger and low scores on loving in relationships with their parents (13%), psychological symptoms (11%), life stress (4%), and coparenting difficulties (4%).

For this sample, which combined boys and girls, only four unique predictors in the mothers' model contributed significant amounts of variance to children's internalizing in first grade: negative coparenting style (5%), the child's negative view of self (4%), mothers' life stress (3%), and the child's view of conflict in the parents' marriage (3%). We believe that, if the sample were split by sex, we would find a substantial contribution to the prediction of daughters' internalizing from mothers' perceptions of their family of origin, as suggested by results reported in chapter 8.

Finally, substantial portions of variance in first-grade academic achievement were explained by mothers' descriptions of relationships with their parents (22%), parenting style (14%), and psychological symptoms (8%), and the child's perception that the parents fight a lot (7%).

First Grade Adaptation: Fathers' Model. The fathers' five-domain model explained a very high 61% of the variance in their children's externalizing, 54% of the variance in internalizing, and 57% of the variance in academic achievement in first grade when the children were 6½ years old. When fathers of preschoolers described their relationships with their parents as low in loving and seemed angry with their parents now (12%), when they described themselves as depressed and anxious (9%), and when we observed high marital conflict during the whole family visit (8%)—especially when the children reported that their parents fought a lot (19%)—their children were more likely to show angry and aggressive behavior in their second year of elementary school.

The pattern predicting internalizing in first grade overlapped partially with that for externalizing. Fathers with more psychological symptoms (14%), negative working models of attachment relationships (7%), life stress (4%), and conflictful coparenting relationships (3%), had children who showed more internalizing behaviors 2 years later. The key differences between the patterns for externalizing and internalizing seem to lie in the anger and fighting in families of students who resort to externalizing strategies, and the stress and distress in the fathers of students who show internalizing strategies at school. That is, it is not simply a matter of behavior that is transmitted across the generations but an emotional atmosphere that appears to encourage the child outward to act out aggressive feelings or inward toward sadness and social withdrawal.

The largest contributor to understanding variance in first graders' academic achievement was the father's perception of life stressors (23%), but other domains contributed their share to predicting that outcome: fathers' working models of relationships (8%), parenting style (8%), and the child's perception of parental fighting (7%), coparenting difficulties (4%), and psychological symptoms (3%).

CONCLUSIONS

The findings summarized schematically in Figs. 12.1–12.4 and Table 12.1 provide an instructive context in which to interpret the results from earlier chapters. Four generalizations can be made from the pattern of findings in this chapter. First, every latent variable contributed unique variance to the prediction of at least one outcome. That is, each of the five family domains assessed in the preschool period with data from parents', children's, and observers' reports, adds something to our understanding of how children adapted to the first 2 years of elementary school.

Second, information from different domains was additive; at least two latent variables from different domains, and sometimes three, four, or five, accounted for unique variance in the prediction of outcomes at two points in time (kindergarten, first grade). These findings provide support for our multidomain model of family factors in children's adaptation to school. As we have argued in this volume, the quality of one parent–child relationship and its impact on the child must be interpreted in light of the child's relationship with the other parent, and the parents' relationships as a couple and with their own parents.

Third, the data in Table 12.1, representing the difference between two equations in the proportion of variance explained in each outcome, do not reveal which family variables were "more important" in some absolute sense to explaining individual differences in children's adaptation. For example, a look across the row of data on parenting style implies that it made a smaller contribution to the outcomes than did information about three-generational attachment or marital conflict. Because we were unable to do separate analyses by sex of child, these analyses obscure the fact that mothers' and fathers' parenting style is associated with internalizing in kindergarten—for girls but not for boys (chapters 6 and 8). It could also be that parenting style is not a unique predictor of internalizing. Especially because parenting behavior was placed "late" in the model, after all of the other parent variables had been considered, the low number of significant associations of parenting behavior with children's adaptation is, in part, an artifact of multicollinearity. The predictive power of observed parenting style is usurped by parents' working models of attachment, depression, life stress, and marital quality, all of which help to shape the quality of the parent–child relationships.

Fourth, different family variables were implicated in different outcomes assessed at different times (kindergarten, first grade). This is relevant to the assessment of risk. Although it may be a matter of concern to see that the marital relationship is not functioning well during the preschool period, we cannot automatically assume that this bodes ill for the child in every aspect of his or her adaptation or for all periods of time. Authoritarian parenting by mothers or fathers during the preschool period constitutes a risk factor for some outcomes in kindergarten and others in first grade.

Although we cannot determine the absolute weights assigned to the predictive power of each family variable, it is instructive to calculate an "average" across the six models, each containing kindergarten and first-grade outcomes. When we average across the rows, we find that the Loving and Anger variables from the Adult Attachment Interview account for 7.8% of the unique variance in the children's adaptation measures, the child's view of the parents' marriage for 6.6%, psychological symptoms for 4.4%, the child's view of self for 4.0%, life stress for 3.8%, parenting style for 3.5%, co-parenting for 3.3%, and marital problem solving for 2.7%. Although another ordering of variables in the model could change the absolute contributions, the general point remains clear: The child's adaptation to school is predictable from the quality of multiple aspects of preschool family life, as well as from how the child perceives himself or herself and key family relationships.

The question of how family functioning relates to children's adaptation cannot be answered with a single static snapshot. Rather, family functioning becomes associated with children's adaptation in a dynamic process in which multiple aspects of family functioning in different contexts (with mothers or fathers) before children enter school may become relevant to their school adjustment at different times. If we want to know whether children from a nonclinical sample of families are at risk during the early elementary school years, we need to specify the outcome we have in mind, whether we are interested in kindergarten or first grade, and whether we are focusing on information about mothers or fathers. This complex set of findings underlines the idea that risks are not a fixed characteristic of a variable, but emerge as specific functional relations in specific analyses. Rutter made this point many years ago (1987) and the field of developmental psychopathology would do well to remember it more often.

13

Family Factors in Children's Adaptation to Elementary School: A Discussion and Integration

Philip A. Cowan, Carolyn Pape Cowan, Jennifer C. Ablow,
Vanessa Kahen Johnson, and Jeffrey R. Measelle

In this final chapter, we provide a perspective on the study findings as a whole. We summarize and discuss the general trends, acknowledge the study's limitations, and explore the implications of the results for family policy, especially with regard to preventive intervention services focused on parents' relationships—as couples and with their children.

SUMMARY: THE FAMILY CONTEXT OF PARENTING

The first three chapters of this volume provided an overview of our five-domain model of family-school connections, described the design and measures of the study, and presented an account of both continuity and stability of adaptation in children and parents over the 2 years from preschool through the end of first grade.

In chapter 4, we showed that parents' granting of autonomy accounted for significant variance in their children's kindergarten adaptation, over and above the parents' provision of warmth and structure (authoritative parenting). This finding supports the recent move toward adding autonomy as a central dimension of parenting style and fits within the traditional research paradigm that examines links between parents' behavior and their children's adaptation to school. Each succeeding chapter placed parenting within the context of family relationships. In chapter 5, when we added a focus on parenting and gender-stereotyped behavior in children, we found that fathers' satisfaction with marriage and involvement in rearing their children were associated with their tendency to support children's behavior when it went against gender-stereotype. Fathers who were more satisfied with their marriage and more involved in caring for their preschoolers tended to encourage daughters' assertiveness and sons' warmth. This style of parenting functioned both as a protective factor and a risk factor, depending on the sex of the child and the outcome, in that it was associated with fewer externalizing behaviors but a greater number of depressed withdrawn behaviors in boys, and fewer internalizing behaviors but a greater number of externalizing behaviors in girls at the start of elementary school.

Although the analyses in chapters 4 and 5 included self-report questionnaires, they emphasized observation of family interactions—the "outsider" perspective. Chapters 6 through 10 shifted perspective to focus on how "insider" information from family members adds to the outsider perspective to enhance our understanding of family-to-school linkages. We noted that the tendency in family research over the decades has been an increasing dominance of observational research over self-report methods of studying families. Our findings suggest that both perspectives contribute unique predictive power when we consider how preschool family processes explain children's achievement, social competence, and problem behavior during their transition to elementary school. Chapter 6 described how children's self-perceptions of their social competence functioned as both mediators and moderators of the link between what we observed in the family process in our project playroom before the children made the transition to kindergarten and the children's externalizing behaviors or social competence as their teachers observed it the next year at school. In chapter 7, we showed that children's interpretations of their parents' conflict, whether overt or disengaged, in combination with our observations of the parents' marital interaction, predicted the children's use of externalizing and internalizing strategies once they entered elementary school, with different patterns of correlation for boys and girls. Thus, preschoolers' perceptions of themselves, their parents' quality of marital interaction, and three different aspects of parenting style, including gender-stereotyping, all predicted substantial variance in the children's academic achievement and social and emotional adaptation during the transition to school—often, but not always, with different patterns for boys and girls.

In chapter 8, we moved beyond the nuclear triad of mother, father, and child, to show how mothers' and fathers' recollections of relationships with their own parents added to the power of structural equation models to predict children's internalizing and externalizing behaviors at school, once again with different patterns for boys and girls. Chapter 9 added parents' perceptions of their work experiences to show how family-friendly jobs and work-friendly parents may be particularly important in considering the influence of mothers' work on young children's school adjustment.

Then, in chapter 10, we found that, over and above dyadic relationships in the family, assessment of the structure and processes in the whole family predicted teachers' ratings of the children's academic competence and their use of both internalizing and externalizing behaviors as they made the transition to school. These seven separate chapters (4–10) revealed how information from different selections of two or three of the five family domains that we believe affect children (individual, marital, parenting, three-generational, outside-the-family) combined to predict substantial amounts of variation in their early adaptation to elementary school.

Chapters 11 and 12 presented two different kinds of integration. In chapter 11, we provided evidence from a randomized clinical trial intervention design that marital conflict and parenting style play a causal role in children's development. When parents had more effective interactions as couples or with their children after the couples group intervention, their children showed more successful adaptations to elementary school than children of parents in the control condition. The intervention results also suggested that there may be more carry-over from marital quality to parenting quality than there is the other way around. In chapter 12, we illustrated how data from each of the family domains, assessed in preschool, contributed unique variance to predicting the children's internalizing behavior, externalizing behavior, and academic achievement. However, as in almost every chapter, specific linkages between family and school adaptation depended on the specific independent variables in the regressions or path models, which outcomes we examined (e.g., problem behaviors or achievement), and which family members we assessed (mothers, fathers, sons, or daughters). Parenting style, an important ingredient in children's functioning, represents only one of many factors that contribute to their early adjustment to elementary school.

THE PREKINDERGARTEN TO FIRST-GRADE PERIOD AS A TRANSITION

In chapters 1 and 3, we described a life transition as involving qualitative shifts in a person's inner view of self and world, major life roles, and central relationships (P. Cowan, 1991). Using data obtained in the children's preschool period, kindergarten, and first grade, we considered whether the results support the idea that the entrance to elementary school constitutes a life transition for children, for parents, or for families.

A Transition for the Child

Qualitative data from interviews and quantitative data from questionnaires and systematic observations indicate that the children in our study, the oldest in their respective families, experienced a major life transition as they moved from the end of the preschool period into the first 2 years of elementary school. This seems true despite the fact that many of the children, like increasing numbers of American children entering kindergarten, had already had some experience in preschools or out-of-home day care (U.S. Department of Education, 1993). As Kagan and Neville (1996, p. 388) argued persuasively, "rather than a discrete event, transition today connotes an extended process that occurs at different times, over different durations for different children. Such differences make *transition to school* difficult to define." We agree that the transition to school is a process rather than an event, and that children are coming to kindergarten with a wide variety of preschool experiences. Still, there are qualitative differences between the more voluntary programs of preschool and day care with their emphasis on exploration and play, and the compulsory world of elementary school with its emphasis on achievement. This difference alone is a substantial one for children, and it creates conditions that tend to produce a major life transition.

We found that a majority of the children in this nonclinical sample of relatively advantaged families were generally faring quite well during this transition—able to meet the challenges posed by kindergarten and first grade and able to respond to complex new school environments with the development of new intellectual and interpersonal skills. Nevertheless, despite the children's generally positive sense of competence as indicated in their responses to the Berkeley Puppet Interview, we have three areas of concern about their well-being or difficulty during the transition to elementary school. First, girls' perceptions of their academic competence became more negative between the last preschool year and their completion of first grade. It was striking to us that, just as mothers had more negative views of themselves and their lives than did fathers (chapter 3), daughters who were 5 and younger began to show increasing doubts about their competence as they set out on their academic and social trajectories. This was not true for the sons in our study.

Second, based on the children's self-reports on the Berkeley Puppet Interview, their scores on the Peabody individually administered academic achievement tests, and their parents' perceptions of them on the Child Adaptive Behavior Inventory, we could see that children at the high end of the adaptation continuum in the preschool period tended to make good adjustments to elementary school, whereas those at the low end tended to remain behind their peers in kindergarten and first grade. This is a troubling although not entirely surprising finding, as it provides support for Alexander and Entwisle's trajectory hypothesis (1988); without some intervention, young students may be at risk for maintaining negative self-perceptions and lower levels of academic and social functioning throughout their school careers. The trajectory notion stimulates our third area of concern. Although a majority of the children in our study were able to meet the challenges of elementary school, we found children and families who were in substantial distress before school entrance, and many of them remained in that position over the first 2 years of school (discussed later).

A Transition for the Parents

Despite the concerns recounted by parents as they anticipated their first children's transition to school, parents showed a number of positive changes in the period between prekindergarten and the end of first grade. As their first child entered school, they were reporting significantly fewer symptoms of anxiety, greater satisfaction with the division of labor in the household, more involvement in their work lives, and fewer stressful life events. They were less psychologically involved in their housework and parenting role (on The Pie), and more authoritative in interaction with their children. Overall, these years were more generally positive for parents than we had expected, with the very important exceptions of a small but statistically significant increase in symptoms of depression and a decline in husbands' and wives' marital satisfaction or adjustment.

We noted that there was even more continuity and stability in measures of parents' adaptation over the 2-year period from preschool to first grade than there was over the 1-year period from preschool to kindergarten. In some ways, then, after a period of change in connection with their children's entrance to school, things appeared to settle down in their family lives and to allow parents more opportunity to look outward, especially to become somewhat more involved in their work lives.

And yet, reported feelings of sadness and depression increased for both fathers and mothers, marital conflict increased from both parents' point of view, and positive ratings of the marriage declined. In part, this decline in marital satisfaction may be attributable to the erosion in relationships experienced by some couples at the 7- to 10-year points in their marriage, rather than to issues triggered specifically by the child's transition to kindergarten. In part, as we suggested in chapter 3, it may also be attributable to the continuing discrepancies in self-esteem, and satisfaction with work inside and outside the family, in each case to the disadvantage of women. These disappointments or dissatisfaction, too, can contribute to the erosion of long-term intimate relationships.

In sum, despite the fact that many measures of parental functioning were quite stable over this 2-year period, parents experienced both negative and positive shifts in self, roles, and relationship quality that seems to define the period in which their first child makes the transition to elementary school as a major life transition.

A Transition for the Family

Family systems theories (Wagner & Reiss, 1995; Walsh, 2003) are based on the assumption that major changes in the life of one family member will have reverberating effects throughout the family system. We have shown that the changes in children's self-view, roles, and relationships as they entered elementary school were accompanied by changes in the self, roles, and relationships of their parents. This period, then, constitutes a life transition for the family.

We could not compare the findings of this study directly with investigations that focus on two other major milestones in families with young children: the transition to parenthood and parents' separation or divorce (Amato & Booth, 2001). In both of those cases, there is a marked change in family structure (the addition of a child, the removal of a parent) accompanied by significant and primarily negative alterations in family processes. By contrast, around the first child's transition to school, despite some concerns voiced by one or both parents or the child, the structure of the family appears to remain quite stable. This may buffer the family system from the potentially disequilibrating, but more temporary reverberations that occur as children enter the formal elementary school system.

FAMILY RISK AND PROTECTIVE FACTORS IN CHILDREN'S ADAPTATION TO SCHOOL

Risk and Protection

In constructing a study that would help us understand links between early risks and negative outcomes in children's lives, we followed leads from developmental psychopathology (Cummings, Davies, & Campbell, 2000) and prevention science (Coie et al., 1993). By using longitudinal designs, risk studies attempt to do three things. First, they identify individuals or families at Time 1 who are more likely to be in distress at Times 2, 3, and later. Next, they attempt to identify mechanisms that may be responsible for the links between risks and negative outcomes. Third, risk studies identify factors that either lead to negative outcomes where we expect minimal or no problems (vulnerabilities), or are related to positive outcomes despite the presence of risks (buffers, protective factors, resilience).

We presented some examples of buffering processes. Parents' encouragement of behavior against stereotype and children's adoption of that behavior had some protective functions, but the same factors that protected also increased the risks for other types of problem behaviors. Children's positive self-perceptions buffered children from the vicissitudes of their parents' conflict. Path models suggested that positive marital relationships helped to break the pattern in which negative parent–child relationships are transmitted across generations. In a sense, participation in a couples group helped to buffer both parents and children in the transition to school period against cumulated risks that begin to take their toll on some children's adaptation.

"Nonclinical" or "Low-Risk" Samples

The concepts of risk, buffering, vulnerability, and resilience—initially applied to public health studies of health and illness, and mental health studies of psychopathology—are now used frequently in developmental psychology to describe "nonclinical" individuals and families (P. A. Cowan, Cowan, & Schulz, 1996). The sample of families that participated in this study can be described as nonclinical by virtue of the fact that they were not recruited from clinical settings, and they were not screened in or out of the study on the basis of preexisting psychopathology, marital distress, or superior functioning. Nevertheless, as we reported in chapter 3, by the end of kindergarten, 1 in 10 of the children had been identified by parents or teachers as having significant academic, behavior, or emotional problems. The normative data we gathered from kindergarten and first-grade teachers on the Child Adaptive Behavior Inventory revealed that the externalizing or internalizing scores of children in the top 8% to 15% of this sample are in the top 10% of a sample of more than 1,400 of their classmates in more than 80 elementary schools.

The nonclinical picture is similar for the parents in the study. To say that life for them was generally stable, predictable, even improving in some cases, is not to say that all were coping satisfactorily. Between 25% and 50% of the parents were coping with symptoms of depression and marital distress, which we know leaves their children at further risk for academic and social difficulties as they proceed with their school careers. The trajectory hypothesis is relevant for parents as well as for their children, because individual, marital, and parenting difficulties and distress tend to persist over time. This information provides a strong rationale for providing universal interventions that are targeted to families in general, not just to families at high risk or already in serious distress.

General Support for the Five-Domain Model of Family Functioning and Children's Adaptation

Throughout the volume and particularly in chapter 12, we show that the findings of our longitudinal study support the utility of a five-domain model of family functioning, in which variables in each of the domains contribute unique variance to predicting children's externalizing problems, internalizing problems, and academic achievement in the first 2 years of elementary school. A combination of latent variables representing preschool levels of adaptation in individual, marital, parent–child, three-generational, and outside-the-family domains accounted for 26% to 65% of the variance in the children's kindergarten and first-grade outcomes. We found even higher proportions of explained variance when analyses were done separately for boys and girls, although some of the increase was probably due to the artifact of reduced sample sizes.

What family systems theories tell us is that each domain of the family provides a context in which the other domains operate. Most studies of child development begin with parenting as a context. It was instructive to find that, in this study, the quality of the parent–child relationships accounted for, at most, 10% to 15% of the variance in the children's adaptation (see chapters 4 and 5). The studies here emphasize the idea that the quality of the parents' relationship with each other—as a couple and as coparents—provides a context for understanding the kinds of relationships they develop with their children. Adding information about the relationship between the parents allowed us to predict another 10% to 15% of the variance in children's adaptation to school (see Ablow, chapter 7). Yet another context is provided by parents' experiences in their families of origin. When we added data from systematically coded narrative memories of parents' early relationships, we could predict another 15% to 20% of the variance in their children's academic achievement and externalizing or internalizing behaviors in kindergarten and first grade (see chapter 8).

With reference to our focus on the importance of the parents' relationship as a couple in their children's school adaptation, the five-domain models provided some essential information. There are actually two conceptually distinct aspects of marital quality in family life: how the partners relate to each other when they are alone, and how they collaborate or fail to do so when they are interacting in their child's presence, which we spoke of as coparenting (see McHale & Cowan, 1996). The models in chapter 12 show that in some equations, the quality of dyadic interaction we observed between the parents was a unique predictor of the children's adaptation, whereas in other equations, the qualities we noticed when the couple was coparenting acted as a unique predictor of school adjustment. In still other equations, information about the couple from both these contexts provided significant predictive power in explaining variations in the children's adaptation to the first 2 years of elementary school. It will be important in future research to investigate the separate and combined contribution of men's and women's intimate relationships as couples, and their relationships as coparents, to the environment of the developing child.

THE INTERTWINING OF METHOD
AND SUBSTANCE IN THE FINDINGS

Jean Piaget (1967), an epistemologist with a constructivist view of the scientific method, noted that how we investigate scientific questions inevitably shapes what we find. A number of design and measurement features of this study contributed directly to our substantive account of the links between family functioning and children's adaptation to school. The study described here was (a) longitudinal, and used (b) multiple data-gathering methods from (c) multiple sources of data from (d) different levels of the family structure (individual, dyadic, triadic), examined with (e) different data analytic techniques. The study (f) took account of different combinations of gender of parent and child, in an investigation of (g) how various aspects of family life combine to explain or predict children's academic and social outcomes as they navigate the first 2 years of their elementary school careers.

Longitudinal

We noted in the introduction that almost all studies of the family-school connection gather concurrent information about parents and children or begin the study after the children start kindergarten. The use of a longitudinal research design with a preschool assessment leaves conclusions about family–child correlations less vulnerable to the criticism that they reflect the child's effects on parents rather than the effects of the parents or the family on the child. But, as Cowan and Cowan (2002b) have written elsewhere, the longitudinal approach does not completely solve the chicken-and-egg problem of "what comes first." Although it is clear that some measurements of parents in the preschool period precede some measures of child outcomes in kindergarten or first grade, it is always possible that the parents' early reactions were to preexisting characteristics of the child that we did not capture in this study. Only with an examination of intervention effects in random assignment designs can we make more definitive statements about parental influence on children's adaptation to school.

Multiple Data-Gathering Methods

In many studies, data describing various aspects of family functioning are gathered using a single method in a single context (questionnaires, interviews, or observations). These studies can be criticized on the grounds that some of the high correlations across domains result from shared method variance, resulting in what Bank, Dishion, Skinner, and Patterson (1990) colorfully named "glop." Most of the analyses reported in this volume avoided the glop problem. The fact that correlations were high across time or across domains when the methods of data-gathering and the sources of information were different adds strong support to the conclusion that there is real rather than method-artifactual continuity across the various aspects of family life we assessed.

Multiple Sources of Information

In this study, data were obtained from children, mothers, fathers, teachers, and many staff observers. Although the correlations across sources were far from perfect, the converging patterns suggest that different observers were triangulating on the same or similar phenomena. Nevertheless, a focus on agreement or overlap between sources misses an important substantive point. The chapters in this volume indicate that the observers' views and the participants' self-reports complement each other and add power to predictions of concurrent and future adaptation. "Insider" views of family life tell us about the meaning that children or adults attach to events and how they appraise stressors. Insider reports are particularly helpful in dealing with low-frequency events that we are unlikely to observe in a laboratory or home visit, or for describing private experiences like feelings of depression, which may not be observable to others. "Outsider" views of family life have advantages, too. They can inform us about events outside the awareness of the participants, record the intensity of exchanges that may be distorted (minimized or maximized) by them, and lead to the discovery of patterns that can be determined only by statistical analysis.

The inclusion of children's perceptions through the Berkeley Puppet Interview assessment represents more than the addition of another methodological perspective. Chapters 6, 7, and 12 showed that children's views of themselves and their parents play a significant role in linking what goes on for them interpersonally within the family with what happens to them interpersonally outside the family. We view children's perceptions as a critical link in our understanding of how family processes shape children's adaptation.

Different Levels of Family Structure

This study included data focused on individuals, dyads (marital and parent–child), and the family as a whole. Consistent with findings from Hayden et al. (1998), and many other investigators, the chapters in this volume suggest that all three levels of analysis contribute unique information to the explanation of variation in children's academic competence, social competence, and problem behaviors in the first years of elementary school (see chapter 10).

Different Methods of Analysis

Going beyond traditional statistical methods that include correlations, regressions, and GLM-analyses of variance, the chapters in this volume relied heavily on the use of Latent Variable structural equation modeling with Partial Least Squares (LVPLS). In contrast to multiple regression techniques, which examine direct effects and the additive or multiplicative contributions of the independent variables to variation in selected outcomes, path models help us to understand the indirect effects in the links among the independent variables. These models not only contribute to the formation of more differentiated theories about linking mechanisms but they help to expand potential targets for preventive and therapeutic intervention. For example, the path models in chapters 7, 8, 11, and 12 suggest (although they do not prove) that the enhancement of parenting quality might be addressed through a class on parenting skills or an intervention to reduce marital conflict or an intervention to help parents break an intergenerational cycle of painful relationship patterns. Other studies using LVPLS or other forms of structural equation models are producing similar results in which positive and negative affect in different domains of family relationships are linked—with each other (Simons, Lorenz, Wu, & Conger, 1993) and with children's social competence (Isley, O'Neil, Clatfelter, & Parke, 1999). We conclude that LVPLS models represent a promising way of dealing with some of the complexities of multimeasure, multidomain family data, especially given their ability to estimate the strength of indirect linkages. In the end, replication will be the premier method of assessing the meaningfulness and generalizability of results from studies of family factors in children's adaptation to school.

The Ubiquity of Sex Differences

Sex of parent, sex of child, or the combination of the two, played a visible role in the patterns of results in most but not all analyses in this volume. We found few systematic mean differences between fathers' and mothers' questionnaire responses or behaviors with one another or with their children. Nevertheless, there were clear differences between the patterns of correlations associated with information about fathers or mothers and children's school outcomes. Data obtained from fathers were implicated in the results of every chapter examining children's externalizing behaviors at school. By contrast, in almost every case, data obtained from mothers were implicated in explanations of children's internalizing behaviors at school.

Marital distress heightened gender differences in parenting. We obtained some support for an earlier finding that unhappily married fathers of daughters tend to treat their children more negatively than do dissatisfied fathers of sons, a trend that received support in Coiro and Emery's (1998) review.

Finally, we found different trends for boys' and girls' school adaptation, and, in several chapters (5, 7, and 8), in which we were able to analyze the data by sex of child or parent, we could not generalize from parents' behavior to children's outcomes without paying attention to whether we were talking about fathers, mothers, sons, or daughters (P. A. Cowan et al., 1993). The interactions of the effects of sex of parent and sex of child throughout the volume are particularly susceptible to criticisms associated with low sample size. For now, we can state that fathers appear to be more closely implicated in externalizing behaviors of both boys and girls, and that mothers appear to be consistently implicated in their daughters' shy, withdrawn, depressed behavior in the early years. This certainly conforms to sex stereotypes that men are more likely to be externalizing and women to be externalizing, but much more research needs to be done to explain how these processes unfold across the generations.

Academic and Socioemotional Outcomes

As we noted in chapter 1, studies of family-school linkage have chosen to focus on either academic or socioemotional competence but not both. Because some of the chapters in this volume were based on individual dissertations, they did not all contain exactly the same outcome measures. Nevertheless, a number included both academic and social competence measures in their analyses. Although we could make the general statement that family functioning during the preschool period predicts academic and social competence or difficulties for children—the specific family-to-school links depended on the family domain and the particular outcome being considered.

The Representational and Practicing Family

In our view, the most important way in which method and substance converge in this study is in the demonstration that parents' and children's perceptions of self, relationships, and life as a family (assessed by the Adult Attachment Interview, the Berkeley Puppet Interview, and questionnaires), and our team's observations of family transactions (assessed in child, parent–child, and couple visits to our project), are implicated in explaining how children fare as the child makes the transition to elementary school. Beyond the statement that inner and outer sources of information are important lies the possibility, as Measelle has shown in chapter 6, and that path models in other chapters suggest, that there is a synergistic combination of these perspectives that shape the child's adaptation trajectory. The findings support, although they do not prove, the hypothesis that men's and women's working models of early experiences in their families of origin affect how partners react to each other when they are working on real-life disagreements and helping their children manage a complex task or solve a challenging problem. In turn, parents' transactions with their children have a direct role in how the children evaluate themselves, in ways that affect their subsequent interactions with teachers and peers at school. In sum, the inner and outer perspectives on the family used in this study suggest that there is a dynamic interplay between representations and transactions that helps to explain the consistent connections we find between the quality of family functioning and children's adaptation to school.

THE THEORY-TESTING FUNCTION
OF AN INTERVENTION STUDY

We have noted the importance of the intervention design in addressing some theoretical issues about the nature of the links between family processes and school outcomes (chapter 11). Participation in groups with an emphasis on marital or parenting issues had differential positive effects on the parents, and explained 31% of the reductions in externalizing behaviors between kindergarten and first grade, 21% in children's perceptions of their adjustment to kindergarten, and 12% of the variance in both kindergarten academic achievement scores and reductions in internalizing behaviors over the same period. Positive changes in parents that were attributable to the intervention were responsible for the positive results in children's adaptation to school. These results allow us to go beyond correlations to discuss causal influences of family relationships on children's adaptation to school.

Implications for Socialization Theories

Parenting Matters. The findings of this study bear directly on the criticisms of socialization theory made by Harris (1998) and others who explain correlations between parenting behavior and children's outcomes by genetic linkage mechanisms (e.g., Rowe et al., 1994). Harris is correct in her criticism of socialization research for exaggerating claims of parental influence based on correlational designs, but mistaken in her sweeping dismissal of the importance of parents' behavior for their children's development and adaptation. From results reported here, we cannot conclude that the direction of effects always moves from parents to children, but we have shown through a random assignment, experimental design that intervention-induced changes in parents were followed by fewer problem behaviors and higher academic achievement in their children as they made the transition from family to school. This finding supports what might be termed a balanced view of socialization theory, in which at least some of the variation in the quality of marital and parenting relationships influences children's development.

Fathers Matter.   At the beginning of the 21st century, it seems strange that family researchers must urge readers to pay attention to the importance of fathers in their children's adaptation. Despite growing interest in research on fathers over the past two decades (Bronstein & Cowan, 1988; Parke, 1996), even recent studies of children's school adaptation deal with "family" factors in children's development by focusing primarily on mothers. As we have shown in each chapter of this volume, how fathers are faring as individuals, how they treat their wives and children, and whether they bring stress home from their jobs, all contribute to our understanding of children's school adaptation.

Couple Relationships Matter.   Converging evidence from the preceding chapters adds to the literature of the past two decades by Conger et al. (1994), Gottman and Katz (1989), and Hetherington (1999), among others, by showing that the quality of the parents' relationship as a couple plays a central role in how the family is functioning as a system. Parents' inability to resolve or contain marital conflict is a risk factor for negative outcomes for their young children, and marital conflict can play a causal role in children's adaptation and development. Satir (1972) described couples as the "architects" of family life. We are not arguing that the architect metaphor, with its emphasis on careful and conscious family-building, is the most apt description of the role couples play in the family. In our view, the quality of the relationship between the child's parents functions like a thermostat. When families are functioning effectively and the weather turns cold, the thermostat turns up the heat to take the chill off. When the environment gets too hot to be comfortable, the thermostat turns on cooler air to bring the atmosphere to a more comfortable level. That is, in a real rather than metaphorical sense, in well-functioning families, partners work together to protect themselves and their children from threatening events. When families are not functioning effectively, the regulator tends to break down so that stressors from inside and outside the family are amplified rather than reduced by maritally stressed parents.

Implications for Family Systems Theories

Our results raise some questions about a simple extrapolation from correlational risk models to expectations about the generality of intervention effects. Despite the fact that we found extensive links among individual, marital, parenting, and three-generational family domains, the direct effects of the maritally-focused and parenting-focused interventions were, by and large, quite specific to the parents' marital and parent–child relationships. At this point, the results suggest a cautionary note about some assumptions inherent in family systems theory. Despite the correlational connections among five major domains of the family, targeting a single risk factor or a single family domain may not buffer children from risks in other domains. In other words, change throughout the family system may be difficult to promote unless interventions are designed to target a number of the central aspects of family functioning.

Our decision to focus on either marital or parent–child relationships was dictated largely by a wish to clarify some theoretical issues about the connection between them. In considering a wider application of this preventive approach, it is not necessary, and may even be counterproductive, to focus an intervention on marital "or" parent–child relationships. We believe that both can be included profitably in preventive and therapeutic services for families. It was also the case that because we did not assess change in parents' working models of attachment that played a prominent role in predicting family functioning and children's adaptation, our account in chapter 11 inadvertently minimizes the importance of couples dealing with past and present relationships with their parents. Our experience in two longitudinal intervention studies suggests that mental health professionals can strengthen the power of programs for couples and parents by including as part of the "curriculum" a focus on three-generational issues, how mothers and fathers can begin to come to terms with the past, and build better relationships with their parents (the children's grandparents) to support their own development and the development of their children.

THE FAMILY CONTEXT OF PARENTING:
A SYSTEMS APPROACH

Given the fact that there are so many statistical links among parenting style, other domains of family life, and children's adaptation to school, two important conceptual questions remain. First, what are the implications of this research for understanding the role of parenting in children's development? And, second, what are the mechanisms or processes that determine how this linkage actually works in families' lives?

Despite the voluminous body of research on parenting (see Bornstein, 2002, a five-volume *Handbook of Parenting*) and the parenting advice books that crowd the shelves of libraries and bookstores, there is no widely-accepted definition of what parenting is and is not. Discussions of the topic usually focus on what a caregiver (most often a mother) thinks or does when interacting with his or her child.

The study described in this volume suggests that it would be profitable to take a broader perspective as Bornstein (2002) does in his handbook. First, from the data presented in chapter 12, it is clear that parents may have an impact on children not only by what they do, but also by the kind of people they are. Second, the relationship between the parents plays an important role in shaping the nurturance and the material, social, and didactic caregiving that the child receives. The effects on the child come in part from the coparenting relationship, in the content and style of the parents' exchanges as they attempt to work together to care for the child. More direct effects on the child come from the fact that parents who do not feel nurtured in their relationship as partners have a harder time providing the warmth, structure, and encouragement of autonomy that are the hallmarks of authoritative parenting. We are arguing, then, that the relationship between the child's parents, even when some of it is hidden from the child, is not something entirely apart from parenting because it has important consequences for the child as a recipient of caregiving and as a future caregiver.

Similarly, understanding the role that fathers and mothers play in the lives of their children can be enriched by a consideration of their roles as transmitters or breakers of family generational patterns (Clulow, 2001). Cowan, Bradburn, and Cowan's analysis of men's and women's narratives about relationships in their families of origin (chapter 8) makes it clear that the business of being a parent to one's child depends in part on one's thoughts, feelings, and perspective on having been a child in one's family of origin.

Finally, sometimes to their young children's astonishment, mothers and fathers are embedded in important networks of relationships that do not include the child—at work and in relationships and aspects of community life outside the nuclear family. The stress and support parents experience in relationships in these settings help to shape the kind of parents they are when they are with their children, and the thoughts and activities related to the child that they engage in when they are not at home (e.g., phoning home, buying toys, arranging play groups, doctors' visits, and so on).

Thus, the five-domain family systems model that we proposed in chapter 1 conceptualizes parenting as occurring within the context of the system of relationships inside and immediately outside the family. Have we broadened the definition so that "everything is parenting" and "nothing is not parenting?" In a sense, perhaps we have. We are suggesting that, once people become parents, most aspects of their lives have a potential bearing on the quality of the relationship they develop with their children, whether or not they live with them. This does not mean that everything that happens to a father or mother affects their children's development. It does mean that understanding the parent–child relationship requires that we look beyond the parents' behavior with the child, or their beliefs about childrearing, to consider how the context of the parents' lives may be affecting the child's development and adaptation.

This systems view of parenting has implications for both research and the planning of interventions to foster optimal caregiving environments for children. Clearly, the five-domain model we suggest has guided the research reported in this volume. And, the contextual model of parenting guided the choice of an intervention for parents—as couples, in a group with other couples and leaders who are clinically trained—as a way of enhancing the family environmental context. This, we hoped, would give children a better chance to begin their academic and social trajectories at more optimal points in their kindergarten-to-high-school years. The results here suggest that parenting classes and other parent-education offerings could benefit by extending the focus from parenting behavior to how parents' lives and relationships affect the environment in which their children begin their academic and social careers.

ISSUES OF GENERALIZATION FROM THE FINDINGS

A number of restrictions in our sample, design, methods, and measures, make it necessary to qualify or be cautious about the conclusions we draw from the data. Here we summarize the limitations of our study, although we do not again address the issues of sample size that we discussed throughout the volume.

Representativeness of the Sample

As we noted in chapter 2, the participants in this study do not constitute a representative sample of the United States population or the population of the 27 communities in Northern California in which they live. The selection was made by recruiting two-parent families, most of whom had a first child in a day-care center or preschool. Although approximately one fifth of the sample came from families with below-median incomes in 1990 to 1993, a majority of the families is relatively well off in terms of education and income. Using data from the Child Adaptive Behavior Inventory to compare teachers' descriptions of the target children in the sample with their classmates in more than 80 schools, we learned that the study children were seen as remarkably similar to their peers, with a similar range of adaptive and troubling behaviors.

Because of our emphasis on preventive intervention, the study was limited to families with a first child making the transition to elementary school. Further research is needed to determine whether some of the tension and disequilibration in both children and parents during the transition to school years shifts systematically as younger siblings begin to knock on the schoolhouse door.

The Intervention As a Confound

It could be argued that, because the intervention effects of the study were statistically significant, the intervention design could have interfered with our conclusions (chapter 3) about stability and continuity. We used intervention vectors as covariates to eliminate the main effects of participation in an intervention on the variables under consideration, but this does not eliminate variation due to potentially complex interactions among intervention, time, and other variables. We are again dealing with trade-off dilemmas here. It is possible to construct a study without an intervention so that the growth trajectories would be clearer, but we would then lose the power to test causal models and direction of effects of marital change on parenting, of parenting change on marriage, and of parents' change on children's development. Alternatively, we could focus on the intervention and omit analysis of continuities and discontinuities over time. We chose to control for intervention effects as best we could, and treat the trajectory findings as hypotheses to be tested in further studies.

Potential Sources of Influence on the Child Not Measured in This Study

Despite the large number of measures from multiple perspectives, domains, and sources of information, there were important family risk and protective factors that were not assessed in the larger study.

Variations in Socioeconomic Status (SES) and Culture and Ethnicity. Although the range in income in this sample was large, the participants did not span the full range of incomes in the nation, especially at lower SES levels. We are quite aware that poverty is an important risk factor with respect to children's achievement (Coleman et al., 1966; Conger et al., 1994), but we suspect that samples with a larger range of SES will produce correlations similar to those in this study, because poverty often affects children indirectly by disrupting relationships—between fathers and mothers and between parents and children (see Conger, Elder, et al., 1994; McLoyd, 1990). We noted in chapter 2 that 15% of the participants in this study were African American, Asian American, or Latin American. Differences in intergenerational patterns, parenting practices, and the importance of focusing on the couple relationship, certainly differ from one culture to another (Parke & Buriel, 1998), but given the fact that each ethnic group had relatively few participants, we were in no position to make generalizations about the impact of cultural and ethnic differences in normative family practices. This topic will have to be the topic of a longitudinal intervention study with a very different sample.

Genetic History or Temperament Markers. As Harris (1998), Plomin (1994), and others have argued, the design of this study does not allow us to rule out the operation of genetic effects in explaining correlations between parents' and children's characteristics. How severe a limitation this is depends on a study's goals. If investigators simply want to identify risk factors in the preschool period that predict later child outcomes to design targeted interventions, then the notion that the linking mechanisms are genetic is not relevant to the findings. Let us assume for the moment that some of the outcomes we assessed in the children were highly heritable. Heritable traits are subject to positive intervention effects (Collins, Maccoby, Steinberg, Hetherington, & Bornstein, 2000). Even when children's difficult temperament is a risk factor for later achievement (Martin, Olejnik, & Gaddis, 1994), interventions with parents could have positive effects on their children's adaptation to school.

The Interconnection Among Outcomes. In this study, we treated academic competence and internalizing and externalizing behaviors as separate outcomes, but they are interconnected in reciprocal fashion (Cole, Martin, Powers, & Truglio, 1996; Hinshaw, 1992). It would be possible to test models in which family processes predict whether a child having academic difficulties would also have behavioral difficulties, or vice versa.

Childcare, Day Care, Preschool. In investigating the sharing of household and family labor, our Who Does What? questionnaire examined the relative contribution of mothers and fathers to each family task. In the parenting tasks we observed, we focused on mothers' and fathers' behavior. We know that other caregivers (day-care staff, grandparents) have short-term or long-term impact on children and their families; those contributions were not examined in this study.

Sibling Relationships: A Sixth Family Domain. There is an important sixth domain of family life that did not receive enough attention in this series of studies—the oldest child's relationship with his or her siblings. Preliminary analyses of this data set (Bondar, 1995) are consistent with results of studies of high-risk families (Bank, Patterson, & Reid, 1996) in suggesting that sibling relationships tend to mirror the style of interaction between the parents. And, like parents' relationships, sibling relationships can either buffer or exacerbate the impact of chronic family conflict on children's ability to establish positive relationships with peers.

The Impact of the School Environment. This study was conducted with a foreground focus on families, and a background focus on schools. As Weinstein (2002) eloquently argued, variations in classroom and school environments can have marked and lasting effects on children's development. This study was designed to examine the contributions of children's family environments in depth. Issues that must be investigated in future studies include the possibility that families and schools each contribute uniquely and additively to variations in children's adaptation, that they may have interactive effects (Epstein, 1996), and that the "fit" or lack of fit between the family and school environments may have separate effects on the children.

Conclusions Concerning Limitations

Despite the fact that this study does not address some questions and is not able to answer others with the data we gathered, we are fairly confident in coming to some general conclusions: (a) the state of affairs in multiple family domains predicts children's adaptation to school, (b) families and children who are at risk for difficulties in elementary school can be identified during the preschool years, and (c) a group intervention for parents as couples, led by mental health professionals, has the potential to enhance the parents' relationships as partners and as parents, with subsequent benefits for their children's adaptation to school. Specific statements about patterns of prediction and longevity of intervention effects await analyses of later data on the families in this study, and studies of new samples of families that use both similar and different methods of measurement and intervention.

SOCIAL POLICY IMPLICATIONS: PREVENTIVE INTERVENTIONS FOR FAMILIES

Issues of the legitimacy of making social policy decisions based on data from empirical studies are complex and not easily resolvable. It is impossible to guarantee that a statistically significant outcome found in any one study or set of studies will have the same magnitude of effects when applied universally to a geographically-defined population (neighborhood, town, state, country). Our tendency toward caution is based on a number of qualifications and limitations of the results we have reported here. Despite this, we feel strongly that it is the responsibility of social scientists to talk about how their findings could contribute to the ongoing public dialogue on social issues and decisions about the public good. In this vein, we offer this concluding section, not as a set of prescriptions, but as speculation about what our findings could mean for parents, politicians, and others concerned with giving children the best possible start in their formal school careers.

In the study described in this volume, we were able to account for as much as half the variation in children's adaptation to school using a battery of questionnaires and observations to assess family functioning. Regardless of how the linkage between family factors and children's adaptation is explained, four implications of the five-domain model for planning preventive services for families are clear.

It Is Possible to Identify Children at Risk for Academic and Social Problems

From the studies reported here and from many others in the literature, we know that it is possible to develop a multidomain assessment protocol for individuals and families before children enter school to identify families whose children are at risk for academic and social difficulties. Although the protocol would not be perfect, judging by the amount of variance in outcome accounted for by the predictors, we can do a reasonably good job of identifying families whose children are at risk for academic and social problems in the early elementary school grades.

Some may question whether we should do this even if we have the technology. They worry that premature labeling of individuals and families could have long-term negative effects. On the other hand, 10% or more of the children entering elementary school already have serious learning and mental health difficulties, and schools do not have the resources to identify these children in a timely fashion so that services can be provided when they are needed. We believe that in the long run, it could be beneficial to intervene earlier, before the problems in children and families are intractable and resistant to treatment.

There Are Important Opportunities for Preventive Intervention With Families Around the Transition to Elementary School

We have shown that it is possible to intervene with parents as couples in a way that produces positive results for their children's ability to meet the challenges of early elementary school. That is, the path models we have presented are not simply descriptions of correlations, but representations of dynamic functional connections among the quality of marital interaction and parent–child relationships and children's academic and social competence in the early elementary school grades.

At present there are very few, if any, mental health or parenting services available to families with a first child entering school, unless the child and family have already been identified as in need of treatment; even then, the chances of receiving adequate help are slim. A few home-visiting programs for high-risk mothers, beginning at birth and focused primarily on parenting, have shown promising effects, and some early school-based interventions have a family component (Slavin, Karweit, & Wasik, 1994). Even so, with the exception of the Abecedarian project (Ramey & Ramey, 2000), these programs have rarely followed children from the early postpartum years into school. Parenting classes are more likely to be available than mental health services, a substantial number of them low cost or free, but almost all are attended by mothers alone, and none that we know of provides information and helps with the marital or three-generational family issues that we have shown are related to parents' and children's adaptation. We suggest that it may be in the interest of society to offer universal preventive services for nonclinical families with a child about to enter elementary school. As we have seen, within such a sample is a substantial proportion of men, women, and couples already experiencing considerable individual or marital distress. The data we have presented make it clear that the children of these parents are likely to be identified as having the kinds of academic, social, or emotional difficulties that tend to persist over the elementary school years.

It Is Time to Consider Extensions of the Findings to Preventive Interventions With Low-Income Populations

As we write this concluding chapter, Congress is debating revisions of welfare reform that would provide substantial monetary support for systematically evaluated intervention programs to increase the involvement of low-income unmarried fathers in the lives of their children, and to encourage "healthy marriages" (Horn, 2002). Although the discussion of the latter programs emphasize marriage, some of the federal money would actually be allocated to programs designed to strengthen couple relationships in low-income families, regardless of the couple's marital status. Proponents of these programs point to the fact that programs for fathers and especially for couples have been shown to work (Fagan, Patterson, & Rector, 2002). Our reading of the literature is that very few interventions for couples have been evaluated systematically, and of the few that have, almost all have been for middle-class families (P. A. Cowan & Cowan, 2002a; Dion, 2003). An important set of findings from work by Heinicke and his colleagues (Heinicke, 2002; Heinicke et al., 1999) showed that extensions of middle-class preventive interventions to facilitate the transition to parenthood, with important modifications and increased intensity, could be successful with low-income women and their partners. Especially given that the new programs for low-income couples will be systematically evaluated, it seems worthwhile to test the implications of this approach to a preschool intervention all along the socioeconomic spectrum. We do not know whether our intervention model can be applied to a low-income sample, or what modifications would be necessary for it to have similar results. We are currently working on a project in five counties of California, sponsored by the State Office of Child Abuse Prevention, which will begin to provide an answer to these important questions.

Our Results Support Increased Efforts Toward Providing Family-Based Intervention

This study was conducted in a context in which school reform rather than family intervention is being discussed on a national level as a remedy for both declining academic skills and a perceived increase in serious behavior and learning problems (United States Congress, House Committee on Education and the Workforce, 1999). Although many school environments undoubtedly need restructuring, variation in schools may contribute less to child and youth outcomes than variation in economic circumstances, neighborhoods, and families (Traub, 2000). The "Coleman Report" argued almost 40 years ago that families and family circumstances account for more of the variation in achievement than do schools, because some children come to school with disadvantages that are maintained or increase over time (Coleman et al., 1966). We are not suggesting an abandonment of school reform, but rather that a "second front" be established that addresses the earlier concerns of Coleman and his colleagues (Coleman et al., 1966). If a large part of the variance in children's adaptation to school is predictable from family functioning in the preschool period, if children tend to remain in the same rank order on their trajectories throughout their school years, and if it is possible to intervene with parents to improve their children's academic and social adaptation as they enter the school system, it makes sense to us to encourage family-based interventions to improve children's chances of successful adaptation to school.

References

Abidin, R. R. (1980). *Parent education and intervention handbook.* Springfield, IL: Thomas.

Abidin, R. R. (1997). *Parenting Stress Index: A measure of the parent–child system.* Charlottesville, VA: Psychological Assessment Resources.

Ablow, J. C. (1997a, April). *Critical role young children's perceptions of their parents' conflict play in the development of psychopathology.* Paper presented at the biennial meeting of the Society for Research in Child Development, Washington, DC.

Ablow, J. C. (1997b). *Marital conflict: Young children's perceptions and adjustment.* Unpublished doctoral dissertation, University of California, Berkeley.

Ablow, J. C., & Measelle, J. (1993). *The Berkeley Puppet Interview: Administration and scoring system manuals.* Unpublished manuscript, University of California, Berkeley.

Ablow, J. C., Measelle, J. R., Kraemer, H. C., Harrington, R., Luby, J., Smider, N., et al. (1999). The MacArthur Three-City Outcome Study: Evaluating multi-informant measures of young children's symptomatology. *Journal of the American Academy of Child & Adolescent Psychiatry, 38,* 1580–1590.

Ablow, J. C., & Suh, Y. J. (1997, April). *Marital conflict across family contexts: Does the presence of children make a difference?* Paper presented at the Society for Research in Child Development, Washington, DC.

Achenbach, T. M., & Edelbrock, C. S. (1983). *Manual for the Child Behavior Checklist.* Burlington, VT: Queen City.

Aiken, L. S., & West, S. G. (1991). *Multiple regression: Testing and interpreting interactions.* Newbury Park, CA: Sage.

Ainsworth, M. S., Blehar, M. C., Waters, E., & Wall, S. (1978). *Patterns of attachment: A psychological study of the strange situation.* Hillsdale, NJ: Lawrence Erlbaum Associates, Inc.

Ainsworth, M. S., & Wittig, B. A. (1969). Attachment and exploratory behavior of one-year-olds in a strange situation. In B. M. Foss (Ed.), *Determinants of infant behavior* (Vol. IV, pp. 113–136). London: Methuen.

Alexander, K. L., & Entwisle, D. R. (1988). Achievement in the first 2 years of school: Patterns and processes. *Monographs of the Society for Research in Child Development, 53*(2, Serial No. 218).

Alexander, K. L., Entwisle, D. R., & Dauber, S. L. (1993). First-grade classroom behavior: Its short- and long-term consequences for school performance. *Child Development, 64,* 801–814.

Al-Issa, I. (Ed.). (1982). Gender and child psychopathology. In I. Al-Issa (Ed.), *Gender and psychopathology* (pp. 53–81). New York: Academic Press.

Allen, J. P., Hauser, S. T., Bell, K. L., & O'Connor, T. G. (1994). Longitudinal assessment of autonomy and relatedness in adolescent-family interactions as predictors of adolescent ego development and self-esteem. *Child Development, 65,* 179–194.

Allen, J. P., Hauser, S. T., Eickholt, C., Bell, K. L., & O'Connor, T. G. (1994). Autonomy and relatedness in family interactions as predictors of expressions of negative adolescent affect. *Journal of Research on Adolescence, 4,* 535–552.

Amato, P. R. (1986). Emotional arousal and helping behavior in a real-life emergency. *Journal of Applied Social Psychology, 16,* 633–641.

Amato, P. R. (1996). Explaining the intergenerational transmission of divorce. *Journal of Marriage & the Family, 58,* 628–640.

Amato, P. R. (2001). Children of divorce in the 1990s: An update of the Amato and Keith (1991) meta-analysis. *Journal of Family Psychology, 15,* 355–370.

Amato, P. R., & Booth, A. (2001). The legacy of parents' marital discord: Consequences for children's marital quality. *Journal of Personality & Social Psychology, 81,* 627–638.

Amato, P. R., & Keith, B. (1991). Parental divorce and the well-being of children: A meta-analysis. *Psychological Bulletin, 110,* 26–46.

Anderson, C. A., Hinshaw, S. P., & Simmel, C. (1994). Mother–child interactions in ADHD and comparison boys: Relationships with overt and covert externalizing behavior. *Journal of Abnormal Child Psychology, 22,* 247–265.

Angold, A., Erkanli, A., Silberg, J., Eaves, L., & Costello, E. J. (2002). Depression scale scores in 8–17-year-olds: Effects of age and gender. *Journal of Child Psychology & Psychiatry & Allied Disciplines, 43,* 1052–1063.

Asher, S. R., & Coie, J. D. (Eds.). (1990). *Peer rejection in childhood.* Cambridge, England: Cambridge University Press.

Astone, N. M., & McLanahan, S. S. (1991). Family structure, parental practices and high school completion. *American Sociological Review, 56,* 309–320.

Babinski, L. M., Hartsough, C. S., & Lambert, N. M. (1999). Childhood conduct problems, hyperactivity-impulsivity, and inattention as predictors of adult criminal activity. *Journal of Child Psychology & Psychiatry & Allied Disciplines, 40,* 347–355.

Bagwell, C. L., Newcomb, A. F., & Bukowski, W. M. (1998). Preadolescent friendship and peer rejection as predictors of adult adjustment. *Child Development, 69,* 140–153.

Ballard, M., & Cummings, E. M. (1990). Response to adults' angry behavior in children of alcoholic and nonalcoholic parents. *Journal of Genetic Psychology, 151,* 195–210.

Bandura, A. (1977). *Social learning theory.* Englewood Cliffs, NJ: Prentice Hall.

Bank, L., Dishion, T. J., Skinner, M., & Patterson, G. R. (1990). Method variance in structural equation modeling: Living with "glop". In G. R. Patterson (Ed.), *Depression and aggression in family interaction* (pp. 247–279). Hillsdale, NJ: Lawrence Erlbaum Associates, Inc.

Bank, L., Patterson, G. R., & Reid, J. B. (1996). Negative sibling interaction patterns as predictors of later adjustment problems in adolescent and young adult males. In G. H. Brody (Ed.), *Sibling relationships: Their causes and consequences* (pp. 197–229). Stamford, CT: Ablex Publishing Corp.

Barber, B. K., & Olsen, J. A. (1997). Socialization in context: Connection, regulation, and autonomy in the family, school, and neighborhood, and with peers. *Journal of Adolescent Research, 12,* 287–315.

Baron, R. M., & Kenny, D. A. (1986). The moderator-mediator variable distinction in social psychological research: Conceptual, strategic, and statistical considerations. *Journal of Personality & Social Psychology, 51,* 1173–1182.

Barnett, R. C., & Baruch, G. K. (1988). Correlates of fathers' participation in family work. In P. Bronstein & C. P. Cowan (Eds.), *Fatherhood today: Men's changing role in the family* (pp. 66–78). Oxford, England: John Wiley & Sons.

Barth, J. M., & Parke, R. D. (1996). The impact of the family on children's early school social adjustment. In A. J. Sameroff & M. M. Haith (Eds.), *The five to seven year shift: The age of reason and responsibility* (pp. 329–361). Chicago: The University of Chicago Press.

Bartholomew, K., & Horowitz, L. M. (1991). Attachment styles among young adults: A test of a four-category model. *Journal of Personality & Social Psychology, 61,* 226–244.

Bartholomew, K., & Shaver, P. R. (1998). *Methods of assessing adult attachment: Do they converge?* New York: Guilford.

Bates, J. E. (1986). The measurement of temperament. In R. Plomin & J. Dunn (Eds.), *The study of temperament: Changes, continuities and challenges* (pp. 181–192). Hillsdale, NJ: Lawrence Erlbaum Associates, Inc.

Bates, J. E. (2001). Adjustment style in childhood as a product of parenting and temperament. In T. D. Wachs & G. A. Kohnstamm (Eds.), *Temperament in context* (pp. 173–200). Mahwah, NJ: Lawrence Erlbaum Associates, Inc.

Baumrind, D. (1967). Child care practices anteceding three patterns of preschool behavior. *Genetic Psychology Monographs, 75,* 43–88.

Baumrind, D. (1971). Current patterns of parental authority. *Developmental Psychology Monographs, 4,* 1–103.

Baumrind, D. (1973). The development of instrumental competence through socialization. In A. D. Pick (Ed.), *Minnesota symposia on child psychology* (Vol. 7, pp. 3–46). Minneapolis: University of Minnesota Press.

Baumrind, D. (1989). Rearing competent children. In W. Damon (Ed.), *Child development today and tomorrow* (pp. 349–378). San Francisco: Jossey-Bass.

Baumrind, D. (1991). Effective parenting during the early adolescent transition. In P. A. Cowan & E. M. Hetherington (Eds.), *Advances in family research* (Vol. 2, pp. 111–163). Hillsdale, NJ: Lawrence Erlbaum Associates, Inc.

Beck, A. T. (1963). Thinking and depression: I. Idiosyncratic content and cognitive distortions. *Archives of General Psychiatry, 9,* 324–333.

Bell, R. Q. (1968). A reinterpretation of the direction of effects in studies of socialization. *Psychological Review, 75,* 81–95.

Belsky, J. (1984). The determinants of parenting: A process model. *Child Development, 55,* 83–96.

Belsky, J. (1999). Interactional and contextual determinants of attachment security. In J. Cassidy & P. R. Shaver (Eds.), *Handbook of attachment: Theory, research, and clinical applications* (pp. 249–264). New York: Guilford.

Belsky, J., & Barends, N. (2002). *Personality and parenting.* Mahwah, NJ: Lawrence Erlbaum Associates, Inc.

Belsky, J., Campbell, S. B., Cohn, J. F., & Moore, G. (1996). Instability of infant–parent attachment security. *Developmental Psychology, 32,* 921–924.

Belsky, J., & MacKinnon, C. (1994). Transition to school: Developmental trajectories and school experiences. *Early Education & Development, 5,* 106–119.

Belsky, J., & Pensky, E. (1988). Marital change across the transition to parenthood. *Marriage & Family Review, 12,* 133–156.

Bem, S. L. (1993). *The lenses of gender: Transforming the debate on sexual inequality.* New Haven, CT: Yale University Press.

Bennett, K. J., Lipman, E. L., Brown, S., Racine, Y., Boyle, M. H., & Offord, D. R. (1999). Predicting conduct problems: Can high-risk children be identified in kindergarten and grade 1? *Journal of Consulting & Clinical Psychology, 67,* 470–480.

Berlin, L. J., & Cassidy, J. (1999). *Relations among relationships: Contributions from attachment theory and research.* New York: Guilford.

Berman, R. A., Slobin, D. I., Aksu-Koc, A. A., Bamberg, M., Dasinger, L., Marchman, V., et al. (1994). *Relating events in narrative: A crosslinguistic developmental study.* Hillsdale, NJ: Lawrence Erlbaum Associates, Inc.

Bernard, J. S. (1974). *The future of motherhood.* New York: Dial Press.

Block, J. (1971). *Lives through time.* Berkeley, CA: Bancroft Books.

Block, J. (2002). *Personality as an affect-processing system: Toward an integrative theory.* Mahwah, NJ: Lawrence Erlbaum Associates, Inc.

Block, J. H. (1976). Issues, problems, and pitfalls in assessing sex differences: A critical review of "The Psychology of Sex Differences." *Merrill-Palmer Quarterly, 22,* 283–308.

Block, J. H. (1983). Differential premises arising from differential socialization of the sexes: Some conjectures. *Child Development, 54,* 1335–1354.

Block, J. H. (1984). *Sex role identity and ego development.* San Francisco: Jossey–Bass.

Block, J. H., & Block, J. (1980). The role of ego-control and ego-resiliency in the organization of behavior. In W. A. Collins (Ed.), *Minnesota Symposia on Child Psychology* (Vol. 13, pp. 39–101). Hillsdale, NJ: Lawrence Erlbaum Associates, Inc.

Block, J. H., Block, J., & Morrison, A. (1981). Parental agreement-disagreement on child-rearing orientations and gender-related personality correlates in children. *Child Development, 52,* 965–974.

Bondar, V. (1995). *Marital discord, differential treatment of siblings, and sibling relationship quality.* Unpublished honor's thesis, University of California, Berkeley.

Booth, A., & Dunn, J. (1996). *Family-school links: How do they affect educational outcomes?* Mahwah, NJ: Lawrence Erlbaum Associates, Inc.

Bornstein, M. H. (2002). *Handbook of parenting* (2nd ed.). Mahwah, NJ: Lawrence Erlbaum Associates, Inc.

Bornstein, M. H., & Suess, P. E. (2000). Child and mother cardiac vagal tone: Continuity, stability, and concordance across the first 5 years. *Developmental Psychology, 36,* 54–65.

Boulet, J., & Boss, M. W. (1991). Reliability and validity of the Brief Symptom Inventory. *Psychological Assessment, 3,* 433–437.

Bowen, M. (1978). *Family therapy in clinical practice.* New York: Aronson.

Bowlby, J. (1951). Maternal care and mental health. *World Health Organization Monograph Series,* No. 2, 179.

Bowlby, J. (1988). *A secure base: Parent–child attachment and healthy human development.* New York: Basic Books.

Bradburn, I. S. (1997). *Attachment and coping strategies in married couples with preschool children.* Unpublished doctoral dissertation, University of California, Berkeley.

Bradbury, T. N. (Ed.). (1998). *The developmental course of marital dysfunction.* New York: Cambridge University Press.

Bradbury, T. N., & Fincham, F. D. (1992). Attributions and behavior in marital interaction. *Journal of Personality & Social Psychology, 63,* 613–628.

Bradbury, T. N., & Karney, B. R. (1993). Longitudinal study of marital interaction and dysfunction: Review and analysis. *Clinical Psychology Review, 13,* 15–27.

Bradley, R. H., & Caldwell, B. M. (1984). The relation of infants' home environments to achievement test performance in first grade: A follow-up study. *Child Development, 55,* 803–809.

Brage, D., & Meredith, W. (1994). A causal model of adolescent depression. *Journal of Psychology, 128,* 455–468.

Brand, S., Cowan, P. A., & Cowan, C. P. (1994). Preparing yourself for letting go. *Parents' Press, 15,* 18–20.

Bretherton, I., Ridgeway, D., & Cassidy, J. (1990). Assessing internal working models of the attachment relationship: An attachment story completion task for 3-year-olds. In M. T. Greenberg, D. Cicchetti, & E. M. Cummings (Eds.), *Attachment in the preschool years: Theory, research, and intervention* (pp. 273–308). Chicago: University of Chicago Press.

Brody, G. H., & Flor, D. L. (1996). Coparenting, family interactions, and competence among African American youths. In J. P. McHale & P. A. Cowan (Eds.), *Understanding how family-level dynamics affect children's development: Studies of two-parent families. New directions for child development* (Vol. 74, pp. 77–91). San Francisco: Jossey–Bass.

Brody, G. H., & Flor, D. L. (1997). Maternal psychological functioning, family processes, and child adjustment in rural, single-parent, African American families. *Developmental Psychology, 33,* 1000–1011.

Brody, G. H., & Forehand, R. (1985). The efficacy of parent training with maritally distressed and nondistressed mothers: A multimethod assessment. *Behaviour Research & Therapy, 23,* 291–296.

Bronfenbrenner, U. (1979). *The ecology of human development: Experiments by nature and design.* Cambridge, MA: Harvard University Press.

Bronfenbrenner, U. (1986). Ecology of the family as a context for human development: Research perspectives. *Developmental Psychology, 22,* 723–742.

Bronfenbrenner, U., & Ceci, S. J. (1994). Nature-nurture in developmental perspective: A bioecological theory. *Psychological Review, 101,* 568–586.

Bronstein, P., & Cowan, C. P. (Eds.). (1988). *Fatherhood today: Men's changing role in the family.* New York: Wiley.

Brooks-Gunn, J., Han, W. J., & Waldfogel, J. (2002). Maternal employment and child cognitive outcomes in the first three years of life: The NICHD study of early child care. *Child Development, 73,* 1052–1072.

Bryant, F. B., & Yarnold, P. R. (1995). Principal-components analysis and exploratory and confirmatory factor analysis. In L. G. Grimm & P. R. Yarnold (Eds.), *Reading and understanding multivariate statistics* (pp. 99–136). Washington, DC: American Psychological Association.

Bumpass, L., & Rindfuss, R. R. (1979). Children's experience of marital disruption. *American Journal of Sociology, 85,* 49–65.

Burlingame, G. M., & Barlow, S. H. (1996). Outcome and process differences between professional and nonprofessional therapists in time-limited group psychotherapy. *International Journal of Group Psychotherapy, 46,* 455–478.

Burnette, D. (1998). Grandparents rearing grandchildren: A school-based small group intervention. *Research on Social Work Practice, 8,* 10–27.

Byng-Hall, J. (1999). Family couple therapy: Toward greater security. In J. Cassidy & P. R. Shaver (Eds.), *Handbook of attachment: Theory, research, and clinical applications* (pp. 625–645). New York: Guilford.

Campbell, A. (1993). *Men, women, and aggression.* New York: Basic Books.

Campbell, F. A., Pungello, E. P., Miller-Johnson, S., Burchinal, M., & Ramey, C. T. (2001). The development of cognitive and academic abilities: Growth curves from an early childhood educational experiment. *Developmental Psychology, 37,* 231–242.

Campbell, S. B. (1995). Behavior problems in preschool children: A review of recent research. *Journal of Child Psychology & Psychiatry & Allied Disciplines, 36,* 113–149.

Campos, J. J., Campos, R. G., & Barrett, K. C. (1989). Emergent themes in the study of emotional development and emotion regulation. *Developmental Psychology, 25,* 394–402.

Caplan, G. (1964). *Principles of preventive psychiatry.* New York: Basic Books.

Capraro, M. M., & Capraro, R. M. (2003). Exploring the APA fifth edition publication manual's impact on the analytic preferences of journal editorial board members. *Educational & Psychological Measurement, 63,* 554–565.

Carlson, E. A., Sroufe, L. A., Collins, W. A., Jimerson, S., Weinfield, N., Henninghausen, K., et al. (1999). Early environmental support and elementary school adjustment as predictors of school adjustment in middle adolescence. *Journal of Adolescent Research, 14,* 72–94.

Caspi, A., & Elder, G. H. J. (1988). Emergent family patterns: The intergenerational construction of problem behaviour and relationships. In R. A. Hinde & J. Stevenson-Hinde (Eds.), *Relationships within families: Mutual influences* (pp. 218–240). Oxford, England: Clarendon.

Caspi, A., & Roberts, B. W. (1999). Personality continuity and change across the life course. In L. A. Pervin & O. P. John (Eds.), *Handbook of personality: Theory and research* (2nd ed., pp. 300–326). New York: Guilford.

Caspi, A., & Roberts, B. W. (2001). Target article: Personality development across the life course: The argument for change and continuity. *Psychological Inquiry, 12,* 49–66.

Chavez, D., Corkery, L., Cowan, C. P., Cowan, P. A., DeMarneffe, D., Epperson, B., et al. (1988, March 31). *Parents and partners: A preventive intervention for parents of preschoolers.* Workshop presented at the American Orthopsychiatry Association Meetings, San Francisco.

Chin, W. W. (1998). Issues and opinion on structural equation modeling. *MIS Quarterly, 22,* vii–xvi.

Christensen, A., & Margolin, G. (1988). Conflict and alliance in distressed and non-distressed families. In R. A. Hinde & J. Stephenson-Hinde (Eds.), *Relationships within families: Mutual influences* (pp. 263–283). Oxford, England: Clarendon.

Cicchetti, D., & Cohen, D. J. (Eds.). (1995a). *Developmental psychopathology, Vol. 1: Theory and methods.* New York: Wiley.

Cicchetti, D., & Cohen, D. J. (Eds.). (1995b). *Developmental psychopathology, Vol. 2: Risk, disorder, and adaptation.* New York: Wiley.

Cicchetti, D., Toth, S. L., & Maughan, A. (2000). An ecological-transactional model of child maltreatment. In A. J. Sameroff, M. Lewis, & S. M. Miller (Eds.), *Handbook of developmental psychopathology* (2nd ed., pp. 689–722). New York: Kluwer Academic.

Clulow, C. (2001). Attachment theory and the therapeutic frame. In C. Clulow (Ed.), *Adult attachment and couple psychotherapy: The 'secure base' in practice and research* (pp. 85–104). Philadelphia: Brunner-Routledge.

Clulow, C., Cleavely, E., Coussell, P., & Dearnley, B. (1982). *To have and to hold: Marriage, the first baby and preparing couples for parenthood.* Aberdeen, Scotland: Aberdeen University Press.

Coates, D. L., & Lewis, M. (1984). Early mother–infant interaction and infant cognitive status as predictors of school performance and cognitive behavior in six-year-olds. *Child Development, 55,* 1219–1230.

Coche, J. (1995). Group therapy with couples. In N. Jacobson & A. S. Gurman (Eds.), *Clinical handbook of couple therapy* (pp. 212–229). New York: Guilford.

Cohen, J. (1988). *Statistical power analysis for the behavioral sciences* (2nd ed.). Hillsdale, NJ: Lawrence Erlbaum Associates, Inc.

Cohen, J., & Cohen, P. (1983). *Applied multiple regression/correlation analysis for the behavioral sciences.* Hillsdale, NJ: Lawrence Erlbaum Associates, Inc.

Cohler, B. J., Grunebaum, H. U., Weiss, J. L., & Moran, D. L. (1971). The childcare attitudes of two generations of mothers. *Merrill-Palmer Quarterly, 17,* 3–17.

Cohn, D. A., Cowan, P. A., Cowan, C. P., & Pearson, J. (1992). Mothers' and fathers' working models of childhood attachment relationships, parenting styles, and child behavior. *Development & Psychopathology, 4,* 417–431.

Cohn, D. A., Silver, D. H., Cowan, C. P., Cowan, P. A., & Pearson, J. (1992). Working models of childhood attachment and couple relationships. *Journal of Family Issues, 13,* 432–449.

Coie, J. D., Watt, N. F., West, S. G., & Hawkins, J. D. (1993). The science of prevention: A conceptual framework and some directions for a national research program. *American Psychologist, 48,* 1013–1022.

Coiro, M. J., & Emery, R. E. (1998). Do marriage problems affect fathering more than mothering? A quantitative and qualitative review. *Clinical Child & Family Psychology Review, 1,* 23–40.

Cole, D. A., Martin, J. M., Powers, B., & Truglio, R. (1996). Modeling causal relations between academic and social competence and depression: A multitrait-multimethod longitudinal study of children. *Journal of Abnormal Psychology, 105,* 258–270.

Cole, D. A., & McPherson, A. E. (1993). Relation of family subsystems to adolescent depression: Implementing a new family assessment strategy. *Journal of Family Psychology, 7,* 119–133.

Coleman, J. S., Campbell, E., Hobson, C., McPartland, J., Mood, A., Weinfeld, F., et al. (1966). *Equality of educational opportunity.* Washington, DC: U.S. Government Printing Office.

Collins, N. L., & Read, S. J. (1990). Adult attachment, working models, and relationship quality in dating couples. *Journal of Personality & Social Psychology, 58,* 644–663.

Collins, W. A. (1997). Relationships and development during adolescence: Interpersonal adaptation to individual change. *Personal Relationships, 4,* 1–14.

Collins, W. A., Maccoby, E. E., Steinberg, L., Hetherington, E. M., & Bornstein, M. H. (2000). Contemporary research on parenting: The case for nature and nurture. *American Psychologist, 55,* 218–232.

Coltrane, S. (1996). *Family man: Fatherhood, housework, and gender equity.* New York: Oxford University Press.

Conger, R. D., Conger, K. J., Elder, G. H., & Lorenz, F. O. (1992). A family process model of economic hardship and adjustment of early adolescent boys. *Child Development, 63,* 526–541.

Conger, R. D., Elder, G. H., Jr., Lorenz, F. O., Simons, R. L., & Whitbeck, L. B. (Eds.). (1994). *Families in troubled times: Adapting to change in rural America.* New York: Aldine de Gruyter.

Conger, R. D., Ge, X., Elder, G. H., & Lorenz, F. O. (1994). Economic stress, coercive family process, and developmental problems of adolescents. Special issue: Children and poverty. *Child Development, 65,* 541–561.

Cooley, C. H. (1902). *Human nature and the social order.* New York: Scribner's.

Cowan, C. P. (1988). Workplace policies: New options for fathers. In P. Bronstein & C. P. Cowan (Eds.), *Fatherhood today: Men's changing role in the family* (pp. 323–340). New York: Wiley.

Cowan, C. P., & Cowan, P. A. (1982a). *Couple Communication Questionnaire.* Unpublished questionnaire, University of California, Berkeley.

Cowan, C. P., & Cowan, P. A. (1982b). *Family Relationships Questionnaire.* Unpublished questionnaire, University of California, Berkeley.

Cowan, C. P., & Cowan, P. A. (1988). Who does what when partners become parents: Implications for men, women, and marriage. *Marriage & Family Review, 12,* 105–131.

Cowan, C. P., & Cowan, P. A. (1991). The pie. In M. S. J. Touliatos, B. F. Perlmutter, & M. Straus (Eds.), *Handbook of family measurement techniques* (pp. 278–279). Newbury Park, CA: Sage.

Cowan, C. P., & Cowan, P. A. (1992). *When partners become parents: The big life change for couples.* New York: Basic Books.

Cowan, C. P., & Cowan, P. A. (1995). Interventions to ease the transition to parenthood: Why they are needed and what they can do. *Family Relations: Journal of Applied Family & Child Studies, 44,* 412–423.

Cowan, C. P., & Cowan, P. A. (1997). Working with couples during stressful transitions. In S. Dreman (Ed.), *The family on the threshold of the 21st century: Trends and implications* (pp. 17–47). Mahwah, NJ: Lawrence Erlbaum Associates, Inc.

Cowan, C. P., & Cowan, P. A. (2000). *When partners become parents: The big life change for couples.* Mahwah, NJ: Lawrence Erlbaum Associates, Inc.

Cowan, C. P., Cowan, P. A., Heming, G., Garrett, E. T., Coysh, W. S., Curtis-Boles, H., et al. (1985b). Transitions to parenthood: His, hers, and theirs [Special issue]. *Journal of Family Issues, 6,* 451–481.

Cowan, P. A. (1978). *Piaget: With feeling: Cognitive, social, and emotional dimensions.* New York: Holt, Rinehart & Winston.

Cowan, P. A. (1991). Individual and family life transitions: A proposal for a new definition. In P. A. Cowan & E. M. Hetherington (Eds.), *Family transitions* (pp. 3–30). Hillsdale, NJ: Lawrence Erlbaum Associates, Inc.

Cowan, P. A., Cohn, D. A., Cowan, C. P., & Pearson, J. L. (1996). Parents' attachment histories and children's externalizing and internalizing behaviors: Exploring family systems models of linkage. *Journal of Consulting & Clinical Psychology, 64,* 53–63.

Cowan, P. A., & Cowan, C. P. (1991). Who does what? In M. A. Straus (Ed.), *Handbook of family measurement techniques* (pp. 447–448). Thousand Oaks, CA: Sage.

Cowan, P. A., & Cowan, C. P. (2002a). Strengthening couples to improve children's well-being. *Poverty Research News, 6,* 18–20.

Cowan, P. A., & Cowan, C. P. (2002b). What an intervention design reveals about how parents affect their children's academic achievement and behavior problems. In J. G. Borkowski, S. L. Ramey, & M. Bristol-Power (Eds.), *Parenting and the child's world: Influences on academic, intellectual, and social–emotional development* (pp. 75–97). Mahwah, NJ: Lawrence Erlbaum Associates, Inc.

Cowan, P. A., Cowan, C. P., & Heming, G. (1995). *Manual for the Child Adaptive Behavior Inventory (CABI).* Unpublished manuscript, University of California, Berkeley.

Cowan, P. A., Cowan, C. P., & Kerig, P. K. (1993). Mothers, fathers, sons, and daughters: Gender differences in family formation and parenting style. In P. A. Cowan, D. Field, D. Hansen, A. Skolnick, & G. E. Swanson (Eds.), *Family, self, and society: Toward a new agenda for family research* (pp. 165–195). Hillsdale, NJ: Lawrence Erlbaum Associates, Inc.

Cowan, P. A., Cowan, C. P., & Schulz, M. S. (1996). Thinking about risk and resilience in families. In E. M. Hetherington & E. A. Blechman (Eds.), *Stress, coping, and resiliency in children and families. Family research consortium: Advances in family research* (Vol. 5, pp. 1–38). Hillsdale, NJ: Lawrence Erlbaum Associates, Inc.

Cowan, P. A., Cowan, C. P., Schulz, M. S., & Heming, G. (1994). Prebirth to preschool family factors in children's adaptation to kindergarten. In R. D. Parke & S. G. Kellam (Eds.), *Exploring family relationships with other social contexts. Family research consortium: Advances in family research* (Vol. 4, pp. 75–114). Hillsdale, NJ: Lawrence Erlbaum Associates, Inc.

Cowan, P. A., Powell, D., & Cowan, C. P. (1998). Parenting interventions: A family systems perspective. In W. Damon (Ed.), *Handbook of child psychology* (5th ed., Vol. 4, pp. 3–72). New York: Wiley.

Cox, M. J., Owen, M. T., Lewis, J. M., & Henderson, V. K. (1989). Marriage, adult adjustment, and early parenting. *Child Development, 60,* 1015–1024.

Cox, M. J., Paley, B., & Harter, K. (2001). Interparental conflict and parent–child relationships. In J. H. Grych & F. D. Fincham (Eds.), *Interparental conflict and child development: Theory, research, and applications* (pp. 249–272). New York: Cambridge University Press.

Cox, M. J., Paley, B., Payne, C. C., & Burchinal, M. (1999). The transition to parenthood: Marital conflict and withdrawal and parent–infant interactions. In M. J. Cox & J. Brooks-Gunn (Eds.), *Conflict and cohesion in families: Causes and consequences* (pp. 87–104). Mahwah, NJ: Lawrence Erlbaum Associates, Inc.

Creasey, G. (2002). Associations between working models of attachment and conflict management behavior in romantic couples. *Journal of Counseling Psychology, 49,* 365–375.

Crick, N. R., & Dodge, K. A. (1994). A review and reformulation of social information-processing mechanisms in children's social adjustment. *Psychological Bulletin, 115,* 74–101.

Crick, N. R., & Ladd, G. W. (1993). Children's perceptions of their peer experiences: Attributions, loneliness, social anxiety, and social avoidance. *Developmental Psychology, 29,* 244–254.

Crockenberg, S. (1988). *Social support and parenting.* New York: Plenum.

Crockenberg, S., & Langrock, A. (2001). *The role of emotion and emotional regulation in children's responses to interparental conflict.* New York: Cambridge University Press.

Crockenberg, S., & Litman, C. (1990). Autonomy as competence in 2-year-olds: Maternal correlates of child defiance, compliance, and self-assertion. *Developmental Psychology, 26,* 961–971.

Crockenberg, S. B. (1981). Infant irritability, mother responsiveness, and social support influences on the security of infant–mother attachment. *Child Development, 52,* 857–865.

Cross, S. E., & Madson, L. (1997). Models of the self: Self-construals and gender. *Psychological Bulletin, 122,* 5–37.

Crouter, A. C., Perry-Jenkins, M., Huston, T. L., & Crawford, D. W. (1989). The influence of work-induced psychological states on behavior at home. *Basic and Applied Social Psychology, 10,* 273–292.

Crowell, J. A., & Feldman, S. S. (1989). Mothers' working models of attachment relationships and mother and child behavior during separation and reunion. *Developmental Psychology, 27,* 597–605.

Cummings, E. M., Ballard, M., & El-Sheikh, M. (1991). Responses of children and adolescents to interadult anger as a function of gender, age, and mode of expression. *Merrill-Palmer Quarterly, 37,* 543–560.

Cummings, E. M., & Cummings, J. S. (2002). *Parenting and attachment.* Mahwah, NJ: Lawrence Erlbaum Associates, Inc.

Cummings, E. M., & Davies, P. (1994). *Children and marital conflict: The impact of family dispute and resolution.* New York: Guilford.

Cummings, E. M., Davies, P., & Campbell, S. B. (2000). *Developmental psychopathology and family process: Theory, research, and clinical implications.* New York: Guilford.

Cummings, E. M., DeArth-Pendley, G., Du Rocher Schudlich, T., & Smith, D. A. (2001). Parental depression and family functioning: Toward a process-oriented model of children's adjustment. In S. R. H. Beach (Ed.), *Marital and family processes in depression: A scientific foundation for clinical practice* (pp. 89–110). Washington, DC: American Psychological Association.

Cumsille, P. E., & Epstein, N. (1994). Family cohesion, family adaptability, social support, and adolescent depressive symptoms in outpatient clinic families. *Journal of Family Psychology, 8,* 202–214.

Curtis-Boles, H. (1979). *Important people.* Unpublished questionnaire, Becoming a Family Project, Department of Psychology, University of California, Berkeley.

Cutrona, C. E., & Troutman, B. R. (1986). Social support, infant temperament, and parenting self-efficacy: A mediational model of postpartum depression. *Child Development, 57,* 1507–1518.

Dadds, M. R., Schwartz, S., & Sanders, M. R. (1987). Marital discord and treatment outcome in behavioral treatment of child conduct disorders. *Journal of Consulting & Clinical Psychology, 55,* 396–403.

Damon, W., & Hart, D. (1982). The development of self-understanding from infancy through adolescence. *Child Development, 53,* 841–864.

Darling, N., & Steinberg, L. (1993). Parenting style as context: An integrative model. *Psychological Bulletin, 113,* 487–496.

Darwin, C. (1875). *On the origin of species by means of natural selection, or the preservation of favored races in the struggle for life.* New York: D. Appleton and Company.

Davies, P. T., & Cummings, E. M. (1994). Marital conflict and child adjustment: An emotional security hypothesis. *Psychological Bulletin, 116,* 387–411.

Davies, P. T., & Cummings, E. M. (1998). Exploring children's emotional security as a mediator of the link between marital relations and child adjustment. *Child Development, 69,* 124–139.

Davies, P. T., & Forman, E. M. (2002). Children's patterns of preserving emotional security in the interparental subsystem. *Child Development, 73,* 1880–1903.

Deal, J. E., Hagan, M. S., Bass, B., Hetherington, E. M., & Clingempeel, G. (1999). Marital interaction in dyadic and triadic contexts: Continuities and discontinuities. *Family Process, 38,* 105–115.

Deater-Deckard, K., & Dodge, K. A. (1997). Externalizing behavior problems and discipline revisited: Nonlinear effects and variation by culture, context, and gender. *Psychological Inquiry, 8,* 161–175.

Demo, D. H., & Acock, A. C. (1996). Family structure, family process, and adolescent well-being. *Journal of Research on Adolescence, 6,* 457–488.

Dempsey, K. (2002). Who gets the best deal from marriage: Women or men? *Journal of Sociology, 38,* 91–110.

Denton, K., & West, J. (2002). *Children's reading and mathematics achievement in kindergarten and first grade* (Rep. No. NCES 2002–125). Washington, DC: National Center for Education Statistics.

Derogatis, L. R., & Melisaratos, N. (1983). The Brief Symptom Inventory: An introductory report. *Psychological Medicine, 13,* 595–605.

Diamant, A. (1993, October 24). More work for the weary. *Boston Globe Magazine, 7,* 7–8.

Dion, M. R., Devaney, B., McConnell, S., Ford, M., Hill, H., & Winston, P. (2003). Helping unwed parents build strong and healthy marriages: A conceptual framework for interventions. Washington, DC: Mathematica Policy Research, Inc. Document No. PR03-02.

Dix, T. (1991). The affective organization of parenting: Adaptive and maladaptive processes. *Psychological Bulletin, 110,* 3–25.

Dodge, K. A. (1990). Developmental psychopathology in children of depressed mothers. *Developmental Psychology, 26,* 3–6.

Dozier, M., & Kobak, R. R. (1992). Psychophysiology in attachment interviews: Converging evidence for deactivating strategies. *Child Development, 63,* 1473–1480.

Dunn, J. (1993). *Young children's close relationships: Beyond attachment.* Thousand Oaks, CA: Sage.

Dunn, J. (1996). Sibling relationships and perceived self-competence: Patterns of stability between childhood and early adolescence. In A. J. Sameroff & M. H. Haith (Eds.), *The five to seven year shift: The age of reason and responsibility* (pp. 253–270). Chicago: University of Chicago Press.

Dunn, J., Slomkowski, C., & Beardsall, L. (1994). Sibling relationships from the preschool period through middle childhood and early adolescence. *Developmental Psychology, 30,* 315–324.

Durlak, J. A., & Wells, A. M. (1997). Primary prevention mental health programs for children and adolescents: A meta-analytic review. *American Journal of Community Psychology, 25,* 115–152.

Eccles, J., Wigfield, A., Harold, R. D., & Blumenfeld, P. (1993). Age and gender differences in children's self- and task perceptions during elementary school. *Child Development, 64,* 830–847.

Eder, R. A. (1990). Uncovering young children's psychological selves: Individual and developmental differences. *Child Development, 61,* 849–863.

Elizur, Y. (1984). The stress of school entry: Parental coping behaviors and children's adjustment to elementary school. *Journal of Child Psychology and Psychiatry, 27,* 625–638.

Elkind, D. (1985). Egocentrism redux. *Developmental Review, 5,* 218–226.

Emery, R. E. (1999). *Marriage, divorce, and children's adjustment* (2nd ed.). Thousand Oaks, CA: Sage.

Emery, R. E., & O'Leary, K. D. (1984). Marital discord and child behavior problems in a nonclinic sample. *Journal of Abnormal Child Psychology, 12,* 411–420.

Entwisle, D. R., & Alexander, K. L. (1993). Entry into school: The beginning school transition and educational stratification in the United States. *Annual Review of Sociology, 19,* 401–423.

Entwisle, D. R., & Alexander, K. L. (1996). Family type and children's growth in reading and math over the primary grades. *Journal of Marriage & the Family, 58,* 341–355.

Epstein, J. L. (1996). Perspectives and previews on research and policy for school, family, and community partnerships. In A. Booth & J. F. Dunn (Eds.), *Family-school links: How do they affect educational outcomes?* (pp. 209–246). Mahwah, NJ: Lawrence Erlbaum Associates, Inc.

Erel, O., & Burman, B. (1995). Interrelatedness of marital relations and parent–child relations: A meta-analytic review. *Psychological Bulletin, 118,* 108–132.

Erickson, M. F., Sroufe, L. A., & Egeland, B. (1985). The relationship between quality of attachment and behavior problems in preschool in a high-risk sample. In I. Bretherton & E. Waters (Eds.), *Growing points of attachment theory and research. Monographs of the Society for Research in Child Development, 50*(1–2), 147–166.

Erikson, E. H. (1950). *Childhood and society.* New York: Norton.

Estrada, P., Arsenio, W. F., Hess, R. D., & Holloway, S. D. (1987). Affective quality of the mother–child relationship: Longitudinal consequences for children's school-relevant cognitive functioning. *Developmental Psychology, 23,* 210–215.

Fagan, P. F., Patterson, R. W., & Rector, R. E. (2002). *Marriage and Welfare Reform: The Overwhelming Evidence that Marriage Education Works* (Backgrounder No. 1606). Washington, DC: Heritage Foundation.

Fagot, B. I. (1995). Parenting boys and girls. In M. H. Bornstein (Ed.), *Handbook of parenting, Vol. 1: Children and parenting* (pp. 163–183). Mahwah, NJ: Lawrence Erlbaum Associates, Inc.

Fagot, B. I., & Leinbach, M. D. (1993). Gender-role development in young children: From discrimination to labeling. *Developmental Review, 13,* 203–224.

Falk, R. F., & Miller, N. B. (1987, June). *A soft-models approach to transitions.* Paper presented at the Family Research Consortium, Second Annual Summer Institute, Santa Fe, New Mexico.

Falk, R. F., & Miller, N. B. (1992). *A primer for soft modeling.* Akron, OH: University of Akron Press.

Feiring, C., & Lewis, M. (1998). Divergent family views and school competence in early adolescence. In M. Lewis & C. Feiring (Eds.), *Families, risk, and competence* (pp. 53–70). Mahwah, NJ: Lawrence Erlbaum Associates, Inc.

Feldman, S. S., Rubenstein, J. L., & Rubin, C. (1988). Depressive affect and restraint in early adolescents: Relationships with family structure, family process and friendship support. *Journal of Early Adolescence, 8,* 279–296.

Ferguson, E., & Cox, T. (1993). Exploratory factor analysis: A user's guide. *International Journal of Selection and Assessment, 1,* 84–94.

Feshbach, S., Adelman, H., & Fuller, W. (1977). Prediction of reading and related academic problems. *Journal of Educational Psychology, 69,* 299–308.

Fiese, B. H. (1992). Dimensions of family rituals across two generations: Relation to adolescent identity. *Family Process, 31,* 151–162.

Fife, C. (1997, April). *Empirical classification of adult attachment status: Scoring adult attachment security on a continuum from state of mind scales.* Poster session presented at the Symposium on Attachment, Society for Research in Child Development, Washington, DC.

Fincham, F. D. (1998). Child development and marital relations. *Child Development, 69,* 543–574.

Fincham, F. D., Grych, J. H., & Osborne, L. N. (1994). Does marital conflict cause child maladjustment? Directions and challenges for longitudinal research. *Journal of Family Psychology, 8,* 128–140.

Fonagy, P. (1996). The significance of the development of metacognitive control over mental representations in parenting and infant development. *Journal of Clinical Psychoanalysis, 5,* 67–86.

Fonagy, P. (1998). Prevention, the appropriate target of infant psychotherapy. *Infant Mental Health Journal, 19,* 124–50.

Fonagy, P., Steele, H., & Steele, M. (1991). Maternal representations of attachment during pregnancy predict the organization of infant–mother attachment at one year of age. *Child Development, 62,* 891–905.

Forehand, R., Armistead, L., & Klein, K. (1995). Children's school performance: The roles of interparental conflict and divorce. In B. A. Ryan, G. R. Adams, T. P. Gulotta, R. P. Weissberg, & R. L. Hamptom (Eds.), *The family-school connection: Theory, research, and practice* (pp. 250–269). Thousand Oaks, CA: Sage.

Forgatch, M. S., & DeGarmo, D. S. (1999). Parenting through change: An effective prevention program for single mothers. *Journal of Consulting & Clinical Psychology, 67,* 711–724.

Fraley, R. C., & Spieker, S. J. (2003). Are infant attachment patterns continuously or categorically distributed? A taxometric analysis of strange situation behavior. *Developmental Psychology, 39,* 387–404.

Fraley, R. C., & Waller, N. G. (1998). Adult attachment patterns: A test of the typological model. In J. A. Simpson & W. S. Rholes (Eds.), *Attachment theory and close relationships* (pp. 77–114). New York: Guilford.

Framo, J. L. (1982). *Family-of-origin therapy: An intergenerational approach.* New York: Brunner/Mazel.

Frosch, C. A., Mangelsdorf, S. C., & McHale, J. L. (2000). Marital behavior and the security of preschooler–parent attachment relationships. *Journal of Family Psychology, 14,* 144–161.

Fuller, B. (1999). *School choice: Abundant hopes, scarce evidence of results.* Policy analysis for California Education (PACE), University of California, Berkeley.

Galinsky, E., Bond, J. T., & Friedman, D. E. (1996). The role of employers in addressing the needs of employed parents. *Journal of Social Issues, 52,* 111–136.

Geary, C., & Boykin, K. (1997, April). *Adolescent autonomy with mothers as a predictor of susceptibility to peer influence.* Poster session presented at the biannual convention of the Society for Research in Child Development, Washington, DC.

George, C., Kaplan, N., & Main, M. (1985). *The Adult Attachment Interview.* Unpublished manuscript, University of California, Berkeley.

Gilligan, C. (1982). *In a different voice: Psychological theory and women's development.* Cambridge, MA: Harvard University Press.

Gjerde, P. F. (1986). The interpersonal structure of family interaction settings: Parent–adolescent relations in dyads and triads. *Developmental Psychology, 22,* 297–304.

Gjerde, P. F., Block, J., & Block, J. H. (1988). Depressive symptoms and personality during late adolescence: Gender differences in the externalization of symptom expression. *Journal of Abnormal Psychology, 97,* 475–486.

Goldberg, W. A., Greenberger, E., & Nagel, S. K. (1996). Employment and achievement: Mothers' work involvement in relation to children's achievement behaviors and mothers' parenting behaviors. *Child Development, 67,* 1512–1527.

Goldenberg, W. A., & Goldenberg, H. (1996). *Family therapy: An overview* (4th ed.). Pacific Grove, CA: Brooks/Cole.

Goldsmith, H. H., & Campos, J. J. (1990). The structure of temperamental fear and pleasure in infants: A psychometric perspective. *Child Development, 61,* 1944–1964.

Goodman, S. H. (Ed.). (2002). *Children of depressed parents: Mechanisms of risk and implications for treatment.* Washington, DC: American Psychological Association.

Gotlib, I. H., & Goodman, S. H. (1999). Children of parents with depression. In W. K. Silverman & T. H. Ollendick (Eds.), *Developmental issues in the clinical treatment of children* (pp. 415–432). Needham Heights, MA: Allyn & Bacon.

Gottfried, A. E., Gottfried, A. W., & Bathurst, K. (1988). Maternal employment, family environment, and children's development: Infancy through the school years. In A. E. Gottfried & A. W. Gottfried (Eds.), *Maternal employment and children's development: Longitudinal research* (pp. 11–58). New York: Plenum.

Gottlieb, B. H. (Ed.). (1988). *Marshaling social support: Formats, processes, and effects.* Thousand Oaks, CA: Sage.

Gottman, J. M. (1993). The roles of conflict engagement, escalation, and avoidance in marital interaction: A longitudinal view of five types of couples. *Journal of Consulting & Clinical Psychology, 61,* 6–15.

Gottman, J. M. (1994). *What predicts divorce?: The relationship between marital processes and marital outcomes.* Hillsdale, NJ: Lawrence Erlbaum Associates, Inc.

Gottman, J. M. (2001). Meta-emotion, children's emotional intelligence, and buffering children from marital conflict. In C. D. Ryff & B. H. Singer (Eds.), *Emotion, social relationships, and health* (pp. 23–40). New York: Oxford University Press.

Gottman, J. M., & Katz, L. F. (1989). Effects of marital discord on young children's peer interaction and health. *Developmental Psychology, 25,* 373–381.

Gottman, J. M., Katz, L. F., & Hooven, C. (1997). *Meta-emotion: How families communicate emotionally.* Mahwah, NJ: Lawrence Erlbaum Associates, Inc.

Gottman, J. M., & Levenson, R. W. (1986). Assessing the role of emotion in marriage. *Behavioral Assessment, 8,* 31–48.

Gottman, J. M., & Levenson, R. W. (1988). The social psychophysiology of marriage. In P. Noller & M. A. Fitzpatrick (Eds.), *Perspectives on marital interaction* (pp. 182–200). Clevedon, England: Multilingual Matters.

Gottman, J. M., & Levenson, R. W. (1999). How stable is marital interaction over time? *Family. Process, 38,* 159–165.

Gough, H. G., Fioravanti, M., & Lazzari, R. (1983). Some implications of self versus ideal-self congruence on the revised Adjective Check List. *Journal of Personality & Social Psychology, 44,* 1214–1220.

Gough, H. G., & Heilbrun, A. B. J. (1980). *The adjective check list manual.* Palo Alto, CA: Consulting Psychologists Press.

Gray, E. B., Lovejoy, M. C., Piotrkowski, C. S., & Bond, J. T. (1990). Husband supportiveness and the well-being of employed mothers of infants [Special issue]. *Families in Society, 71,* 332–341.

Green, R. J. (1995). High achievement, underachievement, and learning disabilities: A family systems model. In B. A. Ryan, G. R. Adams, T. P. Gullotta, R. P. Weissberg, & R. L. Hampton (Ed.), *The family-school connection: Theory, research, and practice* (pp. 250–269). Thousand Oaks, CA: Sage.

Greenberg, M. T., Lengua, L. J., Coie, J. D., Pinderhughes, E. E., Bierman, K., Dodge, K. A., et al. (1999). Predicting developmental outcomes at school entry using a multiple-risk model: Four American communities. *Developmental Psychology, 35,* 403–417.

Greenberg, M. T., Speltz, M. L., & DeKlyen, M. (1993). The role of attachment in the early development of disruptive behavior patterns. *Development and Psychopathology, 5,* 191–214.

Greenberger, E., O'Neil, R., & Nagel, S. K. (1994). Linking workplace and homeplace: Relations between the nature of adults' work and their parenting behaviors. *Developmental Psychology, 30,* 990–1002.

Greenspan, S. I. (1981). *Psychopathology and adaptation in infancy and early childhood: Principles of clinical diagnosis and preventive intervention.* New York: International Universities Press.

Greif, E., Alvarez, M., & Ulman, K. (1981, April). *Recognizing emotions in other people: Sex differences in socialization.* Paper presented at the biennial meeting of the Society for Research in Child Development, Boston.

Grolnick, W. S., & Ryan, R. M. (1989). Parent styles associated with children's self-regulation and competence in school. *Journal of Educational Psychology, 81,* 143–154.

Grolnick, W. S., Ryan, R. M., & Deci, E. L. (1991). Inner resources for school achievement: Motivational mediators of children's perceptions of their parents. *Journal of Educational Psychology, 83,* 508–517.

Gross, J. J., & Levenson, R. W. (1997). Hiding feelings: The acute effects of inhibiting negative and positive emotion. *Journal of Abnormal Psychology, 106,* 95–103.

Grossmann, K., Grossmann, K. E., Fremmer-Bombik, E., Kindler, H., Scheuerer-Englisch, H., & Zimmermann, P. (2002). The uniqueness of the child–father attachment relationship: Fathers' sensitive and challenging play as a pivotal variable in a 16-year longitudinal study. *Social Development, 11,* 307–331.

Grych, J. H., & Fincham, F. D. (1990). Marital conflict and children's adjustment: A cognitive-contextual framework. *Psychological Bulletin, 108,* 267–290.

Grych, J. H., & Fincham, F. D. (1993). Children's appraisals of marital conflict: Initial investigations of the cognitive-contextual framework. *Child Development, 64,* 215–230.

Grych, J. H., Fincham, F. D., Jouriles, E. N., & McDonald, R. (2000). Interparental conflict and child adjustment: Testing the mediational role of appraisals in the cognitive-contextual framework. *Child Development, 71,* 1648–1661.

Grych, J. H., Seid, M., & Fincham, F. D. (1992). Assessing marital conflict from the child's perspective: The Children's Perception of Interparental Conflict Scale. *Child Development, 63,* 558–572.

Gutek, B. A., Repetti, R. L., & Silver, D. L. (1988). Nonwork roles and stress at work. In C. Payne (Ed.), *Causes, coping and consequences at work* (pp. 141–174). New York: Wiley.

Hackman, J. R., & Oldham, G. R. (1975). Development of the Job Diagnostic Survey. *Journal of Applied Psychology, 60,* 159–170.

Haft, W. L., & Slade, A. (1989). Affect attunement and maternal attachment: A pilot study. *Infant Mental Health Journal, 10,* 157–172.

Harris, J. (1997). Where is the child's environment? A group socialization theory of development. *Psychological Review, 102,* 458–489.

Harris, J. (1998). *The nurture assumption: Why children turn out the way they do.* New York: Free Press.

Harter, S. (1982). The Perceived Competence Scale for children. *Child Development, 53,* 87–97.

Harter, S. (1999). *The construction of the self: A developmental perspective.* New York: Guilford.

Harter, S., & Pike, R. (1984). The pictorial scale of perceived competence and social acceptance for young children. *Child Development, 55,* 1969–1982.

Hayden, L. C., Schiller, M., Dickstein, S., Seifer, R., Sameroff, S., Miller, I., et al. (1998). Levels of family assessment: I. Family, marital, and parent–child interaction. *Journal of Family Psychology, 12,* 7–22.

Hazan, C., & Shaver, P. R. (1994). Attachment as an organizational framework for research on close relationships. *Psychological Inquiry, 5,* 1–22.

Hazan, C., & Zeifman, D. (1999). *Pair bonds as attachments: Evaluating the evidence.* New York: Guilford.

Heinicke, C. M. (1984). Impact of prebirth parent personality and marital functioning on family development: A framework and suggestions for further study. *Developmental Psychology, 20,* 1044–1053.

Heinicke, C. M. (1991). Early family intervention: Focusing on the mother's adaptation-competence and quality of partnership. In D. G. Unger & D. R. Powell (Eds.), *Families as nurturing systems: Support across the life span* (pp. 127–142). Binghamton: Haworth.

Heinicke, C. M. (2002). *The transition to parenting.* Mahwah, NJ: Lawrence Erlbaum Associates, Inc.

Heinicke, C. M., Beckwith, L., & Thompson, A. (1988). Early intervention in the family system: A framework and review. *Infant Mental Health Journal, 9,* 111–141.

Heinicke, C. M., Fineman, N. R., Ruth, G., Recchia, S. L., Guthrie, D., & Rodning, C. (1999). Relationship-based intervention with at-risk mothers: Outcome in the first year of life. *Infant Mental Health Journal, 20,* 349–374.

Heinicke, C. M., & Guthrie, D. (1992). Stability and change in husband–wife adaptation and the development of the positive parent–child relationship. *Infant Behavior & Development, 15,* 109–127.

Helgeson, V., Cohen, S., Schulz, R., & Yasko, J. (1999). Education and peer discussion group interventions and adjustment to breast cancer. *Archives of General Psychiatry, 56,* 340–347.

Heming, G. (1985). *Predicting adaptation in the transition to parenthood.* Unpublished doctoral dissertation, Department of Psychology, University of California, Berkeley.

Heming, G., Cowan, P. A., & Cowan, C. P. (1990). Ideas about parenting. In J. Touliatos, B. F. Perlmutter, & M. A. Straus (Eds.), *Handbook of family measurement techniques* (p. 362). Newbury Park, CA: Sage.

Hess, R. D., Holloway, S. D., Dickson, W. P., & Price, G. G. (1984). Maternal variables as predictors of children's school readiness and later achievement in vocabulary and mathematics in sixth grade. *Child Development, 55,* 1902–1912.

Hesse, E. (1999). The adult attachment interview: Historical and current perspectives. In J. Cassidy & P. R. Shaver (Eds.), *Handbook of attachment: Theory, research, and clinical applications* (pp. 395–433). New York: Guilford.

Hetherington, E. M. (1993). An overview of the Virginia Longitudinal Study of Divorce and Remarriage with a focus on early adolescence. Special section: Families in transition. *Journal of Family Psychology, 7,* 39–56.

Hetherington, E. M., Cox, M. J., & Cox, R. (1982). Effects of divorce on parents and children. In M. E. Lamb (Ed.), *Nontraditional families* (pp. 233–388). Hillsdale, NJ: Lawrence Erlbaum Associates, Inc.

Hetherington, E. M., & Kelly, J. (2002). *For better or for worse: Divorce reconsidered.* New York: Norton.

Hill, J., Fonagy, P., Safier, E., & Sargent, J. (2003). The ecology of attachment in the family. *Family Process, 42,* 205–221.

Hinde, R. A. (1995). A suggested structure for a science of relationships. *Personal Relationships, 2,* 1–15.

Hinde, R. A., & Stevenson-Hinde, J. (1988). *Relationships within families: Mutual influences.* Oxford, England: Clarendon.

Hinshaw, S. P. (1992). Externalizing behavior problems and academic underachievement in childhood and adolescence: Causal relationships and underlying mechanisms. *Psychological Bulletin, 111,* 127–155.

Hinshaw, S. P. (2002). Preadolescent girls with attention-deficit/hyperactivity disorder: I. Background characteristics, comorbidity, cognitive and social functioning, and parenting practices. *Journal of Consulting & Clinical Psychology, 70,* 1086–1098.

Hinshaw, S. P., Owens, E. B., Wells, K. C., Kraemer, H. C., Abikoff, H. B., Arnold, L. E., et al. (2000). Family processes and treatment outcome in the MTA: Negative/ineffective parenting practices in relation to multimodal treatment. *Journal of Abnormal Child Psychology, 28,* 555–568.

Hinshaw, S. P., Zupan, B. A., Simmel, C., Nigg, J. T., & Melnick, S. (1997). Peer status in boys with and without attention-deficit hyperactivity disorder: Predictions from overt and covert antisocial behavior, social isolation, and authoritative parenting beliefs. *Child Development, 68,* 880–896.

Hochschild, A. (1989). *The second shift: Working parents and the revolution at home.* New York: Viking.

Hochschild, A. (1997). *The time bind: When work becomes home and home becomes work.* New York: Metropolitan Books.

Hodges, E. V. E., Boivin, M., Vitaro, F., & Bukowski, W. M. (1999). The power of friendship: Protection against an escalating cycle of peer victimization. *Developmental Psychology, 35,* 94–101.

Horn, W. (2002). Welfare reform reauthorization: Promoting self-sufficiency, protecting children, and strengthening marriage. *Poverty Research News, 6,* 3–6.

Horowitz, M., Schaefer, C., Hiroto, D., Wilner, N., & Levin, B. (1977). Life event questionnaires for measuring presumptive stress. *Psychosomatic Medicine, 39,* 413–431.

Hsu, J. (1996). *Gender in the family system: Effects on childhood symptomatology.* Unpublished dissertation. Berkeley: University of California Press.

Hulin, C. L. (2002). Lessons from industrial and organizational psychology. In J. M. Brett & F. Drasgow (Eds.), *The psychology of work: Theoretically based empirical research* (pp. 3–22). Mahwah, NJ: Lawrence Erlbaum Associates, Inc.

Husaini, B. A., Neff, J. A., Harrington, J. B., Hughes, M. D., & Stone, R. H. (1980). Depression in rural communities: Validating the CES-D scale. *Journal of Community Psychology, 8,* 20–27.

Huss, S. N., & Ritchie, M. (1999). Effectiveness of a group for parentally bereaved children. *Journal for Specialists in Group Work, 24,* 186–196.

Huston, A. (1983). Sex-typing. In P. Mussen (Ed.), *Handbook of child psychology* (4th ed., Vol. 3, pp. 388–467). New York: Wiley.

Ingoldsby, E. M., Shaw, D. S., Owens, E. B., & Winslow, E. B. (1999). A longitudinal study of interparental conflict, emotional and behavioral reactivity, and preschoolers' adjustment problems among low-income families. *Journal of Abnormal Child Psychology, 27,* 343–356.

Isley, S. L., O'Neil, R., Clatfelter, D., & Parke, R. D. (1999). Parent and child expressed affect and children's social competence: Modeling direct and indirect pathways. *Developmental Psychology, 35,* 547–560.

Jacobvitz, D., & Sroufe, L. A. (1987). The early caregiver-child relationship and attention-deficit disorder with hyperactivity in kindergarten: A prospective study. *Child Development, 58,* 1496–1504.

Janowsky, J. S., & Carper, R. (1996). *Is there a neural basis for cognitive transitions in school-age children?* Chicago: University of Chicago Press.

Jenkins, J. M., & Smith, M. A. (1991). Marital disharmony and children's behaviour problems: Aspects of a poor marriage that affect children adversely. *Journal of Child Psychology & Psychiatry & Allied Disciplines, 32,* 793–810.

Jimerson, S. R., Egeland, B., Sroufe, L. A., & Carlson, B. (2000). A prospective longitudinal study of high school dropouts: Examining multiple predictors across development. *Journal of School Psychology, 38,* 525–549.

Johnson, V. K., Cowan, P. A., & Cowan, C. P. (1999). Children's classroom behavior: The unique contribution of family organization. *Journal of Family Psychology, 13,* 355–371.

Johnson, V. K., Silverman, R. C., Compton, N. C., & Leon, K. (1998, August). *Disparate mother–child mental representations of fathers in discordant families.* Paper presented at the conference of the American Psychological Association, San Francisco.

Johnston, J. R., Gonzalez, R., & Campbell, L. E. (1987). Ongoing postdivorce conflict and child disturbance. *Journal of Abnormal Child Psychology, 15,* 493–509.

Jones, E. E. (2000). *Therapeutic action: A guide to psychoanalytic therapy.* Northvale, NJ: J. Aronson.

Joreskog, K. G. S. D. (1985). *LISREL-V program manual.* Chicago: International Educational Services.

Kagan, S. L., & Neville, P. R. (1996). Combining endogenous and exogenous factors in the shift years: The transition to school. In A. J. Sameroff & M. M. Haith (Eds.), *The five to seven year shift: The age of reason and responsibility* (pp. 387–405). Chicago: University of Chicago Press.

Kashani, J. H., Allan, W. D., Dahlmeier, J. M., & Rezvani, M. (1995). An examination of family functioning utilizing the circumplex model in psychiatrically hospitalized children with depression. *Journal of Affective Disorders, 35,* 65–73.

Katz, L. F., & Gottman, J. M. (1993). Patterns of marital conflict predict children's internalizing and externalizing behaviors. *Developmental Psychology, 29,* 940–950.

Katz, L. F., & Woodin, E. M. (2002). Hostility, hostile detachment, and conflict engagement in marriages: Effects on child and family functioning. *Child Development, 73,* 636–651.

Kazdin, A. E. (1997). Practitioner review: Psychosocial treatments for conduct disorder in children. *Journal of Child Psychology & Psychiatry & Allied Disciplines, 38,* 161–178.

Kellam, S. G., Ling, X., Merisca, R., Brown, C. H., & Ialongo, N. (1998). The effect of the level of aggression in the first grade classroom on the course and malleability of aggressive behavior into middle school. *Development & Psychopathology, 10,* 165–185.

Kellam, S. G., Rebok, G. W., Mayer, L. S., Ialongo, N., & Kalodner, C. R. (1994). Depressive symptoms over first grade and their response to a developmental epidemiologically based preventive trial aimed at improving achievement. *Development & Psychopathology, 6,* 463–481.

Kellam, S. G., Simon, M. B., & Ensminger, M. E. (1982). Antecedents in first grade of teenage drug use and psychological well-being: A ten-year community-wide prospective study. In D. Ricks & B. Dohrenwend (Eds.), *Origins of psychopathology: Research and public policy* (pp. 17–42). New York: Cambridge University Press.

Kenny, D. A. (1996). The design and analysis of social-interaction research. *Annual Review of Psychology, 47,* 59–86.

Keppel, G., & Zedeck, S. (1989). *Data analysis for research designs: Analysis of variance and multiple regression/correlation approaches.* New York: Freeman.

Kerig, P. K. (1998). Moderators and mediators of the effects of interparental conflict on children's adjustment. *Journal of Abnormal Child Psychology, 26,* 199–212.

Kerig, P. K., Cowan, P. A., & Cowan, C. P. (1993). Marital quality and gender differences in parent–child interaction. *Developmental Psychology, 29,* 931–939.

Kessler, R. C. (2003). Epidemiology of women and depression [Special issue]. *Journal of Affective Disorders, 74,* 5–13.

Kim, A. (1995). *Children's sex-typed behaviors: Early parental influence on childhood gender socialization.* Unpublished senior thesis, University of California, Berkeley.

Kirk, R. E. (2003). The importance of effect magnitude. In S. F. Davis (Ed.), *Handbook of research methods in experimental psychology. Blackwell handbooks of research methods in psychology* (pp. 83–105). Malden, MA: Blackwell Publishers.

Kleinbaum, D. G., Morgenstern, H., & Kupper, L. L. (1982). *Epidemiologic research: Principles and quantitative methods.* Belmont, CA: Lifetime Learning Publications.

Kobak, R. R., Ruckdeschel, K., & Hazan, C. (1994). From symptom to signal: An attachment view of emotion in marital therapy. In S. M. Johnson & L. S. Greenberg (Eds.), *The heart of the matter: Perspectives on emotion in marital therapy* (pp. 46–71). Philadelphia: Brunner/Mazel.

Kobak, R. R., & Sceery, A. (1988). Attachment in late adolescence: Working models, affect regulation, and representations of self and others. *Child Development, 59,* 135–146.

Kochanska, G., & Coy, K. C. (2002). Child emotionality and maternal responsiveness as predictors of reunion behaviors in the strange situation: Links mediated and unmediated by separation distress. *Child Development, 73,* 228–240.

Kohn, M. L. (1969). *Class and conformity: A study in values.* Homewood, IL: Dorsey.

Kohn, M. L. (1979). The effects of social class on parental values and practices. In D. Reiss & H. A. Hoffman (Eds.), *The American family: Dying or developing* (pp. 45–77). New York: Plenum.

Kohn, M. L. (1983). On the transmission of values in the family: A preliminary formulation. In A. Kerchoff (Ed.), *Research in sociology, education and socialization* (Vol. 4, pp. 3–112). Greenwich, CT: JAI.

Kohn, M. L., & Schooler, C. (1973). Occupational experience and psychological functioning: An assessment of reciprocal effects. *American Sociological Review, 38,* 97–118.

Kornstein, S. G., & Clayton, A. H. (Eds.). (2002). *Women's mental health: A comprehensive textbook.* New York: Guilford.

Kraemer, H. C., Stice, E., Kazdin, A., Offord, D., & Kupfer, D. (2001). How do risk factors work together? Mediators, moderators, and independent, overlapping, and proxy risk factors. *American Journal of Psychiatry, 158,* 848–856.

Kremen, A. M. (1996). *Relationships between parenting and children's ego-control: An HLM analysis of stability and change.* Unpublished dissertation, University of California.

Kuczynski, L. (2003). *Handbook of dynamics in parent–child relations.* Thousand Oaks, CA: Sage.

Kuczynski, L., Kochanska, G., Radke-Yarrow, M., & Girnius-Brown, O. (1987). A developmental interpretation of young children's noncompliance. *Developmental Psychology, 23,* 799–806.

Kupersmidt, J. B., Coie, J. D., & Dodge, K. A. (1990). The role of poor peer relationships in the development of disorder. In S. R. Asher & J. D. Coie (Eds.), *Peer rejection in childhood* (pp. 274–305). New York: Cambridge University Press.

Ladd, G. W. (1990). Having friends, keeping friends, making friends, and being liked by peers in the classroom: Predictors of children's early school adjustment? *Child Development, 61,* 1081–1100.

Ladd, G. W. (1996). Shifting ecologies during the 5 to 7 year period: Predicting children's adjustment during the transition to grade school. In A. J. Sameroff & M. M. Haith (Eds.), *The five to seven year shift: The age of reason and responsibility* (pp. 363–386). Chicago: University of Chicago Press.

Ladd, G. W., Hart, C. H., Wadsworth, E. M., & Golter, B. S. (1988). Preschoolers' peer networks in nonschool settings: Relationship to family characteristics and school adjustment. In S. Salzinger, J. S. Antrobus, & M. Hammer (Eds.), *Social networks of children, adolescents, and college students* (pp. 61–92). Hillsdale, NJ: Lawrence Erlbaum Associates, Inc.

Ladd, G. W., Kochenderfer, B. J., & Coleman, C. C. (1997). Classroom peer acceptance, friendship, and victimization: Distinct relational systems that contribute uniquely to children's school adjustment? *Child Development, 68,* 1181–1197.

Ladd, G. W., & Price, J. M. (1987). Predicting children's social and school adjustment following the transition from preschool to kindergarten. *Child Development, 58,* 1168–1189.

Ladewig, B. H., & White, P. N. (1984). Dual-earner marriages: The family social environment and dyadic adjustment. *Journal of Family Issues, 5,* 343–362.

Lamb, M. E. (2000). The history of research on father involvement: An overview. *Marriage & Family Review, 29,* 23–42.

Lambert, N. M. (1988). Adolescent outcomes for hyperactive children: Perspectives on general and specific patterns of childhood risk for adolescent educational, social, and mental health problems. *American Psychologist, 43,* 786–799.

Lambert, N. M., Hartsough, C. S., Sassone, D., & Sandoval, J. (1987). Persistence of hyperactivity symptoms from childhood to adolescence and associated outcomes. *American Journal of Orthopsychiatry, 57,* 22–32.

Lazar, I., & Darlington, R. B. (1982). Lasting effects of early education: A report from the Consortium for Longitudinal Studies. *Monographs of the Society for Research in Child Development, 47*(Serial No. 95).

Lazarus, R. (1992). *Emotion and adaptation.* New York: Oxford University Press.

Lazarus, R. S. (1999). *Stress and emotion: A new synthesis.* New York: Springer.

Leaper, C. (2000). Gender, affiliation, assertion, and the interactive context of parent–child play. *Developmental Psychology, 36,* 381–393.

Leaper, C. (2002). Parenting girls and boys. In M. H. Bornstein (Ed.), *Handbook of parenting: Vol. 1: Children and parenting* (2nd ed., pp. 189–225). Mahwah, NJ: Lawrence Erlbaum Associates, Inc.

Levant, R. F. (1988). Education for fatherhood. In P. Bronstein & C. P. Cowan (Eds.), *Fatherhood today: Men's changing role in the family* (pp. 253–275). New York: Wiley.

Levenson, R. W., & Gottman, J. M. (1983). Marital interaction: Physiological linkage and affective exchange. *Journal of Personality & Social Psychology, 45,* 587–597.

Lewis, M. (1987). Social development in infancy and early childhood. In J. Osofsky (Ed.), *Handbook of infancy* (2nd ed., pp. 419–492). New York: Wiley.

Little, R., & Yau, L. (1996). Intent-to-treat analysis for longitudinal studies with drop-outs. *Biometrics, 52,* 1324–1333.

Locke, H. J., & Wallace, K. M. (1959). Short marital-adjustment and prediction tests: Their reliability and validity. *Marriage & Family Living, 21,* 251–255.

Lodahl, T. M., & Kejner, M. (1965). The definition of job involvement. *Journal of Applied Psychology, 49,* 24–33.

Loeber, R., & Dishion, T. (1983). Early predictors of male delinquency: A review. *Psychological Bulletin, 94,* 68–99.

Lohmoeller, J. B. (1989). *Latent variable path analysis with partial least squares.* New York: Springer-Verlag.

Lowinsky, N. R. (1992). *Stories from the motherline: Reclaiming the mother–daughter bond, finding our feminine souls.* Los Angeles: J. P. Tarcher.

Loyd, B. H., & Abidin, R. R. (1985). Revision of the Parenting Stress Index. *Journal of Pediatric Psychology, 10,* 169–177.

Lyons-Ruth, K. (1996). Attachment relationships among children with aggressive behavior problems: The role of disorganized early attachment patterns. *Journal of Consulting & Clinical Psychology, 64,* 64–73.

Lyons-Ruth, K., Alpern, L., & Repacholi, B. (1993). Disorganized infant attachment classification and maternal psychosocial problems as predictors of hostile-aggressive behavior in the preschool classroom. *Child Development, 64,* 572–585.

Lytton, H. (1994). Replication and meta-analysis: The story of a meta-analysis of parents' socialization practices. In R. van der Veer, M. H. van Ijzendoorn, & J. Valsiner (Eds.), *Reconstructing the mind: Replicability in research on human development* (pp. 117–149). Stamford, CT: Ablex Publishing Corp.

Lytton, H. (2000). Toward a model of family-environmental and child-biological influences on development. *Developmental Review, 20,* 150–179.

Lytton, H., & Romney, D. M. (1991). Parents' differential socialization of boys and girls: A meta-analysis. *Psychological Bulletin, 109,* 267–296.

Maccoby, E. E. (1980). *Social development: Psychological growth and the parent–child relationship.* New York: Harcourt Brace Jovanovich.

Maccoby, E. E. (2000). Perspectives on gender development. *International Journal of Behavioral Development, 24,* 398–406.

Maccoby, E. E., & Jacklin, C. N. (1974). *The psychology of sex differences.* Stanford, CA: Stanford University Press.

Maccoby, E. E., & Martin, J. A. (1983). Socialization in the context of the family: Parent–child interaction. In E. M. Hetherington (Ed.), *Handbook of child psychology: Socialization, personality and social development* (4th ed., Vol. 4, pp. 1–101). New York: Wiley.

Main, M., & Goldwyn, R. (1984). Predicting rejection of her infant from mother's representation of her own experience: Implications for the abused-abusing intergenerational cycle. *Child Abuse & Neglect, 8,* 203–217.

Main, M., Kaplan, N., & Cassidy, J. (1985). Security in infancy, childhood, and adulthood: A move to the level of representation. Growing points of attachment theory and research. *Monographs of the Society for Research in Child Development, 50*(Serial No. 209).

Markman, H. J., Renick, M. J., Floyd, F. J., & Stanley, S. M. (1993). Preventing marital distress through communication and conflict management training: A 4- and 5-year follow-up. *Journal of Consulting & Clinical Psychology, 61,* 70–77.

Markus, H., & Wurf, E. (1987). The dynamic self-concept: A social psychological perspective. In M. R. Rosenzweig & L. W. Porter (Eds.), *Annual review of psychology, Vol. 38* (pp. 299–337). Palo Alto, CA: Annual Reviews, Inc.

Markwardt, F. C. (1989). *Peabody Individual Achievement Test–Revised.* Circle Pines, MN: American Guidance Service.

Markwardt, F. C. (1991). Manual for the Peabody Individual Achievement Test–Revised. Circle Pines, MN: American Guidance Service.

Marsh, H. W., Craven, R. G., & Debus, R. (1991). Self-concepts of young children 5 to 8 years of age: Measurement and multidimensional structure. *Journal of Educational Psychology, 83,* 377–392.

Martin, R. P., Olejnik, S., & Gaddis, L. (1994). Is temperament an important contributor to schooling outcomes in elementary school? Modeling effects of temperament and scholastic ability on academic achievement. In W. B. Carey & S. C. McDevitt (Eds.), *Prevention and early intervention: Individual differences as risk factors for the mental health of children: A festschrift for Stella Chess and Alexander Thomas* (pp. 59–68). Philadelphia: Brunner/Mazel.

Marvin, R. S., & Stewart, R. B. (1990). A family systems framework for the study of attachment. In M. T. Greenberg, D. Cicchetti, & E. M. Cummings (Eds.), *Attachment in the preschool years: Theory, research, and intervention* (pp. 51–86). Chicago: University of Chicago Press.

Mason, M. A., Skolnick, A. S., & Sugarman, S. D. (2003). *All our families: New policies for a new century: A report of the Berkeley family forum* (2nd ed.). New York: Oxford University Press.

Mattanah, J. F. (2001). Parental psychological autonomy and children's academic competence and behavioral adjustment in late childhood: More than just limit-setting and warmth. *Merrill-Palmer Quarterly, 47,* 355–376.

McClelland, G. H., & Judd, C. M. (1993). Statistical difficulties of detecting interactions and moderator effects. *Psychological Bulletin, 114,* 376–390.

McHale, J. P. (1995). Coparenting and triadic interactions during infancy: The roles of marital distress and child gender. *Developmental Psychology, 31,* 985–996.

McHale, J. P. (1997). Overt and covert coparenting processes in the family. *Family Process, 36,* 183–201.

McHale, J. P., & Cowan, P. A. (Eds.). (1996). *Understanding how family-level dynamics affect children's development: Studies of two-parent families.* San Francisco: Jossey-Bass.

McHale, J. P., & Rasmussen, J. L. (1998). Coparental and family group-level dynamics during infancy: Early family precursors of child and family functioning during preschool. *Development & Psychopathology, 10,* 39–59.

McHale, S. M., & Crouter, A. C. (1992). You can't always get what you want: Incongruence between sex-role attitudes and family work roles and its implications for marriage. *Journal of Marriage & the Family, 54,* 537–547.

McHale, S. M., Freitag, M. K., Crouter, A. C., & Bartko, W. T. (1991). Connections between dimensions of marital quality and school-age children's adjustment. *Journal of Applied Developmental Psychology, 12,* 1–17.

McLoyd, V. C. (1990). The impact of economic hardship on Black families and children: Psychological distress, parenting, and socioemotional development. *Child Development, 61,* 311–346.

Mead, G. H. (1934). *Mind, self and society: From the standpoint of a social behaviorist.* Chicago: University of Chicago Press.

Measelle, J. R., Ablow, J. C., Cowan, P. A., & Cowan, C. P. (1998). Assessing young children's views of their academic, social, and emotional lives: An evaluation of the self-perception scales of the Berkeley Puppet Interview. *Child Development, 69,* 1556–1576.

Messer, S. C., & Gross, A. M. (1995). Childhood depression and family interaction: A naturalistic observation study. *Journal of Clinical Child Psychology, 24,* 77–88.

Mikulincer, M., & Florian, V. (1998). The relationship between adult attachment styles and emotional and cognitive reactions to stressful events. In J. A. Simpson & W. S. Rholes (Eds.), *Attachment theory and close relationships* (pp. 143–165). New York: Guilford.

Mikulincer, M., Florian, V., Cowan, P. A., & Cowan, C. P. (2002). Attachment security in couple relationships: A systemic model and its implications for family dynamics. *Family Process, 41,* 405–434.

Miller, N. B., Cowan, P. A., Cowan, C. P., & Hetherington, E. M. (1993). Externalizing in preschoolers and early adolescents: A cross-study replication of a family model. *Developmental Psychology, 29,* 3–18.

Miller, P. H., & Aloise, P. A. (1989). Young children's understanding of the psychological causes of behavior: A review. *Child Development, 60,* 257–285.

Minuchin, P. (1988). Relations within the family: A systems perspective on development. In R. H. J. Stevenson-Hinde (Ed.), *Relationships within families: Mutual influences* (pp. 7–26). Oxford, England: Clardendon.

Minuchin, S. (1974). *Families and family therapy.* Cambridge, MA: Harvard University Press.

Mize, J., & Pettit, G. S. (1997). Mothers' social coaching, mother–child relationship style, and children's peer competence: Is the medium the message? *Child Development, 68,* 312–332.

Moos, R., & Moos, B. (1976). A typology of family social environments. *Family Process, 15,* 357–371.

National Center for Educational Statistics. (1998). National Assessment of Educational Progress, long-term assessment. *NAEP FACTS, 3.*

Nelson, G. (1984). The relationship between dimensions of classroom and family environments and the self-concept, satisfaction, and achievement of grade 7 and 8 students. *Journal of Community Psychology, 12,* 276–287.

Newcomb, M. D., & Locke, T. F. (2001). Intergenerational cycle of maltreatment: A popular concept obscured by methodological limitations. *Child Abuse & Neglect, 25,* 1219–1240.

NICHD Early Child Care Research Network. (2003). Does quality of child care affect child outcomes at age 4 1/2? *Developmental Psychology, 39,* 451–469.

Nolen-Hoeksema, S., Wolfson, A., Mumme, D., & Guskin, K. (1995). Helplessness in children of depressed and nondepressed mothers. Special section: Parental depression and distress: Implications for development in infancy, childhood, and adolescence. *Developmental Psychology, 31,* 377–387.

Nuckolls, K. B., Cassel, J., & Kaplan, B. H. (1972). Psychological assets, life crises, and the prognosis of pregnancy. *American Journal of Epidemiology, 96,* 431–441.

O'Donnel, J. P., & Van Tuinen, M. V. (1979). Behavior problems of preschool children: Dimensions and congenital correlates. *Journal of Abnormal Child Psychology, 7,* 61–75.

Ogbu, J. U. (2003). *Black American students in an affluent suburb: A study of academic disengagement.* Mahwah, NJ: Lawrence Erlbaum Associates, Inc.

Olson, D. H. (1993). Circumplex model of marital and family systems: Assessing family functioning. In F. Walsh (Ed.), *Normal family process* (2nd ed., pp. 384–396). New York: Guilford.

Olson, D. H., & Gorall, D. M. (2003). Circumplex model of marital and family systems. In F. Walsh (Ed.), *Normal family processes: Growing diversity and complexity* (3rd ed., pp. 514–548). New York: Guilford.

Olson, S. L., Bates, J. E., & Kaskie, B. (1992). Caregiver-infant interaction antecedents of children's school-age cognitive ability. *Merrill-Palmer Quarterly, 38,* 309–330.

Osborne, L. N., & Fincham, F. D. (1996). Marital conflict, parent–child relationships, and child adjustment: Does gender matter? *Merrill-Palmer Quarterly, 42,* 48–75.

Osofsky, J. D., & Osofsky, H. J. (1984). Psychological and developmental perspectives on expectant and new parenthood. In R. D. Parke (Ed.), *Review of child development research: The family* (Vol. 7, pp. 372–397). Chicago: University of Chicago Press.

Owens, G., Crowell, J. A., Pan, H., Treboux, D., O'Connor, E., & Waters, E. (1995). The prototype hypothesis and the origins of attachment working models: Child–parent relationships and adult–adult romantic relationships. *Monographs of the Society for Research in Child Development, 60*(Serial No. 244).

Paley, B., Cox, M. J., Harter, K. S. M., & Margand, N. A. (2002). Adult attachment stance and spouses' marital perceptions during the transition to parenthood. *Attachment & Human Development, 4,* 340–360.

Parcel, T. L., & Menaghan, E. G. (1990). Maternal working conditions and children's verbal facility: Studying the intergenerational transmission of inequality from mothers to young children. *Social Psychology Quarterly, 53,* 132–147.

Parke, R. D. (1996). *Fatherhood* (2nd ed.). Cambridge, MA: Harvard University Press.

Parke, R. D., & Buriel, R. (1998). Socialization in the family: Ethnic and ecological perspectives. In N. Eisenberg (Ed.), *Social, emotional, and personality development* (5th ed., Vol. 3, pp. 463–552). New York: Wiley.

Parke, R. D., & Tinsley, B. J. (1987). Family Interaction in Infancy. In J. D. Osofsky (Ed.), *Handbook of infancy* (2nd ed., pp. 579–641). New York: Wiley.

Patterson, C. J., Griesler, P. C., Vaden, N. A., & Kupersmidt, J. B. (1992). Family economic circumstances, life transitions, and children's peer relations. In R. D. Parke & G. W. Ladd (Eds.), *Family-peer relationships: Modes of linkage* (pp. 385–424). Hillsdale, NJ: Lawrence Erlbaum Associates, Inc.

Patterson, G. R. (1986). Performance models for antisocial boys. *American Psychologist, 41,* 432–444.

Patterson, G. R., & Capaldi, D. M. (1991). Antisocial parents: Unskilled and vulnerable. In P. A. Cowan & E. M. Hetherington (Eds.), *Family transitions: Advances in family research* (Vol. 2, pp. 195–218). Hillsdale, NJ: Lawrence Erlbaum Associates, Inc.

Patterson, G. R., & Reid, J. B. (1984). Social interactional processes within the family: The study of the moment-by-moment family transactions in which human social development is imbedded. *Journal of Applied Developmental Psychology, 5,* 237–262.

Pears, K. C., & Capaldi, D. M. (2001). Intergenerational transmission of abuse: A two-generational prospective study of an at-risk sample. *Child Abuse & Neglect, 25,* 1439–1461.

Perry, D. G., & Bussey, K. (1979). The social learning theory of sex differences: Imitation is alive and well. *Journal of Personality and Social Psychology, 37,* 1699–1712.

Perry, K. E., & Weinstein, R. S. (1998). The social context of early schooling and children's school adjustment. *Educational Psychologist, 33,* 177–194.

Peterson, J. L., & Zill, N. (1986). Marital disruption, parent–child relationships, and behavior problems in children. *Journal of Marriage & the Family, 48,* 295–307.

Pettit, G. S., Harrist, A. W., Bates, J. E., & Dodge, K. A. (1991). Family interaction, social cognition and children's subsequent relations with peers at kindergarten [Special issue]. *Journal of Social & Personal Relationships, 8,* 383–402.

Phillips, M., Brooks-Gunn, J., Duncan, G. J., Klebanov, P., & Crane, J. (1988). Family background, parenting practices, and the black–white test gap. In C. J. M. Phillips (Ed.), *The black–white test score gap* (pp. 103–145). Washington, DC: Brookings Institute.

Piaget, J. (1967). *Six psychological studies.* New York: Random House.

Pianta, R. C., Cox, M. J., & National Center for Early Development & Learning. (1999). *The transition to kindergarten.* Baltimore: Brookes.

Pianta, R. C., Morog, M. C., & Marvin, R. S. (1995, April). *Adult attachment status and mothers' behavior toward their spouses.* Paper presented at the Society for Research in Child Development, Indianapolis, IN.

Pianta, R. C., Rimm-Kaufman, S. E., & Cox, M. J. (1999). Introduction: An ecological approach to kindergarten transition. In R. C. Pianta & M. J. Cox (Eds.), *The transition to kindergarten* (pp. 3–12). Baltimore: Brookes.

Pianta, R. C., Smith, N., & Reeve, R. E. (1991). Observing mother and child behavior in a problem-solving situation at school entry: Relations with classroom adjustment. *School Psychology Quarterly, 6,* 1–15.

Pleck, J. (1985). *Working wives/working husbands.* Beverly Hills, CA: Sage.

Pleck, J. H. (1997). Paternal involvement: Levels, sources, and consequences. In M. E. Lamb (Ed.), *The role of the father in child development* (3rd ed., pp. 66–103). New York: Wiley.

Plomin, R. (1994). *Genetics and experience: The interplay between nature and nurture.* Thousand Oaks, CA: Sage.

Plomin, R., & McClearn, G. E. (Eds.). (1993). *Nature, nurture & psychology.* Washington, DC: American Psychological Association.

Popenoe, D. (1993). American family decline, 1960–1990. *Journal of Marriage & the Family, 55*, 527–541.

Pratt, M. W., Kerig, P., Cowan, P. A., & Cowan, C. P. (1988). Mothers and fathers teaching 3-year-olds: Authoritative parenting and adult scaffolding of young children's learning. *Developmental Psychology, 24*, 832–839.

Pruett, K. D. (2000). *Fatherneed: Why father care is as essential as mother care for your child.* New York: Free Press.

Radloff, L. S. (1977). The CES-D Scale: A self-report depression scale for research in the general population. *Applied Psychological Measurement, 1*, 385–401.

Ramey, C. L., & Ramey, C. T. (1992). Early educational intervention with disadvantaged children: To what effect? *Applied & Preventive Psychology, 1*, 131–140.

Ramey, C. T., & Ramey, S. L. (2000). Intelligence and public policy. In R. J. Sternberg (Ed.), *Handbook of intelligence* (pp. 534–548). New York: Cambridge University Press.

Rapaport, R., Rapoport, R., & Streilitz, Z. (1977). *Mothers, fathers, and society: Towards new alliances.* New York: Basic Books.

Reiss, D. (1989). *Families and their paradigms: An ecologic approach to understanding the family in its social world.* New York, NY: Guilford Press.

Renken, B., Egeland, B., Marvinney, D., & Mangelsdorf, S. (1989). Early childhood antecedents of aggression and passive-withdrawal in early elementary school. *Journal of Personality, 57*, 257–281.

Repetti, R. L. (1984). Determinants of children's sex stereotyping: Parental sex-role traits and television viewing. *Personality & Social Psychology Bulletin, 10*, 457–468.

Repetti, R. L. (1989). Effects of daily workload on subsequent behavior during marital interaction: The roles of social withdrawal and spouse support. *Journal of Personality & Social Psychology, 57*, 651–659.

Repetti, R. L., & Wood, J. (1997). Effects of daily stress at work on mothers' interactions with preschoolers. *Journal of Family Psychology, 11*, 90–108.

Richman, N., Stevenson, J., & Graham, P. J. (1982). *Pre-school to school: A behavioural study.* London: Academic Press.

Rodriguez, J. L. (2002). Family environment and achievement among three generations of Mexican American high school students. *Applied Developmental Science, 6*, 88–94.

Rogers, S. J., & May, D. C. (2003). Spillover between marital quality and job satisfaction: Long-term patterns and gender differences. *Journal of Marriage & the Family, 65*, 482–495.

Rolland, J. S., & Walsh, F. (1996). Family therapy: Systems approaches to assessment and treatment. In R. E. Hales & S. C. Yudofsky (Eds.), *The American Psychiatric Press synopsis of psychiatry* (pp. 1097–1126). Washington, DC: American Psychiatric Association.

Rosenbaum, P. R., & Silber, J. H. (2001). Matching and thick description in an observational study of mortality after surgery. *Biostatistics, 2*, 217–232.

Rothbaum, F., & Weisz, J. R. (1994). Parental caregiving and child externalizing behavior in nonclinical samples: A meta-analysis. *Psychological Bulletin, 116*, 55–74.

Rowe, D. C., Vazsonyi, A. T., & Flannery, D. J. (1994). No more than skin deep: Ethnic and racial similarity in developmental process. *Psychological Review, 101*, 396–413.

Rushton, J. P., Brainerd, C. J., & Pressley, M. (1983). Behavioral development and construct validity: The principle of aggregation. *Psychological Bulletin, 94*, 18–38.

Rutter, M. (1987). Psychosocial resilience and protective mechanisms. *American Journal of Orthopsychiatry, 57*, 316–331.

Rutter, M., & Sroufe, L. A. (2000). Developmental psychopathology: Concepts and challenges. *Development & Psychopathology, 12*, 265–296.

Ryan, B. A., & Adams, G. R. (1995). The family-school relationship model. In B. A. Ryan, G. R. Adams, T. P. Gullotta, R. P. Weissberg, & R. L. Hampton (Eds.), *The family-school connection: Theory, research, and practice* (pp. 3–28). Thousand Oaks, CA: Sage.

Ryan, B. A., Adams, G. R., Gullotta, T. P., Weissberg, R. P., & Hampton, R. L. (Eds.). (1995). *The family-school connection: Theory, research, and practice.* Thousand Oaks, CA: Sage.

Sachs-Ericsson, N., & Ciarlo, J. A. (2000). Gender, social roles, and mental health: An epidemiological perspective. *Sex Roles, 43,* 605–628.

Sameroff, A. J., & Haith, M. M. (Eds.). (1996). *The five to seven year shift: The age of reason and responsibility.* Chicago: University of Chicago Press.

Sameroff, A. J., Seifer, R., Baldwin, A., & Baldwin, C. (1993). Stability of intelligence from preschool to adolescence: The influence of social and family risk factors. *Child Development, 64,* 80–97.

Sameroff, A. J., Seifer, R., & Zax, M. (1982). Early development of children at risk for emotional disorder. *Monographs of the Society for Research in Child Development, 47*(7, Serial No. 199).

Satir, V. (1972). *Peoplemaking.* Palo Alto, CA: Science and Behavior Books.

Saxe, L., Cross, T., & Silverman, N. (1988). Children's mental health: The gap between what we know and what we do. *American Psychologist, 43,* 800–807.

Scarr, S. (1996). How people make their own environments: Implications for parents and policy makers. *Psychology, Public Policy, & Law, 2,* 204–228.

Schaefer, E. S. (1965). A configurational analysis of children's reports of parent behavior. *Journal of Consulting Psychology, 29,* 552–557.

Schaefer, E. S., & Hunter, W. M. (1983, April). *Mother–infant interaction and maternal psychosocial predictors of kindergarten adaptation.* Paper presented at the Society for Research in Child Development, Detroit, MI.

Schneewind, K. A., & Ruppert, S. (1998). *Personality and family development: An intergenerational longitudinal comparison.* Mahwah, NJ: Lawrence Erlbaum Associates, Inc.

Schoppe, S. J., Mangelsdorf, S. C., & Frosch, C. A. (2001). Coparenting, family process, and family structure: Implications for preschoolers' externalizing behavior problems. *Journal of Family Psychology, 15,* 526–545.

Schulz, M. S. (1997, April). *Daily linkages between parents' stressful work experiences and the quality of parent–child interactions.* Paper presented at the Society for Research in Child Development, Washington, DC.

Schulz, M. S., Cowan, P. A., Cowan, C. P., & Brennan, R. T. (2004). Coming home upset: Gender, marital satisfaction and the daily spillover of workday experience into marriage. *Journal of Family Psychology, 18,* 250–263.

Schulz, M. S., & Cowan, C. P. (2001). *Promoting healthy beginnings: Marital quality during the transition to parenthood.* Paper presented at the Society for Research in Child Development, Minneapolis, MN.

Sears, H. A., & Galambos, N. L. (1992). Women's work conditions and marital adjustment in two-earner couples: A structural model. *Journal of Marriage & the Family, 54,* 789–797.

Shavelson, R. J., Hubner, J. J., & Stanton, G. C. (1976). Self-concept: Validation of construct interpretations. *Review of Educational Research, 46,* 407–441.

Shaver, P. R., Belsky, J., & Brennan, K. A. (2000). The adult attachment interview and self-reports of romantic attachment: Associations across domains and methods. *Personal Relationships, 7,* 25–43.

Sheeber, L., Hops, H., Alpert, A., Davis, B., & Andrews, J. (1997). Family support and conflict: Prospective relations to adolescent depression. *Journal of Abnormal Child Psychology, 25,* 333–344.

Shonkoff, J. P., & Phillips, D. A. (2000). *From neurons to neighborhoods: The science of early childhood development.* Washington, DC: National Academy Press.

Signell, K. A. (1972). Kindergarten entry: A preventive approach to community mental health. *Community Mental Health Journal, 8,* 60–70.

Simons, R. L., Lorenz, F. O., Wu, C., & Conger, R. D. (1993). Social network and marital support as mediators and moderators of the impact of stress and depression on parental behavior. *Developmental Psychology, 29,* 368–381.

Skolnick, A. (1981). Married lives: Longitudinal perspectives on marriage. In D. H. Eichorn, N. Haan, M. P. Honzik, & P. H. Mussen (Eds.), *Present and past in middle life* (pp. 269–398). New York: Academic.

Slavin, R. E., Karweit, N. L., & Wasik, B. A. (Eds.). (1994). *Preventing early school failure: Research, policy, and practice.* Needham Heights, MA: Allyn & Bacon.

Smith, E. P., Prinz, R. J., Dumas, J. E., & Laughlin, J. (2001). Latent models of family processes in African American families: Relationships to child competence, achievement, and problem behavior. *Journal of Marriage & the Family, 63,* 967–980.

Smith, P. K., & Drew, L. M. (2002). *Grandparenthood.* Mahwah, NJ: Lawrence Erlbaum Associates, Inc.

Spanier, G. B., & Lewis, R. A. (1980). Marital quality: A review of the seventies. *Journal of Marriage & the Family, 42,* 825–839.

Spielberger, C. (1979). *Understanding stress and anxiety.* New York: Harper & Row.

Sprafkin, C., Serbin, L. A., & Elman, M. (1982). Sex-typing of play and psychological adjustment in young children: An empirical investigation. *Journal of Abnormal Child Psychology, 10,* 559–567.

Sroufe, L. A., Carlson, E., & Shulman, S. (1993). Individuals in relationships: Development from infancy through adolescence. In D. C. Funder, R. D. Parke, C. A. Tomlinson-Keasey, & K. Widaman (Eds.), *Studying lives through time: Personality and development* (pp. 315–342). Washington, DC: American Psychological Association.

Sroufe, L. A., Duggal, S., Weinfield, N., & Carlson, E. (2000). Relationships, development, and psychopathology. In A. J. Sameroff, M. Lewis, & S. M. Miller (Eds.), *Handbook of developmental psychopathology* (2nd ed., pp. 75–91). New York: Kluwer Academic.

Sroufe, L. A., Egeland, B., & Kreutzer, T. (1990). The fate of early experience following developmental change: Longitudinal approaches to individual adaptation in childhood. *Child Development, 61,* 1363–1373.

Sroufe, L. A., & Rutter, M. (1984). The domain of developmental psychopathology. *Child Development, 55,* 17–29.

Stebbins, L. (2001). *Work and family in America: A reference handbook.* Santa Barbara, CA: ABC-CLIO.

Steele, H., & Steele, M. (2003). Clinical uses of the Adult Attachment Interview. In M. Cortina & M. Marrone (Eds.), *Attachment theory and the psychoanalytic process* (pp. 107–126). London: Whurr.

Steele, H., Steele, M., Croft, C., & Fonagy, P. (1999). Infant–mother attachment at one year predicts children's understanding of mixed emotions at six years. *Social Development, 8,* 161–178.

Steele, H., Steele, M., & Fonagy, P. (1996). Associations among attachment classifications of mothers, fathers, and their infants. *Child Development, 67,* 541–555.

Steinberg, L. (2001). We know some things: Parent–adolescent relationships in retrospect and prospect. *Journal of Research on Adolescence, 11,* 1–19.

Steinberg, L., Elmen, J. D., & Mounts, N. S. (1989). Authoritative parenting, psychosocial maturity, and academic success among adolescents. *Child Development, 60,* 1424–1436.

Steinberg, L., Lamborn, S. D., Dornbusch, S. M., & Darling, N. (1992). Impact of parenting practices on adolescent achievement: Authoritative parenting, school involvement, and encouragement to succeed. *Child Development, 63,* 1266–1281.

Stevenson, H. W., Chen, C., & Lee, S. (1993). Motivation and achievement of gifted children in East Asia and the United States. *Journal for the Education of the Gifted, 16,* 223–250.

Stipek, D., Recchia, S., & McClintic, S. (1992). Self-evaluation in young children. *Monographs of the Society for Research in Child Development, 57*(1, Serial No. 226).

Stith, S. M., Rosen, K. H., Middleton, K. A., Busch, A. L., Lundeberg, K., & Carlton, R. P. (2000). The intergenerational transmission of spouse abuse: A meta-analysis. *Journal of Marriage & the Family, 62,* 640–654.

Straus, M. A. (1979). Measuring intrafamily conflict and violence: The Conflict Tactics (CT) Scales. *Journal of Marriage & the Family, 41,* 75–88.

Tamis-LeMonda, C. S., & Cabrera, N. (Eds.). (2002). *Handbook of father involvement: Multidisciplinary perspectives.* Mahwah, NJ: Lawrence Erlbaum Associates, Inc.

Tannen, D. (1990). *You just don't understand: Women and men in conversation* (1st ed.). New York: Morrow.

Tellegen, A. (1988). The analysis of consistency in personality assessment. *Journal of Personality, 56,* 621–663.

Thompson, B. M. (1997). Couples and the work-family interface. In W. K. Halford & H. J. Markman (Eds.), *Clinical handbook of marriage and couples interventions* (pp. 273–290). New York: Wiley.

Traub, J. (2000, January 16). What no school can do. *New York Times Magazine.*

U.S. Department of Education. (1993). *Prospects: The congressionally mandated study of educational growth and opportunity: The interim report.* Washington, DC: Author.

Udry, J. R., & Chantala, K. (2002). Risk assessment of adolescents with same-sex relationships. *Journal of Adolescent Health, 31,* 84–92.

United States Congress, House Committee on Education and the Workforce. (1999). In *Comprehensive school reform: Current status and issues: Hearing before the Committee on Education and the Workforce.* Washington, DC: U.S. General Printing Office.

Vaillant, G. E. (1995). *Adaptation to life* (2nd ed.). Cambridge, MA: Harvard University Press.

van Aken, M. A., & Riksen-Walraven, J. M. (1992). Parental support and the development of competence in children. *International Journal of Behavioral Development, 15,* 101–123.

van IJzendoorn, M. (1995). Adult attachment representations, parental responsiveness, and infant attachment: A meta-analysis on the predictive validity of the Adult Attachment Interview. *Psychological Bulletin, 117,* 387–403.

van IJzendoorn, M. H. (1992). Intergenerational transmission of parenting: A review of studies in nonclinical populations. *Developmental Review, 12,* 76–99.

van IJzendoorn, M. H., & Bakermans-Kranenburg, M. J. (1996). Attachment representation in mothers, fathers, adolescents, and clinical groups: A meta-analytic search for normative data. *Journal of Consulting and Clinical Psychology, 64,* 8–21.

van IJzendoorn, M. H., Kranenburg, M. J., Zwart-Woudstra, H. A., & Van Busschbach, A. M. (1991). Parental attachment and children's socio-emotional development: Some findings on the validity of the Adult Attachment Interview in the Netherlands. *International Journal of Behavioral Development, 14,* 375–394.

Vannoy, D., & Philliber, W. W. (1992). Wife's employment and quality of marriage. *Journal of Marriage & the Family, 54,* 387–398.

Vecchiotti, S. (2003). Kindergarten: An overlooked educational policy priority. *Social Policy Report, 17,* 3–17.

Vinokur, A. (1998, August). *Preparing couples coping with the stress of unemployment.* Paper presented at the meeting of the American Psychological Association, San Francisco.

Vondra, J., & Belsky, J. (1993). Developmental origins of parenting: Personality and relationship factors. In T. Luster & L. Okagaki (Eds.), *Parenting: An ecological perspective* (pp. 1–33). Hillsdale, NJ: Lawrence Erlbaum Associates, Inc.

Waddington, C. H. (1957). *The strategy of the genes.* London: Allen & Unwin.

Wagner, B. M., & Reiss, D. (1995). Family systems and developmental psychopathology: Courtship, marriage, or divorce? In D. Cicchetti & D. J. Cohen (Eds.), *Developmental psychopathology, Vol. 1: Theory and methods* (pp. 696–730). New York: Wiley.

Walker, D., Greenwood, C. R., Hart, B., & Carta, J. (1994). Prediction of school outcomes based on early language production and socioeconomic factors. *Child Development, 65,* 606–621.

Wallerstein, J., & Kelly, J. (1980). *Surviving the breakup.* New York: Basic Books.

Walsh, F. (Ed.). (2003). *Normal family processes* (3rd ed.). New York: Guilford.

Walsh, F. (Ed.). (2003). *Normal family processes* (3rd ed.). New York: Guilford.

Watson, D., & Clark, L. A. (1997). Measurement and mismeasurement of mood: Recurrent and emergent issues. *Journal of Personality Assessment, 68,* 267–296.

Webster-Stratton, C. (1994). Advancing videotape parent training: A comparison study. *Journal of Consulting & Clinical Psychology, 62,* 583–593.

Weinstein, R. S. (2002). *Reaching higher: The power of expectations in schooling.* Cambridge, MA: Harvard University Press.

Weisner, T. S., Garnier, H., & Loucky, J. (1994). Domestic tasks, gender egalitarian values and children's gender typing in conventional and nonconventional families. *Sex Roles, 30,* 23–54.

Weissman, M. M. (Ed.). (2001). *Treatment of depression: Bridging the 21st century.* Washington, DC: American Psychiatric Press, Inc.

Weissman, M. M., & Klerman, G. L. (1977). Sex differences and the epidemiology of depression. *Archives of General Psychiatry, 34,* 98–111.

Wentzel, K. R., & Caldwell, K. (1997). Friendships, peer acceptance, and group membership: Relations to academic achievement in middle school. *Child Development, 68,* 1198–1209.

Werner, E. E., & Smith, R. S. (1992). *Overcoming the odds: High risk children from birth to adulthood.* Ithaca, NY: Cornell University Press.

West, S. G., Sandler, I., Pillow, D. R., Baca, L., & Gersten, J. C. (1991). The use of structural equation modeling in generative research: Toward the design of a preventive intervention for bereaved children. *American Journal of Community Psychology, 19,* 459–480.

Westerman, M. A., & Schonholtz, J. (1988). Marital adjustment, joint parental support in a triadic problem-solving task, and child behavior problems. *Journal of Clinical Child Psychology, 22,* 97–106.

Wile, D. (1981). *Couples therapy: A nontraditional approach.* New York: Wiley.

Wilson, B. J., & Gottman, J. M. (1995). Marital interaction and parenting. In M. H. Bornstein (Ed.), *Handbook of parenting* (Vol. 4, pp. 33–56). Hillsdale, NJ: Lawrence Erlbaum Associates, Inc.

Wolchik, S. A., West, S. G., Westover, S., & Sandler, I. N. (1993). The children of divorce parenting intervention: Outcome evaluation of an empirically based program. *American Journal of Community Psychology, 21,* 293–331.

Wold, A. H. (1982). Sequence of information and processing strategies in oral language. *Scandinavian Journal of Psychology, 23,* 267–272.

Wood, J. J., Cowan, P. A., & Baker, B. L. (2002). Behavior problems and peer rejection in preschool boys and girls. *Journal of Genetic Psychology, 163,* 72–88.

Wylie, R. C. (1989). *Measures of self-concept.* Lincoln: University of Nebraska Press.

Yalom, I. D. (1995). *The theory and practice of group psychotherapy* (4th ed.). New York: Basic Books.

Zahn-Waxler, C., Duggal, S., & Gruber, R. (2002). *Parental psychopathology.* Mahwah, NJ: Lawrence Erlbaum Associates, Inc.

Zarit, S. H., & Eggebeen, D. J. (1998). Parent–child relationships in adulthood and later years. In M. H. Bornstein (Ed.), *Handbook of parenting vol. 1: Children and parenting* (2nd ed., pp. 135–164). Hillsdale, NJ: Lawrence Erlbaum Associates, Inc.

Zimmerman, T. S., Haddock, S. A., Current, L. R., & Ziemba, S. (2003). Intimate partnership: Foundation to the successful balance of family and work. *American Journal of Family Therapy, 31,* 107–124.

Zimmerman, P. (1999). Structure and functions of internal working models of attachment and their role for emotion regulation. *Attachment and Human Development, 1,* 291–306.

Author Index

Subject Index

Note. *f* indicates figure; *t* indicates table.